Karmic-Cycle

~

The Chronic
Consequence
Of
Karmic-Bondage

Karmic-Cycle

~

The Chronic Consequence Of Karmic-Bondage

Vijai K. Tiwari

Anant Missionary Ashram
Orlando, Florida

Table of Contents

Preface

The saying, 'One reaps what he sows,' brings to attention a profound natural law of 'sowing and reaping' or 'seeding and harvesting', which states that 'reaping is always of the same kind as is sowing.' In other words: seed creates seed; and it creates of its own kind; but of course, the implied assumption is that it happens only under some suitable conditions.

These two facts that are related to 'seeding and harvesting' hold true throughout the creation when it comes to multiplication of life – biological as well as botanical. All living beings through seeding give birth to their own kind, and so do the plants and trees.

This physical law of 'seeding and harvesting', upon which depends the continuity of life, does not need any proof for its validation. Universally accepted truth is that, when planted, the seed becomes a plant (a tree), bears fruits, and creates more seeds; which in turn, again are planted and many more seeds grow out of that. And thus, the cycle continues. Of course, always, the seed creates of its own kind, and not of any other kind; meaning, reaping is only of what is sown.

Now, if this law holds true in the physical world, then just for the sake of argument, we can also assume that it holds true in the spiritual world, especially, when it is true that God did not create any contradictions in laws He established – the physical as well as spiritual that govern His creation.

It means we could safely assume that the law of 'seeding and harvesting' should work when it comes to planting the seeds of 'good' and 'bad'; meaning, through seeding, 'good' should create further good, and 'bad' should create further bad.

Well, this assumption about 'seeding and harvesting' of good and bad, which we have just made, does not remain an assumption anymore since most major philosophies profess and preach it to be one of the most visibly applied spiritual law instituted by the Divine to regulate the humanity even though its enforcement does not seem always as obvious.

Though in the physical world, the law – the reaping is only of what is shown – is self-witnessing; however, in the spiritual world it is often challenged due to the lack of proof of its enforcement.

For example, how often we see a wicked man flourishing and living a prosperous life, while a righteous man failing and suffering all kinds of hardships.

In such paradoxical situations, it is not easy to stand by the law that dictates 'one reaps what he sows,' with implied meaning that good of man bears good fruits and his bad bears bad fruits, because the obvious seems to be proving quite the contrary at times – which is: the bad giving rise to good and good giving rise to bad.

So we wonder: Why it is the way it is? Why is it that the law that holds true so universally in all physical world fails so badly in spiritual realm? Why does the truth that is so exceedingly exalted by all scriptures at times seem to be failing to stand on its own grounds?

And we try to seek answers to such questions and figure out: Why is there such an opposite outcome of man's deeds – the good resulting in bad and bad resulting in good?

Well, the reality is that, man's rationality has no answer to such questions as: Why does sometimes the good and virtuous suffer and endure life filled with all kinds of hardships? And why does sometimes the evil and wicked prosper and live an affluent life?

His reason fails to provide any adequate explanation for such disparity; and his understanding remains unable to offer any satisfactory justification for such injustice. The truth is that even with all kinds of secular knowledge and material wisdom, man is still totally incapable in providing any ample elucidation for such happenings that are so frequently scattered throughout all segments of human population.

Though the wisdom of man fails to provide a sufficient justification for such unfairness in life, the *Hindu* scriptures however do present a pretty convincing argument about why life, which at times seems so unfair and is filled with so much injustice and at other times looks so arbitrary and coincidental, actually has a very defined order, in which all incurring incidents are no coincidences at all, but are the happenings that have been destined to take place according to some pre-ordinance determined by the Higher power responsible for sustenance of all creation.

The *Vedanta* philosophy, which is the heart of *Hindu* theology, unfolds the great mystery of existence of life through the doctrine of *Karma* that yields a concise but quite clear explanation and provides a very satisfactory and sufficient elucidation why life is the way it is by revealing the following truth:

A - Though the soul is eternal and immortal and is a part of all-pervading Consciousness (God), yet she suffers mortality due to her Karma **(Holy Gita 8:3)**, which she creates during her human embodiment. Karma is a subtle counterpart to human action that demands exhaustion through the expression of suitable life by the soul. It is a silent reaction to man's action that manifests in due time and materializes itself during some future Karmic-life of the soul. In brief, Karma is a debt that results due to actions rendered by the soul during her human embodiment, which in due time demands a definite payoff that is possible only through the expression of further suitable Karmic-life by the soul.

B - Not only Karma is the basis of all life but is also the regulating authority over soul's all material manifestations; it is the Karma that forces her to pass through countless earthly embodiments **(Holy Gita 13:21)** by demanding its expression and exhaustion in small fractions as it matures. All reincarnations of the soul with their good and bad experiences are nothing but the expression of Karma that she creates during her human births **(Holy Gita 2:43)**. The evenness and unevenness of life, which the soul experiences in human life, is not because of anything else but due to her own doings of the past.

C - The cycle of Karma, which starts at the end of human life and completes only when the soul, after passing through countless non-human embodiments, wears the human flesh again, continues until she takes the total refuge in the sanctuary of God where through His grace she is forgiven of all Karma and set eternally free from bondage. Only then, when the soul finds perpetual rest in the sanctuary of God, she is released from the fetters of Karma.

Thus, by revealing the above stated truth about the soul, and by unveiling the *Karmic*-theory and disclosing what *Karma* is, and upon what rules it operates, the *Vedanta* Philosophy surely succeeds in providing the rationalization for injustice and unfairness of life that seems so unjustified.

However, the sticking point is that it holds grounds only when the concept of 'Reincarnation of the soul' is acknowledged first, which happens to be a concept that is not widely accepted in religious world beyond the periphery of *Hindu* belief.

For example, in Christianity, Judaism and Islam, there is no concept of 'reincarnation', or of '*Karma*'; they both are absent in them. Though the Holy Bible professes, **"For whatsoever a man soweth, that shall he also reap – Holy Bible, Galatians 6:7,"** meaning what one sows is what he reaps, it still does not give any further explanation for unjustified life that we all witness almost on daily basis except that the purpose of all life is to make God's work and will manifest **(Holy Bible, John 9:3)** in human life, which of course, is always true regardless of what it is.

Still, the lack of recognition by other religions does not hold back the popularity of concept of *Karma*, which is beyond the theological confinements imposed by various faiths and beliefs, as it is one of those notions that often cross the imposed religious boundaries.

As a proof, often the believers of various faiths as well as nonbelievers across all populations of the world regard happenings in life a result of *Karma*, especially the ones that are extraordinary in some way; and in their spiritual wonderment, they often consider them as if they were manifestations of some consequential effects of their past deeds.

So the concept of *Karma* is quite common in all societies regardless of their professed faith, as there are always some folks in all walks of life who believe in the percussions of *Karma* even without necessarily accepting the notion of 'reincarnation'.

But 'reincarnation' is such a foundation without which the doctrine of *Karma* cannot stand straight but falls flat; therefore, it is absolutely essential that the 'reincarnation' of the soul and her repeated earthly manifestations be taken into account, and all whereabouts of her entire *Karmic*-life be considered to fully explain those questions that otherwise remain unanswered in regard to why life is the way it is, and why at times it is so uneven and so unjustified?

With such basic beliefs of *Hinduism* that *Karma* is the basis of all mortal manifestation of the soul **(Holy Gita 8:3)**, and that the soul, who though is intrinsically immortal, yet wears the clothes of mortality through suitable reincarnations to express and exhaust her *Karmic*-dues, the *Vedanta* philosophy is quite capable in providing a satisfactory elucidation on why all kinds of seemingly unfair happenings take place in life. The laws and statues that it provides to describe the workings of *Karma* are quite capable in yielding a sufficient reason for its justification.

This book that lies in your hands takes a very close look on this very popular subject so called *Karma*, and explains in easy terms what *Karma* is? What are its workings? Upon what principles does it operate? And what are its rules and regulations?

Furthermore, it expounds upon what the *Karmic*-bondage is and how is it caused? How does it bind the immortal soul to the cycle of birth and death and make her a captive of mortality by forcing her to pass through embodiment after embodiment?

These are some of those questions that rise out of a deep inquiry made by an eager heart, which desires to understand the reality of soul's drifting through all kinds of *Karmic*-worlds and wants to know her whereabouts after she leaves this corporal world and resumes her *Karmic*-journey beyond it.

After talking about the *Karmic*-captivity of the soul, the book simply does not leave the matter there, but continues its exploration of scriptures to expound upon the way for her redemption from the incarceration by *Karma* and attaining the unending freedom from bondage.

Thus, this manuscript not only provides details on various laws of *Karma* and their operation and enforcement upon the mortal life of the soul, but also yields an account for the entirety of *Karmic*-life which the soul suffers.

In addition to that, it also gives glimpses of those details that depict how she repeatedly passes through the tunnel of transmigration and how she wanders into all kinds of *Karmic*-worlds, and then tries to bring in focus the descriptions of those detours that the soul takes before her final restoration into her native habitation – the everlasting abode of God.

Since this book is based upon *Hindu* theology and its main purpose is to shed light upon the subject of Karmic-bondage of the soul, it does not try to establish any validation of doctrine of Karma and provides no justification for theory of Reincarnation simply because it does not find it necessary to yield any rationalization for their legitimacy but to simply accept their legality and recognize the authority of their rules and regulations, which as per Hindu scriptures happen to control all of soul's Karmic-manifestations and mortal materializations.

The manuscript also does not try to prove the point that life is governed by the laws of *Karma* but simply accepts the validity of their enforcement in accordance to the *Karmic*-statues as dictated by the *Hindu* scriptures and employs them in contents of its export.

Well, I have written what I was inspired to write about the subject of '*Karma*', but of course, in the light of scriptures as bestowed by the Divine even though there are thoughts in this book that may not find a direct support in the holy text.

However, I have not written anything in its pages that I have made up on my own through my own understanding and is not given by God; therefore, in each and every word of this book, I see nothing but His revealed truth about the *Karmic*-constitution with which He rules and regulates His creation.

So, with much confidence in God I present this book to you in anticipation that it would help you find the truth that has been preordained for you to be found in its wisdom, and thus, it becomes a lamp unto your path leading your soul to reach the land of eternal illumination.

I fully believe that scriptures are windows to the mind of God; they provide a peek into His heart and soul. Their sole purpose is to make man understand the reality and truth of God and know the manners and ways in which He desires him to operate.

Therefore, with a diligence spirit let us seek the wisdom of God through His holy word with a confidence that they would reveal to us the understanding of Karma and its bondage, and open a way for our redemption, and thus, unfold God's plan for our rescue from the captivity to *Karma* by exposing the hidden path to eternal life that He has paved for us by His own hands.

With much reverence in God,

– Vijai K. Tiwari

1

Karmic-Bondage
~
The Burden of Karma upon the Soul

Since the multiplication of life in Creation is based upon the physical law that states that, 'seed creates seed, and it creates of its own kind', it makes sense to accept the spiritual derivation of it, which can be stated as 'the good creates good and the bad creates bad', even though it cannot be confidently confirmed since it lacks a direct verification.

Now, this does not mean, there is no evidence at all of its corroboration because the natural order of unfolding of life often seems to provide quite candid and reasonably convincing proof for its legality.

Furthermore, most scriptures often speak of this law regardless of the orientation of their theology as to whether they accept the concept of *Karma* or not. In fact, many philosophies even profess that 'one reaps what he sows,' which indirectly implies to mean that 'good creates good while bad creates bad'. Thus, regardless of lacking of its formal acceptance by various theologies, the concept of *Karma* is yet highly popular.

Since *Karma* is an integral part of *Hindu* doctrine, the holy books of Hinduism are filled with such texts that describe the basic principles of Karma and speak loudly of its operating rules and regulations especially the one which is the most fundamental and exalted by the Holy *Ramayana* this way:

karama pradhana bisva kari rakha, jo jasa karai so tasa phalu cakha.

These words are translated to mean:

Even though He has made Fate the ruling factor in this world, so that one reaps what one sows.

(Holy Ramayana, Ayodhya-Kanda 126-2)

Meaning, one reaps the harvest according to what type of seeds he sows; his labor bears the fruits according to his actions.

Similarly, when Holy Gita describes the effect of *Gunas*, it is not hard to see that the nature of *Gunas* dictate the fact that 'one reaps what he shows', though she does it quite indirectly, and not directly.

Anyone can study the quality and character of the 'Three Modes of Nature (*Gunas*)', which she unveils in her text, and easily conclude that 'The good creates good and bad creates bad'. Undoubtedly, it is a broad derivation of truth that emerges from her exceedingly extensive analysis of the three modes of nature – the *Sattwa, Rajas* and *Tamas*.

Just look at her following text that describes what type of actions bear what type of fruits?

The wise say that the <u>fruits</u> of virtuous actions is *Sattwika* and pure, the fruit of Rajas is pain, while the fruit of *Tamas* is ignorance.

From *Sattwa* proceeds knowledge, from Rajas greed, and from *Tamas* heedlessness, delusion and ignorance.

(Holy Gita 14:16-17)

Clearly, while *Sattwa*, due to its purity, is enlightener and the giver of health and happiness **(Holy Gita 14:6)**, the *Rajas*, as being of the nature of passion, is the producer of craving and attachment **(Holy Gita 14:7)**, while *Tamas*, being born of ignorance, is the deluder in every way **(Holy Gita 14:8)**. In other words, from purity arises purity, from passion arises passion, and from ignorance arises more ignorance **(Holy Gita 14:9)**.

2

Thus, according to Holy Gita, the fruits of an action are no different than the action itself; meaning, whatever is 'action', so is its 'outcome'. Certainly, the reaping is of the same kind as sowing.

Similarly, Holy Bible also professes the same spiritual law that says 'one reaps what he sows'. It repeatedly says that the wicked reaps the fruits of wickedness, while the righteous reaps the fruits of righteousness:

Even as I have seen, they that plow iniquity, and sow wickedness, reap the same.

(Holy Bible, Job 4:8)

They that sow in tears shall reap in joy.

(Holy Bible, Psalms 126:5)

As per these holy words, one certainly reaps according to his sowing:

Be not deceived; God is not mocked: <u>for whatsoever a man soweth, that shall he also reap</u>.

For he that soweth to his flesh shall of the flesh reap corruption; but he that soweth to the Spirit shall of the Spirit reap life everlasting.

(Holy Bible, Galatians 6:7-8)

Oh! How beautiful are these word of God that clearly tell that if the sowing is fleshly, then so are its fruits; the corporeal seeding brings only the corporeal crop; but when one sows in the land of the Spirit, he reaps the heavenly harvest.

But what if the reaping never comes in this lifetime, then what happens to the law: **"For whatsoever a man soweth, that shall he also reap?"**

Well, when we ask this question, we find it very essential to understand what 'sowing' and 'reaping' really means?

In fact, this question forces us to find out the true meaning of the word 'outcome' of an action; or its 'fruits' or 'result'? So what are they? And what do they really mean? Well, let us investigate a little bit and take a close look at these terms and

3

try to define them first before we go any further so that we have no confusion about them.

Generally, in secular terms, the 'outcome', or 'result' or 'fruit' of an action means whatever has been accomplished through it, and whatever has been materialized out of it.

However, this is not all, when we speak of it in spiritual terms; because then, we not only take into account whatever has been accomplished through an action in its present course but also its rewards that are subtle and unseen, and are yet to come to fruition in the future.

For example: Suppose your neighbor has lost his job, and this month, he desperately needs help in paying his rent. So once you came to know his need, you chip in some money and make it possible for him to pay his dues.

Now let me ask this: What is the total 'outcome', or 'result' or 'fruit' of your action, which obviously can be characterized as being good?

Of course, in this case, your neighbor's rent is paid and he does not need to worry about it at least for another month. So that is the tangible outcome of your action. If we try to measure it secularly, then that is all what has been accomplished by what you did. Isn't it!

But is that really all? Or there is something more, which could be called as the 'outcome' of your action, which happens to be of tremendous goodwill?

Well, secularly speaking, nothing more! Since, that is all what materialized as a result of what you did for your friend, and that's it.

However, when we speak of the same in spiritual realm, we have to not only consider the direct result of your action but also all subtle 'consideration' of the 'good' that you received out of your good deed, which would bring its rewards in the 'future'. Of course, by no means the word 'future' in this reference is limited to this lifetime.

This 'consideration' of 'good' would surely bear its fruits in its due time, although, there is no definite way to know for how and when it would happen except that it definitely would, sooner or later.

Who knows, someday you yourself might face a tough financial situation and you might need help, and all of sudden someone shows up to share your burden just the way you did to your neighbor. Well, that could very well be the reward of the 'consideration' that you hold in your hand for doing good to your neighbor in the past.

So even though the 'consideration' of 'good' is subtle and is not visible by any means, it does not mean that it does not exist; that it is not there; because it always is.

How do we prove that it is there?

Well, if there is nothing else, at least your heart knows that you did something really good. As a result, every time the thought of your neighbor comes to your mind, you feel extremely joyful about what you did. Thus, there is a reward of feeling good in you; isn't it? At a minimum, that much reward of your good deed is already there within you that would lighten-up your heart with joy every time you would think of it in the future.

Now, let us go a bit further and assume that your neighbor is a good man. So quite obviously, he would remain thankful to you for the rest of his life for what you did for him in times of hardships; and not only that, if possible, he would try his best to return the favor by doing some good to you. Well, in that case his good deeds towards you would be counted as even further rewards for your good deed. Isn't it?

Similarly, how about the family members of your neighbor? If they know what you did, won't they be thankful to you? Won't they show their gratitude towards you by doing whatever good they can do for you? Thus, quite expectedly, there will be a consideration of their goodness coming your way. In fact, the chances are that anyone who comes to know what you did for your neighbor would have a kind heart towards you, especially his family and relatives.

So as we can see, there is no doubt that a 'consideration' of 'good' would exist for you, which would bring rewards for you in the future even though it remains beyond quantitative measurements.

Mind it! We still have a lot more to include when counting the rewards of your good that you would earn as 'consideration', because only God knows what else He has in His palm for you as a recompense for your kindness that you showed to your neighbor.

It means the entirety of the 'result' of your action is not just saving your neighbor from the trouble but also the invisible and subtle 'consideration' of 'good' that would come to fruition later and bring much rewards for you by bearing good fruits; however for now, we have no idea of what that is and how and when in the future it would come to materialization?

Well, this is what we mean by such expressions as, 'the outcome of an action', or 'result or fruit of an action' in the context of discussion about *Karma* and its bondage.

After understanding the meaning of the 'outcome' or 'fruit' or 'result' of an action, let us now try to understand the whole meaning of 'sowing' and 'reaping'.

Surely, when we sow the seeds of any grain – wheat, barley, mustard etc. – we reap and harvest of the same. But after reaping is finished and the harvest is over, there is nothing more left that would come to us as a result of our sowing. That's the end of it.

However, as we have discussed above, that when we do the 'sowing' through our actions, the 'reaping' is not limited to just gross 'result' as it also includes the subtle and invisible 'consideration' that comes to fruition but only later in our future and brings rewards of its own kind.

So when the holy word says: **"For whatsoever a man soweth, that shall he also reap,"** it actually means three things:

First: The reaping is of the same kind as is sowing; meaning, the fruits of the harvest, which one reaps, are of the same kind as of the seeds he sows.

Second: The 'reaping' of fruits includes both: the visible and gross fruits, and the invisible and subtle fruits. The visible fruits are direct fruits, which materialize in present due course, while the invisible fruits are indirect fruits that materialize in future; these are those intangible fruits that rise out of 'consideration', which one earns out of the inclination of the intent and the extent of willingness in engaging in the effort behind his action of sowing.

Third: The fruition of the earned 'consideration' comes in fractions over a period of time that may span beyond a lifetime.

In *Hindu* theology this 'consideration', which results from human action, is called *Karma*. Of course, other theologies, which do not have the concept of *Karma*, refer to it as 'reaping', which rises out of one's 'sowing'.

When one sows the seed of 'good', he reaps the harvest of 'good', and when he sows the seed of 'bad', he reaps the harvest of 'bad'.

Meaning, when one sows the seeds of hatred, animosity, jealousy, greed, lust or any kind of evil, so he reaps in return. But when he sows the seeds of love, friendship, compassion, care and plants the kernels of any kind of goodness, then goodness is what his life receives.

Of course, the 'reaping' can come at anytime in the future after the 'sowing' has been done. It has no time constraints whatsoever, since the 'consideration' earned by man, bears its fruits in its own due time and brings forth its rewards as per its divine ordinance.

In fact the biggest reward of human deeds, which comes as a collective 'consideration', comes only after ones death, but only in the form of what happens to his soul after she leaves this world.

Though many theologies profess, 'one reaps what he sows', however, not all yield the same explanation of the rewards that result out of this collective 'consideration', which comes only after one's death.

For example in Christianity, on the 'Day of Judgment', if one is 'saved', meaning one is reconciled with God through his faith in Lord Jesus Christ, and his sins have been forgiven through His death on the cross, then the rewards of the collective 'consideration' of his deeds in this life would be given to him in heaven in the forms of various kinds of privileges. On the other hand, if one is not 'saved', then his torture and torment in hell would also be affected accordingly; meaning, his sowing will determine how dreadful life his soul is going to suffer in hell.

This kind of belief is professed by some other theologies as well, which do not have the concept of *Karma* and do not believe in reincarnation of the soul.

For example, in Islam, which also believes in the 'Day of Judgment', God would judge the man, and based on his deeds reward him accordingly with the pleasures in heavens or sufferings in hell.

However, *Hindu* philosophy is quite different in the sense, that it provides quite a detailed description of what the 'rewards' are that arise out of collective 'consideration' of human deeds, which it calls *Karma*, and sufficiently explains how do they come to fruition by expressing life and exhausting *Karmic*-obligations properly through suitable reincarnations of the soul.

This is why the *Hindu* doctrine is not only able to depict the entire view of the 'reaping' that results out of the 'sowing' done through human actions, but also is able to yield an adequate elucidation on why and how the 'reaping' that spans through countless future 'reincarnations' of the soul, though often may seem unjustified due to lack of understanding of its entirety, is actually very justified.

As can be expected from the title, this book does not focus at all on what the other faiths and beliefs have to say about this widely popular and often quoted spiritual law of 'one reaps what he sows', but pays sole attention to explaining the mystery of 'sowing' and 'reaping' as unfolded through the wisdom of *Vedanta* philosophy, and in doing so, unveils the workings of '*Karmic*-cycle', which encapsulates the entirety of 'reaping' in the form of *Karmic*-consequences, and presents a very clear view of how the soul endures them through countless 'reincarnations'.

Although the concepts of *Karma* and reincarnation are simple to understand, however, their workings as presented by *Hindu* faith are not all that easy; the reason being that there are too many laws and statues of *Karma* that operate in the same domain and have much bearing upon each other.

This book takes up on this subject and dedicates itself to explaining all those things that are required to have a good comprehension of how the 'sowing' and 'reaping' works in the realm of *Karmic*-doctrine.

Well, the word '*Karma*' is quite a common and popular word that not only *Hindus* but also the folks from other societies and cultures all over the world use, and often through it express their wonderment about the happenings in life which possibly could be tied to their past deeds.

How often we hear, "Oh! It must be my *Karma*," or "What can I say, it is my *Karma*!" and the expressions like these that just come out of lips of many all over the world so simply and so naturally that folks can't resist using them so habitually. Surely, *Karma* is such a widely popular and so frequently used word that it transcends languages, cultures, faiths and religions.

And the reason of its popularity is that this word is extremely handy. It is so easy to employ and so simple to communicate, and yet when used with only so few words, it conveys so much meaning. How often the emotions in regard to a particular circumstance, which could take lot more words and sentences to express, are conveyed so simply through the use of this word.

One of the most peculiar things about this word is that, whether one understands all its intricacies or not, yet he understands what does this word refer to. Hardly ever, there is any mistake in understanding the meaning of what this word stands for.

Like when someone says, "Oh! It must be my *Karma*!" what he means to say is that the situation he is referring to is a result of the deeds of his past; and it is a direct outcome of his actions, which he has done previously, either during this life or the life before this.

If the situation in reference is good, then it means it is the outcome of some good deeds of the past, and if not, then it must be the result of some bad things one has done in his past. The vague implied concept is that something good has occurred due to some good of the past; or something bad has occurred due to some bad of the past.

Thus, we find the word 'Karma' pretty handy when we need to refer to some event in life that as per our individual belief occurred as a result of some action or actions of the past, whether done in this life or in some life before this.

This happens to be the most common use of this word; and of course, it happens to be quite correct; meaning, the general understanding of the word 'Karma' is quite good; there is no doubt about that!

But regardless of how much knowledge people have about this word and how many folks actually use it, and no matter how popular it is, the fact still remains, that not everybody agrees with the entirety of its meaning for which it stands especially in lieu of the Hindu philosophy in which lies its genesis.

The reason being, that one can accept the total meaning of word 'Karma' for which it is really meant but only if he accepts the word 'reincarnation' first, since without accepting the word 'reincarnation', the word 'Karma' remains incomplete in its purposefulness.

Thus, whenever one uses the word Karma, there is always an underlying thought of 'reincarnation', with which not everybody agrees, since reincarnation is not a universal concept as many major religions totally deny it.

Not everybody agrees that the soul incarnates over and over, which is what the word 'reincarnation' stands for in this context. It is the Vedanta philosophy of Hinduism that professes the concept of 'reincarnation of the soul', but not many other major philosophies agree with its theological assertions.

Moreover, according to most major theologies, the soul never returns to this world once she ceases her embodiment on this earth and parts away from these mortal territories. So then, how can they ever believe in 'reincarnation' of the soul?

In fact, even the definition of what the soul is, differs from religion to religion. Hindu holy books say that the soul is a part of God **(Holy Gita 15:7)**. She is the Atman – a part of Brahman (The

ParamAtman – The Godhead) – the Eternal - the all-pervading Transcendental Self **(Holy Gita 2:24).**

But that thought is ridiculed by many religions as they have their own understanding of the soul. They also disagree with the *Vedanta* thought that the souls in all beings are equal and are part of one Unity – the *Brahman*.

This is why it is no surprise that the concept of salvation is regarded so differently by various philosophies and doctrines. Some religions do not even believe that there is such a thing called 'The salvation of soul', which by *Hindu* theology is identified as 'The Liberation of the *Atman* (*Moksha* – also called as *Mukti*)'.

Well, in context of this book, considering what its contents are, the expressions like 'The salvation of soul', 'The liberation of the *Atman*', 'The freedom from bondage', 'The attainment of *Moksha*', 'The Self-realization', 'The attainment of everlasting rest and peace', 'The release from the captivity of *Karma*', 'The eternal deliverance from sin', and any such phrases mean only one thing, which is: The freedom of soul from bondage to *Karma* and her attainment of eternal Liberation – the *Moksha*.

Thus, the truth-seeking thoughts differ in various areas of spiritual understanding from philosophy to philosophy, and they vary quite widely when it comes to concepts of '*Karma*' and the 'Reincarnation of the Soul'.

Unlike *Hinduism*, which professes that the soul, if not salvaged during human embodiment, returns to this world again and again **(Holy Gita 5:17, 8:16)**, several other religions dictate that she comes into this world only once, and upon her return, she either ascends to grace and rises to heaven or descends to disgrace and falls into damnation of hell depending upon the criteria their philosophy dictates.

So my fear is that only those folks that agree with the notion that the soul returns to this world and incarnates over and over due to her *Karma*, would be able to enjoy and be truly benefited by the contents of this book, as for all others, it would not make a whole lot of sense because of theological differences between their religious doctrine and *Hindu* philosophy.

One thing needs to be pointed out though, that in *Hindi* and *Sanskrit*, the word '*Karma*' means 'action' but when used in this context, it has a much different meaning, which according to Merriam-Webster's dictionary is: "The force generated by a person's actions held in *Hinduism* and *Buddhism* to perpetuate transmigration and in its ethical consequences to determine the nature of the person's next existence."

Surely, this is the meaning how the word *Karma* is generally used. It means, to a common mind that is oriented with such understanding and uses this word, the *Karma* is a force (reaction) generated by man's action that perpetuates his future life according to its rules and regulations.

Now, even though there is no doubt that the word '*Karma*' is quite often used by people of various cultures and societies, and of various faiths and religions, not much can be said confidently about how much more the folks of other societies who use this word actually know about it and understand anything about its governing laws.

Well, it is anybody's guess!

Surely, the common belief among we *Hindus* is that our lives are pre-ordained by *Karma*; and that, all moments of our day are formed and shaped according to it. What we were before this moment, what we are now, and what we are going to be in the future, is all determined by *Karma*.

Additionally, we also believe that after we die, we go to heaven and hell according to our deeds, and that our soul goes through all kinds of lower and higher embodiments depending upon our *Karma* **(Holy Gita 13:21)**; of course, until eventually, she incarnates as human, and the cycle of *Karma* starts again.

Thus, the soul continually bears the burden of *Karma* till the day comes when through the grace of God she is forgiven of all sin and released from the fetters of *Karma* by attaining *Moksha* (Liberation). Only then she is released from all forced encapsulations of mortal and material existence and get restored into her inherent form of *Sat-Chit-Ananda* (Truth-Consciousness-Bliss).

Surely, most of us think and believe like that! However, there are only few who have the true understanding on how the *Karmic*-laws actually work?

In general, even though some concepts of *Karma* seem to be fairly understood, yet the detailed knowledge of its rules and regulations upon which it operates is widely missing, as there are not many people who truly understand how the laws of *Karma* function. Thus, there seems to be a significant ignorance about it.

It is a fact that most of us do not have a clear comprehension of it, as we speak and hear things that are totally false and misconceived. Quite clearly, there is a lacking in our knowledge about *Karma* and its principles upon which it operates, and that surely has contributed to the rise of all kinds of misconstrued and miscomprehended concepts and beliefs in our understanding, which actually affect our religious life dramatically.

So there is a need that we understand correctly what *Karma* is, and what are its laws and statues that govern all life in the universe.

Surely, it is very important for us to know the workings of *Karma*, since it dictates what happens to us next after we die, and since it has much leverage not only upon our current life but also upon life that lies beyond this.

Well, first thing is first! Let us begin by finding out: What is Karma?

The doctrine of 'Cause and Effect' is the basis of Karma. For every 'effect' there is a 'cause', and for every 'cause' there is an 'effect'. Human life (action) causes '*Karma*', which in turn causes more life (all kinds of creaturely life including human), and then life (human) again causes *Karma* – and thus, the cycle continues (the *Karmic*-Cycle).

Every human action causes an effect – the *Karma*. And *Karma* in turn becomes the cause and creates its effect, which materializes in form of all kinds of life, **"That creative force is known as Karma which is the cause of the existence and the manifestation of all beings – Holy Gita 8:3."** After all kinds of nonhuman creaturely lives **(Holy Gita 13:21)**, *Karma* causes human life again, which causes more *Karma*, and thus, another cycle of *Karma* starts again.

As I have said before, *Karma* is a subtle counterpart and a silent reaction to human action that definitely manifests itself in due time; however, the 'due time' is an unknown factor.

You see! Besides the gross act itself, which is the direct result of an action, there is always an indirect result – a subtle counterpart called *Karma* – which represents the tangibility of the <u>motive</u> and the <u>extent of effort</u> behind the action. Depending upon the motive, the produced *Karma* is good or bad; meaning, the good motive creates good *Karma*, while the bad motive creates bad *Karma*. Thus, the quality and quantity of Karma depend upon these two factors.

As a rule, for each action that man performs there is a reaction associated with it; but since the reaction is subtle at the time of its creation, so he cannot see it; and since its tangibility is not immediate as it manifest itself only in future, it remains unrecognizable and unidentified.

But regardless of its invisibility at its birth, according to the scriptural truth, *Karma* is there, and even in the absence of its tangibility it surely exists.

In fact *Karma* remains invisible in its raw form, subtle and silent, till in due time it matures and becomes ready to get manifested and be expressed in some suitable form of life by the soul, but of course, as a 'reaction' to the action that creates it. This happens to be called as 'The Exhaustion of *Karma*'.

The exhaustion of *Karma*, which is due upon the soul, takes places when it is expressed through some suitable life that yields a way for its manifestation and becomes a medium for the 'reaction' to take place, and allows its tangibility to materialize when the due time arrives. Thus, expression of *Karma* in such manner offers a way for *Karma* to be burned and be exhausted.

It means *Karma* is a debt that the soul as embodied man accumulates when she performs actions, and which she pays back in due time by expressing it in some suitable form of life.

So to state it in more understandable terms, Karma is a subtle and silent counterpart to human action, which is like a delayed reaction that takes place with absolute certainty, in due future frame of time, as an expression of some suitable form of life by the soul.

The above yields a pretty good definition of what *Karma* is? It certainly is complete in its statement and is sufficient enough to describe it.

Please make a note of words that are underlined, since they signify various things about the nature of *Karma*. In the following paragraphs we would refer to these underlined words while trying to explain what does the above definition of *Karma* really mean?

The brief summary of what these words are telling us is: That *Karma* is a definite counterpart of an human action; that it is like a delayed reaction that is subtle and silent at its birth; that its mentality, maneuvering, motion and magnitude are totally dependent upon the mentality, maneuvering, motion and magnitude of the action that creates it; that its materialization is certain, which takes place in its own due time when it manifests itself in some form of life that is suitable for its expression.

Since, *Karma* is a 'reaction' to an action, it is very straightforward to think that the nature of *Karma* is dependent upon the nature of action that creates it; meaning, in terms of its enormity and extent, its motion and magnitude, its direction and degree, the *Karma* is equivalent to its corresponding action and is directly proportional to it.

Therefore, we can confidently say that the character of *Karma* is derived from the essence of the action that creates it.

Thus, keeping the keyword 'reaction' in mind, it is not hard to figure out that good action creates good *Karma* while the bad action creates bad *Karma*; meaning, as is an action, so is its reaction; as is a deed, so is its *Karma*. If action is good, the *Karma* is good; if action is bad, the *Karma* is bad too.

In terms of *Hindu* philosophy, the good *Karma* is created by good deeds called '*Punyas*' and bad *Karma* is created by bad deeds called '*Papas*'.

Well, let us summarize what we have come to understand so far about *Karma*, but of course, without getting too much into details, as the rest of chapters of this book would provide a wider view of all things related to it.

To do so, let us reconsider the definition of *Karma* as stated above and analyze it piece by piece:

Firstly: Karma is a subtle and silent counterpart to an action.

It means even though *Karma* is definitely created as a counterpart to an action, but it is not visible at its birth; though it exists, but at that point it does not have any grossness; surely, it is present, but only as being silent and mute.

Secondly: Karma is created only by human action.

It is essential to know that no other being but human has the capability to create *Karma*; it is only man and no other creature which creates it; it is only his actions that are the reason for birth of *Karma*.

Thirdly: Since Karma is a reaction to action, therefore as is action, so is Karma.

Since *Karma* is a reaction to an action, it means it derives its nature and temperament, character and quality from the action that creates it. Thus, as is action in its nature, so is its *Karma*.

This is why the common understanding about *Karma* is that good action creates good *Karma*, and bad action creates bad *Karma*.

Thus, an action itself defines what its *Karma* would be like; its virtue and vitality, its quality and character, its nature and disposition, all are totally dependent upon the action that is the reason for its creation. In fact, though it is too early to talk about but let me state it briefly anyway while providing its details in later chapters, that the nature of *Karma* also defines the nature of bondage to that *Karma*; meaning, if there is any bondage to action, then so it is with its *Karma*.

Fourthly: Karma is a delayed reaction to an action where the delay is not controlled by any physical law.

It means no one knows when the expression of *Karma* and its material manifestation would occur?

You see! The *Karma* is like a <u>delayed response</u>, where even though the response is equivalent to the action but it is put on hold and delayed till it matures. There is no way to know what that delay is, because its timing is not bound by any physical laws, even though the action that causes it is under their governance.

Therefore, only thing we can say with certainty is that the expression of *Karma* would take place in some future frame of time, which could come during this lifetime or during the life after this; of course, that remains unknown.

Fifthly: This delayed reaction to human action, called as Karma, is an event of absolute certainty.

Even though there is much vagueness about the timing of the exhaustion of *Karma*, which represents the delayed reaction to an action, but there is no uncertainty about whether it would take place or not; because it is an <u>absolute certainty</u> that it would.

Surely, the timing of the <u>due season</u> of maturity of *Karma* is determined by the *Karmic*-laws of God, so no one knows when it would take place, but there is no doubt in its happening.

It means the exhaustion of due *Karma* occurs with an <u>absolute certainty</u>, unless of course, it is forgiven by God, but that can happens only before it matures (The reason why it is so, is explained later in chapter third – *Karmic*-Cycle).

Sixthly and lastly: The exhaustion of Karma comes in due future frame of time as an expression of some suitable form of life by the soul.

We already know that *Karma* is like a delayed reaction to an action, which is going to take place in some <u>due future frame of time</u>. But this 'due future frame of time' is dependent not upon the physical laws but upon the *Karmic*-laws; meaning, the rules and regulations of *Karma* determine when that 'due' time is going to be.

In terms of *Hindu* Philosophy, this 'due' season is when *Karma* matures and becomes ready for exhaustion. Only *Karmic*-laws determine the maturity and readiness of *Karma* for exhaustion, which of course, could take place during the remaining life or some upcoming *Karmic*-life in the future.

Beloved! The maturity of *Karma* is like the maturity of a Certificate of Deposit (CD) in the bank, the terms of which dictate a maturity date when the interest on the amount of CD can be claimed in full according to terms of the CD.

Similarly, *Karma* remains raw till it matures, in due time, and becomes ready to be exhausted. As then, it demands a suitable form of life for the soul to wear so that she could exhaust it.

But this condition has a much broader meaning since it really complicates things for the soul (*Atman*).

How? Well, let us understand that!

The *Karmic*-laws state that the exhaustion of the matured *Karma* can occur only when it is expressed through some suitable form of life by the soul **(Holy Gita 8:3)**.

But it is not hard to conceive that not all *Karma* can be expressed through the human body, especially if it is so bad that it demands lower bodies for its exhaustion **(Holy Gita 13:21)**, or it is so good that she needs to travel to high heavens for its expression by enjoying divine pleasures **(Holy Gita 9:40)**.

This imposes a very serious problem for the soul because the exhaustion of bad *Karma* demands that she passes through all kinds of lower embodiments to exhaust the due bad *Karma*, and similarly, wear heavenly forms and live in heavens to express good *Karma*.

In other words, the 'suitability of form of life' needed to exhaust the portions of matured *Karma* forces the soul to wear all kinds of suitable bodies and travel through all kinds of *Karmic*-territories. There is no rules that defines concretely how portions of *karma* would mature, and when the soul is going to embody in what form?

When we understand this complexity imposed upon the soul, we can understand the meaning of words 'due future frame of time' clearly by confronting the fact that the word 'due' refers to that frame of time in future when not only the *Karma* has matured but also the soul is ready to wear the suitable form of life that would facilitate the proper exhaustion of matured *Karma*.

Well, I am sure, with this understanding of *Karma*, it would be easy for us to understand what the bondage of *Karma* is, since even without our awareness, we already have covered some of its basics in last few paragraphs.

So let us understand now: What is the Karmic-bondage?

The dictionary meaning of the word 'bondage' is: 'A state-of-being bound usually by compulsion' or 'servitude or subjugation to a controlling person or force'.

It means it is a state-of-being bound to someone or something under force, and under compulsion and controlling influence.

Now, if we take this meaning of the word 'bondage', the '*Karmic*-bondage of the soul' would mean to be, 'The state of soul being bound to *Karma* under force'; isn't it! And that is exactly what we find it to be.

You see! Once man performs an action, his soul becomes obligated to exhaust the *Karma* created by his action. It is like a debt due upon her that has to be paid off by her, no matter what. Thus, for the soul, the exhaustion of due *Karma* is such an essentiality that cannot be waived under any condition.

We would learn later, in chapter where we would discuss the rules and regulations of *Karma*, that *Karmic*-rules compel the soul to wear whatever bodies are suitable to express the due *Karma* and endure suffering of those embodiments that are necessary to express it.

Therefore, the soul has no choice in this matter but to bear the *Karmic*-consequences of her human embodiment.

Of course, the due *Karmic*-consequences are as such that they compel her to pass through the suffering of those *Karmic*-lives that are suitable and essential for proper and complete exhaustion of the owed *Karma*.

Thus, the soul is in bondage to *Karma* since she is in 'the state-of-being, where she is bound to *Karma* under its force'.

And it is this bondage to *Karma* because of which, she is tied to mortality; she is tied to the repeated cycle of birth and death and bound to continual series of transmigration.

Well, now we know what is the meaning of '*Karmic*-bondage' of the soul, and how does she get trapped into it?

Next, we should reiterate one more time what the true nature of the soul is, and what she has become due to her bondage to Karma.

Of course, the scriptural truth tells us that the soul (*Atman*) in her absolute form of pure consciousness is nothing but the all-pervading, imperishable, immutable, ancient, eternal, transcendental Self **(Holy Gita 2:12-30)**; she is the *Atman*, an eternal part of God – The *Brahman* **(Holy Gita 15:7).**

Therefore, the soul is also of the same nature as of God, which is of *Sat-Chit-Ananda* (Truth-Consciousness-Bliss), meaning she is imperishable and immortal, and she is of the nature of pure consciousness and everlasting bliss.

This is true not for one or few but each and every soul, no matter what embodiment she is under, whether it is human or non-human. All creatures have a soul that is of pure light and love, and is of pure knowledge and bliss.

But when we look around, it certainly does not seem that way.

So what has happened to such an extraordinary nature of the soul (*Atman*)? Why does she not seem to inhabit her true virtue? Where is gone her true quality and character?

Well, the answer lies in the fact that even though the soul is immutable and unchangeable **(Holy Gita 2:24-25)**, she appears to be altered due to the fact that there is formed an opaque layer of darkness around her due to impurities caused by egocentricity, which happens to be responsible for *Karma*.

It is this encapsulation by egocentric ignorance that has eclipsed the soul and has surrounded her by the darkness of *Karma*, which has hindered her radiance, and hidden her natural sparkle and glow. In other words, the soul (*Atman*) has been conditioned by *Karma*; she has been externally altered into being something that is dark, ignorant, egocentric and full of passion and infatuation.

Oh! That is what she has become – a conditioned and stipulated soul that is confined by egocentric individuality.

To create a better understanding about what the soul is, let us look at the words of *Svetasvatara Upanishad* that unfold much mystery regarding this matter:

The soul can be thought as a part of a <u>point of a hair</u> which divided by a hundred were divided by a hundred again; and yet in this living soul there is the <u>seed of Infinity</u>.

The soul is not a man, nor a woman, nor what is either a woman not a man. When the soul takes the form of a body, by the same body the soul is bound.

The soul is born and unfolds in a body, with dreams and desires and the food of life. And then it is reborn in new bodies, in accordance with its former works.

The quality of soul determines its future body: earthly or airy, heavy or light. Its thoughts and its actions can lead it to freedom, or lead it to bondage, in life after life.

(Svetasvatara Upanishad, Part 5)

The meaning of these words may not be as obvious for now, but I am sure it would become quite visible as we move along further into the contents of this book.

Meanwhile, as we can see from the holy text above, that the soul, who is infinitely smaller than the '**point of a hair**', is in fact so big than she contains the '**seed of infinity**'. Though she is not a man or woman or any creature, but she seems to become that living-being whose body she wears.

Though in her true form she is the embodiment of liberty, due to her dreams and desires, she becomes bound to mortal bodies, which she wears life after life. Due to her affection and attachment to the material world she gets tied to the cycle of birth and death; and thus, her passion and infatuation, makes her prisoner of bondage.

Now, let us understand: Who we truly are; what our true nature is; and what we have become?

Surely, we are the soul!

Of course, we are not the body that dies and becomes ashes but the immortal and eternal *Atman*! Not the blood and bones that perish and pass away but the everlasting transcendental Self. That is who we are – the Atman – the soul!

But if the soul is in bondage, then so are we! Isn't it?

Even though in our purest form, we are of the nature of God, but bondage has changed all that about us. We have lost the eternal glitter and glow of our transcendental Self and have become very dim and dark perishable self.

Oh! Just look at us now and see what have we become!

How many among us are ready to joyfully proclaim that we are immortals; that we are full of true life and light; that we are the immutable, imperishable and eternal beings? Because in truth that is what we are; but look what we have become? Haven't we become the most pitiful self-centric self?

How true! As only a few chosen ones among us have escaped the lowly life of this material world and have ascended to consciousness of the higher Self, but they are very rare because only the most blessed reaches the most enlightened state of Self-realization **(Holy Gita 7:19)**.

As for the rest of us, it remains as an unreachable dream. Because due to ego and pride, and due to inner infection of passion and infatuation, we believe in the reality of our current human existence and consider its entirety as our own because that is what the indwelling ignorance and darkness, which surrounds our soul, has made us believe. The evil of *Karma* has

22

manipulated us, and that is why we are no more what we ought to be.

Thus, the reality for most of us is quite different than what it should be since our soul has been eclipsed by the illnesses of *Karma*; she has been plagued by the passion and infatuation, and infected by the evil egocentricity that feeds them, **"All desires that are born of egoistic will – Holy Gita 6:24."**

No wonder, we are nowhere even close to what we ought to be. Due to bondage we have lost our true nature and have become something we are not. Our immortality has been overshadowed by mortality; our transcendental existence has been tarnished by the transmigration.

After human embodiment, when our soul leaves this world, her *Karmic*-obligations force her to pass through the repeated cycle of transmigration so that she could suffer the consequences of her human-actions and pay her *Karmic*-dues by wearing countless lower and higher embodiments **(Holy Gita 13:21).** Not only that, she is also forced to take a seemingly endless journey to all kinds of *Karmic*-worlds **(Holy Gita 8:16)**, where for her *Papa* (bad *Karma* created by bad deeds), she suffers through the dreadful gutters of lowly hell, and for her *Punya* (good *Karma* created by good deeds), she travels through the pleasurable plains of high heavens.

So, if during human embodiment we do not succeed in liberating our soul from *Karmic*-bondage, then the cycle of *Karma* starts again; and we again go through seemingly a nonstop terror of transmigration which forces our soul to pass through countless lower and higher births. This happens to be the case more often than not.

The fact is that we have been going through this *Karmic*-cycle timelessly; who can say for how long? Only God knows since we have no recollection of the past **(Holy Gita 4:5).** Therefore, it is no exaggeration to say that we have been in this for a very long time.

And this cycle of higher and lower births, which seemingly is nonstop, continues till God in His mercy takes us out of it, and gives us another chance to redeem our soul from bondage by granting us another human embodiment, which of course is the only embodiment that has the empowerment to affect the *Karmic*-course.

But what does generally happen in human embodiment though is quite sad!

When our soul embodies as man, due to our attachments and desires, and our passion and infatuation for this world, she not only exhausts the old *Karma* just like she does in any other embodiment, she also creates new *Karma* with bondage, and thus, adds new load of *Karma* upon her head. In due time, the newly created *Karma* demands exhaustion, which of course, compels the soul to go through all kinds of suitable embodiments again by kick-starting the next cycle of *Karma*.

Oh! Each time, at the end of a *Karmic-cycle*, when God in His goodness gives another human embodiment to the soul and grants her another opportunity to save herself from the *Karmic*-bondage and become eternally liberated (*Moksha*), she often wastes it in enjoying the pleasures of this world and fails to free herself from the captivity of *Karma*.

Thus, the new *Karmic-cycle* commences again.

This is what has been going on since who knows how long? Surely, we have been in *Karmic*-bondage timelessly and would remain so in the future as well if we do not save our soul from its fetters now.

But what can we do to save the soul from *Karmic*-captivity if we already know that we cannot escape the creation of new *Karma*, as each and every human action creates it, and also, that the created *Karma* definitely demands its exhaustion?

Thus, it is certain that our soul would endure the immeasurable suffering, as she would be compelled to pass through all kinds of embodiments that are suitable for exhaustion of load of *Karma*.

So, we wonder, if there is anything we could do to escape the bondage to *Karma*? After all, as it seems, there is no way out of this evil self-sustaining cycle.

Well, such wonderment is quite natural, because we have not learned yet enough about *Karma* and its operating laws; otherwise, we would know better and understand that there are ways that can save our soul from the repeated torture of transmigration.

When we take a closer look at the ordinances that regulate the operations of *Karma*, one of the most important things we learn is that, though each and every human action creates *Karma*, surprisingly enough, not all of them create bondage **(Holy Gita 3:9)**.

We also become aware of the truth that it is not the action, nor the *Karma* that has the power to create bondage, as they both are non-binding in themselves; they both do not possess such potency, since such potency resides only in ego and self-centricity that accompany the action **(Holy Gita 4:22)**.

Oh, the secret! The bondage lies not in action but in the affinity with which the action is performed, because that is what binds the soul to its *Karma*.

It means as long as the action is without the assertion of egocentricity and self-centeredness, it is unbinding; it has no threads of bondage **(Holy Gita 3:9, 9:9)**.

That is why the *Karma* generated by ego-less actions is bondage-free; it does not bind the soul, as she remains out of its grasp.

In the following verse, this is exactly what is being told by Holy Gita:

If one is satisfied with whatever comes <u>without his egoistic effort</u>, and is beyond the pairs of opposites, and if he is also free from jealousy, and balanced in success and failure, <u>then even while acting, he is not bound</u>.

(Holy Gita 4:22)

The scriptural truth from the verse above clearly states that in absence of ego lies the absence of bondage – meaning the actions that are done without ego are non-binding, while the ones that are rendered with ego are binding.

So the bondage in *Karma* comes due to egocentricity and self-centeredness, because due to them we perform our actions with the sense of 'I-*ness*' and 'Mine-*ness*'. Thus, our real problem is not the action, nor *Karma*, but the attachment and desire that we have in it due to our ego and self-centricity.

It means it is our passion and fervor, our attachment and desire that is associated with the action, which is the true reason for our bondage to *Karma*, **"Impelled by desires, attached to the fruits of action, and thereof, goes to bondage – Holy Gita 5:12."**

Thus, though it is true that whenever we perform action, we create *Karma*, but whether we go into its bondage or not depends upon with what motive we render it. If we render it with ego and self-centricity, we go into its bondage, and if not, we remain bondage-free.

Therefore, it is the attitude and intent behind the action that determine whether there is bondage to its *Karma* or not. If an action is done without any attachment and without any desire of its fruits, then there is no bondage; but if it is done with selfish intents and with desire of its fruits, then it brings bondage for the 'doer' **(Holy Gita 5:12)**.

It means if we have passion in our action then it would bind us, otherwise it won't, and we would remain free from its bondage.

This should provide us some comfort, since now we know a way out of the captivity by *Karma*. We also understand now, why our soul keeps living in bondage, because whenever she attains a human life, she lives her days in infatuation with this world, and remains engaged in earning and accumulating its affluence to satisfy her fleshly thirst instead of trying hard to get freedom from bondage.

Thus, due to her affection and adoration for material things, the soul leaves this world without getting freedom from bondage, which in turn, forces the commencement of the next cycle of *Karma* compelling her to pass through countless embodiments again so that she could exhaust the created *Karma* of her previous human embodiment.

Since, it is not the action, nor the *Karma* that creates bondage but the passion, ego, and self-centricity in action that does, we can safely conclude that our soul would continue to live a life of *Karmic*-bondage and endure suffering of transmigration as long as we remain slave to the sensuality of this world.

Surely, that is an established truth, but of course, with only one exception, that through the grace of God, the soul could receive immunity from all *Karmic*-incarceration, which one finds only when he enters into His sanctuary and abides there with his entirety.

In fact, the grace of God is the only way out for the soul to get eternally released from bondage.

Well, there might be some who may not agree with me on this and think differently, and yet there might be some others who may find it hard to believe, but the truth is what it is. The grace of God is the only way for the soul to get out of bondage; this is the only avenue for her to attain the eternal liberation.

Otherwise, without the grace of God, she would continue to endure the torment of *Karma*, and thus, would continually remain entrapped by the *Karmic*-cycle, and not be able to attain freedom from bondage.

Now, what do we really mean when we say, 'Freedom from bondage?'

Before we get to this topic, let us understand one thing clearly, that there are several expressions that are used to refer to this particular state-of-being of the soul, which is of the highest consciousness called *Moksha*, where she is fully free from all bondage and is totally restored into her inherent form.

The literal meaning of the word '*Moksha*' is: 'The Eternal Liberation'. However, it is most often used with its implied meaning, which is: 'The Eternal Liberation of the Soul'; or to say it better even with more clarity as: 'The Eternal Liberation of the Soul from Bondage'.

The use of the word *Moksha* is synonymous with other expressions like: 'Eternal Liberation', 'Freedom from Bondage', 'Salvation', 'Saved', 'Redemption of Soul', 'Deliverance from Sin', 'Deliverance from Bondage', and 'Nirvana'; and there are still some more terms like these that are highly common in our daily language which are used for it.

In *Hinduism*, however, there is yet one very special term that is used to refer to this enlightened state-of-being of the soul called 'Self-realization', which refers to such a state-of-being where one has realized his higher Self and has become established in its truth. But this terminology is common only in communities that are sufficiently learned in *Hindu* Theology.

But no matter what we call it and what expression do we use to refer to it, one thing remains constant, that what we are talking about by these expressions is the state of absolute liberation of soul from bondage – the bondage, which has caused the soul all kinds of grief and is most definitely her main trouble. But how?

Let us look at it, and let us find out, what kind of trouble the soul actually is in?

You see! In her inherent nature the soul is immortal; but because of bondage, she lives a mortal life. Surely, it is the bondage that forces her to wear all kinds of suitable embodiments so that she could express and exhaust the debt of *Karma* that she has upon her head.

Otherwise, intrinsically, the soul (*Atman*) is a part of the all-pervading and eternal Transcendental Self – the *Brahman* – the *ParamAtman* – the Godhead – Who is absolutely pure and pious, holy and hollowed. However, due to bondage to sin she has been separated from Him. So until she is free from all sin, and become separated and sanctified from all un-holiness, she would not be able to have union with Him.

Since her passion for things of this world has made her slave to sin, until she is released from such slavery, she would not be able to see the light of the Spirit, and thus, would not be able to be restored to her authenticity of purity and piousness. Meaning, until all surrounding impurities caused by the passion have been removed and all contamination has been washed off her, she would not be able to have union with the Creator.

The fact is that due to her passion and infatuation – her attachment and desire – she is so thirsty, that until she drinks the cup of living water, she would not be cured of worldly dehydration and cannot be salvaged from earthly bondage.

Oh! Only the living water of the Truth can quench the thirst of a dehydrated soul; only the realization of Reality can rest her in peace; otherwise, her material manifestation would not cease and her restlessness would continue, and she would not be liberated from the fetters of bondage.

Well, what is the Moksha – the eternal liberation – the salvation of soul?

To understand it, let us first get the grip of truth that, as per scriptures, all material manifestations of the soul are due to Karma, **"That creative force is known as Karma which is the cause of the existence and the manifestation of all beings – Holy Gita 8:3,"** but the underneath fact is that it is not the Karma but its bondage that is the real cause of her embodiments. Meaning, the bondage to <u>Karma</u> is the reason of soul's mortality. It is the bondage that forces the immortal soul to pass through all kinds of mortal manifestations.

This happens to be the basic truth about the conditioned Karmic-life of the soul. From this, we would derive the meaning of Moksha.

In the above holy text, the word 'Karma' can be replaced with expressions like 'sin', 'the impurities surrounding the soul', 'the delusion and darkness around the Atman', 'the ignorance', and many other terms like that, and they all would work; they all would imply to be the reason for soul's material manifestations.

Thus, Moksha – the salvation of the soul – is such a state of existence of the soul where she is no more captive of Karma, no more captive of bondage, no more captive of mortality, no more captive of cycle of birth and death.

Meaning, the eternal liberation of the soul is a state of absolute liberty where she is eternally free from all kinds of bondage – free from bondage to Karma – free from bondage to sin – free from bondage to this world. In this state of-being, which is of highest enlightenment, she is free from everything that keeps her tied to the cycle of Karma; that makes her captive of mortality; that keeps her tied to the cycle of birth and death.

To have more understanding of this highest state of existence of the soul – the *Moksha* – the eternal liberation of soul – the salvation – here are some expressions that try to describe it by looking at its multidimensional view:

It is the state of absolute liberation of the soul **(Holy Gita 5:17)**; it is her deliverance from passion and infatuation; it is her redemption from the slavery to sin; it is her independence from the captivity to *Karma*; it is her freedom from all bondage; it is her release from the terror of transmigration; it is her discharge from the cycle of birth and death; it is her total emancipation from the manacles of mortal manifestations **(Holy Gita 8:16)**.

It is the state of true being-*ness* of the soul where she is not living in some conditioned state-of-being caused by her indwelling ignorance that makes her forget who she is and deludes her to believe in a false self-individuality; it is the restoration of Self-awareness where she knows who she truly is and who she is not; thus knowing, it is the rediscovering of her intrinsic form and reclamation of the knowledge about her genesis, and realization of her inherent form of immortal and eternal Transcendental Self.

it is the demolition of all walls of ignorance between the conditioned 'self' and all-pervading Transcendental 'Self' caused due to ego and pride; it is the elimination of all barricades of sin between the soul and the Sprit caused due to her passion and infatuation; it is the removal of all barriers of bondage standing between the *Atman* and *ParamAtman* (the Godhead) caused due to his delusion and darkness; it is the end of seemingly timeless separation of man from God caused by his self-indulgence and self-centricity, and is his eternal reconciliation with Him.

It is the amalgamation of 'created' with the Creator, the merging of 'made' with the Maker and becoming One with that Eternal Being, Who never perishes, even when all else perishes; Who is never destroyed even when all other is destroyed **(Holy Gita 8:20)**; and in Whom finds the *Atman* the unending rest and everlasting peace.

It is the release of the soul from the domains of captivity to darkness and delusion, and her reaching to the providence of divine light and wisdom where through the Self-realization she attains the knowledge about her own intrinsic form of ever-Existence, pure-Consciousness and everlasting-Bliss (Sat-Chit-Ananda), after reaching of which she no more remains the captive of darkness but becomes the embodiment of Light.

It is the arrival of the soul to that imperishable abode of Immortal and Immutable *Brahman,* which she attains through the grace of God after drifting in all kinds of *Karmic*-worlds – which is the home of everlasting peace and bliss **(Holy Gita 14:27)** – upon reaching of which she never returns to this world. The *Moksha* is that finality for the wandering *Atman* from where he never returns to the perishable worlds, **"That is My highest abode reaching which, one does not return this world again – Holy Gita 8:21."**

It is the rescue of the soul from falling into the fouls of hell and her reinstatement into everlasting heavenly life; it is her redemption from sin and restoration into righteousness of God; it is her deliverance from all earthly captivity and re-establishment into everlasting freedom; it is her salvation from timeless condemnation and resurrection into eternal commendation of the providence of God.

It is the satisfaction of that dehydration of timelessly unquenched soul for which she has drifted as nomad in all kinds of *Karmic-Lokas* and wandered through all sorts of planes of varying consciousness, traveled from world to world like a lost wanderer and have repeatedly gone back and forth between the extremities of heaven and hell, and wore repeatedly mortal bodies through innumerable transmigrations and endured all kinds of suffering and sorrow.

In summary, *Moksha* – the liberation of soul – the salvation - is nothing but restoration of the soul to her intrinsically supreme State-of-Being.

Oh! Before she was free but now she is in bondage; meaning, she has to be freed and be reinstated into the eternal Liberation again. Before she was with God but now she is separated due to her misconceived self-individuality; meaning, her false sense of self-identity needs to be liquidated and dissolved so that she could be reunited with Him again. Before she was of the nature of Knowledge but now she is under the clouds of delusion and darkness and surrounded by all kinds of impurities; meaning she has to be cleansed off all ills and be restored into light and wisdom, and resurrected into Knowledge again. Before she was of the perpetual life but now she is living the days of mortality; meaning, she has to regain her inherent immortality and be reinstated into everlasting life again.

2

Laws of Karma
~
The Governing Rules and Regulations of Mortality

The holy books unfold the Truth; they reveal knowledge about God; they unveil mystery of the universe, the heaven and hell and all worlds in between. They describe things that God has intended for man to know and find out.

They expose secrets of Existence as well as Non-existence. They convey understanding about what is the Truth and what is un-truth? What is the Reality and what is unreality? And they divulge knowledge about what exits and also what exists not?

Surely, the scriptures reveal all kinds of sacred knowledge, but there is none other as highlighted as is the unfolding of mystery of life that yields the adequate understanding about its origin, sustenance, and eventual merger with the Creator, and gives a concrete exposure of the purpose of all living-beings, especially the man in the context of overall schema of His cosmic creation.

It is not hard to see that the scriptures are very focused in exposing the supreme knowledge of the Transcendental Self and His altered states of existence as conditioned-soul. They are very attentive in unfolding the mystery of transitory transformations of the *Atman* (soul), which he assumes through transmigration that he passes through due to his *Karmic*-obligations laid upon him because of his bondage to this world. In addition to this, they also yield quite a sufficient account of his travel through all kinds of *Karmic*-worlds, which he not only passes through but occasionally makes temporary stays in them.

They further tell of what happens to the soul (*Atman*) during the times of Dissolution and Creation, and how she goes from manifest to un-manifest during the period of Non-existence, and how she resurrects again into materialization from un-manifest to manifest when the Existence commences again.

Thus, the scriptures unveil many of those secrets that are ever beyond man's ability to know on his own.

Surely, as vouched for by those who have explored them, the holy books expose so much knowledge that it is ever beyond the telling of man.

But one thing is easy to tell that it all has been told by God with a very specific purpose, and that purpose is, that man could know His truth and understand his own reality so that he could salvage his soul from the shackles of sin and redeem himself from the fetters of *Karma*, and thus, liberate himself from the bondage and resurrect his soul into the everlasting life.

Mainly for this reason, God unfolded the mystery of *Karma* and unveiled not only its ordinances that regulate the conditioned-life of the soul in *Karmic*-worlds, but also exposed man to what he must do in order to secure escape for his soul from any further imprisonment to mortality, and save her from the ongoing entrapment by the cycle of birth and death.

We do not need to be genius to realize that holy books are the words of God, which He spoke to man of all times with the primary purpose to help him understand the Reality and Truth, and convey very specific instructions on how to make life meaningful by attaining salvation for his soul, which is the highest goal of human life, and thus, have reconciliation with His creator and end his eternal separation from Him.

The holy books consistently make it clear that man needs deliverance from sin; that he needs release from the bondage of *Karma*; that he needs the liberation from the captivity of the cycle of birth and death; and that he needs the end of his separation from God.

Thus, they give a very specific message to him by explicitly emphasizing the fact that only becoming One with God would end soul's indignant individuality; that only her union with Him would make her eternally whole; and that only her submersion in Him would bring her the everlasting rest and peace.

And they leave no doubt that achieving salvation is the top priority for man, and that the redemption of his soul is the sole purpose of his birth; and that liberating his *Atman* from the fetters of *Karma* is the highest goal of his life.

But that is not all the Holy Scriptures do. Besides rendering every effort to make man aware of the reason why God created him as human, they also continually feed him the guidance in every way possible so that he could successfully live by the plan and fulfill the purpose that God had in His mind when He formed and fashioned his soul into a living human-being.

Thus, scriptures, which are the living words of God, are the greatest guide and the supreme teacher of man; they are the most perfect guiding-light for his soul.

Hear these words of the divine wisdom emanating from Holy Gita where she enthusiastically advises man to seek guidance from the sacred books and commands him to truthfully abide by their truth in his daily life:

Therefore, <u>let scriptures be your guide</u> in determining what is right and what is wrong. Knowing what is in accordance with the scriptures, you must perform duties in this world.

(Holy Gita 16:24)

Please make a note that Holy Gita gives this sound advice, **"Let scriptures be your guide,"** not only once or twice, but quite repeatedly **(Holy Gita 3:7, 13:25, 16:1, 16:23, 17:11, 17:13, 17:24);** of course, not so explicitly.

Look at these most prayerful words of the Psalmist that seek the guiding-light unto his path hidden in the holy text:

35

Thy word is a lamp unto my feet, and a light unto my path.

(Holy Bible, Psalms 119:105)

The wisdom dictates that man should seek light from the scriptures, and live and abide by their truth; because they not only unfold the reality of existence of man, and reveal how he has been caught by the claws of *Karma* and trapped by the shackles of sin, but also unveil God's plan to pull his soul out of the burden of bondage and liberate her into everlasting life, and thus free her forever from the manacles of mortality.

In Holy Gita Lord God says that through the discourse He has revealed the Supreme truth **(Holy Gita 18:64)**, and has unveiled even that layer of the Truth, which is hidden underneath the deep secrets, **"Thus I have imparted to you the wisdom that is the secret of all secrets – Holy Gita 18:63."**

Of course, as per these words of God, He has disclosed to man the deepest secrets of His kingdom, which though is all-existent and all-pervading and yet cannot be seen by man unless of course first God grants him the vision of enlightenment **(Holy Gita 11:8)**.

Nonetheless, the constitution of His government with which He rules and regulates His creation has been described in scriptures, where He has dictated, though not very thoroughly yet sufficiently, the laws and statues, which command and control His Kingdom.

Surely, God has given man all the necessary instructions on how he could live on this earth in most meaningful manner and be right and just with Him during all his days, and finally be united with Him upon his parting from this world.

He has detailed everything what was needed for man to carry out His plan and fulfill His will by walking in His professed ways, and eventually finding the salvation for his soul through His graces, and thus be fully fruitful just as God has intended for him to be.

Thus, God revealed all what He thought was necessary for man to know, yet only those things that He found right in His sight, and exposed to him only what He considered essential for him to know.

He unfolded only what was vital for mankind to understand and nothing more, and intentionally kept hidden the rest, because some of it He thought was harmful to man and some He found unnecessary.

Thus, as per the will of God, many things were not exposed to man for one reason or the other. And even the things that have been revealed to him often lack the details of their workings, as not all secrets about them have been unfolded in their entirety because so was found to be fit in the sight of God.

For example: even the scriptures, which have been worded precisely, yield different meanings to different seekers, as we all come up with our own understanding of the same words of God, because God reveals different things to different people as per His will. Though His words are the same to all in reading, His revelations rising out of them vary from heart to heart, person to person, and seeker to seeker.

You see! The revealed Truth is not an exact science, where all know-how is concrete and clearly defined, so not all the questions, which we all have, are answered precisely in the holy books.

Thus, in our spiritual understanding, there are areas that surely are gray. There are things, about whom much has been spoken in scriptures, yet lack specific details about them.

Such is the case with *Karma*. Though, there is much exposure about this subject in holy books, yet not all and everything about it is explicitly exposed. Even though there is much revelation as to how the *Karmic*-laws operate, yet their concrete understanding is often missing.

For example: if we ask a simple question, **"What action produces what specific *Karma*?"** or **"What *Karma* results into what specific birth for the soul to exhaust it?"** the answer is not specifically documented anywhere in scriptures.

True, that *Vedas*, *Puranas* and other *Hindu* holy books quite often talk about things related to this subject, yet they lack concrete details.

But that does not mean human mind is not curious to know them – because it surely is. It wants to nail down all principles of *Karma* just like anything else; it wants to understand everything about its rules and regulations and desires to know the specifics about how do the laws of *Karma* operate? Of course, it wants to know all things that pertain to it.

I am sure, if we could help, we all would like to know the exact science behind *Karmic*-principles because no matter how ignorant we are about other aspects of it, we all know and believe quite firmly that *Karma*, which is the unseen outcome of our past actions, somehow quite definitely factors into formation of our future life; and this belief alone raises enormous curiosity in us to know all the specifics about it.

But the reality remains that not all the answers about *Karma* can be found in scriptures as clear as we like; however, they unveil many mysteries related to it to a greater extend, which, in a meaningful way, are quite sufficient to satisfy the curiosity of a wise and prudent mind.

However, in absence of details on how the laws of *Karma* operate when we raise such questions for which there are no scriptural answers, an interpreter of the scriptural truth takes the liberty to come up with the answers according to his own understanding and beliefs; and that surely leaves much room for biased interpretation, which often creates confusion in our understanding about the workings of *Karma*.

I just mentioned it so that we could keep this thought in mind as a caution. You see! The Truth is revealed according to the humility and hunger of the heart and not by the eagerness, agility and aggressiveness of the mind.

Beloved! That is the governing spiritual law, which applies to true learning of the wisdom hidden in the holy word of God.

Of course, through mind we comprehend the truth concealed in scriptures but only as a concept, which remains afloat in our intellect until it settles down and becomes a concrete conviction to our inner being. But it becomes conviction only when we live it and experience its liveliness and come in touch with its true essence. Till then, we remain void of the totality of the truth. We see its true face only when our spirit gets awakened by the light of the embedded truth and acquires the vision of love to behold it.

Oh! We come to know the truth only when first we become the truth; meaning, the truth is known by experiencing it and not by learning it:

In truth who knows God becomes God.

(Mundaka Upanishad, Part 3, Chapter 2)

The fact is that human depends upon mind to gain knowledge; that is his instrument of learning; that is his faculty of intangible growth through which he multiplies his understanding. But the scriptural truth is beyond mental comprehension; it is beyond human mind and thought, as so says the *Upanishad*:

Words and mind go to him, but reach him not and return.

(Taittiriya Upanishad, 2.9)

God reveals wisdom to those who seek His heart; He uncovers His mysteries to those who commune with Him in the solitudes of their soul; He unfolds His secrets to those whose spirit receives and reflects the radiance of His spirit.

The truth is revealed to a mind that is pure and pious; it is given to a seeker who is unselfish and altruistic; it is bestowed upon a heart that is extremely devout and humble.

Otherwise, the received truth becomes tainted and defiled because the wisdom received in selfishness and pride becomes covered by the clouds of ignorance caused by the indwelling darkness of the seeking heart.

So even though not all questions about *Karma* are answered in the scriptures, yet if we diligently and devoutly seek the words of God, we find out that they expose enough details on this subject for our purpose and yield adequate knowledge about what the rules and regulations of *Karma* are?

They clearly divulge the sufficient knowledge of the principles of *Karma* and depict the know-how of those rules and regulations upon which *Karmic*-worlds operate including the exceptions and deviations from their regular jurisdiction, if there are any.

They also answer the questions like: How *Karma* keeps the soul under its captivity life after life? How does its bondage force her to pass through countless embodiments **(Holy Gita 13:21)**? What is the reason behind her imposed mortality **(Holy Gita 8:3)**? And what makes her continually tied to the cycle of birth and death?

Thus, there is enough knowledge exposed in the word of God that adequately establishes the laws of *Karma* and defines its life-cycle that governs the total conditioned-life of the soul as an individual *Jiva* (conditioned-soul).

Surely, the words of God take us through many details that explain the principles of *Karma* to a point where we begin to understand the reason and purpose of life, and learn of the destinations that our *Atman* (soul) have traveled thus far and would travel in the future as a part of her *Karmic*-journey, which eventually one day at the end of her spiritual evolution, would end in paradise, but only through the grace of God.

Through them, we come to know the principles behind the cycle of earthly embodiments, and learn the secret of birth and death, and understand the truth why *Karma* is the reason behind all life **(Holy Gita 8:3)**, and finally, we also gain knowledge in great detail about our bondage to *Karma*.

And that surely is a good news since we have to have this knowledge to get reasonably familiar with *Karma* and its bondage, and have an adequate understanding of the principles upon which it operates.

Therefore, it is highly advisable that we chart down the laws of *Karma* before we move any further, since it is this knowledge that forms the basis of all understanding regarding its bondage, which of course, has an ever-continuing cyclic effect upon the future of the soul.

But, since the knowledge of *Karma* is not consolidated at one particular place in scriptures but is scattered all over, we have to extract it in bits and pieces from the related holy texts.

However, before we do that and venture into holy word which unfolds the mysteries of *Karma*, we must have a firm belief in our heart that if something is not revealed in the holy word, then God obviously did not find it necessary to disclose it, and did not think that it was essential for us to know.

With such readjusted attitude, let us now visit the scriptures to find out what God has revealed about the instituted principles of *Karma* and try to understand its laws – which are the governing rules and regulations of all mortality.

Please make a note that descriptions of these ordinances of *Karma* that are given here are quite brief and concise to a point that they yield only the concept of it and leave out all the details that would come later when they become applicable to the subject being discussed in the upcoming chapters.

First: All Karma demands exhaustion.

This is such an essentiality for the soul (*Atman*) that cannot be waived. She has to do this no matter what – meaning if there is any due *Karma* upon her, then the soul has to exhaust it no matter what. Whether the *Karma* is good or bad, it has to be exhausted by the soul as she has no choice in this matter but to live by this rule.

Though the above statement is true, however, as we will see later, the truth stated in it deviates from its absoluteness but only under one condition, that the *Karmic*-penalties imposed upon soul are waived through the forgiveness that comes through the grace of God.

There is one exception to this rule though, that there is no waiver for the <u>matured *Karma*</u> for the soul no matter what, since the body, which the soul wears to exhaust it, once assumed, has to go through all *Karmic*-consequences regardless of the pardon that is received by the soul by entering into the sanctuary of God.

Of course, there is no scriptural text that could support and validate this conclusion, however, such finding holds much ground when we look into the lives of many such Self-realized souls that have suffered exceedingly even after becoming wholly enlightened.

So it is quite reasonable to say that once the soul has begun the embodied life, all ordained *Karma*, which was the reason of this embodiment, demands compulsory exhaustion before she could end her mortal journey in that form.

The reason being that the forgiveness of sins by God, if there is any, does not apply to those *Karmic*-consequences that have been ordained for this embodied life of the soul, as it surely does not excuse her from enduring those pending *Karmic*-expressions, good and bad both, which have been ordained to be exhausted in this life .

So, when man takes refuge in God with his entirety and receives His clemency for his sins through His grace and when he is granted pardon for all of his sins, **"I will verily free you of all sins, do not grieve – Holy Gita 18:66,"** he still has to endure the *Karmic*-life that has been ordained for him, even though his experience of it changes dramatically since now he is in the hands of God and God is his companion through it all. Surely, his sins are forgiven but the sorrow and suffering of life still continues the way it was before; however, being with God, makes it much easier to endure.

Thus, there is a divergence in this *Karmic*-law as it deviates from it absoluteness when the grace of God intervenes and saves the soul from its future *Karmic*-consequences; otherwise, all *Karma* demands its exhaustion by the soul, no matter what.

Second: The Karma is exhausted by the soul by wearing suitable bodies and expressing life accordingly.

When the soul in human embodiment performs an action, right then it becomes definite that she would <u>endure</u> a delayed reaction, the *Karma*; and live it as some <u>suitable life</u> in some future frame of time when that *Karma* matures; and that is how she would exhaust and get out of the burden of this portion of *Karma*, which is, by wearing a <u>suitable form of life</u> **(Holy Gita 8:3)**.

Of course, this is the reason why the soul, after human embodiment, goes through countless other embodiments **(Holy Gita 13:21)**, as in each life she expresses and exhausts some portion of matured *Karma*, and she continues this until, due to grace of God, for her good *Karma* she is given a human form again.

Third: The reason for all existence of life is Karma.

Or, we can say that all life is a medium to exhaust *Karma*. After all, if the soul is not salvaged through the grace of God, then regardless of how a soul has lived life as man, there is always a burden of *Karma* upon her after she ceases human embodiment.

And, since all due *Karma* demands exhaustion, the soul is forced to walk on a *Karmically* suitable path to bear all kinds of embodiments creating more material manifestations for her so that a proper expression of *Karma* could take place.

So it is true that life is needed to make the payoffs of *Karma*, but the question is: Is it also true that all life is made for this purpose alone?

Well, the answer comes through these holy words that say, **"That creative force is known as *Karma* which is the cause of the existence and the manifestation of all beings – Holy Gita 8:3,"** and confirm that *Karma* is the sole reason for all life; and it is that creative force, which is the cause of all material embodiments of the soul.

Obviously, these holy words provide a clear clue about life and confidently state the fact that the reason for soul (*Atman*) to embody as *Jiva* (conditioned-soul) is *Karma*, which compels her to wear all kinds of suitable embodiments for its expression.

Thus, the conclusion is that *Karma* causes life to manifest; and life causes *Karma* to be exhausted. Meaning, *Karma* is the basis of all life; and all life is a vessel for expression and exhaustion of *Karma*.

It means no matter what creature it is, there is a pre-determined purpose for its life, which is to exhaust the due matured portion of *Karma* that was earned by its soul by performing actions in her freewill when she was embodied as human, and now is wearing a creaturely body that is suitable for its expression.

Thus, all life is a vessel of exhaustion of some due matured portion of *Karma* regardless of what it is, as it is the only medium for its expression; there is no other way for its exhaustion.

Worth noticing is the fact that this law, which states that the reason of existence of all life is *Karma*, is a corollary to the last law, which states that the only way for exhaustion of *Karma* is for the soul to wear the suitable bodies and express life accordingly.

So if we combine the two laws then one truth becomes firmly established that there is <u>one and only one</u> way to exhaust *Karma*, which is for the soul to wear suitable bodies and express life accordingly – meaning the *Karma* compels the soul to wear bodies, and the soul wears bodies only to exhaust *Karma*; in other words, *Karma* causes life to manifest; and life causes *Karma* to be exhausted.

Fourth: All human actions create Karma regardless of what they are.

One of the most fundamental things about *Karma* is that all human actions create it.

To each action of man, there is a delayed reaction called *Karma*, no matter what; it is always there as a subtle counterpart that manifests itself in the future. It is like an understated reaction – a discrete side effect – to whatever man does that materializes later in its due time.

So when man performs a bad action (*Papa*), as its counterpart, some bad *Karma* is created, and when he performs a good action (*Punya*), as its complement, some good *Karma* is created. This law holds true in all situations and circumstances, regardless.

Thus, the established truth is that human action cannot take place without creating *Karma*. Its manifestation cannot happen without the birth of *Karma*. It is not an option for man to have it or not have it, as it always is there no matter what.

And there is even a good reason, why man's action creates *Karma*, while no other creature in the creation has such a capability.

You see! It is only man and no other creature in the whole creation which has been granted the privilege of freewill; only he has the faculty to discern and choose his actions as per his will; only he has the power to judge and select. Only human has the empowerment to assert his will, as no other creature has such endowment since they all are driven by the power of instinct.

But because man chooses his actions on his own, naturally he is held responsible for them. It makes sense that he is held accountable for them and bears the burden of their *Karma* since he is the one who chooses and renders them.

Of course, *Karma* is like a token of responsibility a man bears when he chooses to perform an action in his freewill, and for which he is forced to endure the consequences according to *Karmic*-judicial system.

Since man performs actions as per his own discernments and renders them as per his choosing, they become his liability; they become his charge. And that is what *karma* is all about; it is a representative of his liability in performing actions.

It means when a man performs an action, whatever is its counterpart in the form of *Karma* becomes the representative of his responsibility and accountability towards it for which he has to suffer its consequences during some future frame of time.

So it is not hard to understand why man's actions create *Karma*, since it is he who discerns and chooses them to perform. And that is why his soul is held accountable for them in the form of their *Karma*.

Oh! *Karma* is the representative of burden of responsibility laid upon the soul of man for the actions he performs in his freewill.

Thus, it is quite obvious that man has no choice in this matter; whether he likes it or not, *Karma* is always there as a reaction to his action, since it is intrinsically embedded in its performance.

This certainly sounds like a bad news that in human embodiment alone the soul creates new *Karma* and gets further loaded by its burden, no matter what. She does not get a free ride like any other birth.

However, this bad news turns into a good one when we learn that it is the human embodiment alone, during which the soul has the empowerment to change the course of *Karma*.

Fifth: No other creature is capable of creating Karma since none has the empowerment of discernment and the privilege of freewill.

What draws the difference between human and any other creature is that he has the empowerment of such faculties as mind and intellect, and he has the endowment of the power of freewill. All these discriminative faculties set him far apart from all others, since through them he is fully capable of holding the discernment in all matters of life, and is able to act anyway he chooses through the power of his freewill.

Thus, man is very special in the sight of God since so many exceptional privileges have been granted to him only, as no other living being has been blessed with them. Only human is capable of thinking and is able to differentiate right from wrong; only he is empowered with the faculty of intellect that enables him to choose between good and bad.

Oh! Only man has such special privileges as no other creature does.

All other beings are void of such apparatus like mind and intellect. They do not have the power of memory (they possibly have some episodic memory) and recollection; they do not have the endowment of autonomy and independence of freewill; they do not have the faculties of discrimination and discernment.

This is why they are not led by any intellect but by their instinct, and are driven by intuition alone. They have no endowment of rationality since they are totally void of intellectual empowerment. This is what draws the difference between the human birth and all other creatures.

We already know that according to laws of *Karma*, all births are made to exhaust *Karma*, but human birth is very unique in the sense that it not only exhausts *Karma* but also creates new Karma.

Since human is equipped with all resources to think and choose, it is no wonder that he is made responsible for his actions and held accountable for his *Karma*; and because he has been given the mind, intellect and freewill, so he is also

46

given the responsibility for his chosen actions in the form of their *Karma*.

But the same does not apply to all other creatures since they are void of all such discriminative faculties and do not have the empowerment of freewill. And since they live by their instinct, they are not held accountable for whatever life they live, and hence, there is no *Karma* created in their lives; they only exhaust the ordained *Karma* and do not create any new one.

Thus, the conclusion is that all other lives but human have only one purpose, which is to exhaust whatever *Karma* has been ordained for them.

However, this conclusion unveils a much greater truth, that all other births but human truly do not do much good for the soul when it comes to her (the *Jiva* – the conditioned-soul) liberation from bondage, since the sole purpose of all other embodied lives is to exhaust the accumulated *Karma* and nothing else.

Though it is true that all other births facilitate the exhaustion of the pending *Karma*, but also is true that during those fallen births the soul as a living-being has only instinct and intuition, and no mind, intellect and freewill; she has no capacity to discern and no ability to choose anything in life. Thus indirectly, unlike human embodiment, she is barred from having a privilege to will and choose the eternal life over the forced mortal living, since she has no power to choose anything anyway.

As a result, non-human births do not do much good in achieving liberation as the faculties to facilitate such ability is absent in them; only humans are privileged to have such an opportunity, and only they are granted the privilege of such gateway to eternity through the grace of God.

Sixth: As is action, so is Karma – meaning the good action creates good Karma while the bad creates bad Karma.

It seems very logical that *Karma* is created according to the nature of action. Meaning, the good *Karma*, is born out of good action (*Punya*), and the bad *Karma* is born out of bad action (*Papa*).

47

No wonder, when some calamity falls upon a person who has committed some evil, often we hold his bad *Karma* accountable for his disaster. At least that becomes a common view with which people look at him.

This is why folks often try to do good deeds so that they could accumulate good *Karma* for future life. How often we hear our holy teachers encouraging us to do good deeds in order to secure good *Karma* for a better 'next-life'. Surely, the popular belief is that good deeds bear good fruits and bad deeds bear bad fruits of *Karma*; also that good *Karma* takes one to hallways of heavens while the bad takes him to corridors of hell. Thus, both extremities of *Karmic*-worlds lie within the reach of *Karma*.

By speaking the words like, **"As a result of meritorious deeds, they attain the heavens where they enjoy divine pleasures – Holy Gita 9:20,"** Holy Gita not only confirms the belief that good deeds cultivate good harvest of *Karma* but also validates the truth that bad deeds do yield a bad crop of *Karmic*-consequences:

> **Confused because of many evil desires, entangled by the snares of infatuation, intensely attached to the gratification of the senses, they fall into foul hell.**
>
> **(Holy Gita 16:16)**

From these holy words, it is quite clear that the ultimate bad of the soul, which takes place when she fall into fouls of hell, is not caused by anything else but by man's bad *Karma*, which of course, as we would learn soon, is created by his ever-unquenched passion and infatuation, and ever-unsatisfied lust and greed.

Surely, the good deeds done to please God pave the way to freedom from bondage for man, **" Only actions done in God bind not the soul of man – Isa Upanishad,"** while the bad ones draw him further deeper into it. While the unselfish actions done for the good of others make man rise to the pinnacle of enlightenment and bliss, the selfish actions done to fulfill his fleshly desires make him fall into the wombs of delusion and darkness, **"Impelled by desires, attached to the fruits of action, and thereof, goes to bondage – Holy Gita 5:12."**

Just the way life established in the Self is an entrance to eternity, life entangled with the lust and greed is a gateway to hell **(Holy Gita 16:21)**. While one paves the path to heaven for the soul, the other paves the path to hell; while one lays the track to freedom, the other lays the trail to captivity; while one brings the liberty from the fetters of *Karma*, the other ties her hand to confines of bondage.

Surely, this is what the scriptures have to say about it.

However, in life, often there seems to be a deviation from the law that says **"As is action so is its *Karma*;"** because, every day we can find such examples where this law seemingly applies paradoxically. We often see folks that are good but are suffering with bad *Karma* and living a troubled life, while many others that are bad and ever engaged in evil but are living a good and flourished life.

Well, in such situations life seems so unjustified.

How often we see that an evil man in his wickedness commits sins all day long, of course, without any fear of God and without any worry of ill consequences for his filthy deeds, and yet he lives a life of wealth and prosperity; while on the other hand a righteous man labors all day longs and suffers greatly day in and day out and yet he endures a life of poverty and hardships.

This scenario is not uncommon anymore as the society is turning wicked more rapidly than ever before. Day by day the evil is growing while the righteousness is declining. The corruption and the wickedness have rooted in the heart of man. The lust and greed have become the rulers of his soul. The honesty, integrity, decency and dignity are the forgone virtues of his spirit; dignity and decency, the virtue and morality, the goodness and grace, have become just some leftover concepts of the righteousness.

In such times, not one or two, but countless examples we can find everyday where a wicked and evil is prospering, while the righteous and virtuous is declining.

And when we see this, we wonder: Where is God? Where is His justice? Where is the judicial enforcement of His Karmic-rule?

These questions are very valid, no doubt! And they do demand and deserve the satisfactory and correct answers. But before we can come up with answers to such questions as to why an evil man has such an enriched life, and why sometimes righteous suffers so much, we must have a proper understanding of the scriptures, that reveal the knowledge of the laws of *Karma*.

Because, before we understand why it is so, we must first understand the fact that the *Karma* affects not one but countless lives that are yet to come. Meaning, *Karmic*-effect could span over several future lives.

Let me caution that without this understanding one may find the following answer inadequate and not very satisfying; however, the truth is that the overwhelming prosperity in the present life of a man, who happens to be evil, is not necessarily the result of what he has done in this life, but probably is result of what he has done in his past lives.

The worldly wealth, which he is enjoying now, is a result of some deeds he did in his past; it is due to his previous good *Karma*, which of course, is coming to fruition now.

But since our focus is only on the current life, we are basing our judgment solely upon what we see in present and draw conclusion on what we know of his *Karma* in this life alone; however, if we knew the totality of his *Karma* spanning over all applicable previous lives, we would find that the harvest this man is reaping now is what he has seeded in his past.

Now, if we believe in the word of God, then we can count on one thing for sure, that regardless how prosperous life he has now but for his evil ways of the present, this deluded and lost soul would earn such a terrible *Karma* that would force him not just to go through countless lower births but also pass through an immeasurable terror and torture of demonic wombs of hell. It would surely happen, because, so says the word of God **(Holy Gita 16:19)**.

Similarly on the other hand, a righteous man, who is seemingly suffering unjustifiably in this life, would certainly be granted a future life of goodness and grace, peace and joy, and receive as recompense much affluence and abundance in his next-life as per rules and regulations of *Karma*.

Seventh: Both type of Karma – the good and bad – is lived separately, as one type does not cancel out the other.

Only if the good *Karma* were able to nullify the bad *Karma*, the things would have been quite different for the soul (*Atman*). Unfortunately, such is never the case – meaning, she has to exhaust good and bad *Karma* separately. There is no cancellation of one by the other.

One type of *Karma* cannot offset the other kind; they both are independent of each other; they both stand on their own, so they both need their separate exhaustion. If that were not the case, after doing a bad deed, man would have been able to wipe out its ill *Karmic*-effects just by doing an equivalent good deed. Everything would have been just fine then.

However, such is never the case; man just cannot do so.

His soul has to endure the *Karmic*-consequences separately for each of his deeds. When man does a good deed, he forms and shapes a good frame of time in his future, and when he does a bad deed, he does the opposite of it and creates and crafts a bad frame of time, which is to come in his future life.

Thus, man's actions create *Karma* that defines separate consequences in his future life. There is no annulment of one type of *Karma* by the other. Each action, each work, each deed is merited and counted separately towards the total sum of *Karma*.

For his good *Karma*, which a man earns through his good deeds, he enjoys the pleasures of heaven, **"Will attain to the higher worlds - those that are attained by men of meritorious deeds – Holy Gita 18:71,"** and for his bad *Karma*, which he becomes responsible for through his bad deeds, he suffers the unpleasant consequences of hell, **"The worst among men, who are involved in sinful deeds, I hurl them into demoniac wombs – Holy Gita 16:19."**

It is as simple as that.

It is not that the total sum is taken of both types of *Karma* at the end of human life and then smaller is subtracted from the greater, and then the resultant decides whether the soul enjoys the journey through provinces of heaven or endures the suffering of domains of hell. Each action, each deed, good or bad, has its own *Karmic*-journey.

Eighth: The heaven and hell are two extreme territories of Karmic-worlds.

According to scriptures there are 14 *Lokas* – the planes of varying consciousness – that are under the rule of *Karma*. They are under its power and authority; its governing laws and statues regulate them.

Among all *Karmic-Lokas*, the heaven is the highest, while hell is exactly the opposite – meaning it is the lowest of them all.

Furthermore, these *Lokas* define the domain of *Karmic*-consequences for the soul. They form that *Karmic*-kingdom in which the soul lives when she is in under the bondage of *Karma* and suffers its captivity.

Man's highest *Karma* takes him to heaven, **"A Yogi enjoys heavenly worlds for everlasting years – Holy Gita 6:41,"** while his worst takes him to hell, **"Abide in hell for an undeterminable period – Holy Gita 1:44."**

So the reward of man's work lies within these two extremities of *Karmic*-worlds – the heaven and hell.

Whatever he does, his soul suffers its consequences in between the territories of these two extreme empires – the empire of good and the empire of bad. When she cultivates good *Karma* (*Punya*) she travels towards the delightful monarchy of heavens, but when she harvests the bad *karma*, she heads towards the evil kingdom of hell.

Thus, whatever is going to happen in man's future *Karmic*-life is very dependent upon what good or bad deeds he does during his current human life. Whether he ends up in heaven or hell, depends upon what he does in this life.

Now, even though the concept of heaven and hell is very popular, and almost everyone believes in them, no one can say for sure what and where they are? However, according to the scriptures, they are the highest and lowest planes (*Loka*) of consciousness among the *Karmic-Lokas*.

Thus, to sum it up, in higher levels, the soul enjoys the pleasures of heavens while in lower levels she suffers the sorrows of hell; however, the existence in both are nothing but mere means for the *Atman* to exhaust *Karma*.

But the real difference between the two types of *Karma* is that good takes the soul towards the light and wisdom and leads her to even higher levels of consciousness, while bad takes her towards the ignorance and darkness and leads her to further lower levels of consciousness.

Whether, the soul heads towards the heaven or towards the hell, the only purpose they both serve is the expression and exhaustion of *Karma*; whether she passes through the higher planes of consciousness or the lower, the only thing that comes out of it is the payoff of her *Karmic*-obligations.

Of course, the experience in two kinds of provinces is different – in one it is filled with pleasure while in other it is filled with pain – but the outcome is the same, which is the expression of *Karma*.

Oh! What a mirage for a human soul that labors in vain and knows not that her striving to attain the highest merit in *Karmic*-judgment changes nothing in terms of her eternity, with one exception of course, that either she becomes more dark or more light; meaning, either she becomes more deluded or more wise. That's all!

Ninth: It is not the Karma but its bondage that is the real problem for the soul.

This is one of those things that many of us fail to realize, that it is not the *Karma* that is our real problem, but its bondage. This is where lies our great misunderstanding, which badly misguides our approach to all spiritual life. Because if we really understood what the real reason of our bondage is, though not all but surely many among us who are spiritually inclined, would be more sensitive to this issue and be more careful in rendering actions in such a way that they are not caught by their bondage.

The scriptures say that it is not the *Karma* but bondage to *Karma* that ties the *Atman* (soul) to mortality. So as far as the salvation of the soul (*Atman*) is concerned, no matter how good our deeds are, if they create bondage to *Karma*, they are useless; and they are futile. In fact they are even harmful to us since they seed further mortality for our immortal soul (*Atman*).

This is why even the good deeds are really not as good as we might think since often they are rendered out of egoistic and selfish attitude where the underneath self-centricity defiles and destroys the goodness of good *Karma* by creating bondage to it.

Therefore, this kind of good *Karma* does not do much good since it increases the burden of bondage upon our soul and multiplies her suffering through mortality.

Thus, it surely would be nice if we sincerely adopt and live by this truth that the real problem for the soul is not the *Karma* but its bondage, because it would certainly help us walk rightly on our spiritual path by enabling us to be vigilant of falling into bondage as much as possible.

Tenth: Ego creates 'doer-ship' in action and doer-ship creates bondage to Karma.

Just like the previous law of *Karma*, this law also is very important to us, because observance of this law can create very different results for our holy labor.

We already know that it is not the *Karma*, which is the real problem for the soul (*Atman*) but it is the bondage to it. But bondage comes in action only when it is done with egocentricity, and rendered with self-centric attitude.

How does that happen, let's look at it!

The scriptures tell that the soul (*Atman*) lives as a *Jiva* (conditioned-soul) because of her misplaced belief in her individuality conceived due to ignorance:

Avidya Upadhih SanMatamaJeeva Iti Uchhyate – The awareness (Atman) conditioned by Upadhi viz. Avidya (ignorance) is called Jiva.

(Tattwa Bodha of Adi Shankaracharya)

Due to indwelling ignorance caused by attachments and desires she has forgotten who she truly is. She cannot remember that she is not a mortal, changeable, and perishable being but an immortal, immutable and imperishable part of the eternal Self.

The impurities that eclipse the mind have disabled the faculty of memory so badly that she cannot remember that she is not the body but the very consciousness in the body that brings it to liveliness.

You see! The ignorance creates such a delusion for the soul that she begins to believe in her own individual identity. Thus, instead of believing in her true existence, which is of infinite and omnipresent consciousness, she begins to believe in her own separate, though limited, existence as an embodied *Jiva*. This falsely misconceived self-individuality gives rise to ego-sense in her.

Now, even though the soul (*Atman*) is action-less, **"The action-less Self – Holy Gita 3:28,"** and a non-performer of actions, **"The Self is non-performer of action – Holy Gita 13:29,"** yet due to ignorance and ego-sense, she believes that she is the 'doer' of actions.

Thus, ignorance leads to ego-sense and ego-sense to sense of 'doer-ship', **"But if one's intellect is dull due to the development of egoism he feels that I am the doer – Holy Gita 3:27,"** and the 'doer-ship' to bondage. It is the sense of 'doer-ship' that holds the soul responsible for her actions and causes her to bear the burden of *Karma*.

In conclusion, the doer-ship is born due to the presence of ego-sense; the ego-sense is born due to indwelling ignorance and darkness; the ignorance and darkness come due to attachments and desires, which of course are the manifestations of *Raga* (love) and *Dwesha* (hate) that are embedded in our nature right from the day when we are born **(Holy Gita 7:27).**

Now if one can win over his ego, and overcome his attachments and desires, he could definitely go beyond the boundaries of *Karma* where his actions cannot bind him anymore.

The validation of above statement comes through the following words of God, which unfortunately do not seem very convincing because they present an example that is totally unbelievable; in fact, it seems almost impossible. And that is why often they are not taken as seriously as they should be; however, they speak the wisdom of profound truth:

He who is free of ego-sense, and whose intellect is not tainted by the sense of doer-ship (and enjoyer-ship); such a Sage, even if he were to kill all beings, yet he does not kill, nor is he bound by such actions.

(Holy Gita 18:17)

Look at these words of Holy Gita, which speak so boldly of the truth that if one were to kill all beings, but without the sense of ego, he does not go to bondage to such a heinous *Karma* created by the most dreadful deed.

The unbeliever wonders in amazement and expresses disbelief by saying, **"How can that be?"** How can it ever happen that one kills the entire life in creation, and yet not be held accountable for his such a dreadful action just because he commits this heinous crime with no ego-sense; just because he renders it without believing he is the 'performer' of it and does not take any credit for its 'doer-ship'.

It means as long as the 'physical doer' does not consider himself the 'intentional and responsible doer', but regards himself to be just the 'instrumental doer', he is untouched by the bondage to its *Karma*.

Surely, knowing this fact makes a big difference to the one who is trying to find a way out of bondage and investing his life in freeing his soul from the fetters of *Karma*.

What is being said by the words of verse, **Holy Gita 18:17**, is that if one can rise to such heights of enlightenment that he becomes a completely ego-less person, then action has no effect on him; the *Karma* has no hold, and bondage has no ruling over him.

In fact his actions become totally inconsequential to him in the sense that upon his soul, there is no *Karmic*-effect **((Holy**

Gita 3:17)); there is no bondage, no burden of *Karma*, no nothing!

Though the actions are still there but due to absence of egocentricity and non-attachment, their *Karmic*-effect upon the soul is no more; meaning, in them there is no potency of bondage and no power to bind her.

And since such a person who has become free of ego and self-centricity renders all actions as a sacred service to God and performs them not for himself but only for the welfare of the world, the performance and nonperformance of actions really do not mean much to him since *Karmically* they become ineffective and insignificant to him, as he is now far beyond the periphery of their bondage, **"Performance and nonperformance of action does not serve any purpose for one who delights in the Self – Holy Gita 3:18."**

So as long as the actions are performed without egocentric attitude, the soul remains untouched by the sin of *Karma*; it remains free from its bondage.

To prove this point that actions done without ego, without selfishness, without attachment and desire, are nonbinding, the Lord gives His own example and says that He remains free from His actions because He renders them in utter love and performs them with absolutely no selfishness and self-centricity.

And since He performs all actions for the good of His creation, He remains forever untouched and unbound by them, and never goes to bondage:

> **O Conqueror of wealth, I am like one who is indifferent, <u>unattached to those actions</u> (of creation, sustenance and dissolution); those actions do not bind Me.**
>
> **(Holy Gita 9:9)**

To make sure that we understand clearly that the actions done in pure love do not bind a man, the Lord God gives His own example, and says that He is not bound by His actions because He is not attached to them, **"Unattached to those actions,"** and He has no desire for their fruits.

He tells us that since He stays unattached to His actions while performing the functions of Creation and Dissolution, and sustenance and support of all worlds, His actions do not bind Him; and since He is not swayed in any way by their outcomes, He remains untouched by their bondage.

Surely God does not need to do anything for Himself since He is not desirous of anything; of course, what can He not have, not only in this world but in any world if He wants to, **"I have no need to perform any work in the three worlds because there is nothing to be attained by Me. Yet I keep Myself engaged in action Gita 3:22;"** yet He remains ever-busy in taking care of His creation, but absolutely without any desire and attachment; and that is why He does not go to bondage.

He remains free because nothing binds Him since He ceaselessly engages in actions for no personal reason but for the goodwill of others. This is why bondage has no hold over Him **(Holy Gita 9:9)**.

God does all things without any selfishness, because He is a God of love **(Holy Gita 10:28)**; because He loves His creation and His love is the 'love unselfish', the 'love unconditional', the 'love agape'.

Now if we keep in mind that actions do not bind God since He has no attachment, and no *Karma* has any hold over Him since His does everything for the good of the creation, then we can safely infer that human actions also, if they are done in total unselfishness for the comfort and care of others and rendered for the welfare of the world, should not be binding.

And beloved! This derived conclusion is hundred percent true!

It means when we live an egocentric and selfish life and perform actions to satisfy our cravings, no matter how great and grand are our achievements, they still are binding, because through them we assert the attachments and desires of our flesh, and communicate our affection and adulation for things of this world.

Obviously, when we do that, and render actions with self-centric attitude, they become our property and possession, and we become their title-holder and custodian; they become our accomplishment and achievement, and we become their 'performer' and 'doer'. So with self-centric attitude when we author actions, perform and render them, we become their possessor in every sense; we become their legal owner and become responsible for them in *Karmic*-jurisdiction.

Oh! We become associated and affiliated with them in every way; and that is what causes the bondage for us.

It is our '*I-ness*' and '*mine-ness*' that we have in our actions, which is the root cause of bondage. It is the sense of 'doer-ship' that we have in them, which ties us with their *Karma*.

The holy word says, that in reality, even though it is the *Prakriti* (nature) and its *Gunas* (three modes of nature) that perform all actions, yet due to indwelling ignorance and darkness we believe that it is 'we' who are their 'doer':

All actions are performed by the *Gunas* of *Prakriti*. But if one's intellect is dull due to the development of egoism, he feels that, "I am the doer."

(Holy Gita 3:27)

In other words, the belief that we are the 'doer' of our actions is the real reason of bondage, and of course, according to above words of Holy Gita, such belief rises in us because of ignorance that grows out of our ego. The 'doer-ship' in action comes due to our misconceived 'self' recognition.

Thus, no matter how we look at it, we arrive to the same conclusion, that it is our ego, our sense of 'I', which is the root cause of all our problems.

Well, the above conclusion, though is well stated yet often is not understood properly, because the assertion of 'I' or ego is not as easily recognized as we might think, particularly in the reference to what we are talking about, since the 'I-sense' in action is highly subtle and under-realized. Often it expresses itself so quietly that its even conscious affirmation is not so visible. And since it uses 'reason' to hide itself, its manifestation at times is highly unidentifiable.

With this sense, that expression of ego is highly subtle in actions, the problem of bondage can be restated in more specific terms by saying that it is not action but the underneath subtlety with which it is rendered is accountable for the creation of bondage.

So what is really liable for bondage is not the gross action but the cumulative inner force with which it is rendered, which of course is nothing but the attitude and motive, the mentality and mindset, the attachment and affection, the resolution and preference, the inclination and desirability, the expectation and anticipation, and all such considerations that pertain to its outcome.

Surely, these are the things that matter the most in the creation of *Karma*.

Please make a note that even though the central reason for bondage is ego, its manifestation takes place in forms of various characteristics that we have just talked about. Now if we look at these entities a bit closely, it is not hard to identify following three reasons which decide whether in an action there is any bondage or not?

First, if one has the affiliation and association with the outcome of action or not; second, if one has the equanimity of mind in its outcome or not; and third, if one believes that he is the 'doer' of it or not.

By *Karmic*-law, if any of these three are present in action, then they would form a basis for creation of bondage to its *Karma*. However, the fact is that if any one of them is present while performing an action, the others are bound to be there too, though they might be so subtle that they may not be identifiable.

For example: if one is selfish, then obviously his selfishness signifies his self-centricity, his individuality. That establishes his egocentricity, and hence, he would consider himself to be the 'doer' as well.

With the same token, his selfishness also identifies the fact that he is not of balanced mind because he would want the desired outcome, and hence, having an attitude of desired outcome would disturb his equanimity in action.

So no matter how we go about it, if one ingredient is there, the others are bound to be embedded in there too.

Hence, it is not the gross action but the inner emotions and feelings, and thoughts and thinking underneath the action that form the basis of creation of bondage to its *Karma*. Meaning, it is not anything else but we ourselves – our own inner passion and infatuation, and ego and self-centricity with which we engage in actions – that ties us to the bondage. Surely, there is no other outside force that plays any role in it.

It is our own affection and adoration, our own cravings and inclinations, our own wishes and desires, our own yearnings and longings that bind us to *Karma*. It is our own ambitions and aspirations to enjoy pleasures on this earth that create bondage for us:

Dominated by desires considering heaven the highest goal they engage themselves in *Karmas* only for the sake of prosperity and enjoyment. Thus they create a *Karmic*-basis for future embodiments.

(Holy Gita 2:43)

Oh! It is we ourselves who are responsible for creating this evil, which in turn forces us to become its salve as it compulsorily demands its full expression and exhaustion regardless of what other wonderful deeds we may commit to offset it.

Therefore, our problem lies nowhere else but within ourselves.

Eleventh: Though all actions create Karma, but not bondage.

We have briefly learned in the First chapter that, though all human actions create *Karma* but not all create bondage. It means there are actions that are bondage-free. But which ones are those, remains a question!

The previous law of *Karma* states that the reason of bondage to *Karma* is our underneath egocentricity with which we perform actions, because it creates 'doer-ship' in them and doer-ship creates bondage. It means the actions that are done without ego and self-centricity are bondage-less.

Actually, Holy Gita gives us a pretty good measuring-stick with which we can always gauge our actions to see how powerful they are in jumping over the fence of *Karmic*-territory? With it we can easily calculate if they are high enough to reach beyond the threshold of *Karma*? And whether they can jump over the fence of bondage?

Well, here is the formula that defines what actions create bondage and what not:

Only those actions bind a person, which are not performed for the sake of sacrifice (for pleasing God). Therefore, O Son of *Kunti*, perform *Karmas* without attachment and with dexterity, for the sake of Divine Self.

(Holy Gita 3:9)

The wisdom of Holy Gita says in plain words that only those actions that are performed to please God and rendered to Him in the form of sacrifice are not binding and do not create any bondage.

The importance has to be put upon the use of word 'only'. In other words, all other actions that do not fit this criteria, meaning those actions that are not done for God, not performed for His sake, not rendered to please Him, not offered to Him in love as an adoring service, not dedicated to serve the humanity in His name and not devoted to the welfare of the world in for His sake, are in fact binding as they all create bondage for man.

Looking at this formula given by the Lord God Himself in Holy Gita to identify what actions create bondage and what not, it is easy to see that the actions that are rendered to please Him in fact are the actions that are free of ego and self-centricity, and they are the only ones that do not create any bondage.

Quite obviously, the actions that are done for sake of God are ego-less and unselfish, because they are rendered in love for God and for no other purpose, hence they are bondage-free and bear no *Karmic*-percussions. Please know that only love for God can take our attention away from ourselves; only it can absorb all of our worldly passion and infatuation.

Twelfth: All three modes of nature – the Gunas – create bondage.

The following holy words say that all three modes of nature (*Prakriti*) – the *Tamas, Rajas* or *Sattwa* – are capable of creating bondage for the soul (*Atman*):

Sattwa, Rajas and Tamas – these Gunas arising from Prakriti create bondage for the Imperishable Atman abiding in the body, O Arjuna.

(Holy Gita 14:5)

What does it mean? Let us expound upon it.

It means, it really does not matter whether the action is good or bad, or whether it is of the nature of *Sattwa, Rajas* or *Tamas*, it still is fully capable of doing the damage to the soul by binding her to *Karma*, but of course, depending upon whether she has any attachment in action or not; meaning, if the soul has any passion in its rendering, it creates bondage.

Clearly, any harm to the soul comes only when she falls for the glamour of this world and becomes infatuated with the things of *Gunas*; only then she becomes the victim of bondage.

Gunas of *Prakriti* lure the soul into lust and lasciviousness, and entice her into infatuation and obsession; it is they that make her fall into captivity to mortality, and bind her to the repeated cycle of birth and death **(Holy Gita 13:21)**.

Thus, it is the *Gunas*, which cause soul's downfall as they tempt her into their fascination; and quite unfortunately, she falls for them. Their attraction and appeal is too much for the soul to resist, and thus she plummets into their temptation as she pursues their pleasures.

The thirst of enjoyment of worldly things makes her live a selfish and self-centric life and that causes her the *Karmic*-bondage, and forces her to pass though countless higher and lower births.

In a way if we look at it, this whole phenomenon of soul's falling into bondage due to her attachment with the objective world of *Gunas* is quite natural.

How? Let us see!

God created and crafted all things with these three modes of nature. There is nothing in this universe, which is not composed of them, **"There is no entity that is devoid of the three Gunas – Holy Gita 18:40."** On top of that He multiplied the mystery of existence by making Gunas operate among themselves, **"The Gunas operate among Gunas – Holy Gita 3:28);"** meaning, objects react to one another without any other external force; they have built-in inertia to react to each other. It is intrinsic behavior for things to operate among themselves due to Gunas they are made of.

So what happens when Gunas outside of us interact with the Gunas inside of us? Well, such interaction creates reaction in us in the form of emotion and feelings. These sentiments and inner reactions are either of love or hate. This is why we have liking and disliking towards things, but of course we also feel neutral about certain other. However, the reaction is always there due to interaction between the Gunas outside and inside of us.

Also, as greater is the interaction, so is the reaction. Of course, some reactions are positive and some negative; some create attraction and some repulsion; some create feelings of liking, and some of disliking. In regard to this, the scriptures say **(Holy Gita 7:27)**, some give rise to Raga (desire) and some to Dwesha (hatred).

So if the operation between Gunas of an object and Gunas within us resulted in passion and we feel attracted to it, meaning, we feel lured to it, our mind begins to continuously dwell on it, and begins to meditate about it.

This constant contemplation eventually becomes our attachment with that object as it multiplies our affection and adoration for it, **"By constantly dwelling upon objects one develops attachment to them; from attachment there arises desire – Holy Gita 2:62."**

Thus, the inherent and automatic interaction among Gunas creates attachment, which eventually gives rise to desire. And since all things are made of Gunas, and the Gunas are part of invincible Maya **(Holy Gita 7:14)**, their attraction is so powerful than we find it hard to resist.

So it is no wonder that we seek earthly pleasures so obsessively and passionately, because they have tremendous power of desirability in them as they are powered by the potency of divine Maya, and hence, their attraction is extremely hard to overcome. They are so alluring that we find ourselves helpless to resist.

Now the common thinking is, that we must seek *Sattwic* path when we pursue spiritual life because *Sattwa* is best among *Gunas* since it is of the nature of purity and piousness. Definitely, this logic makes sense, however, if we dig into the truth a bit deeper, we find out that we need a whole new approach, since the thinking as stated here, though undoubtedly seems good, yet often falls short of what is truly good for us.

Why it is so? The reason is exposed in verse quoted above **(Holy Gita 14:5)**, which though does not yield an adequate explanation of the real problem, certainly not in an obvious manner – however, a little investigation into it concealed meaning brings it all to the surface.

The verse boldly exposes the truth that all *Gunas* create bondage, regardless; not just *Rajas* and *Tamas* but also the *Sattwa*, which we believe to be good. So, it too can create bondage if laced with egocentricity. It means not only *Rajas* and *Tamas* but also the *Sattwa* is capable of creating this evil.

So even though it's true that adoption of *Sattwa* is a positive approach to spiritual life; however, it is truly beneficial if while operating in it we keep in mind that it too is capable of creating bondage, even though *Sattwa* seems to give an impression that it is all good, while the scriptural facts are quite against such assumption.

Surely, as per holy text, *Rajas* is of nature of passion, and is the producer of craving and attachment; therefore, it binds the soul by bonding her with self-pleasing actions and earthly engagements. The *Tamas*, on the other hand, is of nature of ignorance, darkness and delusion, so it creates bondage through procrastination and laziness.

But anyone who knows anything about *Gunas*, expect these two to behave in manners they do knowing that their nature is of passion and procrastination. So there is no surprise in it.

But, how about *Sattwa*?

Well, even though *Sattwa* is of nature of love and light, of purity and piousness, and of health and happiness, it yet creates bondage by creating attachment to happiness and knowledge, and that definitely is a surprise to most of us **(Holy Gita 14:6-9)**.

Thus, no matter how we operate and what *Guna* we pursue, we still end up creating bondage for ourselves.

But if we keep this fact in mind and pursue higher spiritual life knowing that *Sattwic* path is to pave the way to higher knowledge and understanding, and remain vigilant to not fall into the trap of bondage by acting unselfishly and un-egoistically, of course as best as we can, then that would be our way to victory; isn't it?

Therefore, we must remind ourselves constantly that the ladder of *Sattwa* is only to help our soul (*Atman*) to ascend to those heights of heavenly skies, where she could soar into the power of light and love of the Divine and reach the ecstasy of ultimate enlightenment, where hopefully, by seeking the sanctuary in God, she would be able to secure her release from bondage; because, from there by walking in the radiance of the Spirit she could arrive the illumination of Nirvana and attain *Moksha* (salvation) through the bliss of Self-realization.

Thirteenth: From last argument it becomes clear that both type of Karma – good and bad – is capable of creating bondage.

This is one of those distressing truths exposed by the *Karmic*-laws that both kinds of deeds, good (*Punya*) and bad (*Papa*), that earn us good or bad *Karma*, are instrumental in generating *Karmic*-basis for future lives **(Holy Gita 14:5)**; because, it is not the goodness or badness of action that factors into creating the bondage but is the underlying sense of ego that does.

Since the flame of ego in us is ever-burning, it is very natural that we perform actions with egocentric attitude more often than not; and thus, we become bound by their *Karma*. It really does not matter whether an action is good or bad, as in both, it is our 'I' that is prevalent in its performance, and that is what causes us to fall into its *Karmic*-captivity.

So not only the bad *Karma* is bad but also is the good *Karma*. They both are equally bad when it comes to bondage, since they both are capable of binding our soul with their fetters. They both are obstacles on the way to attaining the liberation of soul (*Moksha*).

The ego and selfishness, the attachment and desire, associated with our actions create bondage for us, **"Thus, they create a *Karmic*-basis for future embodiments – Holy Gita 2:43,"** and not their good and bad.

So even our good deeds, which we render for the welfare of the world, get defiled by these evils since we perform them often with a sense of ego and self-centricity, and thus, they end up creating bondage.

Oh! This is the mistake we often make.

We engage in all kinds of good works, offer sacrifices, and do remarkable deeds of charity, but we do them with egocentric attitude rather than exercising humility and meekness, and being thankful to God that He gave us such an opportunity that we could share His love with others by sacrificing ourselves for their good.

But we all know how often that happens!

Therefore, unless one adopts an attitude of extreme humility, his good works would not bear the fruits that are eternal as his egoistic essence would defile their futility and make them earthly and perishable.

And this, we often fail to realize.

We believe that all good actions are good; and quite definitely they are. However, they become less effective if they are carried out with attachment and desire; they lessen in their goodness if they are rendered with egocentric heart. And even though they create good *Karma*, the soul is still a loser, since as per scriptures, such *Karma* is not bondage-free, and thus, it only furthers her mortality.

Well, let us examine this phenomenon in a bit detail so that we could clearly understand the working of good works and see how it affects our *Karmic*-path?

From previous argument we know that all *Gunas* create bondage. Now, as can be expected, the *Tamas* (the mode of nature that is representative of darkness) and the *Rajas* (the mode of nature that is representative of passion), both kinds of actions, create bondage **(Holy Gita 14:7-8)**, since they have relative prevalence of darkness and passion.

However, the actions that are *Sattwic* (the mode of nature that is representative of purity), are not supposed to do so, as seemingly they should not create bondage, since their fruits are pure and pious **(Holy Gita 14:16)** and since they increase the light of Knowledge **(Holy Gita 14:17)**; but in matter of fact, they still do create bondage according to these holy words:

> **Among them *Sattwa* due to its purity is enlightener and the giver of health and happiness. It causes bondage by creating attachment to happiness and (relative) knowledge, O Sinless *Arjuna*.**
>
> **(Holy Gita 14:9)**

Thus, *Sattwic* actions are also <u>capable</u> of creating bondage. Please make a note that I intentionally use the word 'capable' to signify the fact that they all have only the 'potential' to create bondage; meaning, sometimes they do and other times they don't, of course, depending upon whether they are done with or without attachment and desire, ego and self-centricity, and the sense of 'doer-ship'.

Noteworthy is the fact that the bondage to *Sattwic* actions comes due to **"attachment to happiness and (relative) knowledge."** So even though these actions represent our goodness and purity, we still get trapped by their bondage due to our attraction to their virtue and attachment to their goodness – the happiness and joy, the light and knowledge.

And since the *Sattwic* bondage is no different than any other bondage, it too creates ignorance and delusion in us; thus, our holy actions, which were to increase the divine light, end up creating further darkness in us because they get defiled by the traces of ego.

Therefore, we have to be quite careful when engaging in holy and *Sattwic* actions, and not take their goodness for granted, but be watchful of our defiled mind and heart by making sure that we do not render the deeds of benevolence with egocentric and selfish attitude; otherwise, they would lose the greater part of their goodness and would not yield much benefit to us as they are supposed to.

Now, what are those actions that do fall into this category? Meaning, what are so called the *Sattwic* actions?

The answer is: that all our generous and charitable actions, our good and great deeds, our virtuous and righteous works, all such holy and hallowed engagements, are all *Sattwic* endeavors, since they all carry virtue and value, goodness and righteousness in them, **"The wise say that the fruits of virtuous actions is *Sattwika* and pure – Holy Gita 14:16."**

Thus, the actions that we render for good of others are *Sattwic* actions, since they are virtuous and righteous. But their goodness and greatness shines forth only when they are done without egocentric thoughts; otherwise, though they create good *Karma*, yet put shackles of bondage on our feet.

Beloved! Do we see the problem yet? That good and bad, both types of *Karma*, is a curse! Isn't it?

But this does not mean we should not engage in good works and create good *Karma*, because we should; our goal always should be to do good deeds and engage in righteous things. However, our intended goal in them must always be the liberation of our soul in this lifetime rather than putting this burden onto life next.

What we need to understand is that though our virtuous and upright actions would create good *Karma*, they also would put shackles of bondage on our feet and pull us into this world to be born again if we do not render them without ego and self-centricity.

Therefore, while engaging in good and righteous actions, we must keep in mind that their full benefit is only when they are done without egocentricity and selfishness.

Fourteenth: The actions that are done with attachment and desire bring bondage.

The law of *Karma* states that even though all actions create *Karma* (*Aagami*), we get tied to them only if we perform them with ego-sense and self-centricity; otherwise, we remain free from their bondage.

From what we have learned so far, it is easy to see that selfishness creates bondage since it represents the ego-sense and self-centricity, which, as we know, are the root cause of bondage.

In other words, the attachment and desire create bondage, since they are the conveyers of selfishness, and the representatives of ego and self-centricity, which is what is being conveyed by these words of the *Upanishad*:

> **You have pondered, *Nachiketas*, on pleasures and you have rejected them. You have accepted the chain of possessions wherewith men bind themselves and beneath which they sink.**
>
> **(Katha Upanishad, Part 2)**

Speaking in more broader terms, if an action is done without ego and pride, without selfishness and self-centricity, without attachment and desire, without passion and infatuation, then there is no bondage in it; but if it is done with selfish intents, with desire of its fruits, with sense of ego and pride, then it certainly would bring bondage for the doer, **"Impelled by desires attached to the fruits of action and thereof goes to bondage – Holy Gita 5:12."** Thus, attachment to action brings attachment to its *Karma*, and bondage to *Karma* comes only if there is bondage to action.

Fifteenth: Actions performed for the sake of God are not binding.

The scriptures conclude that only actions that are done in God are not binding. Here is what *Isa Upanishad* has to say about it:

> **Working thus, a man may wish for a life of a hundred years. <u>Only actions done in God bind not the soul of man.</u>**
>
> **(Isa Upanishad)**

As we can see, the holy text above provides a pretty simple formula to judge what actions bind the soul by saying that **"Only actions done in God bind not the soul of man."**

But this formula should fit into what we have already learned about what actions are binding and what not? Surely, these should be those actions that are done without selfishness and self-centricity, without attachment and desire, and without ego and pride.

And so they are!

Holy Gita identifies them in a more insightful manner and says that actions that are performed for the sake of God and rendered to please Him are non-binding; meaning, the actions that are rendered for the love of God do not create bondage, **"Only those actions bind a person which are not performed for the sake of sacrifice (for pleasing God) – Holy Gita 3:9."**

The holy book says that only those actions are nonbinding that are performed for the sake of <u>sacrifice</u> (an act of offering something precious to please a deity).

But sacrifice to who? Of course, to God!

It means the actions that are offered to God as sacrifice and rendered to the Divine to please Him are the only ones that do not create bondage; and they do so because they are done in the purity of love, since the love of God is only power that can raise man above his ego and self-centricity. Only His love and light can overcome the emotions and feelings of selfishness and self-indulgence.

But do we really know how to offer actions to God as sacrifice, and how to render them for the sake of His love?

Commonly, the way we know how to love God is by presenting Him with flowers and sweets, singing the prayers and praises, exalting him through *Pooja* and *Aarti*, and offering Him all kinds of sacred sacrifices via *Yajna* and *Tapa* **(Holy Gita 4:28)**; but I am not sure if that is enough?

Because, 'offering things' and 'offering actions' for the sake of His love seem two quite different things; don't they? And if they are, then we ought to find out how to do this rightly so that we could begin to live a bondage-free life.

Well, the clue is given quite clearly in verse, **Holy Gita 17:11**, where the holy text says that the sacrifices that are done with a sense of duty but without expectation of fruits and rendered according to scriptural teachings are considered the offerings of love to God. You see! Lord God Himself confirms that He should be adored through rendering of duty with love, **"By adoring Him through the performance of one's own duty – Holy Gita 18:46."**

So not only *Yajna*, *Tapa* (scripturally professed and commanded acts of sacrifices) and all kinds of acts of austerity – the rites and rituals of various kinds of sacrifices – but also the acts of care and compassion, the deeds of charity and donations, the works of kindness and generosity, and all such works of goodwill and benevolence, are such sacrifices that God accepts as love-offerings.

Great news! Since a large number of folks among us, especially the ones that are caring and compassionate, are quite involved in such things. However, does it mean that all such deeds that we render with a heart of goodwill are the offerings of love to God? Are they all the sacrifices of devotion to Him?

Disappointingly, I must say: Not necessarily! How come? Let me explain!

As per word of God, performing actions with fleshly affection and attachment is one end of the spectrum on how we perform actions, while performing them without any passion and infatuation is the other.

In other words, one extremity represents the presence of ego and selfishness in action, which ends up creating bondage for the soul, **"Attached to the fruits of action and thereof goes to bondage – Gita 5:12,"** while the other represents the complete absence of these evils, and thus, enabling the soul to stay out of bondage, **"By renouncing attachment to the fruit of action is not touched by sin – Gita 5:10."**

Thus, as we go from one end of the spectrum to the other, the ego and selfishness disappear, and so does the bondage. Meaning, for an action to not create any bondage, it has to be performed with absolute absence of ego and selfishness; there can be no selfish intentions, nor any sense of 'doer-ship'.

But since most often we engage in life to satisfy our inner man and render actions more often than not with self-centric attitude, even the greatest of our works create bondage. And why would they not, if they are done even with the faintest sense of ego and selfishness? Why would they not bind us then?

So there lies our problem!

Of course, no honest thinker would disagree with the fact that most of our actions are tainted with these evils; that even our good deeds are often not free of traces of egocentric emotions.

True, that out of the goodness in our heart, we do many good things for others, of course whenever we can, and engage in all kinds of charitable acts, no doubt! But too bad that even such deeds, which by all means are so good, are not always bondage-free simply because we are not free from the sense of ego while rendering them.

So as we can see, there is a very thin line between what actions create bondage and what not; and that suggests that we must understand this delicacy of the subject of bondage a bit better.

The fact is that whatever we do most often is to please ourselves, to fulfill the hunger and thirst of our flesh, to satisfy the ambitions and desires of our inner man; it just is our nature. Even the most wonderful things that we do for the goodwill of others, we do them to make ourselves feel good and to satisfy our own desire. An honest self-interrogation can easily reveal the reality that often our self-centric motives propel us to engage in acts of benevolence and generosity; however, they are quite subtle and highly unidentifiable.

So it is not hard to see that desire, no matter how hidden it is, is the driving force even when we do good deeds, and that causes the problem, since any attachment in action creates bondage.

Since most actions that we render have attachment, because to a greater degree, we do them to fulfill our flesh and

73

.

to satisfy our inner man, therefore, the bondage in them is unquestionable. Yet, we can wonder, why is there any bondage if we are doing deeds for the goodwill of others?

Because when we engage in good works to bring comfort to others, it is quite obvious that we perform them to meet other people's needs rather than our own. So is it not true that there is no selfishness involved in such actions? And if so, then, how can we ever fall into bondage in doing such unselfish deeds?

Well, let's look at it a bit closely, because we must not forget that in the creation of *Karma*, not the gross act but the intent and the sense of 'doer-ship' behind it is what creates bondage. For this reason alone we cannot just look at what is apparent in an action externally, but rather examine what is hidden internally.

No one can deny that the work done for the good of others is not a good thing because it definitely is; however, regardless of how good it is, it still would create *Karma*; no doubt! Since each and every human action does it. Also agreed is that, the created *Karma* would be good since the action is good.

But the question remains: whether created *Karma* would create any bondage or not, which of course, would depend upon whether there is any attachment to it or not? Meaning: Was the action done solely for the love of God? Or, was there some other purpose behind it?

Surely, millions around the world do good works each day and extend their resources to serve humanity – we all know that; but how many of them do so solely for the love of God? How many of them who engage in such generosity consider it to be a blessed service to God rather than believing it to be an act of self-virtue to excel their own goodness and greatness?

You see! How does one thinks about it is where lies the difference between what creates the bondage and what not while performing such generous deeds.

Great works are considered truly great only when they are done with the absoluteness of goodwill and welfare of others; and that is possible only when they are rendered with purity of humility and meekness, with piousness of love and light, and with the sacred sense of sacrifice to God.

It means for any good work to be right and just in the sight of God, the work of benevolence must be absolutely free of self-centricity; meaning, no ego and no selfishness; and only then there will be no bondage.

Now, why do works of charity often create bondage? Because, even though they are done for the good of others, two things still possibly can play a role in defiling them: first, if there is an ulterior motive in their rendering; and second, if there is sense of ego in their performance.

For example, someone does a work of charity to make himself look good in society. Or, he does it out of his own righteousness because he thinks of himself as being very good.

In either case, the work of charity is done with the sense of ego and self-centricity; and hence, it is defiled **(Holy Gita 17:12)**, and therefore, it cannot be considered a love-offering to God. And since both are rendered with selfishness and sense of 'doer-ship' – meaning, they are rendered without absolute humility and purity of goodwill for others – they end up creating bondage.

You see, the 'selfishness' generally is not a problem especially for those who really wish to do good for others, but ego surely is, because ego by nature is extremely subtle and highly deceptive.

So unless one is watchful of its maneuvers, he could be deceived by the feelings of self-righteousness, which may arise due to rendering of good works; instead of becoming more humble and gratified by the feelings of goodness and grace of God that He made him a vessel of blessing for others, he may become more proud and arrogant due to his self-goodness.

This is the main reason why even the great works create bondage; even the most wonderful deeds get defiled and become laced with sin; even the most glorious accomplishments of man rate low in the sight of God. They become less in value and virtue because they carry the sense of self-goodness and self-righteousness, and wear the badge of ego and pride.

This is why Lord Jesus issues a word of warning and commands us to remain extremely quiet about our good deeds and not take any notice of them, because they can create the feelings of self-righteousness. Through these words He makes us aware of a very hidden problem, which victimizes most of us:

But when thou doest alms, let not thy left hand know what thy right hand doeth.

(Holy Bible, Matthew 6:3)

He says that good works are only good when they are performed in extreme secrecy as they are never to become a public knowledge; they are only good when they are done with the joy of soul and not for the exaltation of flesh; they are only good when they are done with the heart of humility and thankfulness and not with the sense of arrogance and pride.

In other words, Lord Jesus warns us to not take any credit for our good works but to give all glory to God for making us a vessel of manifestation of His blessings to others.

But how many among us heed His warning and cherish the true blessedness of our good deeds that God enables us to render.

Oh! Certainly not many!

Because, often folks brag about how good they are, and how they are so dedicated to doing great works for humanity.

Surely, they are kind and compassionate people – that is hardly ever in question since most of them are quite sincere in their holy vocation; however, the problem lies in their egocentric attitude that is more often than not is self-inclined in taking credit for their good works and applauding their own virtue and righteousness rather than exalting the goodness and grace of God.

So a good deed, which has been done for welfare of others, does not qualify itself to be an holy offering to God unless it is free from egocentric emotions, and hence, it automatically does not stand free of bondage, because the underneath intent and sense of 'doer-ship' evaluate it's qualifications.

Therefore, for any good work to be justified as a love-offering to God, it must meet a threefold qualification. First, it must be done without attachment and selfishness; second, it must be performed without ego-sense – meaning, with a heart of humility and thankfulness; and third, it must be rendered solely for the welfare of the world, and with no other thought in mind but to please God.

The ultimate goal of any and all good works must be to please God **(Holy Gita 3:9)**; they must be done only for the sake of His love.

And if they are rendered in such manner, then there would be no bondage in them, of course, due to the fact that they would be pure and unblemished; they would not be tarnished by ego; they would be sacred and not sinful due to selfishness. Then, they would have one and only purpose, which is to serve and please God and nothing else.

This is what the sages and saints of all times have done, and are still doing, as they ever remain dedicated and **"devoted to the welfare of all beings – Gita 5:25."** Even though they have nothing to accomplish for themselves, they yet remain busy for the goodwill of mankind and render their days as a holy service to God. No wonder their actions do not touch them, and they never get caught by the evil jaws of *Karma*.

You see! The primary reason why God commands us to live a life that is devoted and dedicated to serving the humanity with utmost humility and selflessness, **"The wise should also perform actions but without attachment and for the welfare of the world – Gita 3:25,"** is that by doing so we can arrive to spiritual perfection **(Holy Gita 3:20, 18:45-46)** and attain the vision of light and wisdom **(Holy Gita 2:56-57)** through which we could seek asylum in the refuge of God and find salvation for our soul through His graces **(Holy Gita 18:66)**.

This is why even though the wise and prudent, the holy and pious, godly and saintly, who have arrived such level of enlightenment that their actions have no hold over them, and they are ever free from all *Karmic*-obligations **(Holy Gita 3:17)**, they yet live life by remaining engaged in welfare of all beings **(Holy Gita 12:4)**; of course, by not exalting themselves but by humbly thanking God for giving them the privilege to serve Him in love by loving humanity. This is the secret of love of God that lifts the ordinary life to such an extraordinary light where through the vision of enlightenment the man finds the trail to the sanctuary of God, and in there, through the mercy and kindness of God, he attains the eternal liberation for his soul.

The conclusion is that life can be lived without bondage if we seek God in every manner and ways. We can become free from fear of *Karma*, but only if our actions are the actions of love, and they are only for the admiration and adulation of God.

Karma would have no power over us if our deeds are the deeds of devotion and dedication done as a service to God; it would have no dominance over us if our works are for the welfare of beings and are rendered with the sense of sacrifice to the Creator.

What more promise do we need after listening to these words of the incarnated God – the Lord *Krishna* – who tells us how to be free from all fetters of *Karma* by rendering our intrinsic obligations in a manner that they are nothing but the love-offerings to God, and thus, find salvation for our souls by reaching to His everlasting abode:

Having taken refuge in Me he who performs all his duties at all times he attains the Eternal and imperishable Abode by My Grace.

(Holy Gita 18:56)

From His words it is clear that we can live a life of freedom from fetters of *Karma*, and enjoy our days in liberty from bondage to sin.

Oh! Quite surely, we can do that, and live a heavenly life here on this earth just by taking refuge in the sanctuary of God and living the days of peace and joy under His care.

The truth is that if we seek God first in everything, then we do not need to seek anything else for ourselves as all else will be added unto our life by Him; and there would be no need for us to act in selfishness as He would definitely provide all necessary and sufficient provisions to meet our needs.

What more assurance do we need in this regard after hearing these words of Lord Jesus Christ that reveal the true way of life, and teach us how to live life without any care and curiosity, but confidently and assertively, just by living in the abidance of God and seeking Him first in all things?

But seek ye first the kingdom of God, and his righteousness; and all these things shall be added unto you.

(Holy Bible, Matthew 6:33)

These words are witness to the fact that if we seek God first in all things, He would take care of us in every way. We do not need to be selfish and self-indulged as all needs of our day would be met by Him.

Oh! Listen to these most comforting and assuring words of Lord Jesus:

Consider the lilies how they grow: they toil not, they spin not; and yet I say unto you, that Solomon in all his glory was not arrayed like one of these.

If then God so clothe the grass, which is to day in the field, and to morrow is cast into the oven; how much more will he clothe you, O ye of little faith?

And seek not ye what ye shall eat, or what ye shall drink, neither be ye of doubtful mind.

For all these things do the nations of the world seek after: and your Father *knoweth* **that ye have need of these things.**

But rather seek ye the kingdom of God; and all these things shall be added unto you.

Fear not, little flock; for it is your Father's good pleasure to give you the kingdom.

(LUKE 12:27-32)

Through these words He commands us not to worry about anything and have no doubt in God regarding anything in life, as our Father in heaven knows all things, and it is His delight to take care of us and provide for everything we need.

And, you know why would He do that? Because, He loves us; and He loves us so much that He would do anything for us as long as we are good children to Him and abide by His commandments.

79

Oh! After hearing these words how can we still continue to worry about life and remain of doubtful mind about God?

Sixteenth: In rightly performed duty, there is no sin.

One of the main reasons why Holy Gita so heavily emphasizes duty is that its fulfillment opens the door to enlightenment. Sadly, this secret is not understood by many.

The duty born out of one's nature is highly essential to be fulfilled because this is one of the surest ways for one's reaching to spiritual purity and piousness, **"Men pursuing their own duties with devotion attain spiritual perfection – Holy Gita 18:45),"** which enables him to seek the sanctuary in God, where through His grace, he could find deliverance for his soul from all bondage.

Even though the ignorant and ill-informed often accuse Holy Gita of promoting violence, but in sheer reality, when she asks man to take up arm and fight, she is commanding him to not boycott or ignore the battle of life but to engage in it with a sense that it is a natural service to God which should be rendered to Him without attaching himself to its outcome. Thus, the holy book preaches not the approach of aggression but the path of perpetual peace, for not only this life but all life hereafter.

The main theme of her teachings is not to wage violence and be victorious in worldly wars, but to faithfully follow the inherent path of life as defined through natural duty so that the soul could overcome the inner impurity and darkness, and become pure and pious, and have the vision of truth, and thus, could know how to head towards the land of lasting peace and eternal liberation.

The divine incarnation of Knowledge – the Holy Gita – yields a very clear reason why duty is so potent in leading one to spiritual perfection, by telling that the duty is endowed with the power of spiritual transformation, because it is sinless, **"By performing duties born of one's own nature one does not incur sin – Holy Gita 18:47;"** because it multiplies the light and wisdom **(Holy Gita 18:23)**; because it discourages attachment by lessening the desire for fruits of actions.

And since the duty is sinless, it creates no bondage.

This is why, our holy teachers emphasize duty in our sacred sermons, but due to ignorance, not many among us reach the true understanding of it, and remain without clear knowledge of its spiritual wonderment.

You see! The duty is holy and hallowed; it is pure and pious. In fact it is so sacred that it is considered a sacrifice to God **(Holy Gita 18:46)**. No wonder, the fulfillment of duty is very pleasing to Him, as so say the scriptures.

And since rendering duty born out of one's nature is the most blessed thing to do **(Holy Gita 2:31),** it is no surprise that throughout the exposition of Holy Gita Lord God instructs us to perform our natural duty, **"Therefore, perform your duties in daily life – Holy Gita 3:8,"** and rightly render those actions that have been called out by the scriptures and have been pre-ordained intrinsically in our life.

Since, not the gross act but motive behind an action is what creates bondage to *Karma*, even the imperfect duty, but done in pure love and rendered in utter selflessness, remains untainted and sinless. The reason being, the tangibility of intention in act of duty is of love and affection, hence, it does not increase the burden of bondage on the performer.

Of course, the duty is an act of goodwill; it is rendered for the good of others. So if it is rightly rendered, it produces the product of love. The more pure is love underneath an action, the more pure is its outcome. So if the duty is performed in surrender and submission, in love and light, in wisdom and understanding, it takes the performer towards the liberty by pulling him out of bondage.

Now, to understand why duty is sinless, we need to know its roots; we need to know its genesis; we need to know its true nature. Let us briefly look into it.

As per laws of *Karma*, all embodiments of the soul are consequences of her past *Karma*; they are the vessels of *Karmic*-expression and exhaustion. But the 'way of exhaustion of *Karma*' differs in human and nonhuman embodiments; they are not the same as they are not governed by the same rules.

In nonhuman embodiment it is the instinct, which is embedded in the nature of beings that facilitates the proper exhaustion of *Karma*, while in human it is the mind, which is empowered with freewill and autonomous discernment that rules and regulates all *Karmic*-expressions.

Driven by the instinct, a nonhuman embodiment allows *Karma* to flow freely and naturally; thus, paving a proper channel for its expression; however, in human, since the mind has the power to think, discern and choose, the freedom in natural flow of *Karma* is obstructed by its interfering maneuvers.

Of course, the preordained *Karma* still forces its exhaustion through life, but since our response to its expression depends not upon any instinct but the authority of mind, which has the power to discern and choose response anyway it likes, the correctness of expression of *Karma* and its justified exhaustion becomes a doubtful issue.

Clearly, the exhaustion of *Karma* alone is not sufficient for its perfect dismissal if it is not done rightly; because if it is done wrongly it would create further *Karma*, which is what most often happens. No wonder, the burden of *Karma* continues life after life, and keeps the soul tied to the cycle of repeated birth and death almost indefinitely, of course, until the time comes when in much graces of God she is led to His light through which she finds the eventual freedom from all bondage.

With this background, we can understand the function of duty a bit better.

The main purpose of duty is guiding the proper exhaustion of *Karma* in human life so that man could become spiritually pure and pious through its sinless nature and find the way to enlightenment. Thus, duty guides man onto righteous walk and saves him from wandering on trail of mistakes and blunders, and hence, leads him onto the path of love, light and liberty.

In conclusion, the duty is made by God to pave the way of free flow of *Karma* so that it could be exhausted in a proper manner and get burned without giving rise to new bondage.

God made duty because He loves us; he desires to redeem us. He made it so that we could walk on to the road of righteousness and not unrighteousness; He gave us this safeguard to protect us from further getting harmed by *Karma*; He laid down a road on which we can walk without getting into further trouble with bondage.

You see! By teaching how to properly and beneficially walk on the path of pre-ordained *Karma*, the duty guides the soul towards the safety and security of God by avoiding *Karmic*-hazards and saving her from any further damage from bondage.

God does not give human life just to live the old *Karma* but to get out of its captivity for good by rendering the duty rightfully and gaining the vision of Truth leading towards the providence of eternal liberty.

The *Upanishads* reveal this great secret that all things have been put in our path to eternity:

He placed all things in the path of Eternity.

(Isa Upanishad)

Meaning, each and everything, which has been put in the way of life, is in the path of perfect *Karma*; it is in ideal accordance of the pending *Karmic*-percussions.

This clearly implies that with each and every person whom we meet and encounter, each and every place we visit and spend time in, each and every incident and happening that we endure and experience, we have some *Karmic*-relationship; they are no coincidences by any means; they are not arbitrary happenings, but are predefined occurrences caused by the Divine to fulfill some preordained *Karma*.

From this we can clearly conclude that the more close we are to someone, the more we are tied to him *Karmically*. So if we wish to exhaust *Karma* with this person in a most meaningful manner, we have to fulfill all duties towards him; because only then, a proper expression of *Karma* would take place, and only then, it would reach its finality without giving rise to another beginning.

The duty is a road that eventually leads life to love, from love to light, and from light to eternal liberty. When rendered in love, the duty brightens the vision of the man with wisdom. Through the guiding light of wisdom, man finds the way to the sanctuary of God where he finds the unending peace and everlasting liberty for his restless soul.

Oh! The duty is way sinless, the way without the bandits of bondage, the way without the fall into the deep ditches of *Karma*.

Beloved! God made duty so that we could get the clue what is the right way to live our *Karmic*-life, and what is the way to get freedom from bondage.

Seventeenth: The one who is established in the Self is not bound by Karma.

This virtually is a summary statement for all other things we have talked about so far in regard to what creates bondage to *Karma*.

When one becomes fully surrendered to the Divine, an overwhelming change takes place in him as he reaches such a state-of-being where the realization of higher reality and the understanding of the transcendental 'Self' that rises within, begins to overcome the sense of egocentric 'self'.

This sounds good, but what does it really mean? Let me explain!

It means when one is given to God with his entirety, his sense of individuality begins to fall because of lessening of self-centricity, and the sense of oneness with all beings begins to rise; the significance of the lower 'self' begins to decline, and the consciousness of the higher 'Self' begins to grow.

As a result, the light of the realized truth begins to destroy the indwelling darkness; meaning, the existence of limitation born out of ego begins to lose its significance as the sense of higher existence begins to prevail.

When that happens, the magnificence of the material world begins to fade because not the external earthly empire of the lower 'self' but the inner heavenly kingdom of the higher 'Self' becomes the total source of peace and contentment. As a result, when the inner man finds a continual and harmonious existence in the sanctuary of God, the restlessness in soul, which comes due to passion and infatuation, begins to vanish, and the tranquility begins to pervade.

In such attitude where the attention rests more upon the things of God rather than the things of the world, the corporeal attainments and accomplishments begin to lose their value, and the actions find complete rest in equanimity of mind as the person engages in them not for the sake of their outcome but for the sake of love of God; and thus, even though he engages himself in actions all day long, yet remains untouched by them **(Holy Gita 4:22)**.

Since he performs actions not for himself but for the sake of God, his satisfaction does not come from their outcome but from rendering them as offerings of love to Him. So he engages in them with a heart of goodwill and does everything as if it were the most holy service and sacrifice to God.

This is the reason, when one becomes established in his Self, when he becomes fully submitted and surrendered to God, when he lives a life that is totally dedicated and devoted to His love, when he becomes so enlightened that his 'Self' becomes the sole source of his peace and joy, the 'action' becomes *Karmically* impotent; it has no hold over him as he becomes free from all bondage, since now he does nothing for himself but everything for the sake of the Divine.

Look at these words of Holy Gita, that so beautifully unveil the extremity beyond which the 'action' becomes meaningless, and the *Karma* has no power over the one who has transcended worldly passion and infatuation, and has become totally neutral in life, in fact to a point that his life flows totally free from all conditioning; and his Self-being becomes the sole source of his peace and bliss:

For one who delights in the Self, is satisfied by the Self, and is contented with the Self, there exists no more action that needs to be performed.

(Holy Gita 3:17)

To such a person, who has become firmly seated in his 'Self' and has closed the door to the passion of outside world, the external beauty and wonder, the material magnificence and majesty, do not hold any merit.

To him, who completely abides in God and lives reliant fully upon Him, all definitions of 'action', 'Karma' and 'bondage', disappear, and the performance and nonperformance of action holds no value:

Performance and nonperformance of action does not serve any purpose for one who delights in the Self, because such an enlightened Sage does not depend upon any being for any interest of his own.

(Holy Gita 3:18)

Such an enlightened man who has been sanctified by life of selflessness, and whose indwelling darkness has been destroyed by the light of wisdom and has become fully established in the Self, is never bound by the Karma again **(Holy Gita 4:41)**.

The hands of bondage reach him no more since he does nothing at all even though he remains engaged in actions all day long **(Holy Gita 4:20)**; his actions are dissolved as if they never happened **(Holy Gita 4:23)**.

So, what brings one to such a plane of higher consciousness?

Well, of course, his own search for the Truth; his own longing to love with God; his own craving to arrive to the land of divine light and liberty.

No matter what Yoga one adopts and what spiritual door he enters, if he walks towards God with a firm commitment of submission and surrender, he arrives to this most overwhelming state-of-being that is of highest enlightenment where is left no sorrow or joy, and no pleasure or pain, but only the sense of higher consciousness, only the utter awareness of the Truth, only the sheer realization of the higher Reality.

This is that plane of higher realization where one reaches only when he has risen beyond all physicality of existence and has become established in his true Self. Since in him remains no passion and infatuation for this world, he becomes so Self-satisfied that he begins to live in those provinces of lasting peace and bliss that are far beyond the reach of Karma.

This is where a saint of such *Yogic*-virtue becomes totally liberated from the web of bondage since his actions become free from all affinity and affection, and thus creating no bondage for his soul. And even though, in his daily life, he continues to perform actions – of course, not for himself but for the welfare of the world – there remains nothing to be accomplished by him anymore **(Holy Gita 3:17)**, as in his holy sight the only meaningful accomplishment now remains is the love of God to which he solely renders himself by devoutly engaging in the welfare of the world **(Holy Gita 3:25, 5:25).**

3

Karmic-Cycle

~

The Chronic Consequence of Human Action

The scriptures expose the bitter truth that it is man's attachment and desire that create bondage for his soul and force her to go through countless higher and lower embodiments **(Holy Gita 13:21).**

It is his passion in actions, his egoistic assertion in his physical expressions, his indwelling infatuation in his engagements, that create bondage; it is his egocentric indulgence with earthly enterprises that ties his hands with the chain of *Karma* **"Impelled by desires, attached to the fruits of action, and thereof, goes to bondage – Holy Gita 5:12."**

Thus, even though the soul is immortal and eternal, she yet endures mortality and suffers incarceration by the cycle of birth and death almost endlessly.

The reason being that human actions create *Karma*; but *Karma* that is created by actions rendered with egocentric attitude also creates bondage; which imposes a big problem for the soul, as bondage demands *Karma* to be exhausted.

However, the exhaustion of *Karma* is a slow process since *Karma* has to mature first, which happens in small fractions, before it can be ready for exhaustion. Also, exhaustion of any portion of matured *Karma* happens only when the soul wears a suitable body and expresses it as life.

Thus, to exhaust piecemeal portions of *Karma*, little by little as they mature, the soul wears countless bodies that are suitable to express them, and passes through repeated cycle of birth and death – so called the 'Cycle of Transmigration' – almost timelessly.

In each cycle of transmigration, the soul takes a birth and wears a suitable body to live life duly to express and exhaust a portion of preordained (matured) *Karma*, and then ceases it through death to be born again to exhaust another portion of matured *Karma*; and thus, she fulfills all obligations called out by that qualified portion of *Karma* (called *Prarabdha Karma*).

This cyclic transitioning of the soul through transmigration continues as a part of piecemeal exhaustion of inestimable accumulated *Karma* until the time comes, when through much graces of God, she is given another chance to be born as human again to express and exhaust the remaining good portion of her *Karma*.

But in next human life, if the soul does the same thing as the last time, and fails and falls into the same trap of passion and infatuation, and does not find release from *Karmic*-captivity as man, then even though she exhausts preordained *Karma*, the bondage to new *Karma* commences a new cycle of *Karmic*-embodiments again.

This happens to be the sad reality of the soul more often than not.

And seemingly this unending evil cycle of *Karma* continues for the soul, until of course, through much mercy of God this eventually changes, and the day comes when in a human embodiment she seeks total refuge in God, and through His graces finds the forgiveness for her sins and is released from the captivity to *Karma* forever and ever.

However, noteworthy is the fact that such escape from bondage is only possible for the soul while she is wearing a human body; and that is why, human embedment holds such a high merit in the sight of scriptures which never get tired of singing its glory.

Here are the words of Holy *Ramayana* that speak of human life as the most precious gift from God, since even gods find it hard to attain it. Therefore, it is a matter of highest blessing for the soul to be born as human:

> **baRe bhaga manusa tanu pava, sura durlabha saba gramthanhi gava. sadhana dhama moccha kara dvara, pai na jehr paraloka savara.**

This sacred text has been translated as:

> **It is by good fortune that you have secured a human body, which - as declared by all the scriptures - is difficult even for the gods to attain. It is a tabernacle suitable for spiritual endeavors, gateway to liberation. He who fails to earn a good destiny hereafter even so attaining it.**

> **(Holy Ramayana, Uttar-Kanda 43:4)**

Surely, human embodiment is the only vessel there is that can take the soul across the horrid ocean of Transmigration; it is the only gateway for her escape from the misery of mortality.

The holy book further exalts the human embodiment through following words but here it exposes a mystery: that the human embodiment is not only capable of taking the soul towards the heavens but also capable of leading her to hell and keeping her trapped in the cycle of bondage to the worlds in between these two *Karmic*-extremities. But, human embodiment is a blessed vessel also, that can take the soul to that land of eternal liberty that lies beyond all heavens:

> **nara tana sama nahi kavaniu dehi, jiva caracara jacata tehi. Narka Swarga apabarga niseni, gyana biraga bhagati subha deni.**

These sacred words are translated as:

> **There is no other form as good as human body: every living creature - whether animate or inanimate - craves for it. It is the ladder that takes the soul either to hell or to heaven or again to final beatitude, and is the *bestower* of blessings in the form of wisdom, dispassion and devotion.**

> **(Holy Ramayana, Uttar-Kanda 121(A):5).**

The above holy words confirm that even though the human life is the source of bondage for the soul, it also is the door to her eternal liberation. Please, keep in mind, that liberation from bondage for the soul comes only when, as man, she chooses to take refuge in God and seeks His sanctuary and receives the pardon for her sins; otherwise, no matter how good she does and how great she becomes otherwise, she yet falls back into another cycle of *Karma*, which forces her to go through countless non-human embodiments again.

This is the sad reality of each soul; yours and mine, and everyone else's, as each one is in bondage with so called '*Karmic*-cycle' – which is a process that repeats itself over and over until the soul is salvaged from its grip.

This cycle starts when the soul ceases human embodiment, and goes on a long journey into wastelands of all kinds of *Karmic*-worlds to endure consequences of her deeds as per laws of *Karma* that rule and regulate mortality.

During this journey, the soul not only travels to various *Lokas* (plans of varying consciousness) but also suffers an inestimable misery and pain, which she experiences when forced to wear all kinds of countless non-human embodiments. Her sorrow and suffering that she endures due to passing through the series of transmigrations continues unceasingly until through the grace of God she is given another chance to wear the human body again.

Thus, unless the soul is redeemed from all fetters of *Karma* and rescued from bondage in a human life, she is forced to pass through another cycle of *Karma* as explained above; and she remains tied to this repeated-process, which spans from one human embodiment to the next, almost timelessly.

Well, this briefly describes, what does a *Karmic*-cycle consist of.

Now, when we judge what takes place in this self-repeating and seemingly endless cycle of *Karma*, it is not hard to see that it reflects upon the 'cyclic-effect' of human action, which happens to be so self-sustaining that it keeps the soul trapped in a constant orbit where she goes round and round without any break.

Beloved! The sad truth is that each soul is bound to this self-repeating cycle; each one is under its grip. We all are prisoners of this evil process without any exception and would remain so until our soul is liberated eternally from its grip.

But how can we engineer her rescue until first we understand the workings of this recurring cycle of *Karma* and know how it operates?

Therefore, not only we should learn how the conditioned existence of the soul is ruled and regulated in general by *Karma*, but have a specific knowledge about how her life as man is controlled and commanded, and how her *transmigrational* journey is maneuvered and maintained in between two human lives where she passes through countless lower embodiments.

However, before we could do that, we need to reiterate few things about *Karma*, which we have learned so far, just to refresh our recollection, and then continue our discussion further.

To begin with, let us remind ourselves that each human action creates *Karma*, which is nothing but an understated reaction – a subtle counterpart – a discrete side-effect – that is caused by what man does. Also, worth mentioning is the fact that no other creature but human alone is capable of creating *Karma*.

Man performs action at all times; meaning, there is no time in his life when he is action-less and doing nothing **"No one can stay without action even for a single moment – holy Gita 3:5."** It means man constantly and continually creates *Karma* and he cannot escape its creation no matter what; even if one decides to do nothing and remains totally idle, the very act of 'doing nothing' becomes an action, and hence, it generates *Karma*.

In other words, man cannot remain without creating *Karma* since he cannot remain without action, and action cannot remain without creating *Karma*. Of course, bad action (*Papa*) creates bad *Karma*, and good (*Punya*) creates good *Karma*.

One thing more, the nature of *Karma* depends not on the grossness of action but on the intent and motive and the extent of willingness in engaging in effort with which it is performed. This is why the gross act does not matter as much, since it does not factor into the creation of the character of *Karma*, while certainly the inner subtlety, the intent and motive, emotions and feelings, which carries it out do.

The most important thing about any action is the accompanying subtlety, the inclination of mind and heart with which it is performed because that is what decides whether it creates bondage or not.

Karma, good or bad, is such a debt that demands its definite payoff; which can occur only when the soul passes through appropriate embodiments that are most suitable for its proper exhaustion.

That is why the scriptures say that *Karma* is the basis of all life and is the cause of all manifestations **(Holy Gita 8:3)**, since exhaustion of *Karma* is possible only by expressing it through some appropriate life; meaning, without living it through suitable lives, the burden of *Karma* that is sitting upon the shoulders of a soul cannot be lightened.

Briefly, this is what we have learned so far.

The exception, that no other life but human creates new *Karma* even though each and every life is made to expresses it, is due to the fact that no other embodiment but human has the faculty of freewill. Only man has been given the mind and intellect; only he has been gifted with the ability of reasoning. Human alone has the endowment to discern and decide; he alone has the power to will and choose; and he alone has the privilege to make choice and act as he likes.

Since human is his own master, he is held responsible for all what he does and made accountable for all his actions. This is why his actions create *Karma* and make him bear the burden of his deeds.

However, such is not the case in nonhuman embodiments as they are devoid of all such privileged faculties like the mind and intellect, which empower discernment in human and make him the most special being in creation.

In nonhuman embodiments, there is no empowerment of discernment, and no endowment of freewill; there is no apparatus of thinking and recollection; meaning, they have no faculty of reasoning.

They are totally void of all that; they have absolutely no ability to judge, reason and choose, as they all are driven by their instinct, **"All living beings who obey their instincts implicitly – Holy Gita 3:33,"** where they live life with the guidance of their intuition.

Since nonhumans do not have the privilege of freewill and ability to discern and choose, they are not held accountable for their actions either. They bear no responsibility of how do they live their lives. As a result, their actions have no bearing upon them and that is why they have no potency to create *Karma*. This is why a nonhuman life serves only one purpose, which is to express and exhaust *Karma* and nothing else.

So in reality, none of the embodiments a soul wears in between two human lives has any other significance except becoming a vessel to exhaust the due *Karma*.

Oh! They are mere detours on her path to eternity. Please make a note of this thought since it would prove to be highly significant once we begin to employ it to investigate the working of a *Karmic*-cycle.

Well, let's look into what really happens during the recurring cycle of Karma, and what takes place in it?

Briefly speaking, the way it works is that in human life the soul not only exhausts the preordained *Karma* (*Prarabdha*) – just the way she does during every other life – but also creates new *Karma* (*Aagami*).

When human life ends, the newly created *Aagami* (the *Karma* to come) *Karma* gets converted into *Sanchita* (accumulated) *Karma*, which is like a storage or depository of all *Karma* due exhaustion. It is like a storehouse of all cumulative *Karma* incurred during past human lives as a result of both, the *Punyas* (good deeds) and *Papas* (bad deeds), that is still due to be expressed and exhausted as per laws and statues of *Karma*.

However, any exhaustion of *Karma* cannot take place unless first the *Karma* (*Sanchita*) matures and gets converted into *Prarabdha* (ordained) *Karma*, which by the way happens only in piecemeal potions and not all as a whole.

Once *Karma* (*Sanchita*) has matured and been converted into *Prarabdha* (ordained) *Karma*, it becomes ready for fruition. As a result it demands exhaustion, which requires the soul to wear a suitable body and go through a life that is proper for its expression.

Thus, each fraction of the matured *Karma* (*Prarabdha*) imposes a demand upon the soul to pass through a new life that is suitable for its proper expression and exhaustion.

Since the primary purpose of each birth is to exhaust the preordained matured *Karma* (*Prarabdha*), it is given the endowment and environment that is most suitable for its expression.

To satisfy all such demands to express fractions of matured *Karma*, the soul continues to wear one body after the other, and takes on embodiment after embodiment. To lessen the burden of *Karma*, this process forces her to pass through all kinds of *Karmic*-lives, which continues until somewhere along the way, with the remnant of good *Karma*, God grants her another human embodiment in the hope that this time she would attain liberation from bondage.

Eventually, the cycle of *Karma* that begins after the cessation of human embodiment and continues through countless lower lives comes to an end when, after wearing all kinds of nonhuman embodiments, the soul wears the human embodiment again, where she sows new seeds of *Karma* since in human life the soul not only exhausts preordained *Karma* but also creates new one.

The most significant thing about human life is that, though life unfolds in a predetermined fashion as per due *Karma*, the response to it is not preordained by any means; man is totally free to act as he likes since he is endowed with most privileged faculty of freewill.

Therefore, it is wrong to say that all things in life are predetermined and preordained, because they are not, since only the unfolding of life is but the response to it is not. And whatever way one responds to it, determines what kind of *Karma* he creates for his future.

But all that matters only if one does not surrender to God with his entirety, seek His sanctuary and find the salvation for his soul. Because, in that case, he becomes free from all fetters of *Karma*, and he does not need to worry about its percussions.

On the contrary, if the soul wastes the human life when it is given to her by God and does not free herself from bondage, the old cycle of *Karma* ends by starting the next, which sends her onto another journey of *Karma*. Thus, her irresponsible behavior keeps he trapped in incarceration of *Karma* and continues to torture her almost timelessly.

Well, as we can see, besides being categorized as good or bad, the *Karma* is further identified in three ways: *Aagami* (to come), *Sanchita* (accumulated) and *Prarabdha* (ordained) *Karma*, which signifies the fact, that as the time passes, the form of *Karma* changes.

Of course, if the deliverance of the soul (*Atman*) takes place during a human life, then she is released from all fetters of *Karma*, otherwise, the newly created *Karma* (*Aagami*) starts the next cycle of *Karma* for the soul and sets her off again onto another series of non-human embodiments.

Well, this is a brief description of how the *Karmic-cycle* works and how it operates.

What needs to be understood is that the commencement of next cycle of *Karma* after a human embodiment is not compulsory, since the soul has endowment of freewill and has the power to choose between freedom and bondage. So it is totally up to her to make this choice.

She can choose to remain in bondage by wasting human life in pursuing the pleasure and prosperity of this world and get further deep into the captivity of *Karma*, or get out of bondage by investing human embodiment in search for the Truth and reaching the salvation for his soul through the grace of God by taking total asylum in Him.

You see! Both options are available to the soul regardless of what kind of *Karmic*-life she is given. As the Upanishad says:

There is the path of joy, and there is the path of pleasure. Both attract the soul. Who follows the first comes to good; who follows pleasure reaches not the end.

The two paths lie in the front of man. Pondering on them, the wise man chooses the path of joy; the fool takes the path of pleasure.

(Katha Upanishad, Part 2)

If the soul chooses the path of love and joy, and pursues freedom, her spiritual strivings succeed in finding the way to the sanctuary of God, where, of course through His grace, she finds the forgiveness for her sins and gets released from all bondage **(Holy Gita 18:66)**.

But if due to ignorance, she chooses the path of pleasure and ignores the urgency of freedom from bondage and gets consumed by the pleasures and enjoyments of this world, she continues to live the slavery of sin and remain tied to the manacles of mortality.

In that case, the residual *Karma* from other previous lives plus new *Karma* that she creates in most recent human life, starts the next cycle of *Karmic*-percussions, which of course, sets her off onto another journey into *Karmic*-worlds, and forces her to endure more misery and pain of another round of countless embodiments that are demanded of her as an essentiality to exhaust *Karmic*-dues.

Well, this sums up the main functioning of the *Karmic-cycle*; however, there are certain considerations that we must go over to adequately understand its entirety:

Firstly: Human life is the deciding point for what happens to the soul next?

Of course, it could go either way for the soul!

If she becomes liberated from the shackles of *Karma*, she soars into skies of perpetual freedom and heads towards the abode of God to be eternally united with Him; and if she doesn't, and remains in bondage, then she begins to travel on a dark journey into the lost worlds of *Karma*.

Thus, human life is very critical for the soul while being on the journey into mortal worlds, because at this destination, she is fully empowered to halt all *Karmic*-aggression against her and save herself from its tyranny, forever; and thus, put an end to her mortal life and restore her immortality.

But if that does not happen, and she does not employ her privileges of discernment and freewill properly, and misuses the empowerment of mind and intellect wrongly in accumulating the transient affluence of this world, then she continues to wander in wastelands of *Karma*, and thus, multiplies her misery and pain by drowning deeper into the wombs of bondage.

Secondly: After the soul ceases human embodiment, the course of her future life becomes so definite that by no means it can be altered.

We already know that an unsaved soul, which does not get freed from the shackles of sin, remains under the power of *Karma*, and is repeatedly sent to this world to pay for her fines that are imposed upon her by the laws of *Karma* for the deeds that she has done as man.

Now, with this understanding in mind, we can safely derive quite a insightful conclusion that once the soul ceases the human body, the course of her future life, eternal or corporeal, whatever the case may be, is set for her, one way or the other; because the life beyond this point is beyond her control no matter what. It becomes a definite route for her *Karmic*-walk as she has no power and authority over it.

In fact, during human embodiment, if the soul is not salvaged and does not get rescued from bondage, the course that is decided for her by the *Karmic*-laws becomes a definite path for her future, which by no means can be altered or redesigned by any effort (until she is born as human again).

The reason being, the *Karmic*-laws govern all mortality of the soul. And since, after human life, the soul has no empowerment of freewill, whatever is ordained for her to happen, happens. She has absolutely no say in it as she has no choice in its response since during all nonhuman embodiments her expression of life is solely guided by the ability of instinct and not by the power of freewill.

Thus, after human life, when she enters a new cycle of *Karma*, her conditioned existence goes totally out of her hands as then it is solely governed by the *Karmic*-ordinances, which decide what kind of *Karmic*-course she is going to follow.

So, if the soul is not saved during the human life, her *Karmic*-life beyond that point becomes very much fixed and unchangeable, since there is no variable left that could factor into the calculations and considerations of her *Karmic*-consequences and affect her *Karmic*-fate in any manner.

It means all *Karmic*-destinations, which the soul passes through to endure and experience the consequences of *Karma* created by egocentric actions in human life, become predetermined, as they are nothing but pre-established punishments or rewards as judged and ordained by the laws of *Karma*.

Thirdly: Unless a soul is liberated from bondage in human-life, the odds are heavily on the side that she would endure immeasurable suffering of countless lower embodiments.

Since one type of *Karma* cannot cancel or offset the other type, the soul has to face consequences of both, good and bad, separately. It means good *Karma* cannot make up for bad; they both demand their separate exhaustion; they both require their full expression.

So no matter how much good *Karma* the soul accumulates in her human life, it still does not nullify the effects of bad *Karma*, and hence, she has to live through the experience of bad *Karma* regardless, as there is no way she could escape its misery and pain by neutralizing it with her good deeds.

Of course, the good *Karma* manifests itself by letting the soul pass through the pleasurable experiences of high heaven, while the bad unfolds itself by forcing her to pass through the sorrow and suffering of lowly hell.

But what does it really mean? Let me expound upon it a little bit.

It means, if in human life the soul is not rescued and released from bondage, then it is almost certain that she would go through the suffering of countless embodiments to exhaust her bad *Karma*, unless of course she has lived quite a sinless life.

And, what kind of possibility exists for something like that to happen? Well, we all can draw our own judgment on it!

So, unless a soul is exceptionally holy, the passage of great sorrow and suffering for countless lives is a definite *Karmic-*course for her, because the payback for her each sin, which can happen only by expressing *Karma* through lower embodiments, has to be made at all cost.

Oh! There is no waiver in this clause of laws of *Karma*.

Fourthly: Since the soul has no recollection of suffering during countless previous embodiments, it is quite natural for her to continue the behavior of ignorance.

After the soul has gone through the suffering of countless embodiments and has wandered in all kinds of *Karmic-*worlds, higher and lower, she finally returns to this world again as human, and given another chance by God to save herself from sin and find liberation from bondage.

However, most often than not, that does not happen, since the soul has forgotten all the misery and pain she has endured previously, and does not remember at all what kind of troublesome past she has endured during her previous lives, since she has no recollection from any of her past embodiments:

Bahuni Me Vyateetani Janmani Tav Cha Arjuna; Bahuni Me Vyateetani Janmani Tav Cha Arjuna.

These words of Holy Gita are translated as:

Sri Bhagavan said: O Arjuna, you and I have passed through numerous embodiments. I know them all, but, O Destroyer of Foes, you do not know them.

(Holy Gita 4:5)

And since she does not remember what has taken place prior to this life and what kind of suffering she has gone through before this embodiment, nothing deters her behavior of the past; and her ways of passion and infatuation continue, life after life, every time she is given the human flesh to live.

Too bad, that as man, the soul often gets so lost in the glitter and glow of this world, that she often fails to clearly see the purpose of her human birth; and thus, she ends up wasting the most blessed opportunity, which is not easy to come by.

However, though not many but there are some, who through the grace of God become awakened to the truth, and do not wish to repeat the same mistake of the past that would continue the torture of earthly life for their soul, so they invest their holy labor in securing the eternal life.

Hear these words of an awakened soul that has been enlightened with the truth and has come to realization of the sufferings she has endured during past lives, and now wishes to not get trapped again into the darkness of death but rise to the light of immortal life:

May the life may go to immortal life, and the body go to ashes. OM. O my soul, remember past strivings, remember! O my soul, remember that strivings, remember!

(Isa Upanishad)

Beloved! Just because we cannot remember the torture our soul has suffered during past countless lives, does not mean, it's not there; because it is, and we cannot deny it!

True, that we have no recollection of what has happened before. But it does not mean that, out of ignorance, we continue our ways of darkness, and keep justifying our uncaring conduct simply because we do not remember our most misery-filled past.

Of course, it is understandable that such negligent behavior is not unusual, since it is quite natural for us to behave in such a manner. After all, we are creatures that are driven by passion and desire; and surely, our nature is of greed and gluttony, and our flesh easily inclines towards the lust and lasciviousness. So it is not hard to see that unfathomable yearning to enjoy the pleasures of this world is deeply embedded in us.

It is no wonder, that we fail to standup against our fleshly hunger and thirst, and falter in remaining free from the grip of passion; instead, our infatuation overcomes our resolves and forces us to become most self-indulged by engaging us in such self-centric enterprises that only bury us further deep in bondage.

Surely, it all is true, however, our life is our responsibility, and not of anyone else; therefore, whether our soul remains in bondage or is set free, is solely our problem and of no one else. This responsibility rests upon us whether we want it or not!

So, it is for our own good that we change our ways of ignorance by stopping to satisfy the hunger of our flesh, and adopt the path of light by beginning to quench the thirst of our soul.

This I wish and pray for each one of us.

But alas! Our reality is quite the opposite; as most of us are living life in pursuit of happiness of this world rather than seeking the blissfulness of eternity.

Undoubtedly, we are slaves of our own infatuation; so we invest our day in gaining the pleasures and prosperity of this world; and thus, we totally forget the fact that we are in bondage, and that if we do not save ourselves from its shackles, our soul would be pulled back into its gallows of utter gloom for countless embodiments again.

Beloved! This is our reality that cannot be denied. Of course, few are exempted from this wrath of *Karma*, because they have risen to those heights of enlightenment that is far above the reach of bondage; otherwise, most of us, sadly, are sitting trapped in the sinking ship of Maya. Trust me!

Does anyone of us desire to confirm this truth? If so, then let him take the following test and find out!

Answer me this, please! What is the highest priority in our daily life? Is it the salvation of soul or the satisfaction of thirst of the dehydrated flesh? Of course, it is an undeniable fact that our day revolves around the fulfillment of the flesh. Is it not?

Beloved! Ask yourself: How many of us are truly worried about the salvation of our soul (*Moksha*)? How many of us really are restless and losing our sleep over it? How many believe that attaining release from the cycle of birth and death is the most important goal of life? How many are really doing anything about to inch towards eternity?

How many? The easy answer is: Not many!

Surely, not many are concerned; not many are worried that our soul is living the captivity to mortality; that we are the prisoners of bondage; that our *Atman* is timelessly bound to the cycle of *Karma*; that we have been living away from our Maker since who knows how long; that the greatest sorrow of our soul is that she is suffering the separation from God, life after life, and there is no hope in sight for her release.

Am I wrong in saying so? I hope not!

Surely, I haven't found many such souls who are truly worried about their salvation. Though I am fortunate to meet some who do worry about such things, but they surely are in scarcity.

You see! Most of us are blind to the truth that our most magnificent gains in this material world actually make us the biggest loser of all, since they come out of engagements into things of passion and infatuation, which are nothing more but the enterprises of vanity and narcissism; they are useless as they are the trades of no real value at all.

We do not realize that all our earthly earnings would be wiped out in due time no matter what they are, since there is no eternal tangibility in them; there is no permanence in their value and worth. But the price we would pay for them is immeasurable since they would only create more bondage for our soul and feed to the continuation of her *Karmic-cycle*. In other words, there is no real gain but only an unbearable and inestimable loss. I wish we could see that.

However, regardless of these facts, our behavior of ignorance continues; each time our soul is given the chance to live a human life, she does the same thing, over and over, and wastes the most blessed opportunity that is given to her to redeem herself, and throws herself back into another cycle of *Karma* to suffer immeasurable misery and pain of countless more embodiments.

Also, what we miserably fail to understand is that the real problem is not the bad *Karma* but the *Karma* itself; after all, it is not the quality of *Karma* – the good or bad – but the bondage to it, because that is what is our real problem and not the *Karma*.

It means, even when we do good *Karma* and score high *Karmic*-merit, we really do not gain much, since due to bondage, we still remain tied to it, which only forces us through further lower and higher embodiments. Thus, we remain caged by the mortality rather than being eternally free from it.

Though it's true, that even if not all, the most among us, concern themselves to *Karmic*-consequences, and they do think quite a bit about what would happen to their soul after they die, however, their focus is hardly ever upon getting freedom from bondage now, as they mostly concentrate upon accumulating good *Karma* and contemplate upon how they could better their future *Karmic*-life.

Such belief encourages them to do all kinds of holy deeds and engages them in efforts that are believed to secure the richness of future lives in hope that they are going to be prosperous and pleasurable, affluent and abundant in every way possible. So they invest most of their holy labor in earning and accumulating the good *Karma* to better the *Karmic*-rewards that would come to fruition in their future *Karmic*-life.

Thus, there is no argument in saying that there are quite a good number of people who are worried about their 'next-life', and are laboriously working hard to secure its betterment, but the fact still remains, that the folks who are truly worried about their liberation are not many as they are quite rare to be found.

Fifthly: Human birth is very special since it is privileged with faculty of freewill and power of discernment.

The truth is that each birth is purposed to exhaust some portion of the matured *Karma* – the *Prarabdha Karma* – but no birth except human, creates new *Karma*, called *Aagami Karma*. In human birth, we not only exhaust but also create new *Karma*.

This happens because the new *Karma* (*Aagami*) is created only when actions are performed with the egocentric notion of 'doer-ship'. And since no other creature but man has the mind to assert his ego, he is the only one that has the potency to create new *Karma*.

As we already know from the previous chapter that the human alone is uniquely gifted with mind and intellect and has been privileged with the faculty of 'freewill'; and that makes him able to discern and discriminate, and enables him to make choices. Thus, these discriminative faculties enable him to choose his actions at his freewill, **"Your right is only to the works – Holy Gita 2:47."**

So, not only the man can choose his actions but also choose the way how to perform them. He has the choice in both. In his freewill, he has the power to choose to do something or not. And if he chooses to do it, he has the choice on how to do it.

He can perform an action with selfishness or without selfishness, with ego or without ego, with 'doer-ship' or without 'doer-ship', with self-centricity or without self-centricity. It all is up to him; he has full choice in this matter.

The doer-ship, which causes the bondage to *Karma*, is not forced upon him; no such restriction is imposed upon his freewill by any means. He has the full freedom to accept the 'doer-ship' for an action or not; it is solely up to him to believe in it or not believe in it.

The faculty of discernment, the ability to determine right and wrong, the power to choose between good or bad, is all given to man for a single purpose, that he could walk the path of his day on his own, and could live a life of his choice.

And since human is empowered with the ability to discern and has the authority to choose his actions, he is held responsible for everything he does. It is this special privilege that makes him accountable for his actions, and as a result, whatever he does produces *Karma*, which of course, is like a token of responsibility of his choices and underneath motives.

We also know that human alone is held responsible for all what he does since he is empowered with mind, intellect and freewill, and only his life is directed by mental and intellectual discernment; and that is why, only his actions are capable of creating *Karma*. And since all other births are driven by the power of intuition, as they all are void of all such privileged faculties, there is no creation of *Karma*.

Thus, God has made human life different than any other, in the sense that not only it is a medium for soul to exhaust *Karma* but also is capable of creating new *Karma*. It means all other lives but human serve only one purpose, which is to exhaust *Prarabdha Karma*; however, the human life, in addition to that, also creates new *Karma* (Agami *Karma*)

Now, keep in mind that not *Karma* but its bondage is our real problem, since *Karma* on its own has no effect on us, and it is the bondage that enslaves our soul to mortality and subjects her to its suffering.

And that is where lies the secret why the freewill, the discriminative power, the authority to choose actions in human embodiment is considered a privilege, because it enables man to discern and choose the path of freedom instead of following the power of instinct and remain in bondage; which is what happens to all other creatures.

What a wonderful thing it is that these discriminative faculties, the mind, intellect and freewill, which are the reason behind furthering man's bondage by creating new *Karma*, are also the faculties that can help him get out of it.

Surely, man's actions create new *Karma* but that is not the end of it, because what still remains to be determined is whether he goes in bondage to it or not, which of course, solely depends upon whether he performs actions with the sense of 'doer-ship' or not; whether he renders them without desiring their fruits or not; and whether he does them without any selfishness or not. These things play a major role in determining whether he goes to their bondage or not.

So in reality, the faculties that often get man in more trouble by bonding him to *Karma*, if rightly used, can also pull him out of it, and deliver him from the grip of bondage; meaning, though creating new *Karma* is unavoidable for him, however getting into its bondage is still a matter of his choice; it is still under the authority of his choice.

Of course, by giving the mind and intellect, Gad has enabled human to discern between what is right and wrong, what is just and unjust, what is good and evil, and what is of God and what is not? And by giving him the 'freewill', He also has made him capable of choosing between good and evil, virtue and vice, life and death, freedom and bondage; and thus, has granted him the power to choose to live life with God or without God.

And that is the only real choice man has. Oh! Isn't that the only true decision man has to make in his life?

So, if we humble ourselves enough, we can see that in His mercy, God has yielded us a chance to liberate ourselves from bondage while living our life as a *Karmic*-consequence to our past deeds by responding to it rightly and justly and making the best out of the most blessed empowerment endowed in human embodiment.

In abstract terms, the truth can be summed up this way that surely God has tied us to the creation of new *Karma*, but He also has enabled us to choose to get into its bondage or not. Meaning, though we create *Karma* by everything we do, yet we have full freedom to accept to be tied with it or not. And that's the beauty of it.

This surely highlights the fact why human embodiment is the best, since in it alone God has implemented the provision for man to attain liberation for his soul.

Oh! Quite exclusively He has set us apart from all other beings by granting us the highest privileges such as freewill, mind and intellect – the faculty of discrimination and discernment – but He did it with a challenge for us to accept its responsibility and bear accountability for what extraordinary rights He has given to us.

Sixthly: Once Sanchita Karma matures and gets converted into Prarabdha Karma, it does not change no matter what; its exhaustion becomes compulsory.

As a caution, before I begin to discuss this point, I must state the fact right up front that there is no scriptural proof for this particular conclusion, however, what we see in life seems to support this argument quite reasonably and sufficiently. Therefore, it is up to the individual preference to accept this rationale or reject it.

Now, let me present this argument by saying that even though life is ever-changing, the matured *Karma* (*Prarabdha*) that has been ordained for this embodiment does not change; meaning, no matter how a life is lived, and no matter what takes place in it, the *Prarabdha Karma* remains fixed.

Since this conclusion does not have any proof, direct or indirect, it does not mean that we cannot find sufficient evidence to prove its validity, because we can; especially, if we look at it in lieu of the established facts.

Consider the following:

When a portion of matured-*Karma* demands exhaustion as nonhuman, the soul wears a creaturely body that is suitable for its expression and fulfills all *Karmic*-obligations perfectly by living through the guidance of intuition.

However, during such embodiment she does not interfere with any *Karmic*-ordinances since she does not have any ability to create any new *Karma* or change the one that is the basis of its manifestation **(Holy Gita 8:3)**.

But, when the soul embodies as human to exhaust *Karma*, before a life is conceived for her, its framework is formed and fashioned as per preordained-*Karma*, even though there remains all kinds of holes and empty spots, which by the way, are filled-in later by the *Karma* that not only matures in future but may also be created in future.

Well, besides being endowed with privileged faculties of mind and intellect and having empowerment of discernment and freewill, this happens to be another difference between a human and nonhuman embodiment, where as human the soul has, though not all but quite a bit, control over her *Karmic*-life while as nonhuman she has none.

This explains why human is considered to have power to mold and model his life anyway he likes, since he is endowed with the opportunity and empowerment to fill in the blank *Karmic*-spots in his life by creating new *Karma* as per his will, since not all the pre-ordinance is defined before the soul embodies as human, as much remains yet to be worked out by the actions than she performs as human.

In other words, even though the mainframe of human life becomes fixed at birth, a great portion of it yet remains un-ordained, thus, leaving it *Karmically* quite undefined. It is this undetermined and undecided life that becomes the field of man's *Karma* since it is formed and shaped by the new *Karma* that he creates as life progresses.

However, the new *Karma*, which the man creates, though fills in the blanks spots and provides a basis for originally un-ordained life to become ordained and manifest, yet it never alters or interferes with the *Karmic*-life that has been already ordained prior to it.

Though this conclusion is without any solid scriptural support, yet does not lack rationality since laws of *Karma* prohibit one portion of *Karma* to cancel out or nullify another, thus, preventing the ordinance of any portion of *Karma* from changing or altering the manifestation of the other.

So the newly created *Karma* by the soul, which fills in the blank and completes the voids of her *Karmic*-life as man, cannot interfere by any means with her preordained life, because that would be a violation of *Karmic*-laws.

Therefore, it is quite a safe to conclude that once *Karma* has matured and has been ordained for exhaustion, its expression cannot be altered; meaning, no effort on part of man·can ever change the *Prarabdha Karma*.

The witnessing proof of this fact is found in lives of those sages who happen to suffer greatly and continue to face the repercussions of the *Prarabdha Karma* even though they have reached the highest ranks of enlightenment and have been set free from all bondage.

No doubt! That such spiritually sanctified but physically suffering lives provide a profound testimony to the truth that even the most holy souls cannot escape the burns of ordained *Karma*; that whatever has been written by their *Prarabdha*, cannot be erased from life no matter what.

Therefore, even though it is true that after reaching the higher rungs of enlightenments, such souls are ever beyond the reach of *Karma*, as no action can ever bind them anymore **(Holy Gita 3:17-18)**; however, they still remain tied to preordained *Karma* of their past; they still remain bound by those *Karmic*-threads that have been tied by the *Prarabdha Karma*, and get untied only after all ordained *Karma* has been expressed and exhausted with its entirety through the current embodiment.

It means a man cannot be judged for his righteousness in God by the good and bad of his external life, since the current-life is a consequence of his past *Karma*, and is reflective of its pre-ordinance.

This is why often we see that even though one is virtuous and upright and has lived his whole life in righteousness of God, and yet he suffers tremendously, while there is another who is extremely evil and vile, and remains ever engaged in wickedness, and yet he lives gloriously. We can always find such examples in life and wonder, how can that be!

However, in both cases, the past *Karma* is the reason for such disparity, which is what is vividly reflective in their present reality.

What happens, that in case of the one who is virtuous and upright, though he deserves the best of life because he is so righteous, yet due to bad *Karma* of the past, he receives all kinds of suffering and hardship, while the other, who is evil and vile, though he is supposed to suffer because he is so wicked, and yet his life bestows all kind of prosperity upon him since that is what has been ordained for him due to his past good *Karma*.

Therefore, from these two quite common examples we can conclude that the reality of righteousness or unrighteousness of any man is not truly reflected in the view of his present external circumstances.

The reality is that the affluence of life is never a true measure of grace of God anyway, since it is not the prosperity and pleasures of life but the peace and joy, the wisdom and higher understanding, the inner illumination and enlightenment, the comprehension of the Knowledge and Truth, are the real fruits of God's blessings.

This is why there is an evident disparity in people lives, which often makes us wonder, why an evil and vile man is living a luxurious and lavish life, and has abundant affluence of all things, while a man of virtue and righteousness is suffering all kinds of difficulties and hardships, and is struggling through his days to make his ends meet?

The way to explain this is that once life has been conceived and the soul (*Atman*) has taken a conditioned-form as *Jiva* (creature), from that point on, till she ceases the endowed embodiment, the *Prarabdha Karma*, which not only has caused her embodiment but framed and fashioned into her current personification, cannot be altered by any means; meaning, neither it can be nullified or make less effective nor it can be eliminated and avoided.

There are no exceptions for conditioned-soul (*Jiva*), which she could apply to alter her *Karmic*-course, but only to live through it as ordained for her current embodied life.

It means the exhaustion is the only way to wipe out the *Prarabdha Karma*; its consumption through physical expression is such an essentiality that cannot be waived in any circumstance, since there is no other way to burn it and finish it off.

However, we must make a note of the fact that such is not the case with other two types of *Karma* – the *Aagami* and *Sanchit*. They both can be forgiven through the grace of God, meaning they need not to take their normal course, which is to transform from *Aagami* to *Sanchita* and from *Sanchita* to *Prarabdha* as they can be dismissed by God at His will.

In other words: as long as *Karma* remains in these two forms – *Aagami* and *Sanchita* – it can be forgiven by God, but only if one is blessed to receive His graces; in such a case, the un-matured *Karma* does not go through any transformation process since it terminates right then and there. There remains no more demand of its expression and exhaustion.

Now, does that mean God is incapable of forgiving the *Prarabdha Karma*? No, it never means that!

After all, God is omnipotent, all-powering and sovereign God; so how can there be anything that is beyond His capacity? How can anything remain beyond His potency and power?

Of course, such is never the case!

Then how are we to interpret the above stated conclusion that, as long as *Karma* remains in these two forms – *Aagami* and *Sanchita* – it is forgivable by God, but once it has been transformed into its final form – *Prarabdha Karma* – and is ready to be exhausted, it becomes unforgivable, and its expression becomes unavoidable; that it becomes unpardonable even before God.

Well, the answer lies in the fact that not out of His inability to forgive but as a rule, which He has established to regulate His creation, God chooses not to wipe out the *Prarabdha Karma* even if one is fully abiding in His graces.

And why it is so? There is a good reason for it.

By not eliminating and wiping out *Prarabdha Karma*, God offers a better alternative to man, which is to help him endure all inflictions and injuries of *Karma* by being with him and enabling him to express and exhaust *Karma* properly and appropriately by guiding him to through all ordained adversities with His light and wisdom, and giving him the needed encouragement and empowerment.

Thus, not only God helps man properly express and exhaust the ordained *Karma* (*Prarabdha*), but also provides him the opportunity to grow in His faith and trust, which eventually lead him to His true understanding.

Now, whether one chooses to endure hard times with God or without Him is totally up to him. The choice is very clear. One can go through adverse situations without God and endure their sorrow and suffering with his own might and strength. Or, he can take refuge in Him and take advantage of all provisions that are available to him in His sanctuary, and pass through times of turbulence with His grace-filled potency and power and save himself from much deeper misery and pain. The choice is his to make; one allows him to come closer to God while the other puts him further away from Him.

The bitter truth is that one who lives without God, lives in fear, always. If one has the wealth and prosperity, the affluence and abundance, the name and fame of this world, he lives continually in fear of losing it; and if he doesn't have it, he still endures fear, but of failing to attain it. So, one who lives without faith and trust in God, and does not rely upon Him is always haunted by fear, no matter what.

This is why today's man is so stressed out; because, he is living without faith, without trust, and without any abidance and reliance in God. His dependence is in him only; for everything he has to look up to his own might and strength. So when life hits him hard, he tries to manage it with whatever provisions he has built for himself, which often are insufficient and incapable.

But once his self-sustaining power falls short and fails to save him, and he finds no other place to go, the helplessness and destitution multiply his misery thousand times more. He becomes ceaselessly restless; peace is nowhere to be found in his life as anger and hatred, bitterness and resentment, depression and despair, worry and anxiety, begin to surround him from all sides.

So, as we can see, it is not easy to endure the rage of bad *Karma*, when one is living without faith in God, because his own potency and power is the limit of his protection and preservation; his own might and strength is the limit of his safety and security; and his own provisions and resources are the limit of his reinforcements and fortifications.

Well, let's now consider the case of the one who abides in God. What happens to him when he gets caught by the cruel hands of *Karma*?

Surely, such a man also suffers, no doubt! But his suffering does not deter his spirit of love; it only strengthens him even more, and multiplies him further in the light and wisdom of God. Though he also experiences sorrow and suffering, but he sustains all that through firm faith and trust in God; which only bring him even closer to Him.

Thus, such exceptional situations, though not pleasant for anyone to endure, certainly become extraordinary opportunities to become bold in God, which only enables him to stand before Him with even more confidence.

No wonder, a man of God, when endures adversity, he becomes even more pure and pious; his vision of Truth becomes even more clear and sharp; his faith and trust grow even more firm and strong. And he becomes a man of increasing abidance in God.

Surely, such a man suffers even the worst wrath of *Karma* with much peace, because God is with him. Of course, the misery and pain is no less, but knowing that God is with him, there is a subtle and sure sense of relief in his heart.

You see! Due to firmness of faith, which repeatedly tells him that everything is going to be alright no matter which way it turns out to be because it is always in the hands of God, there is a clear acceptance of circumstances as well as their eventual outcome. Furthermore, in such a person, not only there is a hope but a living expectation for a definite deliverance from all adverse conditions, which keeps reminding him that a sure relief from God is on the way.

And best of all, there is a strong feeling of God's closeness, which constantly enforces an infallible confidence in him, which continually keeps reminding that God is with him during all times even while during the tribulation.

The real benefit of all this is that in a person of faith in God, all such spiritual growth increasingly augments the sense of surrender and submission to Him, which of course, in eventuality, paves the way for his deliverance from all mortal sorrow and suffering by liberating his soul from all *Karmic*-bondage and setting her free into eternal skies.

Thus, being under the grace of God makes it much easier for one to bear any agony and anguish of *Karma* than what it is if he were without it, because the safety and security, protection and preservation, fortification and reinforcement, empowerment and enrichment of God, is available only to those that rely upon Him and live in His sanctuary with complete faith and trust in Him.

So, there is a much greater benefit in what God does, when as a principle, He does not allow the preordained *Karma* (*Prarabdha*) to be altered but permits it to take its course. Because by doing so, in place of forgiveness of just some fraction of matured *Karma*, He offers man the opportunity to do himself a much greater good, which is to get closer to the gates of eternal land by gaining more light and wisdom of God and by attaining more glitter and glow in his vision of Truth.

Otherwise, if such opportunity were not there, not many would rise so easily in their spiritual realm, but remain dull in their pious awakening and continue to walk slow on path to enlightenment.

You see! The hard times brought in life by bad *Karma* are the times of growth. If they were not there, I am not sure if man would have the capacity to develop fully, not just emotionally but more so spiritually. Can we deny the fact that often hard times make one stronger, and make him confident and wise?

Such thinking definitely supports the common belief that suffering grows a person in maturity; it raises him in understanding. Of course, whether one grows in understanding of God or of the world, that is a different matter. Yet, it can be said without any doubt that one often grows in wisdom and understanding when he endures times of tribulations and turbulence.

Thus, as a rule, by not wiping out *Karma* that has been preordained and by not allowing it to be altered by any means, but permitting it willfully to take place, God shows very clearly how much He loves us by giving us the chance to live with Him and grow in His understanding, which is what we are to do while enduring the *Karmic*-agony and anguish in His presence, rather than denying us such blessed opportunity that is most essential for human life to be fully purposeful.

Of course, no man likes suffering, but the sages and saints try to accept it with much joy in their heart, since it yields them the opportunity to come even closer to the Creator; it gives them the satisfaction that they are enduring the distress of life because they love Him; it brings them peace of knowing that they are joyfully abiding in His will.

Surely, this is the reason, why an enlightened man does not consider the sorrow and suffering of life as a curse, but accepts it as an opportunity provided by God in love, because not only it lessens the burden of *Karma* upon his soul but it also enables him to purify her even further by living in the closeness of God, and thus, by sharpening her vision of Truth.

Additionally, such abidance in faith of God also deters the creation of bondage to new *Karma*, since the actions of the day are rendered in conformance to the will of God rather than in adherence to the desires of egoistic-self.

Seventhly: Surely, human embodiment is a privilege for the soul since it is empowered to change the course of Karma; but it is extremely hard to come by.

One of the bitter truths, which we generally do not realize, is that often deeds of our day are much heavier in sin than righteousness. I am sure many would find it hard to believe, but it happens to be true. Well, if we want to challenge it, let us examine the facts of our common daily life.

First, let us consider the rule that every action we do, even the most insignificant one, creates *Karma* – the good or bad – depending upon how we perform it. With this fact in mind, now think, how much *Karma* do we create in a single day and what does it mean it terms of suffering its consequences?

And then calculate it for an average life and see how much it amounts to. We find the aggregate simply overwhelming because it is inestimable; isn't it!

Also the truth of the matter is that often our day gets contaminated by the traces of all kinds of evil. The scorning and contempt, the deceit and dishonesty, the indignity and indecency, the envy and jealousy, the conceit and covertness, the animosity and hatred, the anger and fury, the greed and gluttony, the arrogance and self-indulgence, are only a few such vices, which can be listed here without exhausting the list, which victimize us on daily basis and pollute our day with their poison.

Therefore, it is no exaggeration if we say that for most of us, our deeds of the day earn much more bad *Karma* (*Papa*) than good (*Punya*), because we perform most actions with an impure and unholy heart rather than with one that is pure and pious. We all know that the subtle vices like greed and gluttony, and lust and lasciviousness often drive our day and maneuver our endeavors, so the enterprises that we engage in during the fruitful hours of our daily life, are mostly tainted with sin.

Surely, we do not see it that way, but that does not mean it is not like that. And since the selfishness and self-indulgence dominate our actions, by each passing day their *Karma* increases further the burden upon our soul.

Oh! Forget about the bad deeds, as not only they but even our good and great works that we perform with such a heartening attitude earn us *Karma* **(Holy Gita 14:5)**, and sorrowfully, induce more bondage.

The belief that our good deeds add up to so some meaningful good *Karma*, is very misguiding, because in all actuality our good works often do lot more harm than good, since they not only yield good *Karma*, which they most certainly do, but also create much bad *Karma* due to the fact that most of our righteous actions are accompanied by ego and pride, and often done with deceitful, phony and hypocritical intents.

Another fact also comes in play that good *Karma* does not cancel out the bad *Karma*, since all *Karma* demands exhaustion separately; thus, there is tons of *Karma* that accrue for the soul on daily basis.

Now calculate the total sum and see how much *Karma* the soul accumulates through all her days living as human? And then, just fathom on the idea that most of the accrued *Karma* is in bondage and not in freedom.

Beloved! Calculate the odds on your own and see for yourself that for most of us the chances are very slim, that after this life we would embody as human any time soon. This honest truth, we hardly ever hear even from our holy teachers, forget about coincidently reading in the holy books.

Surely, if we live by the laws of *Karma*, then odds are quite against such possibility, because in between two human lives of the soul, there lies a travel to all kinds of *Karmic*-worlds – bounded by the extremities of heaven and hell – and the countless lower earthly embodiments, which she is demanded to wear to express and exhaust her earthly *Karmic*-dues, before through the grace of God, she is given another chance to be human again.

It is truly sad that most of us do not realize how so rarely the soul passes through the human embodiment in her Karmic-journey; we do not understand how hard it is for her to be born as human and wear the clothes of humanity.

Well, after realizing such odds, of course, if we are wise, we would take this human life of ours most seriously and devote it to the purpose for which it has been given by God – which is to attain Moksha. This truth, that human life is very hard to come by, must undoubtedly convince us to regard it as a precious gift of God, which He awarded to us in His utmost love.

Eighthly: The Karmic-cycle is seemingly endless that is revived every time the soul passes trough the human embodiment.

Since only man among all creatures is endowed with the power to change the course of Karma, and only he has the empowerment to end this seemingly ever-continuing cycle, so if he chooses not to do anything about it, it continues unbrokenly. Oh! It is only he – the man – who has the power to change its course. So if he passes his life without trying to put an end to it, he is the one who is responsible for furthering its continuation.

While living his old Karma man creates new Karma, and that new Karma, which he generates as human, feeds more life into Karmic-cycle and revives it to go for at least one more time.

Meaning, if the soul is not delivered from the fetters of Karma in human life, she has no choice but to pass through at least one more cycle of wandering in all kinds of Karmic-worlds and endure misery and pain of those nonhuman lives that are ordained for her to express and exhaust the newly created and past accumulated Karma.

And at the end of it, after going through all kinds of nonhuman manifestations, through the grace of God, she is given another opportunity to be embodied as human so that she could redeem herself. And thus, the cycle repeats itself at least for one more time.

The secret of continuance of Karmic-cycle lies in the fact that human embodiment is what revives it and feeds new life into it. And even though this embodiment of higher order is given to the soul to free herself from the grip of *Karma*, in her infatuation for this world, she ends up doing just the opposite and engages in things that create more *Karma* with bondage, and thus, she injects new life in its prolongation.

So every time when the soul (*Atman*) passes through the human embodiment, if human life does not yield the liberation for her, and she fails to redeem herself, by default, the same thing happens and a new cycle of *Karma* kicks-in, and thus, forcing her to experience the pain and suffering of countless more nonhuman embodiments.

What we must understand clearly is that after the physical death when the soul leaves a human body, she only leaves its physicality (the corporeal elements), which is a vessel for her material manifestation, but she carries with her the rest, which is the subtleness of the very core of her existence; she takes with her all the subtle elements – the senses – the sublime sensuality, **"When the Lord (of the body and senses - the Jiva) leaves this body, he draws the senses and carries them to the body that he obtains – Holy Gita 15:8."**

This subtlety she carries with her as she travels from body to body and passes through the tunnel of transmigration to wear all kinds of embodiments. No change in her inner integration takes place during all those lower lives and during the time when she travels through other planes of higher and lower consciousness.

So when the soul embodies as human again, she has to deal with the same attachments, same desires, and same problems of passion and infatuation, which she has had in her past human life, since she carries with her the senses throughout the *Transmigrational* journey imposed by the laws of *Karma*.

This may not be such a comforting thought if one is trapped by the web of Maya as it surely is not a good news for the one who is gravely thirsty of the water of this world and is hungry of its pleasures.

Therefore, until there is genuine awareness of this reality, our soul would continue her old wasteful ways, life after life, of living in lust and lasciviousness in every human birth, and keep repeating the cycle of transmigration by going from one mortal form to another enjoying the sensuality of this physical world **(Holy Gita 15:10).**

Beloved! As you can see, until we interrupt this seemingly ever-continuing cycle of *Karma* and do something about it, our soul would continue to remain in bondage.

4

Transmigration

~

Atman's Journey from One Body to Another

Once we accept the laws of *Karma* as the regulating authority over the conditioned existence of the soul (*Atman*) in *Karmic*-worlds, where she wanders like a nomad while living the captivity of mortality that is imposed upon her as a consequence to her *Karma*, we surely wonder about many things like: what happens to her when she goes from one body to another? What happens when she repeatedly passes through the passage of transmigration? Or, what happens when the two most significant cosmic events, the Dissolution and Creation, take place?

And many other questions like that where we wonder about the state of existence of the soul while she is passing through the various phases of her journey. You see! Our curiosity increases when we raise these kinds of questions. Doesn't it!

Well, the last chapter describes in detail the so called '*Karmic*-cycle' and exposes its workings in details including the explanation on how does it operate. It also answers the questions: What is the root cause of soul's falling into its snares? What keeps her continually trapped in it, life after life? And what forces her to endure an inestimable sorrow and suffering rising out of countless lower and higher embodiments, which she is compelled to pass through as a part of bearing the burden of *Karma*?

It not only entails the whereabouts of the soul while traveling through all kinds of *Karmic*-destinations but also speaks of several considerations of the truth that apply to the soul during her conditioned life, which help us understand quite clearly what is needed to happen in order for her to attain release from such seemingly never-ending cycle of *Karmic*-confinements.

So, much is explained in there about the *Karmic*-cycle; however, there is still much curiosity in our mind as there remain so many questions that are unanswered, and we would very much like to understand as to what happens to the soul during her passage through transmigration, where she goes from one body to body; and what happens to her when the Existence is completely dissolved and created again during the cosmic events of Dissolution and Creation?

Surely, such wonderment is quite natural for us, because unless we have the answers to our inquiries, the understanding of the consequences of egoistic actions by the soul in her human embodiments, the operation of the laws of *Karma*, the workings of *Karmic*-cycle, and her eventual redemption from its captivity, would remain incomplete.

Fortunately, the Holy Gita allows us to have a glance at a view that depicts how the soul endures the journey through Transmigration, and unveils the facts about her whereabouts during the period of Nonexistence that takes place in between Dissolution and Creation.

Therefore, let us begin our inquiry by examining the related scriptural texts that unfold the mystery of the soul while migrating from body to body, and continue this investigation into next chapter by exploring the holy word that exposes the truth about the survival and preservation of the soul during the two major cosmic events, which define the repeated birth and death of the Universe.

Well, from verse, **Holy Gita 13:21**, which clearly states that the soul (*Atman*) undergoes higher and lower embodiments due to her attachment and desire, **"Because of its attachment**

to the *Gunas* it attains higher or lower births – Holy Gita 13:21," one very specific conclusion can be derived, though implicitly, that these earthly embodiments of the soul are not just a few but countless, because she is so strongly bounded by passion and infatuation that to get her released from these evils is quite difficult and that is why she remains under the custody of *Karma* almost timelessly.

To understand how tightly the soul is chained by passion and infatuation, we all can take an honest evaluation of our own self and see how desperately we are crazy for the things of this world; how deeply we have been paralyzed by our own passion; and how acutely we have been enslaved by our own infatuation.

So, if during human embodiment, the soul does not get rescued from the captivity to mortality and does not reach *Moksha* (Liberation), which is attained only through the grace of God, then she is thrown back into another cycle of *Karma*, where she faces another long series of countless births and deaths.

Thus, the soul is forced to face countless embodiments again, lower and higher, which she endures till she is given another chance by God to embody as human and granted another opportunity to liberate herself from the incarceration of mortality.

This cyclic process continues till the soul is redeemed through the grace of God and liberated eternally. But while she remains trapped in the *Karmic*-cycle, she continually moves from one body to another to express the fractions of *Karma* that get matured in due times and demand their exhaustion through suitable embodiments.

And, even though the soul (*Atman*) is immutable and eternal **(Holy Gita 2:17, 2:21)**, and is unborn and imperishable, **"The Self is never born, nor does It ever perish – Holy Gita 2:20,"** yet she goes from body to body and passes through successive series of births and deaths, and endures mortality by wearing all kinds of creaturely embodiments due to unavoidable demand imposed by the necessity of the expression and exhaustion of preordained *Karma*.

The changing of bodies by the soul is like a person changing his clothes. Just as one gives up the old clothes and wears the new ones, so does the soul wears a new body after discarding the old one. This happens to be a natural order for her:

Just as a person gives up his old clothes to put on new ones, so the embodied soul having discarded the worn-out bodies, puts on new ones.

(Holy Gita 2:22)

The way, once a dress has served its purpose, we dispose it off and get a new one, so does the soul also, which leaves a body once it has served its purpose and goes to another. For her, body is just a vessel that she uses to exhaust a preordained portion of *Karma* and fulfill the purpose for which it has been given to her.

It is a normal and repetitive course for the soul: to be born as *Jiva* and die, and then be born again.

Just the way a body, which the soul wears, grows from being a child to adult and then becomes old one day, the same way also begins her next *Karmic*-phase – which is to abandon the current body and move onto the next:

Just as an embodied soul attains childhood youth and old age through the body so it attains another body after death – Holy Gita 2:13.

(Holy Gita 2:13)

Once a body has served its purpose by exhausting its ordained *Karma*, the soul discards it and takes a new one that is most suitable to exhaust the next installment of matured *Karma*.

This sequence, so called 'Karmic-cycle', with which the soul (*Atman*) is in bondage, continues till she is born as human again, where she gets another chance to deliver herself from the fetters of *Karma*.

One thing to make notice of is that the reason for changing a body and moving from one to another is not dependent upon the body getting old but the complete fulfillment of its primary purpose for which it is given – which is to express and exhaust that portion of the preordained *Karma* for which it is given to her.

The words of Holy Gita say that all manifestations of life are caused by *Karma* **(Holy Gita 8:3);** meaning, any gross manifestation of the soul remains only till that manifestation is serving the purpose of exhausting predestined *Karma* ordained for it.

So once the predestined *Karma* has been expressed by a body, it is salvaged through the death, and the soul moves on to wear another body in accordance with the ordinances of *Karma.*

Well, from the scriptures quoted above, it becomes quite clear that *Karma* forces the soul to wear all kinds of bodies to satisfy her *Karmic*-obligations; however, when the soul *(Atman)* moves from one body to another, the question is: What regulations apply to her? And also, what really takes place during transitioning process as she moves from one body to another? This we yet do not know. In fact, we also do not know whether the soul moves alone or does she carry some belongings with her while going through the transmigrational transitioning and moving from one body to another?

To answer these questions, we need to examine following four consecutive verses of Holy Gita from chapter fifteen that provide a very close look at what happens during the transmigration of the soul. Therefore, let us begin with the following verse where the Lord God says that each embodied being in this world is a part of His Self-being.

Of course, God is the Supreme and primal Being; He is the eternal Transcendental Self; and each creature in the form of an individual soul (conditioned Self) is a part of Him, *"Mam Ev Anso –* **a ray of My Eternal Self:"**

> **In this world of embodied beings, <u>a ray of My Eternal Self</u> exists as the individual soul which <u>abiding in *Prakriti*</u> draws to itself the (five) senses with the mind as the sixth.**

> **(Holy Gita 15:7)**

So, the true genesis of all creatures is in God, since they all are originated from Him, **"I am the origin of all beings – Holy Gita 10:8,"** and they all have a soul indwelling in them, which is a part of Him.

125

Now, please notice these words **"Abiding in _Prakriti_ draws to itself the (five) senses with the mind as the sixth,"** which the Lord God speaks only after declaring that all beings are part of Him, **"A ray of My (His) Eternal Self exists as the individual soul (in all creatures);"** they uncover two very important facts. Let's look at them:

First fact: A part of the Eternal Self (God) that exists in beings as soul (_Atman_) actually abides under the control and conditioning of _Prakriti_, **"Which abiding in _Prakriti_;"** meaning, _Prakriti_ is the ruling authority over her. In other words, the soul is a captive of _Prakriti_, and that is why she abides by its constraints.

Second fact: The soul, under the influence of _Prakriti_, **"draws to itself the (five) senses with the mind as the sixth;"** meaning, she draws the senses and mind to herself because of the conditioning caused by the _Prakriti_.

What is being said here through these two statements is that, though the soul intrinsically is of the nature of 'liberty', however, due to _Karmic_-curse, she loses her freedom and becomes a captive, a 'slave' of _Prakriti_, under whose egoistic influence she associates herself with the mind and senses, which in fact are the organs of expression of ego (**(Holy Gita 13:20),** and thus, she lives a conditioned life of captivity, of course, to render her due _Karmic_-obligations.

To understand it better, we must learn first: What is _Prakriti_?

Well, we would learn soon that the _Prakriti_ is an agent of ego that expresses soul's egocentricity through a layer of conditioning that surrounds her. This is why it is no surprise that the composition of conditioning-layer that eclipses the soul is a combination of two main elements: the _Raga_ (love) and _Dwesha_ (hatred).

Since _Prakriti_ is a representative of egoistic expression of the soul, it is quite natural that the soul attaches herself to the senses and mind – which of course are the instruments of expression of sensuality including desires, the product of ego, **"All desires that are born of egoistic will – Holy Gita 6:24)."**

This explains how the soul is so doomed in darkness and delusion, because when the mind, which is driven by the self-centric _Prakriti_, engages in endeavors to satisfy the senses expressing the embedded desires, it becomes besmirched and corrupt, damaged and disabled in discerning right from wrong.

So as we can see, *Karma* brings slavery for the soul and puts her in custody of *Prakriti*, where she not only loses her 'liberty' but her 'light' as well because the purity of her 'love' (bliss) gets defiled by the self-centricity embedded in desires being expressed by the senses.

Now, consider a hypothetical case where the soul is totally free; there is no conditioning and no external influence; she is who she is; no manipulation of her behavior by any power or influence. Won't she then have full 'liberty' in her movements? Won't she then behave in the purity of 'love' as she is expected of? Won't her face then shine due to her own 'light'?

Of course, all this would be true then!

But unfortunately, that does not happen while she is in her conditioned state of existence. As we all know from our own experiences that under the influence of *Prakriti* – the nature – the soul behaves egocentrically. Surely, we all understand the power and influence of nature (*Prakriti*), which commands and controls our behavior in such a way that whenever we resent its authority, it prevails more often than not.

So the words, **"Abiding in *Prakriti* – Holy Gita 15:7"** state a fact of very profound reality that the soul lives her conditioned-life under the captivity of *Prakriti* **(Holy Gita 13:21)**.

Now, what happens once the soul has fulfilled the purpose of an embodiment – which is to express and exhaust the preordained *Karma*?

Of course, she discards and ceases the old embodiment to wear another one so that she could pay the next installment of her *Karmic*-debt by living the next portion of matured *Karma*.

Now the question is: When the soul moves from her old home to a new one, what things she leaves behind and what she carries with her, and what takes place during this process – which is called transmigration? Well, these secrets are unveiled quite beautifully in following words of Holy Gita:

When the Lord (of the body and senses - the *Jiva*) leaves this body, he draws the senses and carries them

127

to the body that he obtains even in the same manner as the wind carries fragrance (from the flowers).

(Holy Gita 15:8)

The sacred text says that when the soul leaves a body and goes to another, she takes along with her the senses; and by doing so, she carries with her the total sensuality with which she was surrounded prior to parting away from the previous body. Meaning, during her *transmigrational* transitioning, the soul carries with her the total composition of her self-individuality – the egoistic covering that surrounds her.

In other words, when a person dies, his soul takes with her all constituents that compose the subtle being in him. She carries with her all things that define the very person in him. But do we really understand what does that mean?

It means, along with the soul goes man's virtue, his vice, his quality, his character – everything. She carries with her his learning and knowledge, intellect and wisdom, dullness and smartness, love and hate, likes and dislikes, attachments and non-attachments, desires and non-desires – everything that constitutes his very being – except what comprises his physicality. So when the soul moves from body to body, all this moves along with her.

Now, there are two situations that need be analyzed separately. First, when she moves to a nonhuman embodiment, and second, when she moves to a human embodiment.

When the soul moves to a nonhuman embodiment, since there is no mind and intellect, the egoistic-subtlety of the soul remains contained within her nature and remains inactive and there occurs no thoughtful expression of her self-individuality as all assertions of self-individuality come through its instinct, which is the sole driving force of non-human life. The intuition is such an endowment in creatures that facilitates the expression and exhaustion of all ordained *Karma* in a most proper manner so that the purpose of given embodiment could be fully fulfilled.

On the other hand, when the soul takes a human body, the egoistic-subtlety finds a thoughtful and intellectually capable channel to express itself through the faculties of mind and intellect, which happens to be its home, **"The senses, mind and**

intellect are said to be its dwelling places – Holy Gita 3:40;" so it quits being an inactive dweller and becomes an active power within.

Also noticeable is the fact that when the soul moves from body to body, she not only takes with her the senses but also the intellect – not only the vice but also virtue; meaning, she takes with her not only the bad stuff like attachment and desire but also the good stuff like her intellect and wisdom, which is a very significant thing for her, **"When he (*Atman* – soul) is reborn, he is united with the intellect that he had cultivated in his past lives – Holy Gita 6:43."**

So it is quite a good-news for the soul; meaning, when she repeatedly passes through the cycle of transformation and goes from one nonhuman body to another, the intellect and wisdom, which she has accumulated in her last human embodiment, do not get lost but fully remain intact with her. And that's not it; even their magnitude does not change by the change of sensual covering encapsulating the soul. They continually remain constant and never loose their intensity and sharpness, their brilliance and brightness.

Eventually, when the soul enters a human embodiment, she has with her all the subtlety she had at the time when she departed from her past human embodiment.

Thus, every time the soul passes through human life, she gets a chance to build upon what she has already accumulated intellectually till that point in her *Karmic*-journey. And now, she is given another opportunity to grow even more in wisdom, and multiply in understanding, which eventually becomes instrumental in paving her way to *Mukti* (the eternal liberation), **"So he endeavors again to attain the higher rungs of *Yoga* leading to Liberation – Holy Gita 6:43."**

To dig a little deeper into this subject, let us look into the composite of corporeal conditioned-existence of the soul – which is called *Jiva* (conditioned-soul) – and learn what constitutes it?

Well, this happens to be unveiled fairly well in following two verses of Holy Gita that yield a concise description of what the body (meaning Field – **Holy Gita 13:1**) is, and what are its constituents:

> The <u>great elements</u>, ego-sense, intellect and the <u>non-manifest</u>; the ten *Indriyas* (five senses and five organs of action) and mind, and the five objects of the senses;

> Desire, aversion, pleasure, pain, the aggregate (of body and senses), consciousness, firmness - this in brief is the <u>Field</u> along with its effects.

> (Holy Gita 13:5-6)

Looking at these verses it becomes quite clear that except the '**great elements**', (Earth, Water, Fire, Air, Ether – **Holy Gita 7:4**), which constitute the physical enclosure that encapsulates the conditioned-soul (*Atman* – **the non-manifest**) as *Jiva*, everything else that has been described in these verses, meaning, all other constituents of her composition that form her surrounding environment, are carried with her when she migrates from one body to another and passes through the tunnel of transmigration.

Thus, even though, at the time of death, all encapsulating grossness of the soul in any material manifestation is discarded and dissolved, the inner subtleness still remains with her when she moves from one fleshly home to another, since she carries with her the senses and all their effects in the same manner just as the wind carries with it the fragrance from one place to another **(Holy Gita 15:8)**.

Now what does it really mean in the higher schema of *Karmic*-life of the soul as she moves from body to body to bear her *Karmic*-obligations? Well, the following verse helps us greatly in understanding a bit more of the mystery that exposes the truth that through the senses (which the soul carries with her from body to body – **Holy Gita 15:8**) and the mind, the soul enjoys the objective world, of course, through the sensual power of these physical organs;

> Depending upon sound, sight, touch, taste and smell, and the mind (as well as organs of action and *Pranas*) <u>the soul enjoys the objects of the world</u>.

> (Holy Gita 15:9)

Even though not much is said in this verse (at least so it seems on the surface), but when we dig a little deeper into it, we do find much hidden meaning, which truly widens our understanding of what truly happens to the soul at the end of human embodiment as she begins her journey of transmigration and travels through all kinds of higher and lower births to endure the consequences of *Karma*.

But before we get to it, we need to understand the broader meaning of words **"The soul enjoys the objects of the world"** which becomes. even more clear when we intentionally interpret them as **"The soul engages (enjoys) in the objects of this world."**

With this interpretation, what Holy Gita implicitly is trying to say that the soul engages in things of this world, which produce for her not only joy but sorrow as well; in fact the later is more often the case than not. In other words the use of word 'enjoy' is meant to refer to soul's engagement into objective world, which gives her both types of experience: filled with sorrow and suffering , and filled with pleasure and joy.

But the soul, in her intrinsic nature, is ever in bliss, ever in joy, since she is of the form of 'Sat-Chit-*Ananda* (Existence-Consciousness-Bliss)'; so then why does she experience sorrow at all?

The answer lies in the fact that the soul (the *Atman* – *Purusha*) loses her purest form and becomes impure and tainted, and becomes conditioned because she goes under the influence and control of *Prakriti*, **"Which abiding in *Prakriti* – Holy Gita 15:7;"** which is what a *Jiva* is – a conditioned-soul – an *Atman* confined by misconceived self individuality created by the egoistic-self.

You see! It is not some voluntary act on part of the conditioned-soul (*Atman*). Under the influence of *Prakriti*, she is compelled to engage with the things of *Gunas*, which are the product of *Prakriti*, **"*Purusha* abiding in *Prakriti* enjoys the *Gunas* born of *Prakriti* – Holy Gita 13:21."**

Please make a note that I purposely underlined the word 'compelled', because it has a very special significance. How? Let me explain!

Surely, the soul is free in her choices since she has the power of freewill. She does not have to engage with things of *Gunas* at all if she does not want to. But she still feels compelled to do so, because she is under the authority of *Prakriti* and *Gunas* happen to be its products. So it is quite natural that they have a heavy influence upon her while living the captivity of *Prakriti* where she is heavily exposed to them.

Oh! This influence of attraction (*Gunas*) works upon her like a force of compulsion.

Now, what really causes this compulsion when the soul is exposed to things of *Gunas*? A very good question! Because it is not the things of the objective world of *Gunas* but her ego, her self-centricity that causes her to become so captivated by them; it is her egoistic-individuality, which creates attachment and desire for the things of *Gunas* when exposed, and forces her to engage with them.

Things of *Gunas*, in themselves, do not have any such power to compel the soul in anyway, as all such power lies in her ego, in her self-centricity, in her attachment and desire.

Since the power of attachment and desire for the objects of *Gunas* is extremely strong, so the soul feels compelled to engage with them. Their pull is so powerful that she finds herself helpless to hold back but to engage with them, but of course never with neutrality and nonattachment but with egocentricity and selfishness; and of course, that becomes a problem.

Now, what are the objects of *Gunas*? The whole world! Since all things in it have been made with *Gunas*, **"There is no entity that is devoid of the three *Gunas* (modes) arising out of *Prakriti* (Nature) – Holy Gita 18:40."** The whole creation is the field of *Gunas*; meaning, the world is nothing but a meadow of 'enjoyment' for the soul. In other words, the whole objective world is a field of her 'engagement'.

Thus, no matter what the soul does, under the control of *Prakriti*, she engages with the things of *Gunas*, since there is no possible life without it. As a result, she experiences pleasure and pain when she engages with the objective world; the reason being that the sensuality eclipsing the soul perceives things of this world with attachment and desire, and with *Raga* (love, like) and *Dwesha* (hate, dislike), and that causes the soul to experience sorrow and suffering, pleasure and joy:

O Son of *Kunti*, <u>the objects that are perceived by the senses</u> are subject to birth and death. <u>They give rise to pleasure and pain</u>, to heat and cold; they are transient. Therefore, O *Bharata*, endure them heroically.

(Holy Gita 2:14)

Let me repeat the truth here that the objective world of *Gunas* in itself does not have any potency and power to create pleasure and pain for the soul (*Atman*), which happens only when she perceives them through the egoistic attitude.

This is exactly what Holy Gita means in verse quoted above when she says, **"The objects that are perceived by the senses,"** implying that when the soul perceives the objective world with sensuality, she feels sorrow and joy, **"They give rise to pleasure and pain,"** and thus, it becomes the reason for her such experiences.

Obviously, the conditioned-soul (*Jiva*) herself is the cause of her pleasure and pain, because she inflicts them upon her by perceiving things of this world through the effect of sensuality imposed upon her by the *Prakriti*, which happens to be the controlling authority over her that forces her to live helplessly under its regulation, **"These beings which are helplessly under the control of *Prakriti* – Holy Gita 9:8."**

The *Prakriti* uses the power of *Raga* (desire) and *Dwesha* (hatred), which abide in the senses **(Holy Gita 3:34)** and are the instruments of *Prakriti* **(Holy Gita 13:20)**, to exert its control over the soul right from the time of her birth as *Jiva*. From the day one she is under their influence:

O *Bharata*! All beings at the time of their birth come under the sway of the delusion of pairs of opposites caused by desire and hatred. O *Parantapa*!

(Holy Gita 7:27)

Following holy words verify the fact that the soul herself is the cause of her sorrow and joy, and *Prakriti* is the power that forces her to perceive the objective world with an egoistic attitude and causes her to experience pleasure and pain:

Prakriti is the cause of effect (body), instrument (senses) and their functions. *Purusha* (the soul) is said to be the cause of experiencing pleasure and pain.

(Holy Gita 13:20)

The following words of Holy *Ramayana* also yield the same testimony that all life is subjected to experience of pleasure and pain; that all *Jivas* (conditioned souls) are made to experience this duality without any reservations; that all beings are bound by them without any exceptions:

As for the people, every embodied soul is subject to pleasure and pain according to its fate.

(Ramayana, Ayodhya-Kanda, 12.2)

Well, by going through all these scriptural texts we have established the fact that to exhaust *Karma* by wearing suitable embodiments, the soul moves from body to body under the control of *Prakriti* and experiences pleasure and pain according to her indwelling *Raga* (desire) and *Dwesha* (hatred).

And even though, she endures physicality and grossness over and over during the ongoing *Karmic*-cycle by passing through all kinds of non-human embodiments that are suitable to exhaust the preordained *Karma*, she still continues to keep intact all her subtlety without any loss. Any change in it occurs only when she passes through a human embodiment.

These facts are very important to keep in mind as we move further in our discussion and become ready to take a good look at verse, **Holy Gita 15:9** (quoted above), which says that depending upon the senses and mind the soul engages (enjoys) with the objects of this world; meaning, the soul's involvement with the objective world is dependent upon her surrounding sensuality and eclipsing infatuation.

Oh! It is soul's affinity, her infatuation, her attachments and desires that play the controlling role in all her earthly engagements.

Thus, the precise meaning of verse, **Holy Gita 15:9**, is that in conditioned state of existence, the soul is ever under the captivity of *Prakriti*; and while abiding under her influence when through her senses she interacts with the objects of *Gunas*, which are the instruments of the Prakriti, she experiences pleasure and pain depending upon her attachment and desire, passion and infatuation, and *Raga* and *Dwesha* towards the material world. And it goes on like this for her, life after life.

Now, let us try to sum up the transitioning of the soul from body to body right from the beginning of a Karmic-cycle to the end.

Well, after death, when the soul ceases the human body, though she discards her encapsulating physicality, she yet carries with her all subtlety constituted by her senses. So what is carried by the soul is her egocentrically instituted individuality, which establishes her as a conditioned-soul, including her ego-sense and self-centricity, learning and knowledge, intellect and wisdom, desire and aversion, pleasure and pain, and all things that have been listed in verses, **Holy Gita 13:5-6**.

It means she departs from a human body with all her sensuality, all her passion and infatuation, all her desires and attachments, all her intellect and reason, all her light and wisdom, and all what constitutes the composition of the inner being.

One thing still remains that has not been accounted for, is the bulk of *Karma* (the total sum of *Karmic*-earnings of her past human-lives that are still due materialization), which is to be compulsorily spent as it matures, little by little, through countless embodiments and be exhausted by expressing it through various kinds of *Karmic*-embodiments.

This forces the soul to pass through all kinds of higher and lower lives according to the rules of Kama; some she lives to enjoy the rewards of good works (*Punya*), **Holy Gita 9:20**, while others she endures to express the punishments laid upon her as a consequence to bad deeds (*Papa*).

However, by passing through all kinds of ordained *Karmic*-lives in between two human embodiments, regardless of the magnitude of her experiences of pleasure and pain, the soul becomes light as her *Karmic*-burden lessens, since each life enables her to express and exhaust some portion of accumulated *Karma*.

But since all other lives but human are regulated by the instinct, **"All living beings who obey their instincts implicitly – Holy Gita 3:33,"** while passing through nonhuman embodiments, no change ever occurs in the composition of her surrounding sensual-environment, which she has inherited from her last human embodiment.

And since all those nonhuman lives are driven by mere instinct **(Holy Gita 3:33)**, no change is even possible during those embodiments since there is no mind and intellect; there is no faculty of discernment and discrimination; and there is no empowerment of autonomy and freewill.

Thus, the soul carries everything with her through all nonhuman lives what she has taken away from her last human embodiment, but of curse, as she moves further on her journey of transmigration, the burden of *Karma* lessens, since each life enables her to exhaust some portion of matured-*Karma* as per pre-ordinance.

So when the soul completes a *Karmic*-cycle and embodies as human again, at the time of birth, she in fact is no different than what she was when she ceased the previous human body except that she now has a new body, and new external environment to express her ordained *karma*; meaning, the composition of her conditioning encapsulation – the subtlety of her material existence as human – is exactly the same as it was when she parted from the previous human body. Nothing has changed except the external enclosure of her embodiment, and the surrounding environment in which she is born. So the things that got changed are all external and not internal.

In other words, though one goes through countless nonhuman embodiments to express and exhaust the due *Karma* after his death, but at the end of his *Karmic*-cycle, through the grace of God when he is born again as human, at the time of his birth, he is the same person as he was at the time of his death during his past human embodiment.

Thus, it can be said confidently that, except the physicality of material manifestation of the soul, nothing else changes for her, as the composition of her subtlety remains fully intact in between her two human embodiments – from the death of previous body to the birth of next body.

So at the time of birth, one assumes exactly the same encapsulation of his subtle existence that he had at the time of his death during his previous human embodiment; he has the same sensuality, attachment and desire, infatuation and passion, virtue and vice, ego and self-centricity, intellect and wisdom. Everything is the same; nothing is different, absolutely.

All the subtle elements of his material existence from the previous human embodiment remain preserved even while going through the repetitive cycle of transmigration as the soul passes through all kinds of lower embodiments, and finally, gets to be born as human again.

Well, after understanding the fact that between two human embodiments nothing really changes in the composition of encapsulation that surrounds the soul, as her subtlety remains unaltered from the time of her departure from the previous human body till she is born in the next, it becomes quite clear that in between, whatever nonhuman lives she passes through, and whatever time she spends wearing all kinds of lower bodies due to *Karmic*-obligations, all that serves one and only one purpose for her, and that is to express and exhaust her due *Karma* that she has accumulated during her previous human embodiments.

When the soul is given a chance to wear the human body again, she not only exhausts the old preordained *Karma* but also accumulates new *Karma* due to her ego-sense; and to express and exhaust the new *Karma*, she is forced to go through another cycle of *Karma*, which demands her to pass through countless nonhuman embodiments again and experience their pleasure and pain.

This is what has been happening to her since her initial material conception, and would continue to be like this until she is released from all *Karmic*-bondage, which comes only through the grace of God.

Holy Gita summarizes this theme through her following words and says that those who do not understand this truth about the soul (*Atman*) are ignorant, and those who do are wise:

Though abiding in the body, moving from one body to another, and enjoying the objects of the senses, this

137

soul enveloped by the *Gunas* is not seen by the ignorant, those who are endowed with intuitive knowledge they alone know the true nature of the soul.

(Holy Gita 15:10)

Through all this, one thing has become quite clear that even though the laws of *Karma* decide what embodiments the soul has to go through to satisfy its obligations, but how the *Karmic*-life will be regulated during those embodiments are solely under the governing authority of the *Prakriti* (nature).

Here is another revelation to this regard that not only *Prakriti* is the controlling authority over the soul that directs her material manifestation, it also is the true 'performer of all actions', **"All actions are performed by the *Gunas* of *Prakriti* – Holy Gita 3:27,"** even though, due to darkness caused by the egoistic encapsulation around her, the soul believes herself to be the 'doer', **"I am the doer – Holy Gita 3:27."**

Holy Gita clears this matter even further by saying that the soul (Self) has nothing to do with the actions that are performed by the body, which eventually become the cause of her *Karma*, as all the actions are performed by the *Prakriti* alone; and it is not she but the *Prakriti* that creates the doer-ship in her:

The Divine Self does not create "doer-ship" in people, nor does He work; He does not create the relationship between the works and their fruits. It is *Prakriti* that sustains these.

(Holy Gita 5:14)

So in truth, it is never the soul herself but the *Prakriti* that creates problem of bondage for the soul, **"These *Gunas* arising from *Prakriti* create bondage for the Imperishable *Atman* – Holy Gita 14:5,"** and throws her into the captivity to *Karma*. How sad that due to soul's affection and adoration for the things of *Gunas*, the *Prakriti* is able to enslave her.

These words of Lord God highlight the power of *Prakriti* over the soul, **"Presided by Me, *Prakriti* brings forth the creation of beings consisting of movables and immovable – Holy Gita 9:10,"** and state very clearly that it is the *Prakriti* that brings forth soul's physical materialization as beings, and forces them to live helplessly under its authority, **"These beings which are helplessly under the control of *Prakriti* – Holy Gita 9:8."**

Look at how beautifully the *Upanishad* has stated the same truth about the soul, *Prakriti* (nature), and God through these eternal words:

There is the soul of man with wisdom and un-wisdom, power and powerlessness; there is nature, *Prakriti*, which is creation for the sake of soul; and there is God, infinite, omnipresent, who watches the work of creation. When a man knows the three he knows Brahman.

(Svetasvatara Upanishad, Part 1)

Thus, the *Prakriti* is not only the ruling authority throughout all material manifestations of the soul but also is the 'performer' of all movements rendered by the bodies, which the soul wears.

Before I close this chapter let me highlight the main point again that due to *Karmic*-obligations, when the soul moves from body to body, and passes through all kinds of non-human embodiments in between two human lives, all of her eclipsing sensuality, her intellect and wisdom are well-preserved and kept unaltered till the soul is born as human again.

Worth remembering is the fact that no other embodiment but human has the power to alter the *Prakriti* and also the course of *Karma*.

As far as the transmigration is concerned, this process does nothing but to dissolve one material manifestation of the soul that has fulfilled its purpose and initiate another one to express and exhaust another portion of matured *karma*, but with the same inner encapsulation that the soul had at the time of her departure from the previous human materialization.

5

Karmic-Chastisement
~
Soul's Nomad Wandering in Karmic-Worlds

To express *Karma*, the soul travels through all kinds of *Karmic*-worlds like a lost wanderer and roams around timelessly until through the grace of God she embodies as human again.

But if in human life, she is not salvaged from bondage, which happens most often than not, then a new cycle of *Karma* commences, which forces her back onto another cycle of *Karma* where she not only wears countless earthly embodiments but also wanders through all kinds of *Karmic*-worlds. These higher and lower worlds of *Karma* are called *Lokas* – the planes of varying level of consciousness.

The two extremities of these *Lokas* are heaven (*Swarga*) and hell (*Nark*), which sit at the opposite end of each other in the spectrum of varying consciousness. One end signifies the state of extreme pleasure and enjoyment while the other signifies extreme pain and suffering. However, all the planes of varying consciousness in between and including these two extremities are the field of *Karma*, and are run by its laws.

When the soul leaves a human body, unless she is liberated from bondage, she wanders in these Lokas as spirit and embodies as all kinds of creatures in earthly domains (*Bhumi-*

Loka), and endures the consequences of her *Karma* until she returns back as human again to live a very special life that is endowed with the power to release herself from the bondage to *Karma* through the empowerment of mind and intellect and the privilege of 'Freewill'.

So until (through the grace of God) the soul is released and set free from bondage to *Karma*, she not only repeatedly births and dies in this material world and wears all kinds of creaturely bodies but also wanders in unseen worlds of varying consciousness and experiences their pleasure and pain according to her *Karma*. The extreme pleasure is denoted by the high heaven and extreme pain by the lowly hell.

These two extremities of *Karmic*-life have such a wide spectrum of experiences that its one end spreads into the overwhelming pleasures of heavens while the other dooms into the inestimable pains of hell; one extends into the richness that surpasses the opulence of all worlds while the other extends into those dreaded domains that are marred by extreme suffering and sorrow.

They are two opposite ends of kingdom of *Karma*.

While one is most willingly sought residence by man through the best of good *Karma*, the other is a mandatory dwelling for the one who is due the worst of bad *Karma*. In fact, they are so far apart from each other that to go from one end to the other, can take countless lives, and still not make it for sure.

The plane of consciousness on which the human life exists lies almost in the middle of these two extremities of *Karmic*-life.

According to scriptures, when the soul ceases human embodiment, she begins a long journey into the *Karmic*-worlds existing at various planes of consciousness, which lie in between these two extreme ends of *Karmic*-existence. At the end of her long voyage through all kinds of higher and lower *Karmic*-territories she ends up back again in the earthly provinces as human with a fresh opportunity to save herself from the grip of bondage – the power that forces her to go through this cycle over and over.

Our reality is that we all are caught in this seemingly unending cycle that puts us through inestimable sorrow and suffering each time we go through it to express and exhaust our due *Karma*; and the human life that is given to us to permanently relive ourselves from its misery and pain, we waste in doing everything else but just that.

During this most blessed opportunity, so called human life, we remain extremely engaged in accumulating the abundance of this world, and hardly ever pay enough attention and dedicate any meaningful time to do what the human embodiment is given for.

The possible reason we fail in it is that we do not have sufficient understanding of *Karma* and its laws, and do not realize the seriousness of its consequences. Another possibility could be that we may have adequate knowledge of the rules and regulations of *Karma*, and know sufficiently well the seriousness of *Karmic*-consequences, but we still fail to take them seriously since we do not believe that their enforcement is affirmative and adequately visible.

Though it is hard to pinpoint a single reason as there are several that explain why we are not very serious about the considerations of *Karmic*-life that lies right ahead of us, but our best guess could be that we do not believe enough in the enforcement of the *Karmic*-laws because it is not very visible and not self-validating; and that is why we lack their observation and abidance.

Surely we can debate this as much as we want to, but the underneath fact remains the same: we hardly care for the consequences of our *Karma*; because if we did, our behavior will be quite different than what it is. We all will be a very different type of human beings; not as selfish, egoistic but very unselfish and humble. Because that is what the true realization of *Karmic*-consequences would make us.

To prove this point, we should ask this question to ourselves: How many and of what kind of lower *Karmic*-lives can we expect for ourselves after we die, and for how much time we will live in lower planes of consciousness and endure severe suffering of hellish domains before coming back to this world as human again? Surely for our good deeds we will visit the heavens and enjoy its pleasures and prosperity, but how much pain and suffering we will endures in the provinces of hell to account for our bad *Karma*?

How often in our solitudes or among family members and friends, or in any gathering, formal or informal, religious or non-religious, we raise these kinds of questions and discuss the most fundamental issue of what would happen to us after we die?

The honest answer we all come up with: Not often! Or, to say it more modestly: Hardly ever! A great majority of folks of Hindu belief hardly ever raise these kinds of questions that demand us to look at the scripturally spoken *Karmic*-horrors awaiting us in the aftermath of our death.

Even though we often refer to word '*Karma*' in our daily communication but we hardly ever take a pause, and examine those *Karmic*-repercussions that we would definitely face right after our soul ceases this human embodiment.

For this, there could be only two possibilities: either we do not understand the totality of the consequences of *Karma*; or, may be we understand them, yet we choose to ignore them.

Well, often the later is the case, since most of us know adequately what *Karma* is, and what its consequences are; but we simply do not care for them. That is why we do not pay much attention to what would happen after we die.

Now, why do we not care and pay attention to it, has several possibilities, which of course, we would consider one by one as our discussion progresses. Yet, the fact remains, that knowingly or unknowingly, we are extremely careless about the consequences of *Karma*. Surely, if that were not the case, we would not be behaving so ignorantly.

Consider the same questioning again as above but with a different paraphrasing: Though most of us know that after death the soul goes through all kinds of lower births to make the payoffs of *Karma*, but how many of us are worried about what would happen to our soul after we die?

Not many! We all know that. No body loses sleep over it.

Beloved! Even if we just consider it to be a mere possibility, still how many among us do take time to reflect seriously upon this truth? Again the answer is the same: Not many! And this should not be a surprise to anyone!

Therefore, it is not hard to see that our negligence about this whole matter is quite obvious. You see! *Karma* is not some foreign notion to us; it is a highly significant subject in our theology and is a very popular concept of our spiritual understanding.

Yet, because we are so busy in life taking care of all other needs of the day that we hardly have any time for anything else. We are mostly focused upon how to meet our immediate goals and do those things that we think we ought to do in order to have life the way we want it.

Obviously, when our day in consumed in such priorities, who has time to think about *Karma*. No wonder, the questions like, "What will happen to us after we die?" hardly ever surface in our mind and get any meaningful attention.

So, one thing we can confidently say that lacking in our interest about the subject of *Karma*, which without any doubt is so crucial to us especially in regard to life after our death, is due to the fact that everything else in life seems to have higher priority than this, and that is why we have no time to take a serious look at what are its percussions and how are we going to handle them?

However, there is another factor that also contributes significantly to our lacking of interest in this subject is the lack of knowledge of the rules and regulations of *Karma* and their overall operation and enforcement during the total *Karmic-cycle*.

Still, to say that we are ignorant about the consequences of *Karma* would be a big mistake since most of us are fairly aware of them. True, that our understanding of this matter is not much, but it surely is sufficient to know at least this much that we are in big trouble because of it.

No doubt, most of us understand adequately what *Karma* is and what are its percussions? Our common belief is that our life, whatever that is, has been given to us according to our *Karma*, and whatever future life we are going to have would also be as per its accordance. At least this much, or even a bit more, most of us do understand.

However, I have to say this quite openly, that ignorance is still our primary problem; the knowledge, we have about *Karma*, is simply not enough as it requires a much deeper comprehension of it, especially, if we are to have any hope to get liberation from its bondage.

Therefore, it is essential for us to understand not only the workings of *Karma* but also how the soul drifts in all kinds of *Karmic*-worlds, like a nomad, and ignorantly remains captive of their incarceration. Because there are several important facts, which we ought to know, that apply to the soul when she wanders like a vagabond in these non-consequential domains to endure the consequence of *Karma*.

Please make a note that I purposely called *Karmic*-domains as 'non-consequential' because that is exactly what they are, of course, except the one, where we all are now – the earthly province – because this is the only providence where, when the soul embodies as human, is made privileged to pursue the path of true life and liberty.

We would learn more about this as we proceed further in our discussion, and come to realization that regardless of how high is the wandering of soul in the heavenly worlds, it really is of no true good for her; because her true good is only when she becomes awakened by the Truth and begins to walk towards God to seek His sanctuary in the hope of her eternal redemption from the hold of bondage.

But for now let us try to understand, how the *Karmic*-life of the soul is regulated in *Karmic*-territories that are bounded by the two extremities – heaven and hell – and examine several facts that would definitely enhance our vision to see the truth that relate to the soul when she goes astray and drifts in wastelands of *Karma*.

One consideration that is very essential to keep in mind while trying to understand how the soul can find a way out of bondage is that, for sure the good *Karma* by the soul earns her trips to heavens, but that is not all! The highest reward she gets is a special gift from God; which is, that her surrounding darkness is removed and replaced by His light, **"As an act of divine compassion, dwelling within their self, I destroy the darkness born of ignorance with the shining lamp of wisdom – Holy Gita 10:11."**

Of course, as per *Karmic*-laws, for her good deeds (*Punya*) the soul enjoys the pleasures and prosperity of highly placed heavens, and for her bad deeds (*Papa*), she is forced to endure the dreadfulness of misery and pain of degradingly placed hellish worlds. For the expression of good *Karma* the soul travels through the higher worlds **(Holy Gita 9:20)**, while for the exhaustion of bad, she goes through the lower worlds **(Holy Gita 16:19).**

But the *Karmic*-rewards of good deeds, which earn heavenly trips for the soul, do not last forever as they all come to an end even if they are to last for thousands of years; but once they are over, the soul falls back to the human world:

With the exhaustion of meritorious deeds, having enjoyed the expansive pleasures of the heavens, they fall into human world. Thus, the followers of ritualistic portion of the Vedas continue to come and go driven by their desires.

(Holy Gita 9:21)

This is the point we must understand quite clearly, that regardless of time spent in high heavens, after the soul finishes her quota of heavenly pleasures, she falls back to earthly provinces. So, if we estimate the material gains for the soul out of her *Karmic*-excellence, in all reality they are none since whatever she gains, she loses it by enjoying heavenly pleasures. Hence, all such profits are temporary and transient.

So it is no more than taking a pleasurable detour, which the soul takes on her path to eternity; which though feels good, but only delays her arrival to the destiny divine and lengthens her *Karmic*-journey. After all, all heavenly pleasures are nothing but fleeting experiences; they all are transitory just like the ones we have on earthly realm. Surely, they have no permanence, and no potency to last for long.

Thus, after the rewards of good *Karma* are exhausted and the soul has enjoyed her shares of the pleasures in high heavens, she eventually descends down to earthly provinces and continues the cycle of material manifestations again.

Well, the same also applies to her when due to bad *Karma* she is compelled to travel the lower regions of consciousness, and is sent there to endure the hellish suffering according to her *Karmic*-penalties. Then also, regardless of time for how long she has to live in those degraded domains, once she has lived through all the consequences of bad *Karma*, she returns back to this world.

In either case the soul comes back to the material world after her travel to the lands of higher and lower regions of *Karma* ends, and in eventuality of her *Karmic*-progression, she is given another chance to wear the human body again so that she could hopefully do the right thing and get redeemed from the bondage to *Karma* and attain the eternal liberation.

In verse, **Holy Gita 9:21** (quoted above), we hear the reality of what has been so often spoken by the sages of the *Upanishads* that good and bad, both kinds of deeds, cause the *Atman* (soul) to drift in all kinds of *Karmic*-worlds and make him wander in the regions of heaven and hell, but at the end of it, he returns back to the land of humanity again:

Rising by one of them, the living power of *Udana* leads to the heaven of purity by good actions, to the hell of evil by evil actions, and if by both again to this land of man.

(Prasna Upanishad, Third Question)

Now the question is, how much travel the soul does in what direction, towards heaven or hell, and how much life she lives in what kind of *Karmic*-worlds, depends solely upon what kind of *Karma* she earns in the human life, because it is the human life alone that creates new *Karma* and has the power to change her *Karmic*-course.

One thing to remember though! That nothing else has any true significance for the soul in terms of her liberation from bondage except what happens to her during her human embodiment, as all other embodiments and all other *Karmic*-life that she lives on this plane and other planes of consciousness, higher or lower, all are made for her to experience pleasure and pain, and to express and exhaust *Karma* and nothing else. There is no other purpose but just this, as all life in any *Karmic-province* is imposed upon her to endure joy or sorrow for her deeds according to *Karmic*-ordinances.

Now, since nothing else has any true significance for the soul as far as her salvation is concerned except what happens in her human embodiment, it is highly desirable that she does her best to earn the highest *Karma*, because if for some reason she fails to redeem herself in this life, then the good *Karma* can at least put her in higher level of Self-awakening in her next human life.

But what *Karma* the soul earns during a human life greatly depends upon the circumstances under which she lives through and the environment she is given, of course, besides her nature that controls her.

Therefore, even though the good *Karma*, which earns the soul a heavenly life in the higher worlds, and the bad *Karma*, which causes her to endure the hellish life in the lower worlds, become immaterial in her pursuit to regain immortality, it still has a great impact upon her next human embodiment, because both types of *Karma* play a major role in determining what kind of human life she is going to have the next time?

And that is what we need to investigate further and understand how the human life is ordained for the soul and what factors have greater impact upon it?

Even though it is always the good *Karma* that brings the soul a human embodiment, but what happens in human life is dependent upon both kinds of *Karma*. The highest of all *Karma* earns her the life of light and wisdom, while the lowest of good *Karma* including the bad *Karma* brings her life of delusion and darkness. So, what takes place in a human life of the soul solely depends upon her *Karmic*-merit.

For her good *Karma*, she is given such a good life that she could go even higher in her *Karmic*-evolution, and for her bad *Karma*, she is given such a bad life, which only pushes her further deep into the fallen *Karmic*-regression.

Thus, on one hand, the *Karmic*-cycle can lift the soul further towards the higher worlds, while on the other, it can push her deeper into the lower worlds.

So, if the soul has a momentum in moving rapidly towards one end, then it would be very difficult for her, if not impossible, to change its direction, because due to *Karmic*-inertia each cycle would naturally feed more momentum into her swing towards the direction she is already inclined and heading to.

It means if she is heading speedily towards the higher worlds, then each *Karmic*-cycle would induce more light into her and establish her more in wisdom; thus, placing her every time at a higher level of consciousness by increasing her awareness to the Truth.

This fact is validated by the Holy Gita when she speaks of how the spiritual progression comes into the soul:

O Delighter of *Kuru's* Race, when he is reborn, he is united with the intellect that he had cultivated in his past lives. So he endeavors again to attain the higher rungs of Yoga leading to Liberation.

(Holy Gita 6:43)

She says that during each *Karmic*-cycle when the soul passes through the human embodiment, since she has the same intellect as she had at the end of her past human life, she is given the opportunity to continue to build upon it to grow further in light and wisdom. This way, by increasing in radiance of the spirit during each human life, the soul reaches such heights of spiritual realm where she finds the grace of God, which lifts her out of all bondage.

Similarly, if the soul is heading rapidly towards the lower worlds, then each *Karmic*-cycle multiplies her descent and makes it a quick fall for her into the lower worlds, because each human life increases her darkness even further, which drown her deeper in the filthy wombs of vice.

Look at these holy words that tell of what happens to such soul that is infected by human immorality, and unveils the bold truth that evil of man only takes him towards the gates of hell:

There are three gates of hell which are the destroyers of the soul. They are Lust, Anger and Greed; therefore these three must be renounced.

(Holy Gita 16:21)

Thus, the most significant return of *Karma* is what the soul eventually receives in her next human embodiment; externally, the environment and surroundings, the situations and circumstances, and the life she endures; and internally, the intellect and wisdom she is endowed with, and the kind of virtue and vice she embodies.

In other words, the most meaningful reward of *Karma* is what the soul is born with, internally and externally, and what kind of pre-ordinance she has to endure in her next human embodiment.

So, even though, the good *Karma* can bring the soul good times of heavens but it really does not do whole lot of good unless it earns the soul a human life that becomes a useful conduit for her spiritual evolution. If that happens, then that is the true gain for her.

Thus, there is an opportunity for the soul, which she gets due to good *Karma* (*Punya*), where she is risen to the higher orbits of reincarnation that are extremely helpful in finding way to her eternal liberation. But that happens only if she is extremely blessed; otherwise, if the soul does not capitalize on the light of the Spirit, which she acquires through much blessing of God, then all goes in vain.

On the contrary, the bad *Karma* always does the opposite of good *karma* and brings the soul down to lower rebirths, which only multiply her darkness; sometimes, even to a point from where her recovery is not just difficult but almost impossible.

But mind it, please! Through the grace of God, the soul can always recover even from the deepest pit of hell, and not only soar into heavens but also reach the sanctuary of His eternal abode.

Praise God! In Him all things are possible!

But Jesus beheld them, and said unto them, With men this is impossible; but <u>with God all things are possible</u>.

(Holy bible, Mark 19:26)

Surely, often man is helpless in his own, especially, when it comes to light and wisdom, and understanding the higher reality and truth, but through the grace of God, nothing is impossible for him, as in God he is fully capable of attaining anything.

But how can man arrive to such graces unless first he becomes able to know Him? No wonder, he needs light and wisdom, so that he could recognize His face, but that comes to him only when through surrender and submission to God his soul gets cleansed through good *Karma* by living a life of selfless service and sacrifice.

Thus, the true reward of good *Karma* is not the pleasures of heaven, which the soul is granted to enjoy, but the goodness of life that she receives in her next human embodiment, because that can empower her to attain the abode of highest consciousness – Oh, the realm of the Self-realization!

This can be understood better by considering an example of a person who is born in lowly environment. Let us say, he is born in a family, which worships all kinds of spirits and offers sacrifices to demons and dark images. Obviously, such a person is not going to have an environment of light and wisdom, purity and piousness, sanctity and holiness; since his family is sinisterly eclipsed by darkness and delusion, ignorance and illusion, and thus, most probably, is headed by all kinds of misguidance.

Now, let us ask this: What kind of chances this person has for getting out of such darkness and reaching the light? And, what kind of possibility does he have to lift her soul to the land of eternal liberation?

Clearly, not much! I am not saying, never; but we all know that possibility for such a thing is very little. No one can argue with that.

However, if this man was born in a family that is righteous, rich in virtue, and filled with light and wisdom. In that case, don't you think, he would have a great chance to multiply in Knowledge and Truth, and may even find the grace of God to save his soul from the manacles of mortality? Don't you think, he would have everything in his favor then?

Surely, he would!

Let us look at the following verses of Holy Gita that bring this scenario to light quite successfully, when man raises this question before incarnated God, Lord *Krishna* and asks, **"He who is unable to control himself despite his faith, whose mind wanders away from the state of Yoga, thus failing to attain Yogic-perfection, what end does he meet - Holy Gita 6:37?"**

There is wonderment in the heart of a seeker of truth that is eager to know what happens when a sacred soul, which has ascended much on the *Yogic*-path and has successfully begun the spiritual journey of her self-purification, yet due to some failure in her spiritual walk, she falters and fails in attaining salvation? Then, what becomes of her? What kind of *Karmic*-course she faces after such a spiritual fall?

Now look at the reply that Lord God gives through following verses, which He begins by saying the most assuring words a seeker can ever hear: **"A Yogi is never destroyed, neither in this world nor in the next."**

Oh! What a confidence builder are these words! Who would worry about anything after hearing such a promising words by Lord God that proclaim of no harm ever to the soul that has begun the walk towards His sanctuary:

Not only any harm can come to the walker of faith in God as he is ever in His supreme hands, but also no holy labor ever is wasted, **"When he is reborn, he is united with the intellect that he had cultivated in his past lives – Holy Gita 6:43,"** even if he gets lost in the detours of temptations or falls into the traps of luring objective world.

Lord God says that such a man regains all of his holy wealth what he had before (in his previous human life), and in next life begins his march again towards the eternal kingdom with even more spiritual endowment.

Of course, after exhausting her *Karmic*-dues that would rise out of her spiritual fall, such an *Yogic*-soul is given another human life to redeem herself from the shackles of *Karma*; and this time, she is born in a family of such folks that are pure and pious, prosperous and righteous **"He may even be born in the family of wise Yogis – Holy Gita 6:42;"** and she is endowed with the intellect that she has accumulated in her previous human embodiments.

So, she is given just about everything she needs, of course without any loss of what she had before, and even better in terms of holy and scared environment, so that she could easily rise further in her spiritual evolution and become able to attain the highest goal of human life – the eternal liberation.

These holy words provide a witness to the fact that *Yogic*-life is a life that is well-secured in the hands of God. Even with obstacles of all kinds of temptations standing along the way, such life which is of higher quality and good *Karma*, due to loving care of God, has the power to lead the soul towards further heights of light and wisdom, and provide it with such a favorable environment where the she could be purified even further and grow in her spiritual perfection.

Of course, when such a cycle of increasing multiplication in light and higher learning continues through each human life, in eventuality, the soul reaches such a wisdom, **"After many lives (of progressive spiritual evolution) one acquires wisdom – Gita 7:19,"** that washes away her darkness and delusion, enables her to see clearly the truth of God.

And, when the soul comes to know the truth of God, she recognizes her own reality, and realizes who she truly is; and thus, she finds freedom from bandage to all darkness.

Thus, an upward swing towards the light and wisdom can set such an eternal course for the soul, after completing which, she never has to travel through any *Karmic*-worlds again, **"Following the path of Light one does not return – Holy Gita 8:26,"** as she becomes eternally free from the cold grip of *Karma*.

However, reversibly, if the soul is on a downward swing, and is drifting towards the lower worlds, then a lower quality life, of ignorance and delusion, leads her further into *Karmic*-degradation and takes her further into dark worlds.

In such defiled and lowly environment, more attachment and desire, more ambition and aspirations, more passion and infatuation, more yearning and craving, more mania and obsession, more fixation and fascination, more zeal and fervor, grows around the soul, and infects her further with their diseases.

Moreover, due to her affection and adoration for things of this world, she gets caught more tightly by the grip of greed and gluttony, lust and lasciviousness, voracity and covetousness.

Eventually, her fleshly desires, her uncontrollable infatuation, her unending passion, brings her the most horrific downfall and takes her further deep into hellish worlds.

Hear these words of Lord *Krishna*, which leaves no doubt in what happens to a man who gets entangled by his infatuation:

(Thus deluded by ignorance) Confused because of many evil desires entangled by the snares of infatuation intensely attached to the gratification of the senses they fall into foul hell.

(Holy Gita 16:16)

Oh! He falls into the deep wombs of hell. And once the soul begins to decline in virtue and immerses in sin and gets further eclipsed by the human vice, she becomes further void of the sense of God.

And, as more malevolence and evilness, the perversion and wickedness, the immorality and sinfulness, the ill-will and badness, penetrates the human heart, more impurity and pollution, filth and uncleanness, grime and grunge, mire and muckiness, sludge and slush, surround his soul.

In such lowly environment, man becomes so perverted and ungodly that he almost begins to behave like he is an enemy of God; he reaches such a point of degradation that he begins to hate everything that is pious and piteous, holy and divine. Thus, by being against the things of God, he becomes a hater of God **(Holy Gita 16:18)**.

Remember! One does not have to hate God to become His hater; all he has to do is to be against His quality and character, morality and virtue, righteousness and rectitude, and His sanctity and holiness; meaning, one who is disrespectful to His words and commandments, and is rebellious against the authority and rule of His holy kingdom and engages in things that are against His believers, is a hater of God.

Today, we can see how man has become such an enemy of God that he does not even want to hear His name in school classes or read it in any government documents, or display His words in any public places. This is what the man has become. He does not want to see anything of God anywhere, which is within his domain.

Look around and see how man has become the enemy of God.

Turn on the television and watch; as there is always a channel where someone is making mockery of God, and making fun of His words and throwing mud on His followers. It is sad that for a modern man, everything about God has become a matter of ridicule and laughter, as he has no hitch in calling Him names and cursing Him.

How often we hear a comedian on the stage making fun of godly things. This is not happening just in one society but in societies all over the world; of course, more or less. There is no doubt that everywhere, man is becoming more and more wicked by each day.

But such evil against God does not go unpunished as God has drawn the line; and once man crosses that line, he is subjected to the punishment brought against him due to consequences of his crimes; as such blasphemy against the Holy Ghost is the only sin that is unforgivable in the sight of God.

Listen to these words of Lord Jesus Christ that declare the condemnation of such perverted and doomed soul, who has no shame in making fun of the Holy Spirit, and indulges in blaspheme, and speaks against Him:

But he that shall blaspheme against the Holy Ghost hath never forgiveness, but is in danger of eternal damnation:

(Holy Bible, Mark 3:29)

The holy word boldly declares that there is no forgiveness for any blasphemous acts of man committed against the Holy Spirit.

Out of all chapters in Holy Gita, the Sixteenth chapter is quite peculiar in the sense that it shows the thinking in the mind of God about how He despises the sin and disapproves the sinfulness of the sinner? How He detests the unrighteousness in the wicked and abominates the impiety in the evil?

The scriptures point out the truth that the ultimate end of hopelessly degraded and badly besmirched soul is the pit of demonic womb:

These cruel haters of Myself the worst among men who are involved in sinful deeds I hurl them into demoniac wombs.

(Holy Gita 16:19)

The above words of Lord *Krishna* declare the most severe penalty designated as punishment for a perverted man – the man, whose malevolence has crossed the line where he has become an enemy of God:

These words of Lord God give an idea, how strongly He dislikes man's lack of respect for His holiness and righteousness.

Therefore, for our spiritual wellbeing, one thing we must not forget that God loves His holiness and righteousness the most, and nothing would He spare to protect them.

So when man engages in sinfulness and cares not for morality, and his conduct becomes solely against the holiness and righteousness of God, then, according to these words, there is hardly any hope for his redemption, as he wanders timelessly in the wilderness of hell. Because, the grunge and grime of demonic gallows grasp him so tightly into their grip, that his soul suffers the misery and pain almost timelessly:

O Son of *Kunti* having entered into demoniac wombs deluded from birth after birth unable to attain Me they continue to fall into lower births.

(Holy Gita 16:20)

Thus, as the scriptures illustrate clearly, that if the soul has an inclination to one direction, she generally creates such *Karma* that pushes her deeper into that direction even further.

Meaning, if she is on the path of spiritual evolution, then she would do those works that are going to create good *Karma*, and would engage in those enterprises that are holy and hallowed, pure and pious, virtuous and upright; but if her inclination is towards the ways of sinfulness, then she would be very prone to naturally engage in those things that are only going to create bad *Karma* that would further push her deeper into vice.

So in summary, except as man in human world, no matter where else the soul wanders as nomad to exhaust her *Karmic-*dues, and no matter in what *Karmic-*worlds she drifts, it really has no other significance, but that through all such wandering she is able to exhaust her *Karma* and reduce the burden of bondage by experiencing the *Karmically* ordained pleasure and pain.

Thus, truly significant *Karmic*-life is only when the soul embodies as human where she not only endures and exhaust preordained *Karma*, but also has the power of freewill that enables her to shape her future *Karmic*-life the way she wants to.

6

Karmic-Extremities
~
Soul's Passage through Creation and Dissolution

The last chapter describes what happens to the soul (*Atman*) as she goes through the *Karmic*-cycle and repeatedly travels through the tunnel of Transmigration, and how she wanders in all kinds of *Karmic*-worlds and transitions from body to body to wear all kinds of fleshly enclosures that are suitable to express and exhaust the due *Karma* and experience their pleasure and pain according to the *Karmic*-ordinances.

The laws of *Karma* state that, each time the soul passes through human life, unless she is redeemed from the fetters of *Karma*, she is forced to endure another cycle of countless embodiments.

And this continues almost timelessly until through the grace of God, she finds way to her eternal home.

But what happens to the soul, if before she has not been redeemed yet, and the Dissolution incurs and ends all creation? What happens to her when the Creation takes place after the Dissolution and starts the manifestation again? What happens then?

What happens when these two major cosmic events take place and disrupt the cycle of *Karma*? What happens to the soul when the whole universe collapses, and there is no existence left anymore? What happens when all manifestation is dissolved, and all existence, as we know of, ceases? What happens to her then?

Does she survive? Or, she is dissolved for good? This is the main topic for this chapter.

Though not much, the Holy Gita speaks on this subject, however, she speak enough to yield sufficient insight into what happens to the soul in between and during these two cosmic events – the Dissolution and Creation.

She begins to reveal this knowledge by saying that the day of Brahma extents for a thousand Yugas, and so does his night; and the Yuga in itself, though has quite a debatable time span, yet safely can be assumed to be thousands of years to say the least; meaning, the day and night of Brahma are periods of quite sizeable time that could easily extend for millions and billions of years.

Those who know that the day of Brahma extends for a thousand Yugas, and His night lasts for another thousand Yugas, they are the *knowers* of day and night.

(Holy Gita 8:17)

After giving an idea of how long is the time-span of the day and night of Brahma, the Holy Gita begins to unfold the mystery about these two cosmic events – the Dissolution and Creation – by telling: When do these supernatural happenings take place and what happens to the creation when they do occur?

According to her following words: With the day of Brahma comes the creation of worlds, and with his night comes their dissolution. But the materialization of all creation comes not from some other manifestation but from an *unmanifest* into which dissolves all creation at the time of dissolution of all worlds:

With the coming of the day, all these manifested beings and objects proceed from the *unmanifest*, and with the coming of the night all these enter into the state of dissolution known as *unmanifest*.

(Holy Gita 8:18)

It is this *unmanifest* where take refuge all beings when the night of Brahma falls upon the Creation, and the Dissolution dissolves all its manifestations; and from where emerges the manifestation of all beings again when the day of Brahma rises and commences another cycle of creation.

Oh, but higher than this *unmanifest* is yet another *Unmanifest* – the eternal Being – the *Brahman* – Who is the container of all existence and non-existence; Who is imperishable, all-pervading and eternal; Who is the only existence there is even in times of non-existence, but of course without any material form and shape, without any physical attributes and traits, without any corporeal qualities and characteristics.

Higher than this *unmanifest* there exists yet another *Unmanifest* - the Eternal Being who is not destroyed when all beings perish.

(Holy Gita 8:20)

This *Unmanifest* is the eternal keeper of all things; it consists of, not only what exists but also what exists not. Oh! It is the Container supreme – the eternal abode of *Brahman* – the Brahman Himself.

Thus, from scriptures we learn that at the time of Dissolution when all Existence ceases and all materialization of the Universe is dissolved, the Creation, along with all beings, merges into an *unmanifest*, which yet is contained in another *Unmanifest*.

And when the Creation comes, all Existence resurrects; all emerges back from this *unmanifest*, and the materialization along with all beings manifests itself back again.

Now, if the higher Unmanifest is God, then what is this lower unmanifest that is contained in Him?

Well, an indirect clue to this mystery comes from these words of Holy Gita, which say that at the time of Dissolution, all beings merge into the *Prakriti* of God, and remain there till the next *Kalpa* (the period beginning from Creation till *Dissolution*) commences, and emerge out of it when the cycle of Creation starts again. As per following word of God, it is His *Prakriti* that is the holder of all Existence and non-existence during the Creation and also Dissolution:

O Son of *Kunti*, all beings merge into My *Prakriti* at the end of *Kalpa*, and with the commencement of the next *Kalpa* it is I who send them forth.

(Holy Gita 9:7)

Now if the *Prakriti* of God holds all beings in an *unmanifest* form during the period of non-existence that spans from the time of Dissolution till the beginning of Creation, then it must be that unmanifest housing which has been referred in verse, **Holy Gita 8:18**.

Following verses of Holy Gita shed much light on the *Prakriti* of God and say that God has two *Prakriti's* – the higher and lower – which uphold the entire Universe. The higher *Prakriti* is the sustainer of all what is imperishable, while the other, the lower, is the sustainer of all what is perishable.

The eight elements: Earth, Water, Fire, Air, Ether, Mind, Intellect and Ego-principle constitute God's lower nature (*Prakriti*), while the soul (*Atman*) comprises His higher nature:

Earth, Water, Fire, Air, Ether, Mind, Intellect and Ego-principle - these eight divisions go to constitute my *Prakriti* (the Lower Nature).

This is my Lower Nature, O Mighty-armed *Arjuna*! Different from this is My Higher Nature which is the soul, by which this entire world is sustained.

These two (*Prakritis* of Mine) are the source of all beings. Thus, I am the origin of this entire world as well its dissolution.

(Holy Gita 7:4-6)

These two *Prakriti's* of God are the Source of all beings, as from them emerges the entire creation. All what is permanent and perpetual comes from His higher nature, while all what is impermanent and transient comes from His lower nature.

Now we know why God says that He is the Source of all things as in Him lies the genesis of all what exists **"All this has proceeded from Me – Holy Gita 10:8."** Not only lies in Him the creation of all but also the dissolution since at the end of it all, when all existence ceases, He pulls it all back into Him in an *unmanifest* form **"Thus, I am the origin of this entire world as well its dissolution – Holy Gita 7:6."**

By now, looking at the scriptures it becomes quite clear that God Himself is the *Unmanifest* **(Holy Gita 8:20)** and His *Prakriti* is yet another *unmanifest* container that preserves all beings when they cease their existence during the cosmic events of Dissolution and Creation and becomes their holding place.

God uses His *Prakriti* to make it all happen. From the time of Dissolution to Creation, He uses it to preserve all beings in an *unmanifest* form so that when the Creation commences again, they all emerge from it and manifest again.

Please keep all this in mind as we move our discussion on this subject a bit further. Remember! Our soul abides under the control of *Prakriti* **(Holy Gita 13:21, 15:7)**; meaning, we are under the control of our nature. However, such is never the case with God. Unlike us, not only God does not abide by His *Prakriti* but His *Prakriti* abides by Him; meaning, instead of being controlled by His nature, He controls it.

This point happens to be of high significance, so let us make a note of it. Look at the following verse where the Lord God Himself testifies to this truth, and in a way highlights a huge difference between Himself and the man:

> **Keeping *Prakriti* under My control, I, again and again, send forth these beings which are helplessly under the control of *Prakriti*.**

> **(Holy Gita 9:8)**

Please notice two things that are being said here:

First, the Creator recreates the creation over and over but by having the command and control over His *Prakriti*, **"Keeping *Prakriti* under My control, I, again and again, send forth these beings."**

Second, created beings go forth from creation to dissolution and then back to creation, over and over, but only **"helplessly"**, since they are under the power and direction of their *Prakriti*, **"Under the control of *Prakriti*."**

Noteworthy is the fact that unlike God, Who keeps *Prakriti* under His controls, all beings are controlled by their *Prakriti*, and that is why, in above verse, the word 'helplessly' is used to highlight the fact that power of *Prakriti* over all beings is so overwhelming that they powerlessly abide as captives under its authority and rule.

The same truth has been spoken by Lord God in following verse too, as it too uses the word '**helplessly**' to describe the powerlessness of the soul before the power of *Prakriti*, which rules over it during all times of her *Karmic*-existence including the times of Dissolution and Creation:

Thus, O *Partha*, these beings come forth again and again with the coming of the day, and are <u>helplessly</u> led to dissolution (in the *unmanifest*) at the coming of the night.

(Holy Gita 8:19)

Thus, the underlying conclusion in these verses is that under the presiding authority of God, it is His *Prakriti* that sustains the Dissolution and Creation during which the souls (beings) are drawn from their manifest form and are preserved in its *unmanifest*, and then sent back to manifest form when the Creation commences again. Contrarily, it is the *Prakriti* in beings that forces them to go back and forth through these two cosmic events.

Furthermore, during the time in between these two cosmic events, the *Prakriti* of beings remains intact while they exist in the *unmanifest* form; and of course, it is the *Prakriti* that is the reason for their re-rise into materialization again when the Creation inaugurates.

Following verse reveals the secret how the world comes into existence, and how it continues to exist, because all beings (souls) are under the control of their *Prakriti*, which forcefully brings them back and forth from *unmanifest* to manifest and vice versa. They also unfold the mystery of how the cycle of Creation and Dissolution continues:

Presided by Me, *Prakriti* brings forth the creation of beings consisting of movables and immovable. O Son

of *Kunti*, it is for this reason that the world continues to undergo (endless modifications).

(Holy Gita 9:10)

Remember! It is the *Prakriti* under whose control abides the soul *(Atman)* no matter what creaturely embodiment she wears **(Holy Gita 13:21, 15:7)**. It means *Prakriti* is the authority over the soul no matter in what state she is in during her captivity in all *Karmic*-existence including the periods of Creation and Dissolution.

This is why God is called the Self Supreme, **"(I am) beyond the Imperishable *Prakriti*, therefore I am known as the Supreme Self – Holy Gita 15:18,"** because unlike all beings He is beyond the influence of *Prakriti*. Instead of Him being under its authority, His *Prakriti* is under His authority.

The ability to control His *Prakriti* enables God uniquely to embody Himself in any form and shape, and in any era, time, and environment, by using the power of His own *Maya*:

> I am unborn, imperishable, and the Lord of all beings. Yet, by controlling My own *Prakriti*, I embody Myself by My own *Maya*.

> **(Holy Gita 4:6)**

So it makes a lot of sense that even though the soul is a part of God **(Holy Gita 15:7)** and is the eternal Self, yet under the influence and authority of *Prakriti* lives as *Jiva* – a conditioned-soul – and experiences pleasure and pain.

The scriptures say that, just the way the *Purusha* (The Transcendental Self) is beginning-less, so is the *Prakriti*, **"Know both these - *Prakriti* and *Purusha* to be beginning-less – Holy Gita 13:19."** Just like *Purusha*, it too exists even when the soul ceases the materialization and is preserved as *unmanifest*.

Look at the following verse that unveil the truth that just the way *Purusha* (the transcendental Self – the soul) is the cause of experiencing pleasure and pain, so is *Prakriti* the cause of effect (body), instrument (senses) and their functions:

> *Prakriti* is the cause of effect (body), instrument (senses) and their functions. *Purusha* (the soul) is said to be the cause of experiencing pleasure and pain.

(Holy Gita 13:19-20)

The *Prakriti* causes the soul to embody so that her *Karma* could be expressed; and once the soul is embodied, she is forced to experience the sorrow and joy of her ordained embodiment.

Chapter thirteen of Holy Gita is filled with such revelations. If anyone diligently meditates upon its words, it can easily overwhelm him since it unfolds so many mysteries that are ever beyond our ordinary comprehension. Here is something from this chapter that we must talk about next since it is quite significant to the discussion that we are having now.

Well, as mentioned above, the holy text tells us that not only is the *Purusha* (*Atman* – Soul – Transcendental Self) is beginning-less but also is the *Prakriti*. But what does that mean in the realm of higher understanding? Surely, a good question, since it makes us realize something we do not easily do otherwise. Let's look at it.

We do know that the word 'nature' is used in two ways: to refer to the nature of a being like nature of man, nature of an animal etc., and also to refer to the creation outside in general.

Now do we ever notice the difference in our use of this word? While on one side we use it to refer to something that is subtle, which of course is the case when we use this word to mean the 'nature of a being', and on the other side, we use it to refer to something that is gross, which of course is the case when we use this word to mean the 'creation'.

I am sure, many of us have never thought of it before, and never paid any attention to this difference, which happens to be so obvious.

Well, in Hindi language the word for 'nature' is *Prakriti*. And we use the word '*Prakriti*' in same two ways as we do the word 'nature' in English; meaning, we use it to refer to the nature of a being, and also as the creation in general. So we use the word '*Prakriti*' in two very different ways: to refer to something subtle, and to refer to something that is gross.

But mind you! The *Prakriti* is beginning-less **(Holy Gita 13:19)**, meaning, it is imperishable and eternal; and since it is imperishable, hence it cannot be physical or mutable, or something that could be altered and modified. It means *Prakriti* is something that is unchangeable.

Now, in both uses of this word, it refers to something that varies; that changes. The nature of a being has potency to change and so does the nature outside, meaning both uses of this word are contrary to its character, as they both refer to something that is changeable, even while the *Prakriti* itself is unchangeable. Interesting, isn't it!

Well, we surely cannot hold a view that scriptures can be untrue, and at the same time, we also cannot deny the truth of something, which is so obvious in its physical existence. So then, how do we explain this paradox that the *Prakriti*, though is unchangeable, yet refers to things that are changeable?

This contradiction can be resolved, but only if we believe that the scriptures never lie. And if we do that, then we can begin to explore the truth a bit deeper, and only then we find the answer and come to understand why does this paradox exist?

Beloved! Whenever we face such inconsistencies that rise in our comprehension, it is always due to lacking in our understanding of Truth rather than the lacking of truthfulness in the Truth as stated in scriptures. And, so is the case here as well.

The Holy Gita, over and over, states that *Gunas* come from *Prakriti*, **"The Gunas born out of Prakriti – Holy Gita 3:5, 3:27, 3:29, 13:19, 13:21, 14:5, 18:40,"** and they give rise to 'body'. Thus, it is they that cause the effect (body), **"Gunas which give rise to the body – Holy Gita 14:20."**

This further clarifies what she says in verse, **Holy Gita 13:20,** that *Prakriti* is the cause of effect (body). In fact what she indirectly implies is that it is its Guans that are responsible for causing the effect. This, Holy Gita confirms by her own words, **"All the Gunas and their effects – Holy Gita 13:19."**

It means the grossness referred by the word *Prakriti* (Nature) in its both uses, is the grossness of *Gunas*, which rises through their manifestation in creating the material world. After all, the whole universe is their field; the whole existence is their 'effect' as nothing is devoid of them:

On this earth (among the mortals) as well as in the heavenly worlds, among the gods, there is no entity that is devoid of the three *Gunas* (modes) arising out of *Prakriti* (Nature).

(Holy Gita 18:40)

Thus, even though the *Prakriti* never changes since it is imperishable and immutable, the changes we see are in its grossness are caused by its *Gunas*; and that happens because its grossness is the grossness of *Gunas*, which of course, always vary as their manifestation is ever-changing.

So the physical world that we see is the manifested grossness of *Prakriti*, since it is nothing but the grossness of *Gunas*; it is their manifestation. Of course, it is their material effect of the *Gunas* that gives rise to whole creation and it is they that nourish and sustain it, **"Nourished by the *Gunas* (the modes of Nature) the branches of this tree (the World) – Holy Gita 15:2."**

Thus, even though the *Prakriti* is imperishable, just the way the *Purusha* (*Atman* – soul) is, but to embody the *Purusha* as conditioned-soul and to facilitate his manifestation demanded by the laws of *Karma* to exhaust its obligations, and also to give rise to the material world of manifested consciousness, the *Prakriti* has to become the cause of Effect, and become the reason of all grossness.

In other words, it is the beginning-less *Purusha* and *Prakriti* — the eternal and everlasting – that are behind all creation.

Oh! How beautifully, this relationship between these two has been spoken by these words of Holy Gita that iterate the same truth in so many ways:

Arjuna said: I wish to learn (the distinction between) *Prakriti* (Matter) and *Purusha* (Spirit); *Kshetra* (the Field) and *Kshetrajna* (the Knower of the Field); and also knowledge and that which is to be Known, O *Keshava*!

(Holy Gita 13:0)

While one is spoken as Matter (*Prakriti*), the other is spoken as Spirit (*Purusha*); while one is referred as *Kshetra* (the Field), the other is referred as *Kshetrajna* (the Knower of the Field); while one is called the Knowledge, the other is called the One, which is to be known through that knowledge.

Holy Gita not only exposes the truth behind them but also unveils the mystery of how these two are the cause of Effect (Grossness) behind all material existence as well as non-existence, and how they are behind not only what is perishable but also behind what is imperishable?

There are two *Purushas* (beings) in this world: *Kshara* (the perishable) and *Akshara* (the imperishable). All the objects of the world are called *Kshara* while *Prakriti* sustained by the Immutable Self is called *Akshara*.

(Holy Gita 15:16)

Thus, all manifestations of the soul are nothing but effects caused by the *Prakriti*. It is ever with the soul as long as she is under the *Karmic*-detention, because as long as the soul has the burden of *Karma*, she is under the captivity of *Prakriti*.

To understand what kind of authority the *Prakriti* holds over the soul, and how it conditions her behavior, let us consider following four primary functions that it performs:

First function: The Prakriti commands and controls the Karmic-journey of the soul.

Surely it is the *Prakriti* that compels the soul to take the *Karmic*-path that has been ordained for her so that she could suitably and sufficiently express and exhaust the ordained *Karma*. In other words, *Prakriti* is the main facilitator of exhaustion of *Karma*, which makes sure that it has been expressed properly.

To understand how that happens, we must first understand how the *Prakriti* is formed?

Human deeds leave imprints on his mind called impressions – good and bad – depending upon the intensions with which he performs them. This is what the *Karma* is all about. When the soul leaves the human body, the impressions are still there with her since she carries with her the storehouse of sensuality – the senses – as she transitions from body to body **(Holy Gita 15:9)** to express and exhaust her *Karma*.

These impressions are so deep that in each embodiment of the soul, they form and shape the *Karmic*-power around the soul, so called *Prakriti* (nature), in such a way that she is forced to express and exhaust her ordained *Karma* in a proper manner.

Thus, the nature (*Prakriti*) of a being is a direct result of what has been imprinted on the mind during the past human lives of the soul. This is why there seems to be a direct correlation between the *Prakriti* (nature) and *Karma* since *Prakriti* defines embodiments, and all embodiments are the direct result of *Karma* **(Holy Gita 8:3).**

Now we can see how powerful is the *Prakriti*? In fact it is so powerful that it forces man to do even those things that he does not wish to do. How often, an addict wishes to get out of addiction and become free of its grip, but he cannot do that so easily, simply because his nature (*Prakriti*) forces him to remain engaged in it almost helplessly.

When *Arjuna* refuses to take on the war and fight, **"Na Yotse Govinda – O Govinda, I will not Fight – Holy 2:9,"** look at what Lord *Krishna* has to say about it:

Sustained by self-conceit, if you think, "I will not fight," this resolve of yours is vain, because your very nature will compel you to fight.

(Holy Gita 18:59)

Lord God makes it clear that human is so heavily under the influence of his nature (*Prakriti*), that it forces him to do what he is inherently inclined to.

Second function: The Prakriti becomes a vessel for manifestation of attachments and desires.

Remember! What happens when the soul transitions from body to body and travels through the long tunnel of transmigration, she carries with her all subtlety surrounding her; meaning, she brings with her all sensuality, all attachments and desires, **"When the Lord (of the body and senses - the Jiva) leaves this body, he draws the senses – Holy Gita 15:8."**

Now, where do the desires and attachments live?

Of course, in the mind and intellect and senses, **"The senses, mind and intellect are said to be its dwelling places – Holy Gita 3:40."**

And who affects all these physical faculties?

Of course, the *Prakriti*; they all are its instruments. And since the owner – the soul (*Atman* – the *Purusha*) – herself is under its control. So who is the big boss? The *Prakriti*, of course! It means the *Prakriti* is the vessel through which flow all attachments and desires.

Third function: It is the Prakriti that performs all actions, and not the soul.

We have gone through this before and know it well that, though it is not obvious but it happens to be true that all actions are done by the *Prakriti* and not by the soul, **"All actions, in every form are performed by *Prakriti* alone, while the Self is non-performer of action – Holy Gita 13:29;"** meaning, our belief, that we are the 'doer' of our actions is totally wrong. These holy words provide witness that our soul is totally passive in performing actions; the Self is ever a 'non-performer' in them.

So we are not the 'doer' in anything we do, as always it is the *Prakriti* and *Gunas*; but due to ignorance caused by the egocentric nature, we believe that it is we who are the performer of actions:

> **All actions are performed by the *Gunas* of *Prakriti*. But if one's intellect is dull due to the development of egoism, he feels that, "I am the doer."**
>
> **(Holy Gita 3:27)**

Due to ego, the concept, that we are not the 'doer' of our actions, does not easily become our integrated belief even though quite clearly we understand this scriptural truth and unarguably accept its validity.

Surely, we understand it intellectually and accept its reality, however, our egocentricity is so prevalent and potent that it never allows us to internally accept the notion that not us but someone else in us is the actual 'performer' of our actions, and thus, does not allow this truth to become a part of our integrated being.

So, let us try to understand what these kinds of scriptures are really telling us?

According to them, the *Prakriti* and its *Gunas* are the actual 'performer' of actions, and not the soul (Self). Please keep in mind that the senses are the instruments of *Prakriti*; the mind and intellect are also under its influence. Since *Prakriti* performs all actions, the work that is performed by mind and intellect, like the recollection, discrimination and discernment, is also accomplished by it, which of course, takes place under the power of 'freewill'.

It means whatever needs to happen, happens under the influence of *Prakriti* including what is 'desired, discerned and decided' by the freewill. So as we can see all things happen from the time of their conception to their completion by the *Prakriti*.

Surely, the soul does not participate in anything, but she still experiences the pleasure and pain resulting from whatever is done by the body and controlling authority, the *Prakririt*, and this is how she pays the dues of *Karma*, which is by expressing life and enduring its sorrow and suffering.

Of course, worth mentioning is the fact that the soul is so influenced by the *Prakriti* that her freewill gets very conditioned by it; meaning, it leads the soul to make choices that often are not made autonomously but are predisposed by the *Prakriti*; meaning freewill, in true sense, is really not freewill as it gets conditioned by the *Prakriti*.

Fourth function: The Prakriti creates and sustains the sense of 'doership'.

Again the soul (*Atman* – the Self) has nothing to do with 'does-ship'; however, due to inner darkness she believes that it is she who is the doer of actions.

Even though it is almost the repetition of what we already have read in scriptures quoted above, but the following words of Holy Gita do yield something new, which is worthy of our attention:

The Divine Self does not create "doer-ship" in people, nor does He work; He <u>does not create the relationship between the works and their fruits</u>. It is *Prakriti* that sustains these.

(Holy Gita 5:14)

We have just learned that the soul does not do anything, since she is action-less, **"The action-less Self – Holy Gita 3:28;"** and also, that it is not the soul who creates or sustains the 'doer-ship'. Both of these things are done by the *Prakriti*, which performs all actions as well as creates the egoistic sense of 'doer-ship'.

We already knew this. So what is new about it? Well, the new thing that is being revealed by the holy words above is that the soul (Self) **"does not create the relationship between the works and their fruits;"** meaning, it is not the inner Self but the *Prakriti* that creates a relationship between the action and its fruits.

You see! The soul (*Atman* – the Self) is without any passion and infatuation; however, the *Prakriti* that eclipses her is infected with these evils. So, when it performs an action it renders it with the attachment and desire, and with expectation of a particular outcome. Thus, it is the *Prakriti*, which is the creator of relationship between the work and its fruit.

Since we are bound by our *Prakriti*, we are captivated by attachment and desire, and are enslaved by passion and infatuation. So when we engage in any action, we engage with a hope that it produces what we desire and brings the intended fulfillment.

Well, after going over all these things that relate to *Prakriti*, one thing should become clear that the *Prakriti* is such an imposed authority over the soul (*Atman*) that governs her total *Karmic*-life, whether it be repeatedly passing through the tunnel of transmigration to assume all kinds of embodiments as demanded by *Karma*, or wandering through higher and lower *Karmic*-worlds commanded by high and low *Karmic*-merits, or enduring the passage through *unmanifest* during the times of Dissolution and Creation.

In other words, all phases of conditioned-life of the soul (the *Purusha* – *Atman* – Self) imposed by the *Karma* are ever controlled and commanded by the *Prakriti*. It is such a chain around her neck that comes off only when she is totally liberated from all bondage.

So as we can see, the Holy Gita, though does not speak much about all this, yet paints a pretty good picture as to what happens during the times of Dissolution and Creation, and tells us adequately how at the night fall of Brahma, the conditioned-soul (*Purusha*) is pulled into the *unmanifest* under the authority of *Prakriti* and placed in the *Prakriti* of God, where she is preserved and protected in *unmanifest* form during the time in between the Dissolution and Creation, and excelled back into manifest form when the night of Brahma ends and his new day dawns, and another cycle of Creation commences.

The following words of the *Upanishad* speak of the same truth and tell how all things come to rest in God during the times when all existence terminates:

At the end of the worlds, all things sleep: he alone is awake in Eternity. Then from his infinite space new worlds arise and awake, a universe which is a vastness of thought. In the consciousness of Brahman the universe is, and into him it returns.

(Maitri Upanishad, 6.17)

And then, how He (God) alone remains; and how at His will, the universe, merely as His thought, emerges back from Him into materialization:

Oh! Into the *unmanifest* of God merges all, and then emerges back from it when in sheer joy He wills their manifestation. Hear these words of the *Upanishad* that give a glimpse of what it is like in the beginning (before Existence) when God alone is:

In the beginning all was Brahman, One and infinite. He is beyond north and south, and east and west, and beyond what is above or below. His infinity is everywhere. In him there is neither above, nor across, nor below; and in him there is neither east nor west.

> **The Spirit supreme is immeasurable, inapprehensible, beyond conception, never-born, beyond reasoning, beyond thought. His vastness is the vastness of space.**

> **(Maitri Upanishad, 6.17)**

And what happens in His aloneness, and how it all comes into being:

> **When the time came, *Kabandhi Katyayana* approached the sage and said: Master, whence came all created beings?**

> **The sage replied: In the beginning the Creator longed for the joy of creation. He remained in meditation, and then came *Rayi*, matter, and *Prana*, life. 'These Two', thought he, 'will produce beings for me'.**

> **(Prasna Upanishad, First Question)**

Oh! During the times of Non-existence, when all is sleeping as unmanifest and God alone is, there rises a longing of joy in His heart that causes a will in Him for the commencement of Creation. It is when in sheer solitudes He meditates upon the joy of love, that there rises a will in Him to become from One to 'many'.

7

Attachment and Desire
~
The Root Cause of Human Bondage

The *Karmic*-laws dictate that *Karma* is always there in each and every human action; however, the bondage to it may or may not be there depending upon the presence or absence of ego in action. Also, it is the bondage and not the *Karma* that causes *Karmic*-consequences for the soul.

The laws further state that all actions create bondage except the ones that are performed for the sake of sacrifice. In other words, the actions that are done for the love of God and rendered for the good of society, **"Only those actions bind a person which are not performed for the sake of sacrifice (for pleasing God) – Holy Gita 3:9,"** are the only ones that are exempt from the penalty of bondage; meaning, only unselfish and egoless actions are bondage-free.

But how often do we do that? Not often! We all know that.

No wonder! We remain in bondage, life after life, and yet there is no end in sight. The bitter truth is that there are hardly any actions during our day that are without selfishness and self-centricity. Even when we quite genuinely engage in things of charity and goodwill, and render ourselves to the welfare of others, yet how often our ego hovers underneath such praiseworthy works.

Now the question is: Why do we do that? Why are we so incapable of acting without ego and selfishness? Where do these diseases – the selfishness and self-centricity – come from? And what grows and multiplies them in us?

Well, we are the victims of these vices because we are made with ego. We are the creatures of self-centricity and selfishness. Looking at the constituents as listed by the scriptures, one of the elements that constitute us, besides Earth, Water, Fire, Air, Ether, Mind, Intellect, is 'Ego-principle' – the sense of 'self- being' **(Holy Gita 7:4-6).**

You see! The ego is the cause for our soul to be separated from God. Her belief in her own individuality is the reason that has encapsulated her and made her *Jiva* – a conditioned-soul. If she were not eclipsed by the sense of ego, she would not be in bondage as there would be no impurities surrounding her.

In that case, there would be no darkness and delusion, no ignorance and illusion; she would then have no lacking of Self-knowledge. She would be fully established in her reality and truth, in her true Self-being, in her true virtue of love and light, in her true liberty and bliss. But since she is encapsulated by ego, she knows not who she is since darkness created by self-centricity and selfishness has hidden her own truth from her.

Thus, it is the ego-sense that causes the soul to behave the way she does. It makes her self-centric and selfish, and as a result there grows attachment and desire in her.

Holy Gita says that 'desire' is the offspring of 'egoistic will', **"Desires that are born of egoistic will – Holy Gita 6:24;"** meaning, the desire is an expression of self-centric 'will' by the soul under the influence of ego. In another words, the desire is an egoistic assertion of the soul in her free-willed expressions.

The ego-sense in the soul creates the darkness and delusion, and makes her so ignorant that she forgets her own reality. She loses the sense of her own true being and begins to believe in a false self-identification, which causes her to behave ignorantly and egoistically.

Thus, the presence of ego in the soul is her real problem, no doubt! Because it is the ego that causes the bondage to *Karma*, and it is the ego that binds her to mortality.

Well, look at these words of Holy Gita that go far beyond the limit to make this point as boldly as possible, by saying that if one is egoless, then even if he were to kill all beings, he still would not be touched by the sin of such horrid deed as killing all living beings; meaning, he would not be bound by the *Karma* of such vile and dreadful act:

He who is free of ego-sense, and whose intellect is not tainted by the sense of doer-ship (and enjoyer-ship); such a Sage, even if he were to kill all beings, yet he does not kill, nor is he bound by such actions.

(Holy Gita 18:17)

Ego in action is responsible for bondage to *Karma* because it creates attachment to it. It is our self-centricity and selfishness in action that is the reason for our slavery to *Karma*.

Since ego is embedded in us since the time we are born and ego is what identifies who we are, it is hard to do anything without ego. It is such a reality that cannot be ignored. Our whole life is driven by the ego since we are made in such a way that our consciousness is never without it. So then, how can we ever live without asserting ego when it is ever present in us no matter what state of mind we are in? May be not impossible, but it surely is extremely difficult.

Ego causes passion and infatuation and gives rise to attachment and desire **(Holy Gita 6:24)**, because when we constantly look at the objects of this world with selfishness and self-centricity, we get attracted to them, **"By constantly dwelling upon objects, one develops attachment to them; from attachment there arises desire – Holy Gita 2:62."** Thus, due to ego, we become so enslaved by the sensuality of objective world that we do anything we need to do to satisfy our passion.

And what is passion and infatuation? The expression of ego!

It is this expression of ego, which forces us to behave in a manner that it makes us a captive of *Karma*; it is this embedded wanting and craving in the soul that causes her to remain in bondage, life after life.

Oh! It is our fleshly hunger and thirst that has made us a slave to sin; it is our attachment and desire that has imprisoned our soul in mortality; it is our passion and infatuation that has made us captive of bondage, **"Impelled by desires, attached to the fruits of action, and thereof, goes to bondage – Holy Gita 5:12."**

Even though the action in itself has no such power, but it is the attachment and desire that are implanted in it, what create bondage for the soul (*Atman*); it is the embedded infatuation that binds her to its *karma* and ties her to the cycle of birth and death; it is the passion in performance of actions that forces her to go through countless higher and lower embodiments and endure their misery and pain **(Holy Gita 13:21)**.

But what can we about it when we know well that man is born with this disease. Right from his birth he has this infection, which contaminates his whole life and eventually makes him perish. He is infected with attachments and desires right from the day he is born.

Remember! When the soul moves from body to body, she brings with her the senses **(Holy Gita 15:8)**. And what do the senses carry with them? Of course, the attachments and desires **(Holy Gita 3:40)**!

So the attachments and desires, which were there at the end of previous human embodiment of the soul, are there again at the time of her next birth as human.

Now, what else is there from her previous embodiment?

The *Raga* (desire) and *Dwesha* (hatred) **"*Raga* and *Dwesha* pertaining to the sense-objects abide in the senses – Hoy Gita 3:34;"** and the sensing of pairs of opposites, **"All beings at the time of their birth come under the sway of the delusion of pairs of opposites caused by desire and hatred – Holy Gita 7:27."** These are there in man from the day one!

But these can be expected since we know that the soul carries with her the senses as she moves from body to body and travels through transmigration, however, one more very important thing is there – the intellect – the wisdom and

Knowledge. It is there since the soul carries the 'reason' and 'intellect' with her, **"When he is reborn, he is united with the intellect that he had cultivated in his past lives – Holy Gita 6:43."** Surely, it is a good news!

Good news, because there is a whole horde of forces of darkness – the ego and pride, self-centricity and self-indulgence, attachment and desire, passion and infatuation, and *Raga* (love, passion, desire) and *Dwesha* (hatred, dislike) – and they are ready to engage the soul in life of vanity and narcissism, but the intellect – the power of light and wisdom, knowledge and higher understanding – is such a power that is there is to fight these hidden human evils.

However, these evils in man are highly potent and prevalent; and they are so dominant because man cannot control his desires; contrarily, he lives under their power and becomes their slave.

To get an idea how powerful and dominant the human desire is, let us take a look at the answer that Lord *Krishna* gives when *Arjuna* raises this question:

Arjuna asked: O Krishna, what makes a person commit a sinful deed even against his will, as if he were compelled by force?

(Holy Gita 3:36)

Why man sometimes is so helpless that he engages in things he doesn't even like, but he does them anyway as if he is under some compulsion and seemingly has no other choice.

Lord God says that it is man's *Kama*, his desire, his passion and infatuation that forces him to act even against his own will:

Sri Bhagavan Krishna replied: It is Kama (desire) as well as Krodha (anger) arising out of Rajas (passion and externalization). This Kama is great eater and a great sinner. Know this to be your <u>enemy</u> in this world.

(Holy Gita 3:37)

It is his love for this world, his passion for objects of pleasure, his affection for things of enjoyments that compels him to do even those things that he knows are not right and does not want to do them, and yet, under the influence of greed and gluttony, lust and lasciviousness, he does them and commits all kinds of sins even against his own inner person.

How often desires of man make him blind, that in their pursuit he commits the most dreadful sins! We see it happening everyday. Such cases are not hard to find. Even in our own lives, we ourselves have done so many things, which we would not do otherwise, if we were not so tempted by our desires. Is there anyone who is willing to say otherwise?

Surely, our desires have such a stronghold upon ourselves that often we walk quite willingly the path of unrighteousness, and often we commit sin even though we don't want to, and often we go against even our own convictions that have been implanted in us through the goodness and grace of God. And under the influence of greed and lust, we violate those boundaries of righteousness of God that are never supposed to be broken by man no matter what!

This is why Lord God calls the desire an 'enemy', because it can destroy a man completely. He considers it a foe because it destroys one's Knowledge and understanding, and fills him with ignorance and illusion; it destroys the basic person in him.

Oh! It replaces virtue with vice by taking away ones wisdom and filling him with delusion and darkness:

O Son of *Kunti*, wisdom is enveloped by desire, this constant <u>enemy</u> of the wise, which is as insatiable as fire.

(Holy Gita 3:39)

The desire is such a vice that spreads like a fire; the more we try to quench it, the more it multiplies; the more we try to fulfill it, the more it grows. We do not have to go too far to prove it. We can look at our own lives and see if we have been able to quench our own thirst; if we have been able to overcome our own desire; if we have been able to control our own passion.

Even though we have been working all our lives to satisfy ourselves and have been busy to fulfill our carvings and longings, our wanting and desires, but have we achieved this goal? How many among us have succeeded in doing so? How many have been able to defeat the enemy? I am sure, not many!

This is why Lord God asks us to exercise caution against this wicked adversary, **"Know this to be your _enemy_ in this world – Holy Gita 3:37,"** and be vigilant of this evil that can make us spiritually blind and mislead us to walk on the path of destruction and death.

Beloved! We are definitely helpless creatures before our hearts, no doubt! We are captives of our own desires. They are our darlings, whom we raise day and night with all our affection and adoration; and we never get tired of it. Whole life has gone by doing just that; and we still never complain; we still are as devoted and dedicated to them as we ever were before. Isn't it?

But have a heart because we surely are made that way. So, take solace in this thought and then look at this problem with a renewed understanding and with more acceptance of this truth.

I agree that we are born with all this grunge and grime around our soul; we are filled up to the rim with all kinds of impurities and uncleanness, and yes, we are infected by all kinds of diseases like greed and lust right from our birth; but who is to say, that we have to continue living this way and be under the dominance of our passion and infatuation that has accumulated so much filth and dirt around our inner person. Don't we have the freedom in that? Don't we have the freewill that is autonomous and sovereign?

Why can't we turn the table around, and for once, make this evil of selfishness and self-centricity – the desire and attachment, the passion and infatuation – live under our authority and rule, and change the course of its tide by forcing it to flow in direction that is under our command and control, under our authority and rule, and not the other way around.

Isn't it what the Lord God commands us to do and tells us to slay this enemy that has caused inestimable harm to our soul by keeping her under the incarceration of _Karma_?

Therefore O Best of _Bharatas_ (descendants of King _Bharata_), having first subdued the _Indriyas_, slay this

sinful enemy, the destroyer of knowledge and realization.

(Holy Gita 3:41)

Surely, that is exactly what He wants us to do. He commands us to **"slay this sinful enemy."**

Please make a note that Lord *Krishna* addresses the 'desire' as 'enemy' four times in verses, **Holy Gita 3:37, 39, 41, 43,** in range of six verses and asks twice to slay it with wisdom, and have victory over it. Now, the question is why? Because, desire is the destroyer of knowledge; and without knowledge, man is nothing but a host of darkness. His soul is like a drifter that wanders as nomad in all kinds of dark worlds.

The death is not what destroys the soul, because that causes just a change in her attire; it is the darkness that does. Surely, the flesh dies with death, but not the soul; she lives on without any harm. But whence the light and wisdom ceases her path, thence comes her destruction.

Oh! Then she falls into ruins. When her reason becomes handicapped and when her intellect becomes disabled, she heads to her destruction, **"From the loss of reason one heads towards destruction – Holy Gita 2:63."**

Man's destruction comes when his understanding and knowledge gets destroyed; when he loses the sight of truth and reality; when his vision becomes vague and blurred. He gets ruined when the light and wisdom cease his way, and darkness and delusion hover over his path; and when his discrimination and discernment become disabled, and his reason and intellect quit the trail of righteousness.

It is then, that a man dies even though he may be alive in body and flesh, but surely with a dead spirit and a destroyed soul. Of course, he still remains alive physically but due to loss of righteous reason, he becomes totally dead spiritually **(Holy Gita 2:63).**

So what else could be as harmful as desire, if it is so potent that it could bring the ultimate destruction of man? This is why Lord God calls it the enemy of the wise **(Holy Gita 3:39).** Surely the infatuation and passion, the attachment and desire, are the real enemy of the soul; they are the primary and sole cause of her destruction.

Now if the 'cause' behind the bondage is 'desire' and 'desire' is under the control of 'freewill', then why can't we win this battle which seems so unconquerable? After all, we have the total authority over our choices, so why can't we, under the provision of 'freewill', choose and act in such a way that we control our attachments and desires rather than be controlled by them? Why can't we design our responses to life in such a way, that they could become a proper and right 'cause' to create the most suitable and favorable 'effect'; meaning, they could create such a *Karma* that is without bondage? Why can't we do that?

Of course we can, if we really want to!

Look at these words of Lord *Krishna* that not only command us to **"slay this sinful <u>enemy</u>, the destroyer of knowledge and realization – Holy Gita 3:41,"** but also tell how to accomplish it; which of course, is by **"having first subdued the *Indriyas* – Holy Gita 3:41,"** meaning, by controlling our senses and bringing them under our authority. Thus, we accomplish this seemingly impossible task of gaining control over our desires by keeping in check our embedded sensuality.

Beloved! The control of senses is what the *Yogic*-life is all about. It is such a way of life where one overcomes his infatuation by the mastery over his body and mind, and becomes winner over attachment and desire by exercising self-discipline:

> **Devoid of cravings, with the body and mind under his control, having renounced all objects of pleasure, a Yogi performs actions only to maintain body. He does not enter into the evil of the world-process.**
>
> **(Holy Gita 4:21)**

When that happens, one does not get swayed by the temptations of this extremely sensual world, but remains unattached to life, and thus, attains liberation by parting from this world unbounded by *Karma*. Thus, he becomes eternally free. His soul attains salvation and reaches the abode of *Moksha* (Liberation).

We all know that the temptations are a major part of life. They are ever present, as there is no life without them. No wonder when Lord Jesus teaches how to pray, he does not ask us to pray that there be no temptations but that we are not led into them:

> **After this manner therefore pray ye: Our Father which art in heaven, Hallowed be thy name. Thy kingdom come. Thy will be done in earth, as it is in heaven. Give us this day our daily bread. And forgive us our debts, as we forgive our debtors.**
>
> **And lead us not into temptation, but deliver us from evil: For *thine* is the kingdom, and the power, and the glory, for ever. Amen.**
>
> **(Holy Bible, Matthew 6:7-13)**

And He issues a strong warning to that effect through following words and says:

> **Watch ye and pray, lest ye enter into temptation. The spirit truly is ready, but the flesh is weak –**
>
> **(Holy Bible, Mark 14:38)**

He knows that no matter how much we are desirous of life of holiness and no matter how hard we are willing to walk in righteousness, yet our flesh is so weak and feeble that there is a great probability of her falling into sin due to surrounding temptations and sensual enticements.

So the desire and attachments will always rise in us because the worldly temptations are always out there, and hence, no matter what we do and no matter how much life of solitude we adopt, we can never escape them and be completely isolated from their influence; we can never totally shield ourselves from their effects.

It means to break the captivity of bondage to *Karma*, the right thing to do is to learn how to save ourselves from falling into fleshly enticements and avoid getting trapped by the temptations of this sensual world.

And the way to do it and overcome attachment and desire, is to learn how to control our senses; how to tame our mind; how to discipline our body and flesh, **"Keep his body and mind**

under his control, and renounce desires and cravings for possessions – Holy Gita 6:10."

Of course, if we could learn how to have such *Yogic*-control, then we could become free from the fetters of *Karma* even while living our lives the way we are now, **"Such a Sage is untouched by actions, even though he continues performing them – Holy Gita 5:7."**

But how does this trick work, may we ask? Because, the suppression often results in revolution; does it not! So how the suppression of senses could be any different from that, and be without any risk of rebellion?

Well, in ignorance, though it may seem 'suppression', but in truth, what is being required here, such is never the case. It is not a suppression of desires by any means because the control of senses being commanded here is not by suppression but by understanding; it is not by forcefully imposed restraints but by willful submission through knowledge and wisdom, which is attained through the meditation and contemplation:

Having seated himself in a meditative pose and having brought the mind to a state of one-pointed-*ness*, he should attain mastery over the senses and mind, and practice Yoga (Samadhi) for the purification of the soul.

(Holy Gita 6:12)

So what is being told here is that the control over attachment and desire is brought by exercising discipline and self-control that is arrived through meditation and contemplation upon the truth, and through higher understanding and wisdom.

However, that is not all what is being conveyed in verse above, as something significant is still missing in our understanding! And that something is being point out by words, **"Practice Yoga (Samadhi) for the purification of the soul."** Let us look at these words a bit closely.

One of the greatest mysteries of spiritual wonderment, which is revealed to a person, but only through much graces of God, is that meditation and contemplation are effective only when he tries to live life in selflessness and exercises detachment in all things and devotes his life to the love of God:

A Yogi (following the Yoga of action) continues to perform actions merely with body, mind, intellect and senses. With detachment he performs actions for the <u>purity of his heart.</u>

(Holy Gita 5:11)

The reason being that only through selflessness and purity of love one attains **'the purity of heart'**; only through action-in-love he rises in sanctity and sacredness of his inner being; only through doing all things in love of God, he grows in piety and piousness of the soul.

This is the secret why *Karma-Yoga* is emphasized repeatedly by Lord *Krishna*, because only through selfless-action man attains the ability to rise in spiritual realm, **"*Janaka* and others attained perfection by following the *Yoga* of Action – Holy Gita 3:20;"** only through the life devoted to the love of God can he bring perfection to his soul, **"Then be intent upon doing actions for My sake, you will attain perfection – Holy Gita 12:10."**

No wonder, the duty is so sacred because in it there is no sin, **"By performing duties born of one's own nature, one does not incur sin – Holy Gita 18:47."** And what is duty? The obligation to life as it unfolds, moment by moment, in most natural sense. And how are we supposed to respond to the fulfillment of our obligations to life as it unfolds? With sheer love and joy; with utmost purity and piety; with absolute selflessness and self-centricity!

And that is why there is no sin in duty; because, the duty involves actions that are scripturally called to be performed by man to fulfill his intrinsic obligations, which of course, happens only when he renders them in the purity of love and in sanctity of selflessness.

The actions called by man's inherent duty demand unselfishness and altruism in their rendering; they demand love and light in their performance. This is why the performance of duty is an easy way for man to attain spiritual perfection, **"Men pursuing their own duties with devotion attain spiritual perfection – Holy Gita 18:45,"** because they encourage him to be unselfish, and engage him in doing things that are good for others. And that is what grows him in love and light even further.

The selflessness-in-action is such a detergent that cleanses the heart **(Holy Gita 5:11)**; the love-in-action is such a medicine that cures all illnesses of the spirit; the life-of-unselfishness is such a remedy that slowly but surely perfects the soul.

And when the soul begins to heal from all kinds of infections, and begins to get cured from the diseases rising out of sin, and when the impurities surrounding her begin to get washed away through a life of selflessness and sacrifice, she begins to elevate towards the light and wisdom.

The action-in-love begins to wipe out all kinds of grunge and grime off her, and she begins to grow in knowledge and wisdom, which of course, sharpen her spiritual vision that eventually enables her to see the truth of God more clearly than ever before.

So the real reward of selfless engagement in life is actually the gaining of sharpness in spiritual sight; it is the augmentation of understanding of God; it is the growth in His wisdom and knowledge; it is the increased intensity in our inner light that enables us to see God more clearly and enhances our feel for His live presence around us.

But not many know this secret, as most of us try to increase our spiritual vision by studying the holy text and gaining more and more sacred knowledge. We try to rise in piety and piousness by practicing more and more holy ritual and rites; we try to grow in godliness by engaging more and more in chanting and praying, and try to become more spiritually established in ourselves by regularly practicing *yoga* and meditation.

That is why none of it is as effective as it ought to be because we are not doing it right. Our holy approach is very faulty because we are adopting it without all essential elements especially not adopting love as the natural way of our day and not living a life of altruism and unselfishness.

So how can our holy approach work if the main ingredient is missing from our recipe? How can we succeed in making our soul pure and perfect? How can we ever make any true progress in our ascension to enlightenment?

Surely, during recent years, the *Yoga* and mediation have become very popular in all societies, especially in western world, as more and more people are adopting and bringing them into their daily life. Yet, do we see any real gain out of it in spiritual terms?

Obviously not! But, why? Because, most often they are adopted without clear understanding of what they are, and what their true application is!

People engage in *Yoga* and meditation often for physical fitness rather than spiritual uplift. I am not saying that there is no spiritual motivation at all, but it certainly is not their main focus. And even when it is, there is not a clear understanding of what else is needed besides performing *Yogic*-and meditative practices, so that they could produce the right results.

Beloved! Know it for sure that unless there is an inner revolution against the 'self', and a firm resolve to cut down the tree of 'ego', not much progress can ever be made no matter what spiritual and physical restraints are exercised.

Oh! The 'life of love' is the only way to 'life of light', and the 'life of light' is the only way to 'life of eternal liberty'. How can we make any real progress in spiritual realm without having such understanding!

So unless we learn how to live life in love, and exercise it in all encounters and engagements of life by operating in selflessness through the surrender to God, not much good we would reap out of the harvest of our spiritual sowings no matter how good of a champion we become of *Yoga* and meditation. Until we learn how to operate in selflessness and render our day to holy service to God, our *Yogic*-labor would not bear much spiritual fruits.

When the holy word says that the selfless-action cleanses the soul by removing the impurities surrounding her, **"With detachment he performs actions for the purity of his heart – Holy Gita 5:11,"** what it really means is that, all the filth and dirt encapsulating the soul is removed because the egocentricity begins to die, because the pride begins to fall, because the self-centricity begins to decrease, because selfishness begins to vanish away, because the egoistic rule begins to dwindle. That's why!

The only way to cut down the tree of stubborn ego is by performing actions selflessly, and by rendering oneself for the good of others, as there is no other channel to arrive there. Only by living life for the sake of God, can we defeat the selfishness and overcome self-centricity; only by living the day in love and engaging in all things with the light of the Spirit can we bring down the evil empire of ego.

And as the soul begins to emerge out of the shell of ego, she does not remain blind, as she now has the enhanced spiritual vision to see the Truth better, which eventually enables her to find the way for her eternal liberation.

So the whole idea of any spiritual endeavor is to become humble and be out of dark shadows of ego. Because until we are truly humble and meek, and find ourselves helpless without God, there is no knowing of Truth; there is no getting close to Him; and hence, there is no hope for the freedom from incarceration by bondage.

But how often does a seeker set the elimination of ego as the prime goal of his spiritual enterprise? How often does he know that humility is that essentiality without which he cannot have any true communion with God? And how often is he aware of the fact that without selfless-action and without a life of unselfish love, there is no way to become truly humble, which of course is a mandatory requirement to make any significant progress in any spiritual pursuit?

Sadly, not often!

And when such thoughts are missing in the mind of a seeker, how can he ever attain the true rewards of his spiritual toiling? Too bad! He is not even aware of this reality. He does not even know what are the true gains of holy endeavors? He is not even aware of the purpose for which they have been given to man by God?

This is why most often than not people get very little out of their *Yogic*-labor; there meditative practices hardly ever bear any meaningful fruits. No wonder, their spiritual life remains so empty, because often there is no real enlightening substance in it.

This is a lesson to all of us, that no matter what *Yogic*-approach we adopt to rise in our spiritual realm, there is one essentiality that cannot be ignored by any means, which is to adopt a life of love and care, service and sacrifice, surrender and submission.

Because if we do not do that, we would not gain much spiritually no matter how hard we work in exercising meditation and contemplation; no matter how laboriously we toil to gain scriptural knowledge and wisdom; and no matter how faithfully we perform our holy ritual and rites, and engage in prayers and praises of God.

Look at the argument *Arjuna* brings forth to Lord *Krishna* and asks Him the reason why does He command him to engage in war and perform his duty, and follow the path of 'selfless-action' rather than following the path of Knowledge, which as per holy word is a direct way to enlightenment:

> **Arjuna said: O *Janardana*, if you say the intellect lit up with the light of wisdom is superior to the path of selfless action, then why do you lead me, O *Keshava*, to the performance of terrible Karmas?**
>
> **(Holy Gita 3:1)**

Now look at the answer Lord God gives him but by revealing a profound truth that there are two main paths for spiritual seeking: the path of selfless-action (*Karma-Yoga*) and the path of Knowledge (*Samkhya-Yoga*):

> **O *Arjuna*, one who has restrained his mind and senses, and engages his organs of action in the performance of actions enjoined in the scriptures, is far superior to the <u>former</u>.**
>
> **(Holy Gita 3:7)**

He says that the selfless-action is a better path than the path of Knowledge (which is referred in here by the word **'former'**), and commands *Arjuna* to engage in life selflessly and render his intrinsic duty with which he is born, **"Therefore, perform your duties in daily life – Holy Gita 3:8."**

This is the recommendation the disciple receives from his master. Well, why the path of selfless-action is better than the path of Knowledge, there are at least two main reasons:

First reason: The action is ever attached with life as there is no life without action, **"No one can stay without action even for a single moment – Holy Gita 3:5;"** so to beautify life, why not to perform the action the best way we can since it is attached with it and cannot be separated from it. In other words: perform action selflessly and become a *Karma*-Yogi **(Holy Gita 2:48-49).**

And second reason: The path of Knowledge (*Samkhya*) is extremely difficult without selfless-action and is filled with much troubles, **"Without *Karma Yoga* the path of *Samkhya* is beset with troubles – Holy Gita 5:6,"** mainly because renouncing the action externally does not do much good unless one renounces internally all desires of its fruit.

Meaning, one has to renounce the objective world internally if he wishes to pursue the path of Knowledge but by assimilating in it the path of selfless-action (*Karma*); otherwise, his effort is deceitful and hypocritical; the reason being that his thoughts continue to ponder upon the sensual things, **"Those who have restrained the organs of actions, but continue to think of the objects of the senses, are foolish and hypocritical – Holy Gita 3:6,"** which is what the case is most often than not. And it happens because it is not easy to not be attracted by the beauty and bountifulness of the objective world.

To attain such enlightening feat one must be a champion in forsaking his emotions and feelings, and must have an extreme *Yogic*-control over his mind and senses so that he could resist the alluring temptations and keep control over his cravings and desires. Without such mastery over sensual self, one cannot succeed in his spiritual pursuit through *Samkhya* (Knowledge).

Thus, the path of *Samkhya*, though looks very attractive as we can see in case of Arjuna **(Holy Gita 3:1)**, but it is not very practical since it is not easily adoptable; and it is not as effective due to a greater probability that the seeker would fail in controlling his sensual-reaction to the material world and would fall into fleshly temptations which are extremely hard to overcome just by external renouncement.

This is why *Karma-Yoga* (selfless-action) is so glorified in Holy Gita; because, it is highly effective – even though slowly but surely – in overcoming the ego and pride, and defeating the attachment and desire. This unique usefulness of the action-in-love (*Karma-Yoga*), which brings the self-purification so easily and so successfully, is that it is the most valuable tool in all spiritual growth. No wonder, without its assimilation, no *Yogic*-effort, no matter how great it is, can ever be truly meaningful.

The lesson here is that life of selfless-action is a must in all spiritual endeavors. In bringing any meaningful self-control, it is a must; because, without it we cannot make any true progress in walking towards the enlightenment. We can never succeed in any *Yogic*-discipline unless we assimilate this *Yogic*-restraint in our adopted spiritual enterprises. This is why most *Yoga* and meditation fails to produce any radical change in the seeker's life, because often he does not incorporate in it the life of selfless service and renders it as if it is a holy sacrifice to God.

Yes, I agree that we can tame the body and mind through *Yoga* and meditation, but such control, since it is egocentric, is not of much use, unless first it is made egoless. Surely it is effective in controlling the equilibrium of our temperament and balancing the overall attitude of our day, but that is all as far as it goes.

However, should we be satisfied with just that much or demand more out of our spiritual labor? Should we be contented with just temporary and mostly external gains and not seek the total benefit of out holy toiling including our ascension to everlasting enlightenment?

This is why we ought to integrate the selfless-action in our all *Yogic*-approaches, since action-in-love is so complementary to them that it makes all *Yogic*-disciplines fully fruitful.

You see! The body and mind control, without extreme humility, remains highly egocentric; and as long as, there is ego, there can be no light in the soul. Therefore, the mind, body and senses must be brought under control through humility and meekness, so that the restraints could be adopted willingly and joyfully, and of course through higher understanding and wisdom but without any suppression and enforced external inhibiting forces.

Now-a-days, *Yoga* and meditation, which are applied more often than not as a remedy to cure the physical fatigue and mental weariness, are so highly popular that they are being adopted increasingly in just about all societies. No more these are confined to *Hindu* populations as much of the western world has begun to deploy them even commercially.

Surely, these spiritual approaches have proceeded from *Hindu* philosophy, but today, their application and deployment has broken the boundaries of all faiths and beliefs, as they have been embraced by millions around the world without any religious holdbacks and theological considerations.

The reason being that during last few decades, the materialism has risen beyond all imaginations. Man has become slave to things. He has become addictive to objective world. And since the objective world is the subject of mind, the human mind has become readily crowded and complex more than ever before.

This has made the taming of mind more attractive to man than any other alternative which is available to him to relieve himself from all kinds of stress and strain of the day, which of course, is caused by his extremely busy and occupied life that hardly knows any rest.

The fact is that demand of mind-control in life has taken such a turn that it has jumped to the forefront of all human development. The increase in its application is almost phenomenal. Now-a-days, it is not hard to find folks at any gathering, home or at work who are involved in such disciplinary practices and are engaged in *Yoga* and mediation regularly.

According to the educators of human-health, such practices are essential to give the needed break to mind, which happens to process thousand times more information daily today than ever before, and which ever remains tangled with all kinds of complicated situations and circumstances presented by day's' most demanding ultra-fast life.

No wonder, among doctors, prescribing *Yoga* and mediation to their patients has become a common practice to alleviate the stress and strain and calm down the mind that hardly finds any peace in today's extremely tense life filled with chaos and confusion.

So in truth, the *Yoga* and meditation that is deployed so commonly today, is not what it used to be; it has lost its authenticity, its true essence. It was supposed to be the main ladder of *Yogic*-progression but has become merely a mind relieving medicine.

Thus, quite obviously, these spiritual disciplines have lost their true luster, since they are being deployed without their full understanding, and without their full implementation; however, even after all kinds of earthly evolution of these *Yogic*-practices, the object to bring the body and mind under control is still there regardless of all other physical and mental restraints that are being sought through them.

Well, it is a no secret that mind is a powerhouse; it is a resource of unlimited potential; however, the extent of its potentiality and power that can be realized depends upon how much it can be utilized under control. And that is where often lies man's failure; because, there are only few such souls that know how to reach the pinnacle of its potential, and the reason being, that they have learned how to tame it with understanding and wisdom, and how to keep it under their authority.

On the contrary, most of us are so taken over by our infatuation that we do not know how to exercise our dominion over mind; our attention is so scattered because of things we want in life, which keeps our mind very crowded by cravings; it is ever busy passionately in pursuing our desires, and thus, it hardly ever sees peace, and we fail to realize its full potential.

True! That man has progressed so well, that now he has begun to venture the other planets, but he still is a slave to his mind due to his entangling desires **(Holy Gita 2:43, 9:12, 21, 16:12, 16)**. He still has not learned how to tame his mind, and that is why he is trying to learn so aggressively how to have control over it so that he could maneuver it the way he likes.

You see! The scriptures repeatedly speak that the mind has power to guide man to his ultimate good or lead him to his eventual destruction, of course, depending upon how pure or impure it is:

The mind of man is of two kinds, pure and impure: impure when in the bondage of desire, pure when free from desire.

(Maitri Upanishad 6:24)

These holy words give us a clue that the mind rises in purity if it is not in bondage to desire, but it falls into impurity when it is enslaved by infatuation. Of course, the pure mind takes man towards the life of light and liberty, while the mind of impurity takes him towards the life of darkness and bondage. Meaning, a man could head either way, depending upon how pure and pious or impure and maligned his mind is.

Also, it is not hard to see that purity and impurity of mind is directly related to the degree of how much it acts under restraints and how much it behaves as autonomous. How much it conducts under control, and how much it behaves as a rebellion.

Of course, a mind that is out of control drives man to destruction, but the one that knows how to conduct under restraints, reaps richness of life.

Surely, we all are familiar with the problems that rise when mind is not under control; because, then it remains restless; and in restlessness it ventures all kinds of thoughts, and ponders over all kinds of material things.

This constant and continual attention to things creates attraction towards them, which eventually gives rise to desire to have them. Of course, depending upon how strong the desire is, the mind engages as hard in efforts to fulfill it; and it does everything it can to quench its hunger and thirst that rise out of deep lust for the luscious objects of pleasures.

As a result, the mind becomes very consumed by their desires, which further increases its restlessness. And sometimes, if a desire is too strong it captures its attention even to a point that it becomes an obsession.

Thus, by contemplating upon the alluring sensuality of this material world, a wild mind gives rise to destructive desires, which keep it continually engaged in their nourishment and fulfillment. And when, for some reason, they are not satisfied, it gets agitated and angry, which of course, ultimately becomes a reason for destruction of its intrinsic powers of light and wisdom such as discrimination and discernment, reflection and judgment, and thus, causing man's spiritual death **(Holy Gita 2:62-63)**.

So, as we can see, an uncontrolled and wandering mind is ever dangerous as it can cause the total spiritual destruction of man.

However, to have control over body and mind is never easy – we all know that! In fact it is much harder in modern times than it ever were before. The reason being that today's life is extremely materialistic, and hence, the mind is ever filled with much mud of wanting and carving, and occupied by all kinds of ambitions and desires.

So as expected, due to fleshly hunger and thirst, **"this mind is ever so restless – Holy Gita 3:43;"** and that is why it is so hard to tame it. Following words where *Arjuna* expresses wonderment about the difficult nature of the mind, which is so ever turbulent and tumultuous, further testify to this reality:

> **Verily, O Krishna, the mind is fickle, impetuous and turbulent. To me it seems more difficult to control the mind than it is to control the wind.**

> **(Holy Gita 6:34)**

One reason why mind is so hard to control is because the indwelling desires **(Holy Gita 3:40)**, which continually crowd it, are hard to overcome, **"Which is so difficult to conquer – Holy Gita 3:43."** Of course, the mind conceives desires by constantly pondering upon attractive things, but it also nourishes and satisfies them by compelling man to do everything that is needed to be done to fulfill them; and it often forces him to act even against his own will **(Holy Gita 3:36)**.

Thus, conclusively speaking, the desires make mind highly restless and impulsive, tumultuous and turbulent; they make it distracted and multi-branched, **"But the thoughts of one who desires the fruits of action are many-branched and endless –**

Holy Gita 3:43;" and that is why it is so hard to discipline it **(Holy Gita 3:40)**.

However, regardless of the difficulty involved in controlling the mind, which Lord *Krishna* himself acknowledges, He yet exposes a way to discipline it, and unveils a secret that by the practice of *Abhyasa* (repeated effort) and *Vairagya* (dispassion), the mind can be brought under a rule:

> *Bhagavan* **Krishna said: Indeed the mind is restless and difficult to control, but can be brought under control by the exercise of** *Abhyasa* **(repeated effort) and** *Vairagya* **(dispassion).**
>
> **(Holy Gita 6:35)**

Well, the message seems to be that if one desires to bring his mind under control, he ought to repeatedly practice the *Yoga* and meditation and exercise dispassion (*Vairagya*), which seems pretty simple, isn't it? But trust me, it's not so! These words are hiding much deeper meaning. Let us find out what it is?

First, let us expand upon what has been said here and interpret the message by saying that the key to disciplining the mind is the repeated-effort (*Abhyasa*) of trying to abide under the supervision of intellect (*Buddhi*) rather than doing it under the command and control of emotions and feelings (*Chitta*), and of course, the continual growth in life of dispassion (*Vairagya*) and renunciation (*Sanyasa*), and of sacrifice and relinquishment (*Tyaga*).

Now, let us pay attention to the word '*Abhyasa*', which means 'repeated-effort', which has a very special meaning in this reference. You see! What Lord God is saying here is that repeated-effort is needed to overcome the mind; meaning, it cannot be tamed just by telling it once, or twice, or few times, or even several times, but is told and taught over and over; and only then it learns; only then it comes under control.

You must be thinking, so far we have not really added anything anew to the meaning of the verse as stated above; and you are right, I agree! Surely, we have done nothing more than that. Yet, what we have done is that we have expanded our understanding of these words; but nothing new has been unfolded in addition.

So where is the mystery? Well, here it is!

Did you notice that Lord God says *"**Abhyasa (repeated effort) and Vairagya (dispassion)?**"*

Please pay attention to these words! He is not saying it is one or the other. He uses 'and' instead of 'or'. It is both together; meaning, it demands *Abhyasa* (repeated effort) and *Vairagya* (dispassion); it requires not just one but both. And that is highly significant. How? Let's look at it by expounding upon it a little bit more.

Well, keeping this fact mind from holy words above, it is not hard to understand that repeated-effort (**Abhyasa**) – meaning, the practice of *Yoga* and meditation – by itself is not enough. It has to be accompanied by the follow-up of dispassion (*Vairagya*) and detachment; it has to be harmonized with renunciation (*Sanyasa*) and denial; it has to be complemented with a life of relinquishment (*Tyaga*) and sacrifice.

Both types of spiritual disciplines are needed to overcome the mind; one without the other is not as effective as it must be. Surely, they both singularly are effective too, but not as much as they potentially can be while being coordinated and complemented by each other.

Therefore, for effective use of this spiritual approach, both disciplines have to be assimilated as one, and then be adopted and applied as if they are two strings of the same instrument, which together create the sound of music and give rise to a delightful melody.

The verse, **Holy Gita 6:35**, does validate this fact, that *Yoga* and mediation is ineffective if it is not accompanied with dispassion, renunciation and relinquishment. The meditation alone surely yields peace, but only a transitory and transient; there is no permanence in it and no stability. Too bad! That this is exactly what is happening everywhere. Most of the practices of *Yoga* and meditation are hollow and empty; they are vain and void; there is hardly any power to transform man's inner being and renovate him spiritually.

Now, if the same mediation could be yoked with a life of love and affection, compassion and care, service and sacrifice, it definitely would increase the peace and joy of the day, and would raise the person to higher levels of tranquility and equanimity. There is no doubt about it. We all can try it and confirm to ourselves!

This is what provides the power to overcome the mind and senses; this is what enables one to attain self-control; this is what empowers one to conquer his lower 'self'.

By assimilating love and light with *Yogic*-practices, one reaches the utmost rungs of *'Yoga'* and gets established in the higher Self **(Holy Gita 4:41)**, by attaining which even while remaining bound in this body, he becomes eternally liberated, **"He attains the Absolute State of Liberation – Holy Gita 2:72,"** as no fetters of *Karma* binds him anymore.

Therefore, if we wish to bring a real change in our life and wish to rise to higher levels of enlightenment, then the only real way of reaching there is to bring self-discipline by adopting a life of love and affection, care and compassion, service and sacrifice, surrender and submission, and then complementing it with *yoga* and mediation, contemplation and reflection.

That is what we ought to do to overcome our attachment and desire by taming and disciplining our mind through higher understanding that is arrived through life of love and light, and by teaching ourselves how to rest in the peace of God by letting go all we have and all we are.

We must understand this clearly that the repeated-effort (*Yoga* and meditation) – the *Abhyasa* – is effective only through a life that is dedicated to sacrifice and service rendered with love of God. This is exactly what is being told by Lord God through these words, **"(The mind) can be brought under control by the exercise of <u>Abhyasa</u> (repeated effort) <u>and</u> Vairagya (dispassion) – Holy Gita 6:35."**

You see! The change has to occur at much deeper level within us. The control of mind gained externally is not of much value. In fact, it may even turn out to be harmful because of a false sense of attainment of enlightenment, which may come due to temporary tranquility experienced during vain and void *Yogic*-practices.

Any enlightening transformation at the deeper cores takes place only when one is rendered to love; when he is devoted to

199

life of selflessness; when he is given to service and sacrifice for others; when he is dedicated to the welfare of the world; and when he is yielded with his entirety to the will of God. Only then a real change takes place in a man.

And when such a person engages in *Yogic*-practices of meditation and contemplation, he conquers all temptations, and all desires of ever-alluring world, and becomes firmly established in the 'State of absolute contentment'.

You see! The selfless-life is very effective in cleansing the human heart. When one is given to a life that is dedicated to love of God, a divine transformation takes place in him.

The rendering to selfless service and sacrifice for others increases a man in purity and piousness; the adaptation of renunciation and dispassion increases him in detachment and impassiveness; the application of *Yoga* and meditation multiplies him in understanding and knowledge; the practice of reflection and contemplation increases him in light and wisdom. And all these things of heavenly transformation take place in him because his *Yogic*-exercises are assimilated with love and light of God.

Thus, with a mind that has been purified through meditative practices, and a heart that has become the home of love for God, one is able to see the truth of the higher Self and experience His bliss:

When it is restrained by the practice of Yoga (Samadhi), the *Chitta* reaches the state of supreme withdrawal from the world-process. Then the Yogi sees the Self with his purified mind, and rejoices in the Self.

(Holy Gita 6:20)

It is that state-of-being where one is free from the fetters of attachment and desire, and is liberated from all manacles of infatuation and passion. And when that happens, he becomes the abode of such a lasting peace that he can withstand any violent winds of the day, and yet remain fully-composed without ever being disturbed and turbulent:

Just as a lamp does not flicker restlessly in a place where there is no wind, so the mind of a Yogi that has

been subdued by the practice of Yoga does not flicker due to the absence of the wind of desire.

(Holy Gita 6:19)

Surely, such a person, after overcoming his self (lower) through *Yogic*-practices, arrives to that abode of existence where his mind ceases all restlessness and finds the total peace. The only thing then remains is the experience of joy.

Oh! Nothing else but joy!

Here are the words of utter wisdom that bear witness to this truth:

Just as waters from different rivers enter into the ocean from all sides, and yet the ocean continues to be immutable, in the same way he in whom all desires enter without affecting him, he alone attains peace, nor the desirer of sense-objects.

(Holy Gita 2:70)

He becomes such an ocean of peace and joy into which though desires enter violently, yet he remains unmoved by absorbing all disturbances and maintains his bliss so steadfastly that no turbulence is ever able to upset his peace and tranquility.

Beloved! The key is not the control of mind and senses, but to overcome the desire and attachment through the discipline of self-control as we have just discussed.

However, if we do not keep our focus upon why are we trying to grow in self-control, then we probably would not care to exercise renunciation and dispassion. We may forget to pay much attention to the fact that we ought to become humble and meek, egoless and unselfish (which happens only when one moves into the sanctuary of God and no where else). But without these qualities, our exercise of self-control would remain empty and void, and would not produce any meaningful fruits.

We can easily verify this fact by looking at folks that are heavily involved in *Yoga* and meditation, and see how many among them have truly made significant headway towards the abode of enlightenment? Sadly, we have to prepare ourselves for disappointment; don't we!

Of course, the reason is the same, which we have gone over so many times by now that such folks are engaged only in mind-control and not doing things they need to do to remove the indwelling impurities, which are removed only by selfless-action done in the vision of equanimity – meaning through *Karma Yoga* **(Holy Gita 2:48)**.

Therefore, let us not forget, why are we doing anything that is of spiritual nature? What is the ultimate goal of all what we do in our holy life? Let us ask these kinds of questions repeatedly until we get some clear answers; and then check to see if our *Yogic*-approach can sufficiently enable us to achieve that goal.

You see! We can summarize the whole problem this way: Since the attachment and desire are the root cause of bondage **(Holy Gita 13:21)**, one has to overcome them if he desires freedom from *Karma*. And because these evils dwell in the mind and senses **(Holy Gita 3:40)**, the control of mind becomes necessary, otherwise, how can one overcome his passion and infatuation?

However, as per holy word, **Holy Gita 6:35**, the discipline of mind and senses, and the self-control needed to overcome the attachment and desire, requires <u>not only</u> *Abhyasa* (repeated-effort), meaning *Yoga*, meditation and contemplation, <u>but also</u> *Vairagya* (dispassion), *Sanyasa*) (renunciation) and *Tyaga* (relinquishment), which are unavoidable essentialities to arrive to such feat.

Therefore, unless both are exercised concurrently and harmoniously, the spiritual effort would fall short in producing its maximum benefit due to the fact that they are complementary in nature, and hence, they both need to work together and operate simultaneously, since one helps the mind to not flicker but be at rest, and the other helps lessen the ego and pride by inducing in it more humility and unselfishness, which further reduces the flame of desire and increase even more rest and peace.

One thing needs to be reminded here is that the ultimate reward of all such spiritual effort is the light and wisdom – the higher understanding and Knowledge – and the knowing of the true Self, which obviously are such virtues that dawn in human

202

heart only after he has come far beyond the boundaries of passion and infatuation.

This is why, when dies the attachment and desire, so does the ignorance and darkness; and when dies the self-delusion and darkness, the wisdom shines forth upon the face of the *Atman* (soul) like a sun **(Holy Gita 5:16)**.

Beloved! Let us meditate upon the following words of Holy Gita that unveil the mystery of why it is most essential for man to overcome desire and unfold the truth that by winning over this enemy, 'desire', one becomes enabled to attain the ultimate reward of self-control, so called 'Self-realization' – which comes only after the soul has been washed off all impurities through the selfless-action (action-in-love), and her spiritual vision has been re-instated to her original shine through the meditation and contemplation.

Having abandoned all desires, he who moves without the feeling of mine-*ness*, without egoism and without craving, he attains the supreme peace (of Self-realization).

Such is the state of Self-realization, O *Arjuna*. Having attained this, a Yogi is not deluded. Being established in this even at the moment of death, he attains the Absolute State of Liberation.

(Holy Gita 2:71-72)

The holy word says that if a person is able to overcome his ego, and free himself from the bondage to desire, no more he remains bound by ignorance and darkness. Surely, he becomes established in the wisdom of 'Self-realization', where his soul begins to reflect the radiance of the Truth and his spirit begins to emanate the light of The Spirit.

The truth is that if one attains such a Yogic state of higher enlightenment even at the last moment of his life, he still finds the peace supreme here in this world as well as hereafter – so say the above words of Holy Gita.

Therefore, with a diligent and devout heart let us pray that Lord God liberates us from passion and infatuation, and sets us free from all cravings so that we could become the embedded truth in these words of the *Upanishad* and be delivered from the manacles of mortality by being liberated from all chains of bondage:

When all desires that cling to the heart are surrendered, then a mortal becomes immortal, and even in this world he is one with Brahman.

When all the ties that bind the heart are unloosened, then a mortal becomes immortal. That is the sacred teaching.

(Katha Upanishad, Part 6)

Beloved! Know that only after becoming free from the hunger and thirst of this world, can we be fully surrendered to God; only then, can we wholly dedicated to His love; only then, can we be completely rendered to his will; only then, can we entirely abide in His sanctuary, peacefully and joyfully; only then, can we thankfully receive the light of his spirit; only then can we find His grace leading our way to His heavenly providence.

8

Ignorance and Darkness
~
The Main Reason for Soul's Karmic-Fall

Today, when we look at the world, we see that even though man has progressed so well and has risen to glory with such an unbelievable development in science and technology, and has created much wonderment by making life so luxurious and resourceful, and yet he has declined in virtue and value rather than rising in it. Surely, his knowledge is greater than ever before, but it is the ignorance that increasingly hovers in his heart, day and night. Though all avenues of his life are shinning with a glow, yet his inner chamber is filled with utter darkness.

True, that mind of man is becoming sharper everyday, but that does not mean his spiritual vision is also sharpening. Because the facts are pointing to quite a reverse reality, which tells that his mind is only getting darker and darker by each day.

Surely his attainments seem to be of the highest degree, but his losses are so severe that they cannot be counted. Of course, his accomplishments can be seen everywhere because they are corporeal and concrete, and they can be spoken of all day long because they are so apparent and evident that their tangibility demands their open and forceful acknowledgment. So it is not hard to gauge his glory.

However, how can we measure up his losses? How can we calculate the consequence of his decline that is not only affecting today's humanity but is affecting the humanity of all generations that are yet to come? How can we assess the fall of his moral man when we do not even have any realistic hope that he could be restored back in virtue and value in any foreseeable future?

The undeniable reality of man is that he has lost the quality and character; he has devastatingly declined in morality and righteousness. The honor and honesty have left his heart, and dignity and decency have deserted his soul. Today, his spirit knows not the difference between the light and darkness as he is standing very close to being bankrupt of all goodness and grace, all virtue and value, all morality and righteousness.

Oh, how sad! What has become of today's man!

It is not that his vision is fuzzy only a little bit, or he is losing it slowly. Not so! It is weakening rapidly, and declining fast day by day; surely, it is deteriorating very speedily. The fact is that his vision has already become so dark that he is unable to see anything beyond the boundaries of his self-centric world. And considering how rapidly he is losing his moral sight, there is not much time left before he would become totally blind. The most disheartening thing about that is, that he himself is the reason of his darkness and decline; he himself is responsible for his disaster and doom.

It is man's own affection and adoration for things of this world that has veiled his knowledge **(Holy Gita 3:38)**; it is his own passion and infatuation that has doomed him into darkness, **"Wisdom is enveloped by desire – Holy Gita 3:39;"** it is his own attachment and desire that has drowned him in delusion; it is his own material longing and craving that has made him spiritually blind.

Surely, today's man has quit the way of righteousness. No more he follows the trails of virtue. Who can deny that man has fallen so deep into lust and lasciviousness that all his pursuits thrive not for morality and justice but for wealth and affluence, not for virtue and value but for name and fame, not for quality and character but for power and prosperity, not for honor and nobility but for authority and influence, not for integrity and honesty but for riches and resources, not for dignity and decency but for command and control, not for goodness and grace but for acknowledgement and recognition.

Oh! He has fallen into vice in each and every way possible.

When I was young, I knew this man, who even though was not wealthy or powerful, yet was very respected by people and was regarded highly by the local community just because he was an honest and dignified man; he was a man of principles and ideology, and of honor and nobility. Even though his position offered him all kinds of opportunity to take bribery, he never accepted any. He had a position where he could have become quite rich, of course, through immoral means, yet he chose not to, and remained moral and upright. He chose to live with less but with honesty and honor, and not with more riches and affluence, which would have robbed him of dignity and decency. Instead of becoming a man of wealth and prosperity, he chose to be a man of character and quality, and of virtue and value.

Oh! It wasn't so long ago when we honored men who had character and bore virtue. Until only few decades ago, we held high those who were embodiment of righteousness. But now, it seems as if all that has vanished and long gone. The admiration for the right and just, and the appreciation for upright and virtuous has become a thing of the past. It all has been washed off our minds; no more we think like that.

Those times are long gone when the righteousness was the basis of man's being, and virtue was the measure of his greatness. He had pride in who and what he was. He had self-respect, and self-regard; he endowed honesty and honor; he embodied dignity and decency; he wore virtue and value. As I recall, that was a generation of character and quality, of morality and nobility. But what happened to all that?

Today, if one refuges to accept bribery, he is rebuked by his own family; he is considered a fool. Since wealth and prosperity are the highest priorities of life; everyone is being driven by the same pursuit. It doesn't matter how one gets there as long as he does it. That's all what matters.

There is no shame left even in discussing openly the immoral and wicked ways. We do that everyday sitting in our living rooms; we talk about all kinds of sinful stuff while eating at our dinning tables. We do it right in front of our wives, husbands, and children – openly and without any reluctance and hesitation – without any shame and embarrassment.

How often we boast about our dubious ways that we use to make money and gain power. How often without any shame we proudly tell stories about our immoral and dishonest accomplishments even though they are not the feats of any moral courage and righteous dedication but are the disgraceful enterprises of depravity and wickedness, which of course, are nothing but the works of hidden sins.

So how can we deny our moral decline and degradation, which considers everything to be okay no matter how malignant we become in accomplishing success of the day, but of course, as long as we prevail in our ventures to gain wealth and riches, name and fame, and power and prosperity.

I am sure most of us have heard these kinds of stories from folks who feel very proud of their accomplishments even though they have applied all kinds of illegal ways to succeed in them.

The truth is that misdemeanor and misconduct does not bother us anymore, unless of course it is gruesome, because we have become insensitive to immorality; we have become immune to evil and vice; we have become numb in sensing the wickedness. Our spiritual skin has become so thick that we do not sense any scratches of evil. So, it is quite natural that we do not feel anything wrong in our sinful ways.

In fact anything, no matter how illegal and immoral it is, as long as it makes money and helps us gain power and prosperity, we embrace it without any hesitation. We consider the schemes of folly our smartness, and regard the ways of wickedness as our brilliance as long as we succeed in attaining what we want.

The truth is that the darkness has come upon us from all sides; but sadly, our common belief is that we are living the days of light. Though the murkiness of immorally is hovering all over our humanity, but the progress in science and technology has made our life so beautiful and bright that we have become disillusioned to believe that each new sunrise would only increase and spread the shine of our accomplishments into our living rooms.

But in truth, such observation and expectation, such optimism and hope are very deceiving. Please ask yourself: Are we truly going towards the light? Or, are we heading towards the darkness?

Oh! Let us not be fooled by the glitter and glow of our progressive day, because along with it also is falling upon us the darkest night. Let us not rush to thinking that we are heading towards a better tomorrow, because tomorrow is drowning into darkness and we do not even know that we are slipping into sinister wombs.

We are so busy in chasing the prosperity and wealth that we have no time to examine our reality; we are consumed by our passion so badly that we have forgotten to pay any attention to the fact that we have morally declined beyond limits; that we have descended to pitiful depths of human lowliness; that we have fallen into those gallows of immorality from where there is no easy return.

What a sad state of human existence? Is this what we are born for? Is this for which God has made us human? Oh! I am sure He must be wondering about that!

We surely have become numb to the righteousness of God, as our senses have become mute to spirituality; we have gone numb to non-materialism of higher and holy kingdom, as now we only respond to sensuality and seduction of the secularism of this world.

Our mind has gone so blind that it does not even see the depth of its blindness; it sees illusions and believes them to be actuality. Our intellect is so infected with impurities that it does not even know the malignancy of its infection as it judges the ignorance and finds it to be the knowledge; it looks at transient and temporal world that is made of falsehood and fabrications, and believes it to be the manifestation of truthfulness.

Our soul is so deluded that she does not realize how lost she is; her fall into unrighteousness is so deep that she does not even have a sense of depth of her downfall. How strange it is, that she is living the days of slavery to sin, and yet she finds them to be pleasurable.

Alas! Such is the state of our fallen being.

In the lost vision of truth our thinking has been so deformed that in its distorted view we see everything incorrectly; everything is upside down. Everything that is wrong seems right, and everything that is right seems wrong.

What we must value and what not, and what we must hold high and what we must disregard, we just do not know. Often we do what we must never do, and do not do what we ought to do. No doubt! Our judgment has become so defiled that often we engage passionately in those enterprises that have no true value in the sight of God, in fact, they are even against His righteousness, and consciously ignore those endeavors that are a must as per His will.

Thus, our reality is nowhere even close to what it ought to be; since we are what we should not be, and are not what we should be. Honestly, the whole picture of what we have become is very disheartening. Of course, we can deny it, but our denial cannot change the reality.

The problem is that we are not just going from good to bad, but from bad to worse. Consider the following that describes what kind of spiritual decline the soul already has suffered:

When we are born, our soul is already laced with sin; she is already dark and deluded because even then she is surrounded by impurities from past lives. So, she is already defiled and sinful; otherwise, she would have never come into this world, which is a field of *Karma*.

And what we are becoming now, and how, day by day, we are falling deeper and deeper into unrighteousness does not help the situation, but only makes it worse. We are only darkening our soul further and further, and making her more unholy and impious.

Rather than recovering her from the fallen state of sinfulness, we are pushing her further deep into wombs of darkness. We do not even pause and take a break to think about what is her true nature and character, and what is her true beauty and splendor? And look what she has become?

Too bad! That we never reflect meaningfully upon our own true reality, and take a good look at what has changed for our soul? We are supposed to be the eternal and imperishable beings, but here we are, living in perishable bodies that are marred by mortality. We are the transcendental Self and are of the nature of permanence, but because of darkness, we have been eclipsed by earthly embodiments that are vessels of impermanence and transience.

Oh! Before we were the resident of the country of God – the nation of perpetual freedom – but now we are living the imprisonment of *Karmic*-worlds; before we were beings of blissfulness and truth with unending life, but now we have become bodies of flesh, blood and bones that are plagued by birth and death.

So how can we forget that our true nature is of purity and piousness, and look what has happened to us that we have become the embodiment of impurity and un-holiness.

Remember! Our soul is of the nature of consecration and sanctification, but now she lives in desecration and defilement. Her truth has been tarnished by untruthfulness; her imperishable existence has been marred by mortality; her everlasting blissfulness has been overshadowed by the sorrow and suffering of transient life; and her liberty has been shattered by incarceration in bondage.

Surely, we know that we are not the body but the soul, but sadly, we do not abide by this truth, because if we did, we would never live the way we are living; our soul would never be in the state she is in, which is of bondage and slavery.

Oh! She was supposed to be only a witness of all things, but sorrowfully, due to her defiled nature, living as a witness has become secondary to her direct experience of all happenings. Her true nature is utterly sinless, but quite sadly, now she does not even mind living with the filth of sin.

So, as we can see, all that has changed for our soul; even to the point that, though she is supposed to remain passive in all activeness, yet in her altered state of existence, the activeness naturally arises out of her, **"He feels that, 'I am the doer' – Holy Gita 3:27."** Though she was supposed to remain untouched by all experiences, but now it is the experiences of this world that keep her in *Karmic*-captivity.

The problem is that, rather than trying to stop the downfall of our soul, we are often multiplying it; rather than correcting the problem by righteous conduct, we are making it worse by our immoral behavior.

You see! We are handling things wrong; we are doing them totally the opposite. Instead of fixing, we are breaking them down further. Though culturally we think that we are very advanced and developed people, but quite sadly, we have totally lost our truly civilized ways.

In truth, if we had any sense, we would ask: how our soul who in truth is imperishable, but has become the victim of mortality? How has she lost her freedom and become the captive of *Karma*? How has she fallen from the glory and grace of her true existence, and now living in grunge and grime of sin?

Of course, if we raise such questions and ponder upon such concerns, then we would not find any rest as such inquiry would make us impatiently wonder about what has made us so lost that we cannot even remember who we truly are? And we would repeatedly ask: How come our recollection has been so incapacitated that we cannot recall our own reality? How can we not remember our glorious genesis (Sat-Chit-*Ananda* – Existence-Knowledge-Bliss) that we inherited from our supreme father, God?

Surely, our wonderment would grow to a point that we would not stop asking questions like these until we find out: How such a degraded state of existence of our soul has come about? How our self-knowledge has been vaporized to a point that we cannot even remember what our true character is? How our comprehension of truth has become so distorted that we cannot understand rightly what our intrinsic nature is? How the ignorance and darkness has taken such a toll on us that we have forgotten who we truly are?

And we would continually and constantly wonder why our soul has fallen into such disgust that she cannot recall the magnificence of her own glory? Why has she plunged into such depth of sin that she has lost the sense of her inherent sanctity? And what has she done so wrong that she has become the victim of such a disgraceful downfall?

I am sure if we were not so deluded by the increasing evil in our perverted hearts, all these questions certainly would keep rising in our mind restlessly until they are brought to rest by truthful and satisfying answers; and then only, we would know the truth and realize that it is her own fault that the soul has fallen from grace; that it is her own doing that she is doomed in such darkness; that it is her own sin that she has forgotten her true identity and cannot recall who she is?

Of course, then we would understand that even though in her true nature the soul is a part of the Transcendental Self, and is imperishable and immortal, yet due to darkness and delusion she behaves quite the opposite and lives in perishable bodies and endures mortal embodiments; that even though she is eternally liberated, yet she lives in captivity to *Karma* and endures earthly imprisonment; and that even though she is of the nature of bliss and peace, yet she lives a life of sorrow and suffering, and is ever restless and discontent.

Surely then, we would realize the truth, that all things for the soul are quite opposite to what they ought to be and we would become aware of the fact that a great tragedy has struck her; that she has become the victim of her own ignorance.

But alas! Since we have lost our sense of righteousness, none of this ever agitates our awareness; none of this disturbs our thoughts; none of this ever shakes our sight; none of this ever perturbs our heart; and none of this ever troubles our soul. How sorrowful!

Now the question is, why have we become so deadened? The answer lies in the fact that due to self-indulgence we have become so numb that immorality and unrighteousness do not bother us. Our desire and discontentment have hypnotized us in such a way that our senses have ceased responding to right and just things. Our passion and infatuation have made us so deaf, mute, and blind, that we cannot perceive the ugly reality of our own existence.

Oh! It is our love for this world that has blinded us and has made us the creature of ignorance and illusion.

Surely, our soul has fallen from grace because she is extremely passionate about the pleasures of this world; because she is deeply engaged in infatuation of the earthly enjoyments; because she is madly in love with her own fabricated self.

She is suffering through such severely degraded situation because she loves earthly life; because she loves what she believes she has falsely become; because she loves her erroneously established self-identification and adores its glorified gratification. She is enduring these extremely excruciating circumstances because her misconceived self-individuality has taken charge over all things of her conditioned existence; and that is why she is being held accountable for them, and has been thrown into bondage with *Karma*.

So whatever has gone wrong for the soul (*Atman*) is no one else's but her own fault. It is her own doing that she has become so dark and deluded. Surely, it is her falsely established self-individuality that is the root cause of her conditioned existence in mortal states.

It is her misconceived self-identification that has made her forget what her true nature is. It is her taking charge of life of mortality, what has tied her to the chains of *Karma*. It is her accepting the accountability of her malevolent embodiment what has thrown her into the captivity to sin. It is her becoming responsible for all deeds of her embodiment as human what has made her fall into deep detention of *Karmic*-imprisonment.

This is the reason why the soul is in so much darkness that she believes falsely into being something she is not, and is not able to recall who she truly is. Her recollection is so destroyed that that she has no idea of her genesis and cannot recall her true ancestry.

No wonder, man hardly ever thinks about his reality of being a part of God **"Mam Ev Anso – a ray of My Eternal Self – Holy Gita 15:7;"** he hardly ever ventures the idea that God is his father, **"It is I who am the seed-giving Father, while Mahat is the conceiving Mother – Holy Gita 14:4;"** and that in Him is his genesis, **"From Whom all these beings have proceeded – Holy Gita 18:46."** He hardly has any sense of his true lineage. Too bad that he never finds joy in the fact that his heritage is so majestic, and never acknowledges the fact that he is of the family of God.

Though he proudly carries his family name as his last name and often boasts about it, but hardly ever takes pride in the name of his Spiritual family – the family of God – and never fondly speaks of it. Tell me if I am wrong in this. How many of us really do that?

Man never takes pride in the fact that he is the most beautiful creature of all. Oh! He is so beautiful that he resembles His father – God – who is most regal and royal. After all, in his purest form he is of the same nature as of God. He is of the same essence, same virtue, same quality and same character as His heavenly father – which is of true life, love, light and liberty. How sad! That of this truth, man never feels proud of.

What an unfortunate thing that man hardly ever ventures over such thoughts, or rejoices his spiritual heritage and takes pride in his godly genesis. The sad truth is that he never becomes conscious of his true ancestry, and leaves this world even without ever realizing from where he came and of whose offspring he was?

Hear these words of Lord Krishna where He proclaims that we are an extension of His self-being, **"Mam Ev Anso – (You) are the extension of my Being – Holy Gita 15:7;"** and that we are His offspring.

Now, let us hear these verses of the very first book (Genesis) of Holy Bible which tell how God formed and fashioned the man in His own image and resemblance, and how He created and crafted him in his own quality and character, and how He breathed His loveliness and liveliness into him and made Him a living-being **(Holy Bible, Genesis 2:7)**:

> **And God said, Let us make man in our image, after our likeness: and let them have dominion over the fish of the sea, and over the fowl of the air, and over the cattle, and over all the earth, and over every creeping thing that *creepeth* upon the earth.**

So God created man in his own image, in the image of God created he him; male and female created he them.

And God blessed them, and God said unto them, Be fruitful, and multiply, and replenish the earth, and subdue it: and have dominion over the fish of the sea, and over the fowl of the air, and over every living thing that *moveth* **upon the earth.**

And God said, Behold, I have given you every herb bearing seed, which is upon the face of all the earth, and every tree, in the which is the fruit of a tree yielding seed; to you it shall be for meat.

And to every beast of the earth, and to every fowl of the air, and to every thing that *creepeth* **upon the earth, wherein there is life, I have given every green herb for meat: and it was so.**

(Holy Bible, Genesis 1:26-30)

After reading these words, does there still remain any doubt that God formed and shaped man with utmost fondness; that He constructed and composed him with highest affection and adoration. In fact, in so much adoration that He made him with the beauty of His own image and modeled him to be just like Himself.

Following words confirm that we are no ordinary beings but are very special creation of God. And since we are made in His image, we widely reflect His resemblance. So it is right for God to expect from us to act and behave like Him. Look at what Lord Jesus has to say about it:

<u>Be ye therefore perfect</u>, even as your <u>Father</u> which is in heaven is perfect.

(Holy Bible, Matthew 5:48)

He demands perfection from us, **"Be ye therefore perfect,"** because our Father in heaven is perfect, **"even as your Father which is in heaven is perfect"**; He wants us to be good and graceful, holy and hallowed, pure and pious, virtuous and righteous, just the way our father God is in heaven.

Since we are made in the image of God, we have the endowment of His quality and character; we are the reflection of His virtue and vitality; we are the manifestation of His personality and persona. Surely, we have no lacking of any kind; after all, according to the words of the Upanishads, we are of the form of the Truth, Knowledge and Bliss (*Sat-Chit-Ananda*).

Beloved! That is who we are; that is what our true nature; and that is why that is what we ought to be!

When Lord Jesus commands us to be perfect, **"Be ye therefore perfect,"** He is speaking of the perfection that we have inherited from God as being made in His image. Since our father God is perfect, we ought to be too since we have His genes in us, **"Even as your Father which is in heaven is perfect."**

Lord Jesus reminds us that we should be established in our true nature of purity and piousness, which we have inherited from our heavenly Father and abandon our assumed nature which is of sin and evil.

Now, just for the sake of argument, let us assume that we are not like God; then, is it ever possible that Lord Jesus would ask us to be something we are not, and become someone we are not capable of becoming?

Surely that is never possible. He only asked us to be like our father God, because we are made in His image. We do have the capability of reflection of His quality and character because we have been made that way. And that is why we have the endowment of expression of God's virtue and vitality.

Therefore, by saying, **"Be ye therefore perfect, even as your Father which is in heaven is perfect,"** Lord Jesus commands us to be only what we are fully capable of, and nothing more. We definitely have that potentiality in us. And if we didn't, He would have never asked us.

Surely, we are born in imperfection and sin; but that does not mean we are not created in the image of God. So, no matter how sinful is our outer nature, and no matter how much evil and vice surrounds our soul, it still does not mean that our true inner nature is not of perfection.

The truth is that our perfection is an inheritance from God because we are made in His image. And it is that perfection, which Lord Jesus is demanding us to wear, and get rid of this sleeve of sin that is covering our true beauty.

This is why Lord Jesus further says that we ought to be filled with love and light and be endowed with goodness and grace. He implies that by no means our behavior is to be ordinary and average, but be of exceptional excellence and exquisiteness, of outstanding character and quality, and of extraordinary virtue and value.

He says that we ought to mirror God in every way possible. Hear His words that tell us how exactly we ought to act and behave in life:

Let your light so shine before men, that they may see your good works, and glorify your Father which is in heaven.

(Holy Bible, Matthew 5:16)

But sadly, we never heed these words no matter how often we read and hear them. We never believe in our privileged ancestry, in our heavenly heritage, in our glorious genesis; we never believe that we are the children of God, and that He is our first father. And since this belief, that we are made in the image of God, and that we are like Him in so many ways, never instill in us, so we never care to behave like Him.

Of course, we accept our reality of being made in the image of God but only intellectually, and acknowledge that in our true nature we are like Him, but this truth never becomes our conviction; it never becomes our integrated belief.

And since it never instills into our inner being, it never becomes our integrated reality. This is why we never even think to behave like God, forget about being like Him; because, the belief of our true reality of being made in His image never truly materializes in us. The sense of our true heritage, which is in God, never sinks in our heart, and thus, we never truly come to grip of this reality.

The words of Lord Jesus above say that we ought to be the light for this world; meaning, our behavior should be as such that it emanates God's radiance, that it shines forth His beauty before men, **"Let your light so shine before men,"** and that, it becomes the reminder of what our inheritance is? It should be reflective of who do we come from and what our genealogy is? And thus, through godly radiance emanating from our virtuous conduct, we let others know that we are made in the image of God; that we are created in his resemblance; that we are His glorification, **"And glorify your Father which is in heaven."**

But alas! For most of us, that never happens. We never even come close to what we are expected of. We have badly letdown God in every which way possible.

Oh! Rather than becoming like Him we have become totally opposite to Him. Rather than being embodied with His virtue value, we are filled with worldly wickedness and vice. Rather than emanating light like our heavenly father in heaven, we are only multiplying the darkness even further in everything that we engage in.

We have become blind to our own reality. The sad truth is that our blindness is so dark that we consider our darkness to be the light. We think of our shrewd smartness to be our wisdom and take it as if it is our most blessed guiding-light. We are so deluded that we admire our evil ways because they earn us prosperity and power and give us name and fame.

Oh! It is unbelievable, how blind we are!

Though, very definitely we are lost, but we do not realize that we have gone astray. We are so ignorant that we have no idea of what kind of dreadful place we are heading to.

In pursuit of fleshly happiness we have become so consumed that we cannot even sense our own rapid decline. We are so immune to evil that even though it has grabbed us from all sides, and yet we do not feel its pinch. We are so resistant to vice that we engage in all kinds of immorality but we still do not feel vacillated by its venom.

We keep busy counting the gains of our day, not realizing that we have lost the count of our losses; we are consumed in admiring the achievements of our toiling, but without realizing that we are laboring in vain, and that the things for which we are sacrificing everything including our purity and piousness, our sanctity and morality, are not of much worth at all, since they have no lasting value, no true meaning, and no true significance.

We all know that no matter how hard we have worked and no matter how many sacrifices we have made in earning the earthly opulence, yet none of it would come with us when we part from this world. The only thing we would carry upon our soul would be the burden of *Karma* of those deeds that we committed in gaining all that material affluence.

So the gains of this world are actually the losses of the world next, since all the pleasurable benefits now, would demand the future payments of sorrow and suffering in the form of *Karma*. The compensation would be so huge that our soul would suffer an inestimable misery and pain of countless lower lives **(Holy Gita 13:21)**. Thus, we are making an exchange of loss rather than profit, and in ignorance happily giving away our eternal peace and joy for corporeal pleasure and enjoyment.

We are so lost in pursuit of worldly pleasures that our hunt for happiness of today is making us the captive of unhappiness of tomorrow. We have become so sightless that we do not see the devastating truth about our own spiritual destruction. And we have become so delusive that we do not realize that our quest for secular prosperity of the present is sowing the seeds of spiritual poverty in the future.

Our lust and lasciviousness have grown so much darkness around our soul that it has swallowed all the light emanating from our spirit. And because of it our inner chamber is so dark that our moral-man is wandering in utter murky and dim corridors of ignorance with no hope of finding any light of godly wisdom.

Beloved! Do you want to know, how deep is our darkness?

Well, before we try to measure that, let us briefly go over what we have learned so far about *Karma*, and what binds the soul to its bondage, because a quick review of that knowledge would help us rightly measure the depth of our darkness.

First we learned, that it is the *Karma*, which is the main problem for the soul (*Atman*), because *Karma*, which is created by her actions in human embodiment, creates bondage for her;

and it is this bondage that ties her to mortality even though she is imperishable and immutable Self.

Then we found out that even though all human actions create *Karma* but not all of them create bondage **(Holy Gita 3:9)**, as only those actions bind the soul that are done with ego-sense **(Holy Gita 18:17)**, and are rendered with attachment and self-centric attitude **(Holy Gita 14:6,7)**.

After that, we arrived the understanding that it is not the action but affection in action, which is the root cause of soul's bondage. It is the attachment and desire, which grow in her due to association with *Gunas* while living under the captivity of *Prakriti*, that force her to be bound with *Karma* **(Holy Gita 13:21)**.

And finally, we learned that it is what the soul (*Atman*) adores and admires, and what she likes and loves, craves and longs for, meditates and contemplates upon, that ties her hands with the chains of bondage.

Thus, we go from one thing to another in an effort to figure out what is the root cause of bondage of the soul. And we continue our investigation into the truth until we reach to its bottom, and there we learn that regardless of what the actual cause is, the ultimate truth is, that it is the soul's own darkness and delusion that is responsible for her fall into mortality and her drifting in all kinds of *Karmic*-worlds.

So regardless of what is the cause of her bondage, the responsibility is still hers for her downfall from grace; she is the one who is liable for her incarceration in sin; she is the one who is to be blamed for her bondage; and she is the one who is accountable for her captivity by *Karma*.

Surely, it is her own ignorance, which allows such a manipulation of her character and virtue, that even though she is immortal, she yet endures immortality; that even though she is imperishable, she yet lives in perishable homes; that even though she is beyond the claws of birth and death, she yet passes through countless embodiments; that even though she is pure light and wisdom, she yet lives in extreme darkness and delusion.

To understand better the depth of darkness surrounding the soul, let us take a good look at the following words of Holy Gita even though we have browsed over them several times, because they speak of the reality of soul (*Atman - Purusha*) so profoundly that it is hard to comprehend their entirety through casual reading:

> **Purusha (Atman) <u>abiding</u> in Prakriti <u>enjoys</u> the Gunas born of Prakriti. Because of its attachment to the Gunas it attains higher or lower births.**
>
> **(Holy Gita 13:21)**

Beloved! This scriptural text exposes so much truth in so few words that I wish we all could get a good handle on what it has to say!

Don't these words look so simple, **"*Purusha abiding in Prakriti – Prakriti Isthato Purursha*,"** which casually speak of the reality of the soul (*Purusha – Atman –* the Self), and state a simple fact that she is living under the rule of *Prakriti*. But please, do not be fooled by their simplicity as there is a huge meaning hidden underneath; it just isn't obvious, so we do not see it.

Holy Gita uses the word **'abiding'** to describe the condition of the soul under the captivity of *Prakriti*. She uses the *Samskrit* word **'Isthato'**, which means 'situated', but the translation uses the word **'abiding'**, which actually is more appropriate, since it not only reveals the fact that the soul is 'situated', but also unfolds the condition how it is situated? Meaning, it not only exposes the truth that the soul is living under *Prakriti*, but also that she is abiding under its influence as well.

Thus, the word **'abiding'** captures the total view of the soul by communicating the fact that she is not living freely but abiding under the influence of some authority and rule.

Certainly, it is clear from above that the soul is a captive of *Prakriti*. But please keep in mind, she still is not completely under the authority of *Prakriti* since she has the endowment of 'freewill' and is fully able to choose to act any way she likes; because, that is what the power of 'freewill' all about. Isn't it!

So it is better to say that the soul is under a heavy influence of *Prakriti* but surely not under its complete control. This is why, though it is true that most of the choices the soul makes are under heavy influence of *Prakriti*, however, the soul can assert her endowed privilege authoritatively and choose to go against the dominant power of her captor if she wants to and act any way she likes.

It means even though the soul lives under the power of *Prakriti* and abides almost totally in its influence, she still has the endowment of power to act according to her freewill. In other words, the soul has the indwelling power that can overcome the influence imposed by the *Prakriti* under which she abides.

Well, it is nice to know this truth! However, one thing we still do not know: how does the soul abide under the captivity of *Prakriti* – happily or unhappily – willingly or unwillingly?

Though one would expect the soul to be living unhappily and unwillingly under *Prakriti*, since she is her captive and is forced to abide under its influence, but surprisingly such is never the case.

Well, let us look at the answer that comes from these holy words: **"Enjoys the *Gunas* born of *Prakriti*,"** which tell extensively about the state of existence of the soul. They reveal the fact that the soul enjoys (the things of) *Gunas*, which of course are born of *Prakriti*.

As per the natural order of conditioned existence of the soul, when she lives as a living-being (*Jiva*) in this objective world, she has no way but to experience the things of *Gunas*, because everything in it is made with them **(Holy Gita 18:40)**, and thus, there is no escape for the embodied soul from experiencing the *Gunas* as each and everything is made of them.

Now, Holy Gita uses the word **'bhunyate'**, which has been translated as **'enjoys'**. But this word is inclusive of enjoyment of both kinds: of pleasure as well as sorrow; it means the soul enjoys both, the good as well as the bad things of *Gunas*. Meaning, the soul experiences both: the sorrow and joy of the objective world, and experiences good as well as its bad as she has no choice in this matter.

Well, it's true that we all want to enjoy the good of life; however, also is true that no one wants to experience its bad. Can we find anyone who willingly and joyfully wants to endure sorrow and suffering? Surely, none! Everyone wants happiness but no one willingly wants to endure the days of misery and pain.

Even Lord Jesus, when faced with death on the cross, asks the Father God to take the bitter cup away from Him:

And he said, Abba, Father, all things are possible unto thee; take away this cup from me: nevertheless not what I will, but what thou wilt.

(Holy Bible, Mark 14:36)

However, Jesus was so given to God, that to Him His father's will was the highest, and for that He willingly bore death by sacrificing His life at the cross.

So if no one willingly wishes to suffer then why the soul does not resist the temptations of this world which only brings her more sorrow, more suffering, and more mortal life, which is so filled with misery and pain that Lord *Krishna* calls it the ocean of sorrow, **"This world which is the abode of pain – Holy Gita 8:15."**

Do we see the problem yet? Well, let me put it quite plainly! It is an not universal truth that no one likes to endure suffering willingly and joyfully. In fact we all try to do everything we can to avoid misery and pain. But how surprising it is that we hardly ever do anything to avoid the misery and pain for good by attaining *Moksha* (Liberation)!

You know how foolish it is that even though we do not want ever any sorrow and suffering, and we do everything we possibly can to escape them, and yet we hardly ever engage in any effort to eliminate them for good. On the contrary, due to ignorance and darkness, in an effort to overcome misery and pain and to add more pleasure and enjoyment to our lives, we often multiply suffering by creating more new *Karma*.

Oh! True as it is, but surely very surprising that though life is nothing but misery and pain, of course with few enjoyments and pleasures here and there, and yet we never want to give it up. We all want to live forever. We all love life beyond all measures regardless of how much miserable and difficult it is.

Here is another surprising fact: that even after knowing that at the end of our human life, the *Karmic*-cycle would begin again, and would force our soul to endure inestimable misery and pain for countless future embodiments, we yet do nothing to change it.

But why – we all can wonder about that?

Who can argue the reality that we all are busy living this life without hardly ever thinking about life that is certain to follow it. How many among us are really worried about the fact that dark clouds of *Karma*, which are hovering over us, are waiting to take our soul on to a continual trip to repeated transmigration for immeasurable time where we would endure the inestimable pain of countless lower lives?

Surely, not many!

Oh! How terrifying is the fact that death and destruction of the soul is looming upon our head, and each passing day is bringing us even closer to this horrible reality, and yet, we do not seem to care.

Are we wrong in this observation? Definitely not!

Then, why are we so busy in doing everything else but this, and are so consumed by our passion for this objective world, **"Enjoys the Gunas born of Prakriti,"** which only would bring us more death and destruction? Why such a casual behavior and careless conduct on our part about something that is only going to result in sheer dreadfulness?

Well, the answer lies in words of the same verse that raises the question **(Holy Gita 13:21)**, which say, **"Because of its attachment to the Gunas it attains higher or lower births,"** and reminds us that it is our infatuation that has marred our immortality and made us perishable.

Of course, we already are familiar with this fact. We already know that desire is the root cause of our bondage; that attachment is the reason why our soul is living the incarceration of mortality; that passion and infatuation is causing her to endure the captivity of the cycle of birth and death. We know this quite well.

And yet, do we find any change in our behavior? The answer is no! Now, the question is why? Why it is that this truth does not affect us? Why it is that it does not have any bearing upon our thinking? Why are we so insensitive to it? Why are we not scared of this horrible reality that is standing right before us, from which we would have no escape but to face it right after we die?

Beloved! The answer is that we are filled with tremendous darkness. In fact with so much darkness, that we are unable to see our own destruction that is right before us. And it is because our eyes are so dim that we cannot recognize our own devastation.

The most mind-boggling thought about it is that, though we are facing destruction and death of our spiritual being, and yet we are busy celebrating the captivity of our soul. Isn't she living the incarceration of *Karma*? Isn't she captive of death and mortality? And isn't it true that even after knowing this truth the soul is a prisoner of bondage, we are still busy celebrating life by enhancing its beauty as much as we can?

How surprising it is that even though the soul is living under the slavery of *Prakriti*, and yet, she is busy celebrating her engagements with the things of its born *Gunas*, the products of her captor **(Holy Gita 3:5)**. Oh! Can we ever imagine the depth of darkness that is surrounding our soul?

Surely, we all can look at our own lives and realize the truth of our uncontrollable passion for the things of this material world, regardless of who we are, and know in our hearts how madly we are in love with its sensuality.

How sad it is that we are under the captivity of *Karma* and we are happily living it. We have no objection to a life which is of imprisonment. In fact, day and night, we are busy celebrating it. Each day, from morning till evening, we are searching for more happiness, more pleasure, and more enjoyment out of our *Karmic*-imprisonment. Can we deny that?

Is there anyone who is bothered by the slavery of his soul to *Karma*? Surely there are some who think about it and are trying to release the blessed ones, who through the light and wisdom of the Spirit have become awakened to the higher reality and have chosen to take the journey of enlightenment. Only they have abandoned the magnificence of the material world and are seeking the exquisiteness of the eternal kingdom by taking the total refuge in God.

Beloved! Only few are such blessed souls that have saved themselves from the seduction of this world; otherwise, most of us have been duped by its sensuality.

Oh! Blessed are those that have been awakened to the Truth through much graces of God. Otherwise, most of us are living under such darkness that we cannot even see how dark is the reality of our own existence?

Do we want to have another measure of how lost we are? How dark is our darkness? How thick is our ignorance? How deep is our delusion?

Well, listen to this! The scriptures say that all works that we perform are done by the *Gunas* of *Prakriti*, **"All actions are performed by the *Gunas* of *Prakriti* – Holy Gita 3:27;"** and it is the *Gunas* that constantly propel a person to act, **"The *Gunas* born out of *Prakriti* (through attachment and hatred) impel a person to constantly perform actions – Holy Gita 3:5."**

But even though we read and listen to these words, over and over, and intellectually comprehend their truth, yet we fail to believe them. Surely we understand what the truth is, yet we fail to integrate it in ourselves, and you know, why? Because of our darkness!

Our ignorance is so deep that even after hearing this truth time after time, we continue to believe that it is we, who are the 'performer' of our actions and the 'doers' of our deeds, **"But if one's intellect is dull due to the development of egoism, he feels that, "I am the doer" – Holy Gita 3:27."**

So, even though we comprehend mentally that we are not the 'doer' of our actions but the *Prakriti* is, **"All actions, in every form are performed by *Prakriti* alone, while the Self is non-performer of action – Holy Gita 13:29,"** we still do not accept it internally, and thus, fail to make it our concrete conviction.

As a result, we never really accept it as an absolute spiritual law just as we accept the 'Law of gravity' or any other physical law as an absolute reality of earthly existence.

The truly sad thing is that we know it all and yet do not try to change our behavior. We do not even think of improving our belief. And, you know why? Because we are so filled with darkness that our fallen sight cannot see beyond our death; in fact, it is so dim that it does not even see that far.

Look around and you can always find folks that have done quite satisfactorily in their professional lives and now they are well into their retirement age. They are all done raising their children as even they have successfully entered their adulthood. Meaning, in every sense they are done with their responsibilities. For them, now the time has come that they concentrate upon their spiritual life and invest the remaining days on this earth in walking towards enlightenment and in attaining *Mukti* (Liberation).

But if you talk to them, you would be surprised to hear their plans. There are no signs of them slowing down; no lessening in their ambitions and desires. In their mind there is no consideration of the fact that the end of their life is very near; that it is not that far, and that the day of departure from this world is nearing day by day.

I am sure the fear of death is there, which flashes in their dark mind but only like some occasional lightening, just once a while, as they are ever busy in gathering and collecting more and more futile abundance of the material world.

This is not a very uncommon practice. Most of us are guilty of it. By nature we are obsessed with earthly attainments. We have so much darkness that we cannot think straight. We have become so earthly smart that we can always find some logic to justify our lustful ways, no matter how delusive and misguiding they are.

What we do not know that our secular-smartness, of which we are so proud of, and which we use as our main guiding-light for our lives, is nothing but a dark cloud that has hidden our intellect and made our spiritual vision so dim that we cannot discern our ways rightly and justly, and as a result we are so lost that we do not even think about where are we going, and what is our end?

To validate this view, we can ask ourselves, if we have ever contemplated upon our own death and the aftermath of it as seriously as the topic of death itself? I am not talking about a casual interrogation into the subject but a serious deliberation which takes into account all things which possibly can and probably will happen to us after we die and begin the next phase of our *Karmic*-journey.

Well, if you answer is "Yes", then I would say, you are blessed among men; but if not, then please take a glance at what is lying ahead on the road that we would have to take once we move ahead beyond this world?

You see! The reality is quite evident but only to the one who wants to see it. Only he understands that we are living in dreadful darkness. How else to think when we know all the dangers ahead of us, and yet we do nothing to escape them? What other cue can we get from it when we understand it all and yet act as if we have no awareness of it?

I can't blame the folks from other beliefs, but I certainly feel sorry for the folks of *Hindu* belief, because they are quite reasonably aware of the horrible consequences of *Karmic*-bondage, and yet most of them do not try to do anything to save themselves from its agony and anguish.

Though it is quite disheartening, but this surely gives an idea of the darkness we have within us. How sad, that it is so deep, that it habituates us to escape all thoughts of most terrifying life, which our soul would definitely endure due her *Karmic*-transgressions.

Oh! We are so lost that instead of resisting the imprisonment imposed by *Karmic*-ordinance, which has forced our soul to live under the authority of *Prakriti* and indulge in its *Gunas* and commit further *Karmic*-crimes, we are happily living and enjoying it, and ceaselessly celebrating it futile fertility. That's how lost we are!

So the truth is quite evident that because of indwelling darkness and self-delusion, we have become a friendly prisoner of *Karma*; in fact, so friendly that we accept our captivity most willfully and happily, and exceedingly rejoice its vanity.

Surely, the darkness that surrounds the soul is the prime reason of why she is wandering in the wilderness of untruthful and fallacious worlds, and why she is so blind to the truth that every time she gets a chance to find her way out of *Karmic* captivity, she wastes it without even realizing that she is lost and drifting like a nomad.

Oh! It is her own darkness that has encapsulated her light; it is her own ignorance that has eclipsed her knowledge. And since she does not have true understanding, she lacks the discernment to judge between the fiction and nonfiction, between the fabrication and factuality.

No wonder! She has become so unaware of her own true nature that she has completely forgotten who she is. At this point she has no recollection of her own identity, since she has no consciousness left of the reality of her own true being.

Surely, the objective world is very seductive; its temptations are unending. That is why its attraction is so irresistible that we find ourselves almost helpless in falling in love with its things. More we meditate and contemplate upon it, more we become attached and desirous of it; and more we ponder and deliberate over it, more we become infatuated by it.

The fact is that our association and affiliation with the material world only creates more obsession with its things, since we do not know how to interact with it without passion and infatuation, without lust and lasciviousness, without gluttony and greed; meaning, we become possessed by its sensuality because of our selfish and egoistic engagement with it **(Holy Gita 2:62)**.

So what are we to do?

Well, there is no lacking of holy ritual and rites in our daily life, which is ever so filled with all kinds of sacred activities that are professed by our holy authorities. And of course, there is no lacking of holy teachings either. In fact, we do not even need to go anywhere to listen to them as the sermons come daily to our living rooms through the television.

But of what good is our religiosity and of what good are our holy teachings if they are not able to awaken us from this delusion, and make us understand the most important truth about our life, which is that we have been made human with a specific purpose, and that purpose is to salvage our soul from the grip of mortality by liberating her from the bondage of *Karma*.

Of course, we know enough what *Karma* is, and what is its bondage, and also what are its consequences, but of what good is all this knowing if it does not benefit us in any real sense, because just knowing and boasting about it and preaching it to others does not do any good.

Surely, we can continue forever to gain more and more scriptural knowledge and try to become real expert in our holy understanding, but it is of no good until we recognize the fact that our soul is suffering due of her own ignorance, and that is why she has been choosing to walk the path of darkness in all her previous embodiments, and as a consequence to her erroneous choices she has been living the captivity to *Karmic*-cycle for countless lives.

And once we acknowledge and accept this truth and stop looking at everything else, and focus on the fact that it is our own darkness, which has become our curse, and that it is our own unawareness of truth, which has made our soul to wander like a lost traveler in *Karmic*-worlds, we can begin to head up towards the path of light.

True! That all such knowledge about what are the reasons, why our soul is in *Karmic*-bondage, and how has she fallen into this trap, is all very benefiting, but also is true that it is we who have to take the responsibility of getting her out of it.

Therefore, we must choose a right course for our life and take the first step towards that goal by realizing that now is the time to break the ongoing cycle of bondage so that our soul could find the path to her perpetual freedom.

The law of nature is that the path of darkness leads life into further darkness while the path of light leads it into more light. This truth has been spoken by all scriptures. According to holy word the path of light leads the soul to freedom while the path of darkness leads her into further bondage:

These two paths - the path of Light and that of Darkness are considered *beginningless*. Following the path of Light one does not return while following the path of darkness one returns.

(Holy Gita 8:26)

In the light of such scriptural understanding, we can see that due to her indwelling darkness the soul has constantly made wrong choices, life after life, and as a consequence to those ill choices, rather than finding the freedom from bondage, she has gotten further into the bondage.

So to have any hope of redemption for our soul from such fallen state, we must put an end to walking further towards the darkness, and turn around and begin a new march towards the light.

Oh! Only then our soul can be saved from falling into gallows of bondage. But to reach such light and wisdom, we definitely need the grace of God, because without it the radiance of the Spirit would never enter our soul.

Even though, out of ego, most often man thinks he can do it on his own. But it is not so! Because the light enters human heart only through the goodness of God; and wisdom comes into him only through His graces **(Holy Gita 10:10-11)**.

Yes! One can become expert in scriptures, and master any theology on his own, yet the true knowledge does not dawn into his heart through his own wonderfulness; it does not grow in him until it has been given to him by God. Please know that only in His granting comes His knowledge; and only in the giving of His endowment comes His wisdom.

Man is born with darkness that can be destroyed only by the grace of God and not by man's own goodness; it can be overcome only by the light of God and not by man's own wisdom.

Yes, he can make himself worldly smart, but cannot enable himself to be smart in God. Yes, he can make himself wise in the holy text, but he cannot raise himself high in the godly understanding.

Only God can grant such a privilege; only He can give such a gift; and only He can bestow such a blessing; and which He does only out of His love and compassion, and mercy and kindness for man, so that he, whom He loves so much, could be rid of darkness and see His light, and thus, could recognize the brilliance of His being and come to know Him.

As an act of divine compassion dwelling within their self I destroy the darkness born of ignorance with the shining lamp of wisdom.

(Holy Gita 10:11)

Being well-versed in the holy text does not make one smart in the knowledge of God because all that knowledge remains superficial until it is infused into his inner being, which happens only when one constantly lives in the reality of that knowledge and abides by it faithfully and truthfully. But such devoted abidance in the truth embedded in the gained holy knowledge demands one to faithfully live by it in daily life, which is possible only by first letting go of his own worldly understanding and smartness, and living by the radiance and light of the Spirit.

It means one learns of the hidden truth in any knowledge only by living it, by experiencing it, and by making it a part of his responses to daily life. By living it constantly and continually it becomes embedded in his being; it assimilates into composition of his inner man; it becomes an integral part of his intrinsic being.

The bare truth is, that no knowledge, no light, no wisdom can ever come to man without him first making a connection with God, because how can he get it without touching Him first, if God is the sole source of it all. Surely, God is the only light there is as no one else has any glitter and glow, and any brilliance and brightness. From none other emerges any radiance as all else has only darkness. Know, that the light in the sun and moon is not of their own, but of God, **"I am the light in the sun and the moon – Holy Gita 7:8."**

Surely, all luminosity, which pervades the universe, originates from Him and Him alone, as the light in all else is the light of God. He is all light and luminosity, all shine and sparkle, all illumination and radiance; Oh! He is all in all. Regarding this truth let us hear this joyous proclamation by Lord Jesus Christ:

Then *spake* Jesus again unto them, saying, <u>I am the light of the world</u>: he that *followeth* me shall not walk in darkness, but shall have the light of life.

(Holy Bible, John 8:12)

His words reveal the great truth that He is the light of this world, **"I am the light of the world,"** and whoever walks in Him shall never walk in darkness. Who has Jesus in him has His light; meaning, who has God in him has His radiance. Only God can lighten up the human heart and no other.

These words of Lord Jesus echo the same truth that has been spoken by Lord *Krishna* before Him:

He is the Light of all lights beyond the darkness (of ignorance). He is the knowledge the object of knowledge and the goal of knowledge. He abides in the heart of everyone.

(Holy Gita 13:17)

So if God is the Light, and if He is the source of all light, then how can man remove the darkness in him on his own, unless of course, the power of light is given to him by God first; only then, such endowment can be embedded and embodied in him. It is that simple!

If a man thinks that he is sufficient in removing darkness in him and believes that he is fully able of attaining light, then obviously he is very deluded, because in himself he has no capacity and capability to overcome his darkness; and that is why he needs help from God.

Through following words Lord God reveals this secret and tells that in His kindness and compassion only, He showers light upon the darkness of man's spirit; that out of His goodness and grace, He bestows wisdom upon the ignorance of human soul:

As an act of divine compassion, dwelling within their self, I destroy the darkness born of ignorance with the shining lamp of wisdom.

(Holy Gita 10:11)

It is an act of divine compassion on His part. Oh! How I wish, we all knew this.

Therefore, we must become very established in the truth that we would never find the way to the light from darkness if we do not have the consideration and compassion, goodness and grace of God, which of course is reached only through unceasing love and affection, determined devotion and

234

dedication, unwavering faith and trust, constant worship and veneration, and persistent prayers and praises rendered to Him:

To them whose minds rest in Divine Self who worship Me ceaselessly with devotion I give the *Yoga* of Wisdom by which they attain Me.

(Holy Gita 10:10)

When a man is hungry of God's love and light, when he is thirsty of His knowledge and wisdom, when he is restless in his pursuit to know Him, and when he is desperate to reach His closeness, God in His mercy and kindness reveals Himself to Him; in His goodness and grace, He makes Himself known to him.

To only such a rendered soul is granted the wisdom of God, and given His light. Only she becomes devoid of darkness; only she finds freedom from bondage; only she attains the liberation from the fetters of *Karma;* and only she reaches the abode of everlasting peace:

One who is filled with faith, devoted to the pursuits of knowledge, and endowed with the self-control attains wisdom. Having attained it, he hastens to everlasting peace.

(Holy Gita 4:39)

9

Yogas
~
The Spiritual Ladders to Enlightenment

The Holy Gita says that man can seek God in two ways: inside of him or outside of him. To find the truth, either he could take the blissful journey into the inside world; or go on to the holy expedition in the outside world. In one, man finds the self-perfection by exploring the internal world, while in other he does so by venturing the external world. Both ways are good, as they both take him to the enlightenment; they both lead him to Nirvana.

According to Lord *Krishna*, these two paths are: the path of *Samkhya* (Knowledge), and the path of Selfless-action (*Karma*). Former is for those who seek the Truth internally, and the later is for those who seek it externally.

Lord Krishna replied: O sinless *Arjuna*, since ancient times I have taught two paths: the Yoga of Knowledge for those who are qualified for *Samkhya* (attainment of *Brahmakara Vritti* or intuitive revelation of the Self), and the Yoga of Action for those qualified for action.

(Holy Gita 3:3)

All other spiritual paths that are spoken of in scriptures lie in between these extremities that denote the two opposite ends of the same spectrum, which depicts the collection of all *Yogic*-disciplines. While the path of Knowledge (*Samkhya*) is most subtle and intangible, the path of Selfless-action (*Karma*) is most material and gross (tangible). So the subtleness of the discipline increases as we move from one end of the spectrum to the other.

Even though Holy Gita is quite small in volume, she yet exposes many spiritual disciplines called *Yogas*, which have been adopted and applied by sages and saints of all times as ways to reach such enlightenment, where these *Yogic*-approaches became the ladders for their ascension to the land of eternal liberty.

Highly glorified in *Hindu* philosophy, and spoken throughout the *Hindu* scriptures, the *Yogas* are such spiritual restraints that slowly but surely dissolve all impurities surrounding the soul and lead her to such a spiritual perfection where through the enhanced vision of Truth she finds her way to the sanctuary of God and attains eternal rest and peace through His grace.

Following is a quick study that even though does not cover all *Yogas* but sufficiently sheds light on some of them, especially the ones that are highly popular among *Hindu* seekers and often talked about in holy sermons.

The discussion below yields an adequate knowledge about what these *Yogic*-disciplines are? What are their underlying philosophies? How do they operate? How different they are from each other? What does their distinction from each other really mean? And finally, how do they enable one to reach such levels of enlightenment where he is able to properly seek the asylum in God, and find in His sanctuary the everlasting rest and peace for his soul?

First: Karma Yoga (the Yoga of action), which dictates Action-in-nonattachment, lays down a firm track for eternal expedition.

Karma Yoga, denoted by Action-in-nonattachment (Selfless-action), is an easy but highly effective approach among all spiritual disciplines to reach enlightenment just because it is embedded in action itself; and of course, the action we perform all the times as there is no time when we are without performing action.

Life is attached to action, and action is attached to life; meaning, there is no life without action, and there is no action without life. So the very fact that we are intrinsically ever-engaged in action **(Holy Gita 3:5)**, yields a straightforward conclusion that *Karma-Yoga* is the easiest of all spiritual disciplines to adopt since we already are involved in doing physically what we ought to do to apply it except that we would need to change our attitude and inclination, our mind and heart about it so that our daily life could conform to philosophical restraints of this *Yogic*-approach. And, that's all!

Additionally, not only its adoptability is easy, but getting on with it is also quite straightforward. Surely, to become its student, we do not need any schooling or training or any other change in our daily lifestyle; we need none of that. We do not need to add, alter or quit anything that we do in our day, as all that remains just as it is.

The only thing that changes is our inner attitude towards actions we perform during our day; meaning, it requires an adjustment in our mental approach to daily life; and that's it!

Now the question is: What is that change which is required by *Karma-Yoga*, which we need to integrate in our attitude while engaging in actions?

Well, the answer lies in verses that follow after Lord God says: **"Now listen to the wisdom of Yoga – Holy Gita 2:39"** and explains first the glory of action rendered in selflessness, and then commands us to perform action-in-love without attachment, **"Perform actions devoid of attachment – Holy Gita 2:48,"** and without selfishness, **"Perform selfless actions – Holy Gita 2:49."**

But the commandment of 'Selfless-action' is not as stand-alone as we think since it comes with a note attached to it, which says that it needs to be accompanied with a very special state-of-being where one is **"established in Yoga"**.

Look at the following verse where this condition is attached to the commandment of **"Perform actions devoid of attachment"** as a prequalification:

O *Dhananjaya* (conqueror of wealth) be established in *Yoga* and perform actions devoid of attachment. Be balanced in success and failure, for balance of mind is known as *Yoga*.

(Holy Gita 2:48)

And this condition says that we ought to **"be established in Yoga"** while meeting the main condition of *Karma-Yoga*, which of course, calls for action-in-nonattachment, **"Devoid of attachment."**

Well, the meaning of **"Devoid of attachment"** is easy to understand because it tells us that we ought to perform actions without desiring their fruits; but what is the meaning of **"Be established in Yoga?"** We need to figure this out, don't we! However, the good thing is that the lower part of the verse does explain what does it mean?

It says that **"Balance of mind is known as Yoga;"** that *Yoga* is the **"balance of mind,"** meaning, we ought to have the mental equanimity towards any pair of opposites; for example: hot and cold, gain and loss, winning and defeat etc.

So now, if we combine the two requirements, we learn that *Karma-Yoga* not only dictates the performance of actions without wanting their outcome, but implicitly also demands an attitude of acceptance of the outcome regardless of all other considerations.

You see! The two things have to play together; otherwise, the quality of action would not be of the highest degree. This is why Lord God says that, first **"be balanced in success and failure,"** and **"be established in Yoga,"** and then **"perform actions"** but with **"devoid of attachment."**

As we can see, the two restraints have to be applied simultaneously to produce the highest result of this *Yogic-*discipline; meaning, the application of one without the other would not enable us to attain the level of enlightenment that we would reach otherwise.

Surely, the Selfless-action by itself is good but not as good as it is when it is complemented with the balance of mind; meaning, to make it most meaningful, one must perform actions without desiring their fruits but also without being attached to their favorable or unfavorable outcome, whatever the case may be. This distinction is noteworthy since total selflessness in action comes only when it is performed with equanimity of mind; and when ego is completely a non-player in it.

This conclusion is further verified by what Lord God says in verse that follows the verse quoted above:

O *Arjuna*, Karma (performed with desire) is far inferior to the practice of *Buddhi* Yoga (the Yoga of wisdom). Therefore, <u>seeking refuge in the intellect</u> (that flows to Brahman), <u>perform selfless actions</u>; for miserable are those who desire the fruits of action.

(Holy Gita 2:49)

According to Him, performance of action without wisdom is not of much good. *Karma-Yoga* (action-in-nonattachment) is fully fruitful only when it is performed with *Buddhi-Yoga* (The *Yoga* of Wisdom – The *Yoga* of equanimity of mind).

This is why the commandment of God, **"Perform selfless actions,"** again comes with a clause, **"Seeking refuge in the intellect,"** which imposes a condition that selfless-action must be performed with an attitude of equanimity to make it most beneficial.

The holy text below says that, **"The performance of actions with a balanced mind is indeed the skill in Yoga;"** meaning, the Selfless-action is at its highest glory only when it is rendered in wisdom; the action-in-nonattachment is most effective only when it is accompanied with the equanimity of mind; the action-in-love is fully efficient only when it is rendered in light; The *Karma-Yoga* is totally complete only when it complemented with *Buddhi-Yoga*.

Following words of God validate this claim by saying that the best way to perform an action is to perform it with the balance of mind:

If one can maintain a balanced mind, <u>one is able to abandon virtue and vice</u>. Therefore, engage yourself in the practice of *Buddhi* Yoga. <u>The performance of</u>

actions with a balanced mind is indeed the skill in Yoga.

(Holy Gita 2:50)

And why it is so? Because such an action is not bonding! Surely, such action also creates *Karma*, but in its *Karma* there is no power of bondage since it is totally sinless.

The holy word unveils the reason for it. When one has mastered the equanimity of mind, he becomes able to rise above the virtue and vice, **"One is able to abandon virtue and vice;"** meaning, he is beyond the 'good' and 'bad' of what he does; and thus, he is beyond the consequences of his actions, and is no more bound by his *Karma*.

And when one is not bound by the definitions of 'virtue' and 'vice', and by the good and bad of action, surely he has attained the vision of equanimity and has become established in wisdom – which happens to be a definite door to eternal liberation.

Thus, the *Karma-Yoga*, which is at its peak when it is integrated with *Buddhi Yoga*, defines how we ought to live our daily life, and how we ought to engage in our day if we wish to reach such enlightenment that could become the gateway to the kingdom of God:

Endowed with a balanced mind, renouncing the fruits of action, the Sage breaks the fetters of birth and death, and goes to the disease-less abode of Brahman.

(Holy Gita 2:51)

Now the question is, how does the Action-in-nonattachment (Selfless-action) leads one to enlightenment and paves the way for his eternal liberation (*Moksha*)?

Well, one thing that we all must have a good grasp of that the Selfless-action removes the inner pollution, and increases purity and piousness, **"With detachment he performs actions for the purity of his heart – Holy Gita 5:11."** This is why the Holy Gita says that actions of austerity and charity should not be abandoned, **"because *Yajna*, *Dana* and *Tapa* promote purity of mind – Holy Gita 18:5;"** because they grow purity and perfection. And this we must not forget!

You see! The Selfless-action has been not only a popular *Hindu* tradition, **"For *Janaka* and others attained perfection by following the *Yoga* of Action – Holy Gita 3:20,"** but also has been highly professed by other religions as well. Look at these words of Holy Bible that command man to engage in good works so that he could be perfect in the sight of God:

That the man of God may be perfect, *throughly* furnished unto all good works.

(Holy Bible, 2 Timothy 3:17)

Thus, the main yield of the Selfless-action is not the good *Karma* for future *Karmic*-lives, but the cleansing of the soul and removal of impurities off her. That is the real gain of *Karma-yoga*.

Of course, once the impurities have been washed off the soul, she begins to shine; she begins to glow. The radiance of the Spirit begins to reflect upon her face and heavenly light begins to emanate from her.

No more she remains dark and dim, but becomes lighted and illuminated. For her, everything changes for better. The surrounding ignorance vanishes away and the wisdom begins to shine forth through her. The delusion and Self-unawareness get destroyed, and the understanding begins to dawn in her as she becomes reestablished back in Knowledge **(Holy Gita 5:16).**

Now what does it mean for the soul to be reestablished back in Knowledge?

Well, remember from the previous chapter, that ego gives birth to desires, **"All desires that are born of egoistic will – Holy Gita 6:24,"** and desire hides knowledge, **"Desire veils knowledge – Holy Gita 3:38;"** meaning, due to ego we become dark and deluded, and all kinds of impurities make home in our inner chamber.

Well, the impurities we are talking about are: greed, gluttony, lust, lasciviousness, jealousy, hatred, animosity, anger, and kinds of other vices that pervade and pervert the human heart. Of course, they all are born of ego and pride; they all proceed from the selfishness and self-centricity. The inherent ego is the source of all evil in man; meaning, ego is the reason of his vice and wickedness, delusion and darkness, and ignorance and illusion.

Now consider what would happen if the process is repeated reversely; meaning, the impurities surrounding the soul are removed by adaptation and application of Selfless-action of *Karma yoga*; the darkness and delusion are wiped out by the action-in-nonattachment; and the ignorance and Self-unawareness are replaced by the wisdom and knowledge that grow by performance of action-in-love-and-light?

Of course, we would think that a reverse process would end in reverse-result and would lessen ego in us. And, so is the case! It surely does bring the demise of ego.

Due to action-in-nonattachment and with the equanimity of mind, our soul becomes well-established in her truthful Self, because as the purity and piousness increases, and the spiritual perfection multiplies, the assertion of her ego declines; and as a result, the false sense of self-identification, which is caused by ego, also begins to fade away.

Now, one thing is quite important to understand before we move on, that there is a great danger in falling into a folly if we are not careful and are not fully aware of the extremity of expression and assertion of ego in our actions. Let's look at this very possible peril by briefly considering the following example.

But before we do that, let us be clear about something that is quite often misspoken and misunderstood, which is that in a person, the ego never dies; it always lives. No matter in what state-of-being the mind is: the emotion (*Mana*), reflection (*Chitta*), or intellect (*Buddhi*), but the ego (*Ahamkar*) is always there.

So then, what do we mean when we use expressions that imply 'the death of ego?' For example if we say: The ego dies in a person when he becomes well-established in equanimity of mind. It only means that one has mastered how to have a balanced mind.

Well, through such expressions we only mean that the significance of ego has been drastically reduced; the acknowledgement of its assertion has been severely cut-down; its power and influence over 'freewill' has been sternly diminished. This is what we mean when we use such expressions. So please keep in mind, that there is no death of ego as it is always there; may be in extreme subtlety, and in most unrecognized state of existence, but it is always there. One only masters on how to overcome and make it powerless through non-recognition and non-acknowledgement, but he is never able to kill it.

Now, let us examine the extremity of subtle nature with which ego works by considering a very common scenario where one does a great charity work.

For example, let us consider a scenario where I donated a large sum of money to a charity organization. Great! Who wouldn't say that I did well, because I surely did – at least so will be thought commonly!

But let us analyze a bit this highly generous action of mine by considering three quite different attitudes with which I could have performed it:

First scenario: Let us consider a case, where I did this for two reasons. First, that I calculated in mind that someday I will get some favor in return from the executives of this organization to which I gave money; and second, that I felt good and was very proud of the fact that I am such a great giver and wanted others to think of how such a great person that I am.

Now, it's true that outwardly it seems as if I have done a great deed and definitely shown that I am quite a generous person, but let us ask God if He thinks of it as highly as it looks? Well, asking Him is the same thing as judging this action against the truth that He has embedded in His word. Isn't it!

No doubt, the scriptures will not think much highly of this action of mine where I did this work of charity with two very sneaky intents. The first represents my selfishness, and the second depicts my self-centricity; the first expresses my sense of 'self-possession', and the second my 'self-assertion'. So even though outwardly it seems to be an act of goodness and godliness, but only I know inside my heart, that in both ways, it is not, since I did it purely for the selfish reasons and got engaged in it to either get something in return to benefit myself or to exalt and applaud my ego.

Of course, the desire is being expressed in both but its form is different. The ego is being asserted in both but in different ways. The first form highlights the sense of 'me' and 'mine', and the second underscores the sense of 'I'. One expresses selfishness and the other self-centricity. The ego is asserting itself in two forms: first as selfishness, and the other as pride.

Second scenario: Now consider a case where I did the same charity, but I genuinely did not wish any return of favors from anyone; however, my intent was still to glorify my name in the society.

Well again, though my action looks good from outside but in the sight of scriptures, since it is to exalt ego, it is of not much value again except that it would earn some good *Karma* for my future life; however, it surely would increase further darkness in me due to nurturing of my ego.

Third scenario: Finally, look at the scenario where neither I wished any favors in return for my charity, nor I wished to glorify my name. I just did it for the sake of good of others; meaning, I did it out of pure love. And that's all!

Well, if we examine this case from the scriptural point of view, I would reap the highest reward since in this case I acted without any selfishness and without any ego. This is the scenario that describes the highest form of rendering action where one performs it with utter selfishness and self-centricity.

I presented these three scenarios, so that if we want to, we can map our own good works against them and see how do they measure up?

Surely, the first scenario where one expects a return out of his charities and good works is not very common, because most charities are done without expectation of any personal tangible return. However, the second one is; it is quite common since most of us have a strong desire that people come to know about our good deeds and praise us for them. Undoubtedly, this happens most often than not.

For example, isn't it true, whenever there is a function of charity, the donors always try hard for their names be announced and glorified; they always wish others to know of their charitable act?

Recently I visited a local temple, where I saw in its outer hall, as soon as we enter into it, a long list of the patrons and donors with their names engraved on one of the stones of the temple specifying the level of their charity. Their generosity was categorized by the amount of money they provided.

Surely, an act of charity, no matter what it is, is always good; so these men must be praised for what they did. Their act of benevolence to help build a temple for the local community of Hindu believers is highly commendable.

However, their desire to have their names on the list displayed for every visitor to see and recognize their contributions to good works, made their holy act tarnished in the sight of God.

According to His sacred word, their holy deed would surely create good *Karma* for their future *Karmic*-life, but sadly would not earn much merit in the sight of God. These kinds of good works are simple trades where man buys good name for himself as far as God is concerned, and of course, good Karma for his soul.

You see! Each human is embedded with an inherently egocentric nature; he is intrinsically selfish and self-centered. He is born with this disease, and he has this infection in him from the day one. After all, the ego surrounding his soul is the sole reason for his birth, and ego is what he needs to get rid of if he wishes to redeem his soul from bondage.

Surely, this is what he must do in order to make his life meaningful, and fulfill the very purpose for which he is born. And quite fortunately, that is exactly what the faithful practice of the spiritual discipline of *Karma-Yoga*, the action-in-love, the action-in-nonattachment, accomplishes.

Too bad! That even the works of charity and generosity done for the good of others, do not remain pure and pious, but get tainted and tarnished with impurities, because most often folks, out of ignorance, render them with selfishness and self-centricity, and if nothing more, then at least, they get laced with a desire of good *Karmic*-fortune in return. Oh! They do not know that *Karmic*-rewards, no matter how great and grand they are, are not of the degree of the highest return for works of man's benevolence.

Beloved! The main yield of our good deeds is that they cleanse our soul from all impurities and wash all kinds of vice off her. It is because the selfless-action is a cleanser of mind and heart, which in eventuality of its faithful adaptation and continual application brings forth shine and glow unto otherwise the fainted and faded soul.

Actually this is the main reason why Holy Gita has emphasized duty so repeatedly, since the unselfishness is often already present in it. So all we need is to render it with the sense of passivity in its possession, which comes only with a mind that has mastered equanimity.

But quite unfortunately, this is where most of us go wrong. Although, we often do render our duty, however, with selfishness, ego and pride; and thus, because of such self-centric attitude in it, we lessen its glory and lose its highest reward, which can enable us to be free from bondage because it is inherently of nature of sinless-ness, **"By performing duties born of one's own nature, one does not incur sin – Holy Gita 18:47."**

The duty is holy and hollowed. It is a sacred sacrifice that God desires from us. Look at how Lord God commands us to worship Him with faithful rendering of duty and adore Him by its fulfillment with a heart that has been fully submitted to Him in utmost humility:

From Whom all these beings have proceeded, and by Whom all this is pervaded, by adoring Him through the performance of one's own duty, one attains spiritual perfection.

(Holy Gita 18:46)

Also, beloved! Look at the reward that rises out of such sacrificial offering of fulfilled-duty? Oh! The spiritual perfection of the soul!

So, not only in the acts of duty but in all things, if we have an attitude that God is working through me to accomplish them, and accept whatever their outcome is and receive them with much thankfulness since it is from God, then surely we would make a rapid progress in becoming a *Karma*-Yogi. And in no time, we would reach the highest enlightenment, because the action-in-love would wash away our inner impurities, lessen our ego, and fill us with the light and wisdom; and as a result, we would begin to see clearly the Truth and Reality that would enable us to find our way to eternal liberation.

And then, we would no more be the captives of *Karma*!

Second: With boat of wisdom one can cross the ocean of sin.

We already know that attachment and desire, which are born out of ego **(Holy Gita 6:24)**, are the root cause of bondage, **"Impelled by desires, attached to the fruits of action, and thereof, goes to bondage – Holy Gita 5:12."** Surely, it is not hard to figure out, even if we apply only a little bit of reasoning, and try to see how do these enemies of man create problem for him? So let us do just that, and try to refresh our understanding on how desire creates bondage for the soul?

Remember! When the soul (*Atman*) moves from body to body, she carries with her the senses **(Holy Gita 15:8)**. And, where do the desires live? In senses and the mind **(Holy Gita 3:40)**! It means all the unquenched and unfulfilled desires of man are carried by the soul from body to body, and eventually reappear when she is born as human again **(Holy Gita 7:27)**.

Now, when *Jiva* (conditioned-soul, the living-being) is made, his lower-self is made with the lower nature of God, and the higher-Self is made with higher nature of God, **"These two (*Prakritis* of Mine) are the source of all beings – Holy Gita 7:6."**

So when man is made, his physicality is made with constituents of God's lower nature, which are Earth, Water, Fire, Air, Ether, Mind, Intellect and Ego-principle **(Holy Gita 7:4)**. Please make a note that the ego is one of them.

It means ego is there in man when he is born, but so are the attachments and desires **(Holy Gita 7:27)**. And since attachment and desire are there in him at his birth, then so are the delusion and darkness, **"All beings at the time of their birth**

248

come under the sway of the delusion of pairs of opposites caused by desire and hatred – Holy Gita 7:27."

Thus, as we can see, that not only ego but attachment and desire also are present in human right at his birth even though they are not manifested yet – which is a responsibility that falls upon ego.

It is ego that facilitates the expression of attachment and desire, and makes them manifest; and that is why it is held responsible for their birth, **"All desires that are born of egoistic will – Holy Gita 6:24."**

Now, even though the ego has the responsibility and power to facilitate the manifestation of the attachment and desire, but it is able to do it only if the 'freewill' allows it. Please understand this very important fact that unless the freewill of man allows, his ego cannot facilitate the manifestation of his attachment and desire.

However, the 'freewill' allows the expression of attachment and desire only if it finds the sought discernment and reasoning about them to be suitable to nature (*Prakriti*), otherwise, it acts against it and does not allow their manifestation.

It means the manifestation of attachment and desire is agreed and allowed only if the discernment about them is thought to be suitable and favorable to nature (*Prakriti*) in freewill. And that is exactly what happens, and that is how we are trapped by attachment and desire. Our nature chooses their materialization in freewill, which otherwise never happens.

So in conclusion, we can say that we willingly allow the desires to grow in us because the discernment of our freewill finds them favorable and desirable.

In other words, we think of our enemies, not as enemies but friends, and we invite them in. And, by doing so, we confirm the fact that our discernment is wrong and misguided, erroneous and mistaken; otherwise, how else can we ever engage in something that we intellectually find bad and harmful.

Surely, it is so! Oh! we engage in a wrong because our discernment that we arrive to in our freewill wrongly finds it to be right; otherwise, there is no way we would get involved in something that is bad and judged to be bad in our free-willed deliberations.

You see! We always act according to our discernment that we arrive to in our freewill, because during any decision making process, that is the environment we have been given by God. Therefore, if we are engaged in a wrong, it has to be because our discernment that we arrive in full freedom of thought is wrong. Isn't it?

But the discernment would be wrong only if the discerning faculty is wrong, which of course is our mind and intellect. And for mind and intellect to be dysfunctional, they ought to be operating without true understanding and knowledge, without true wisdom and light. Surely, that is the case.

The mind of man is surrounded by delusion and darkness – which is an established fact. So even though the ego has the power to facilitate the manifestation of desire, it has to be yet permitted through the discernment by our freewill, thus leaving the matter fully hanging on to our freedom of thought and determination.

However, more often than not, the freewill does allow these evils to be birthed and nourished and be multiplied, because it operates and seeks deliberations regarding attachments and desires in such an environment where mind and intellect are highly misguided by the delusion and darkness created by love (*Raga*) and hatred (*Dwesha*) towards things, which are present in man right from the day when he is born **(Holy Gita 3:34, 7:27)**; and therefore, his faculties of discernment are under the influence of ignorance.

And as a result, we fail in our discernments, and instead of staying away from the web of desires, we get trapped by them, and in fact so badly that we find ourselves helpless against them; and thus, we get deeper and deeper into bondage and become habitual and willing victims of it.

To confirm how badly we are marred by this disease, we all can examine our own heart and judge how tightly it is bound by desires. Can we deny that our whole life is driven by them, even though we fully know that they are our enemies, **"Know this to be your enemy in this world – Holy Gita 3:37?"**

So, it is our own darkness that, even though we have the power of freewill, we do not yet resist the takeover of it by the attachments and desires, and we willfully surrender ourselves to them and become their hostage. Not only that instead of defying them we often accept their slavery quite gladly knowing fully that they are the destroyers of our soul **(Holy Gita 2:62-63).**

Oh! We become their slaves most willingly and joyfully!

Of course, it sounds surprisingly stupid, but the truth still stands tall that our desires slave us and throw us into the imprisonment of bondage. But what plays the most significance role in all this is the ignorance and unawareness, the delusion and darkness; because, even though the ego is the driving power, but as we have concluded, it is the darkness that misguides our freewill and aligns it with ego to permit the expression and manifestation of attachment and desire.

Otherwise, if the darkness were not there, our freewill would never encourage our ego and allow it to empower the attachments and desires to flourish and rule over us.

We know that we are filled with delusion and darkness, but that is not it! it is multiplying even more by each day due to the simple fact that life is full of alluring enticements and temptations, so it is extremely hard to remain without attachments and desires, and that creates further ignorance in us, **"The delusion of pairs of opposites caused by desire and hatred – Holy Gita 7:27,"** and makes us blind by inducing more and more darkness, **"Darkness born of ignorance – Holy Gita 10:11."**

Along with darkness also increases our bondage, because any involvement with the alluring world means involvement with *Gunas* **(Holy Gita 18:40)**, and *Gunas* create bondage, **"*Sattwa, Rajas* and *Tamas* - these *Gunas* arising from *Prakriti* create bondage for the Imperishable *Atman* – Holy Gita 14:5."**

So, unless one knows how to live a life that is heading towards the light and moving towards the freedom from bondage, he is bound to have more and more ignorance, more and more darkness, and therefore, more and more bondage by each day.

Unfortunately, this happens to be our reality; of course, not for all, but quite surely for most of us. Great many among us are traveling on this road and heading towards further darkness and day by day falling further deep into bondage without realizing the dreadful consequence of their unfulfilled passion and unsatisfied infatuation.

Just as a caution, let me remind once more that even the *Sattwa* (the most pure and pious out of three modes of nature) – the *Guna* that symbolizes purity and piousness, light and wisdom, peace and joy – does create bondage by creating attachment to happiness and knowledge **(Holy Gita 14:6);** meaning, it is not exactly what we often think it is.

Therefore, we must be very clear about the fact that all *Gunas* create bondage by giving rise to some sort of attachment **(Holy Gita 14:6-8).** There is bondage in all things no matter what we do. Surely, this is one of the reasons why many get tempted to abandon the interaction with the objective world and take *Sanyasa* (renunciation). This is quite a popular tradition among *Hindu* believers.

However, the effort of avoiding engagement with the things of this world is not enough to escape bondage, because we can never completely avoid our engagement with all things no matter what; it just isn't possible. It means the creation of bondage is inescapable as long as we keep engaging with the objective world having a self-centric attitude.

Of course, the only way we could change that, if we act reversely and do exactly opposite to it. Rather than living in darkness and sanctioning of ego, which only gives rise to attachment and desire, we cultivate light and wisdom to empower our mind and intellect so that they could become most effective faculties for our freewill in discerning rightly and justly, and choosing the path of freedom from our passion and infatuation.

Surely, it makes sense! Doesn't it! Because, if the ego creates desire, and the desire creates darkness, which in turn disables our freewill and misguides us to choose the path of bondage, then how about doing the opposite to it? Won't it be true as well? Surely it will.

If we cultivate light and empower our freewill with healthy mind and intellect so that they are well-equipped with understanding and wisdom, then won't they function better and deliberate correctly about all things in life, and not lead us to walk on the path of ambitions and desires, and get enslaved by passion and infatuation? Of course, they will!

So, it makes sense that we seek light and wisdom; otherwise, how else we would be able to overcome ignorance and darkness? Without higher understanding, which could enable us to have a good view of our reality, how else we would be able to discern the path of life rightly and justly?

Therefore, it is not hard to see that wisdom is the only cure for malignantly ill soul infected with ignorance; the higher understanding is the only remedy for the *Atman* who is acutely ailing by the disease of delusion.

But how can man reach wisdom, when it is not the earning of his intellectual labor but is a gift of grace of God **(Holy Gita 10:10-11)**. So, there has to be a way; and surely there is one – that opens a door to such blessedness.

Remember, what is the true gain of *Karma-Yoga* (the selfless-action)? Is it not the purification of the soul! Is it not her reestablishment in wisdom! Of course, it is! Surely, the main goal of *Karma-Yoga* is to destroy soul's darkness and fill her with wisdom so that she could find her way to the sanctuary of God and attain salvation through His grace. The sole purpose of the selfless-action (with the equanimity of mind) is to destroy the indwelling ignorance of the soul and restore her into wisdom.

Thus, the reality of *Karma-Yoga* (action-in-nonattachment) is a witness to the same truth that the wisdom is such a ladder that could raise the soul to the heights of eternal liberty.

Look at these words of Lord God that provide the most powerful witness to how potent the wisdom is, where He so emphatically declares that no sin is greater than the power of wisdom, and no darkness is deeper that the power of light:

Even if you were the greatest of all sinners you could cross over all sins by adopting the boat of wisdom.

(Holy Gita 4:36)

Surely, all dark scaffolds of sin can be overcome by the radiance of the understanding of higher reality, and all oceans of bondage can be crossed by the vessel of God's wisdom.

Oh! The wisdom is such a virtue that has been praised over and over by Lord *Krishna* throughout Holy Gita. Hear these delightful words of the incarnated God where He expresses His most intimate emotions about the man of wisdom and says that such a man is very dear to Him **(Holy Gita 7:17)**, and that he is His own very Self:

All these (four types) are indeed the best; however I consider the man of wisdom as My very Self. For with his mind fully established in My Self, he considers Me his highest goal.

(Holy Gita 7:18)

These words speak of Lord's intimate feelings that He has for the man of wisdom. Look how He identifies Himself with him, and says that such a man is His very own being. What more is left to be said by God to express His love for the one who has light and is well-established in wisdom!

Oh! The wisdom is such a virtue that is repeatedly praised by the Holy Gita through words like these:

"There is nothing in this world as pure as wisdom – Holy Gita 4:38),"

and **"O *Arjuna*, *Karma* (performed with desire) is far inferior to the practice of *Buddhi Yoga* (the *Yoga* of wisdom) – Holy Gita 2:49,"**

and **"Even if you were the greatest of all sinners, you could cross over all sins by adopting the boat of wisdom – Holy Gita 4:36,"**

and **"The fire of wisdom turns all actions into ashes – Holy Gita 4:37,"**

and **"Wisdom shines forth like the sun, revealing the Reality of the Transcendental Self – Holy Gita 5:16."**

Surely, the wisdom has been glorified much by the scriptures, but do we yet precisely know, what a man of wisdom behaves like and what the spiritual discipline of wisdom (*Buddhi / Jnana Yoga*) truly is, and what it involves?

Well, this is the same curiosity, which *Arjuna* also expresses to Lord *Krishna* **(Holy Gita 2:54)**, and in response, before yielding the details **(Holy Gita 2:56-72)**, Lord God first summarizes His answer by saying that wise is he, who after overcoming his desires through the self-control, becomes fully and firmly established in his higher Self:

> **Sri Krishna said: O *Arjuna*, when a man thoroughly renounces all the desires of the mind and is <u>satisfied in the Self by the Self</u>, he is called a man of steady wisdom.**
>
> **(Holy Gita 2:55)**

And then he goes on to speak about the virtues, which a man of wisdom embodies, and says that the person of steady wisdom is he, **"who is not agitated in the midst of sorrowful conditions,"** who **"is devoid of craving,"** and **"who is free from attachment, fear, and anger;"** meaning, he has attained the self-control in every way **(Holy Gita 2:56)**, and has attained the mastery over his senses to a point that he **"is able to withdraw his senses from the sense-objects, even like a tortoise that withdraws its limbs from all sides – Holy Gita 2:58."**

But the 'self-control' is not the only thing Lord God talks about, as He further adds a highly significant virtue that must exist in a man of wisdom, which of course, is the balance of mind, **"while meeting with good and evil, neither rejoices nor hates – Holy Gita 2:57;"** meaning, in all things, he has the vision of equanimity – the main producer of nonattachment.

Thus, according to the word of God, the man of steady wisdom is he, who remains calm and composed in all situations and circumstances of life no matter what they are; who has overcome his passion and infatuation; who is free from fear and anger **(Holy Gita 2:56)**; who meets the good and evil with equal heart **(Holy Gita 2:57)**; who has overcome his sensuality **(Holy Gita 2:58)**, who has mastered his passion **(Holy Gita 2:61)**; and whose mind is full of bliss **(Holy Gita 2:65)**, and senses are completely restrained from the sense-objects **(Holy Gita 2:68)**. Such a man is considered well established in godly light and wisdom. These are the sign that tell if a person if of true wisdom or not?

Of course, if we look into these virtues a bit closely, we find that all these virtues can be summed up in two main attributes of a wise man: that he has self-control, and he has the vision of equanimity.

Mind it, that these two virtues are complementary since they feed growth to each other. The self-control increases equanimity of mind by lessening indulgence and involvement, while the balance-of-mind multiplies self-control by decreasing the value of all outcomes. And together they drive out the ignorance and darkness from human heart and fill it with light and wisdom.

These two virtues lead a man to such a state of existence that is exceedingly exquisite and extraordinary. It is a condition when one's inner-being is so Self-contained that he remains totally unaffected by the turbulence in external environment. No matter how much the outer world changes, yet he remains in a steady state of Self-contentment.

He becomes so steadily established in himself (in his very Self) that he is not moved by the outside world. The external disturbance does not penetrate into his internal being. He becomes fully established in the state of constant peace.

The well-known truth is: that the reason for all sorrow and suffering is attachment and desire. This is what Buddha found out in his search for the higher Reality. His search for Truth began with this truth that desire is the ground under all suffering. This truth set him off onto the expedition of Nirvana. His search for lasting peace began with the conviction that the desire is the root cause of all sorrow.

Here are the Four Noble Truths discovered by Buddha that became the sole basis of his teachings:

1. The Truth of Suffering – That Life is suffering.

2. The Cause of Suffering – That the attachment and desire are the root cause of suffering.

3. The Cessation of Suffering – That the suffering can be ended by overcoming the attachment and desire.

4. The Path Leading to the Cessation of Suffering – That the eightfold path of Love will overcome attachment and desire.

The eightfold path is: Right Understanding, Right Thoughts, Right Speech, Right Action, Right Livelihood, Right Effort, Right Mindfulness, and Right Concentration.

So when the desire ceases, peace comes to man quite naturally. And that is what happens to the one who has mastered over his senses and whose mind is well-placed in equanimity:

But the self-controlled Sage, though moving among the sense-objects, with his senses restrained and free from attachment and hatred, goes to Peace.

In that peace of mind all sorrows are brought to their cessation, because the intellect of the Sage, whose mind is full of bliss, becomes established in Brahman.

(Holy Gita 2:64-65)

In such a state of existence where one has overcome his lower self, his inner-being becomes firmly established in his higher Self; he becomes pulled out from the outside world and begins to rejoice the inner kingdom that is extraordinarily rich in peace and joy due to divine the light and wisdom.

Oh! No more such a man derives peace and joy from the outside world as his own inner-kingdom becomes the source of his lasting bliss.

Look at the expression **"Satisfied in the Self by the Self – Holy Gita 2:55"** used by Lord *Krishna* that describes this uniqueness in the man who is well-established in wisdom. Surely, this is a state-of-being of a person where one is fully content and is at peace within himself because he has reached the understanding of his higher reality; he has realized the truth about his Self; he is no more a captive of delusion and darkness, and is a victim of ignorance and Self-unawareness.

In following words, the Holy Gita speaks of this most enlightened state-of-being so called 'The Self-realization', and says that when one has realized his very Self, he goes beyond all darkness and delusion, and becomes so established in light and wisdom, knowledge and understanding that even while living in earthly domains, he attains the state of eternal Liberation:

Such is the state of Self-realization, O *Arjuna*. Having attained this, a Yogi is not deluded. Being established in this even at the moment of death, he attains the Absolute State of Liberation.

(Holy Gita 2:72)

After attaining such spiritual feat in life, where one has reached the pinnacle of wisdom and has become Self-realized, one does not remain prisoner of *Karma* as he becomes fully free from bondage, **"Who has realized the Self, has Liberation even here, not to mention hereafter – Holy Gita 5:26."**

One more thing! Having wisdom is not just 'knowing of the wisdom' but 'being established in that wisdom'. Of course, being established in anything means, that not only one intellectually knows the truth embedded in it, but that it has penetrated his being; that it has been integrated in him internally and has become a part of his natural self.

Until that happens, having wisdom and having higher knowledge has no real meaning. Till then, it is only void and vain treasure that has no real value.

Thus, just learning and knowing of the higher understanding and truth is not enough to be established in the wisdom, but to have them internally integrated in such a way that they have been assimilated with one's natural self, and that the integrated wisdom has become the underground of his daily experiences and responses.

When such wisdom dawns, one becomes fully aware of the truth that because of her attachment and desire **(Holy Gita 13:21)**, his soul is a slave of *Prakriti* (nature) and is a captive of bondage, and knowing this truth, he does not allow this captivity of his soul to continue and puts a halt to her imprisonment by the *Karma*, and engages in those efforts that are provided by God to save her from the manacles of mortality through the guidance of divine light and wisdom.

With such an higher understanding and self-control when a man destroys the dominance of desire and attachment and drives out the darkness through the vision of equanimity, he becomes established in wisdom.

Oh! He becomes established in his true Self!

Third: The Samkhya (the Yoga of Knowledge) paves the way to Moksha (Self-realization) through intuitive Self-knowledge.

The scriptures tell us that due to ignorance, we have lost the consciousness of our own reality; due to darkness we have become unaware of our own truth. Oh! We have forgotten our own authenticity and genuineness. We have lost the sense of our own loveliness and liveliness, our own vitality and vivacity, our own immensity and vastness. We do not even remember our own very nature of everlasting peace and harmony, and of unending joy and bliss.

Our own darkness has made us forget that we have the genesis in God; that we are an extension of His being, **"Mam ev Anso - a ray of My Eternal Self exists as the individual soul – Holy Gita 15:7;"** and that our true nature is of *Sat-Chit-Ananda* (Knowledge-Consciousness-Bliss), which is the same as of God.

Of course, because of ignorance, we are so deluded that we believe in our misconceived individuality, even though we intellectually know that it is a false notion. We know that we are not the mortal body but the immortal *Atman*, and yet we are unable to get out of darkness and restore ourselves unto the light of the Truth.

Therefore, if somehow our *Atman* could realize that he is a part of all-pervading and immutable Transcendental Self, and recognize the truth about himself that he is an extension of *Brahman* Himself, then he would not remain a captive of *Karma* but would be released from all bondage of darkness **(Holy Gita 5:16)**.

Since, ignorance is the reason why the immortal *Atman* is suffering the cyclic-captivity of *Karma*, which keeps him in bondage to the repeated cycle of birth and death, surely the most direct way for his release from detention by mortality would be the realization of the truth about his own Self, and knowing of the reality of who he truly is and who he is not.

Of course, it makes much sense; however, it remains to be seen if our conclusion holds any validity. The two things are fairly clear from all this. First, man is living in darkness; he is surely ignorant of the Truth; and second, he needs light to destroy the darkness and be established in Knowledge to overcome the ignorance. These two facts are unarguably true, no matter how we look at human bondage.

Well, consider this: after hearing *Arjuna's* grief about the war **(Holy Gita1:29-2:8)**, when Lord *Krishna* begins to speak, it is no coincidence that He speaks of the Knowledge *(Samkhya)*. His words highlight one very important truth about man that he is ignorant; that he is filled with delusion and darkness; that he is void of the Truth and Reality.

> **The Blessed Lord said: You are grieving over those who are not fit to be grieved for, yet you speak words like a great man of wisdom. But the wise do not grieve neither over the living nor over the dead.**
>
> **(Holy Gita 2:11)**

So the very first words of wisdom, which come out from the mouth of God in the discourse of Holy Gita, tell very boldly that man is a misguided being and is a self-deluded creature because what he thinks to be Real is actually unreal and what he sees as the Truth is actually untruth.

However, against this reality, man's view of himself is quite the opposite. He thinks of himself to be wise and prudent, filled with light and wisdom, and has knowledge and understanding; but the fact is, his self-assessment badly fails on all counts.

The point being made by Lord God in His words above **(Holy Gita 2:11)**, is precisely just that, where He noticeably underlines the fact that *Arjuna's* grief is misconceived due to his misunderstanding of the reality.

The words, **"You are grieving over those who are not fit to be grieved for"** clearly underscore the fact that *Arjuna* is ignorant of the Truth; that he is void of true understanding; and that he does not know what the Reality is?

The measurement of depth of *Arjuna's* ignorance comes in words, **"Yet you speak words like a great man of wisdom,"** which ridicule his understanding by making him face the fact that his expressed wisdom is of no good as it is filled with delusion and darkness.

So, as we can see, Lord God begins the discourse by revealing to man his dark reality that he is void of the Truth: that due to darkness, he cannot see his actuality, and hence, he needs light.

Then in verses, **Holy Gita 2:12-38**, He unveils the secrets of *Samkhya* (Knowledge), and exposes much truth about the *Atman* (Self – soul), and finally concludes unfolding of the mystery of the Transcendental Self by saying that **"O *Partha*, this is the wisdom of the *Samkhya* (Knowledge) which I have given to you – Holy Gita 2:39."**

Lord God speaks of wisdom of *Samkhya* (Knowledge) through these verses that dictate the reality of the Transcendental Self and expose the Truth of the *Atman* by saying that we are the *Atman* and not the body; and that we are part of that all-pervading Transcendental Self who is imperishable and eternal **(Holy Gita 2:17)**.

He tries to wake man up from deep ignorance by telling him that he is not what he thinks he is; and that he is not a mortal being but is the immortal *Atman*. He unveils the truth that just like the eternal Transcendental Self, the *Atman* (soul) too is immutable and unborn **(Holy Gita 2:21)**, stable and ancient **(Holy Gita 2:24)**, un-manifest and unchangeable **(Holy Gita 2:25)**; therefore, he neither is ever born, nor he ever dies **(Holy Gita 2:20)**.

All these things Lord God reveals to man right as soon as He begins His discourse to him and unveils to him the wisdom of *Samkhya* (Knowledge) so that through the understanding of Truth he does not remain surrounded by ignorance and darkness.

Well, judging the response that Lord God gives to man, it makes a whole lot of sense that the Self-realization through Knowledge is the most direct path to *Moksha* (Liberation).

Why? Because once the soul realizes the truth about her-Self, the delusion, which creates darkness in her to make her believe in her own individuality, vanishes away. And hence, no more she bears the sins of her falsehood; and thus, she becomes free forever from the fetters of *Karma*, and hence, never returns to this mortal world.

Those who have their intellect centered in the Self and who are supremely devoted to the Self destroy all sins by knowledge and attain the state of Liberation whence there is no return (to the world-process of repeated birth and death).

(Holy Gita 5:17)

Also, the common sense is that if one is doomed in darkness, light is his only natural savior; if one is suffering with ignorance, knowledge is his only definite cure. Any other therapy would not work. Isn't it!

Surely, *Arjuna* has the same thought in his mind when he expresses his confusion and wonders why Lord *Krishna* commands him to engage in Selfless-action rather than render himself to the pursuit of wisdom even though the later is considerably superior to the former as per the following words of Holy Gita where *Arjuna* says:

Arjuna said: O Janardana, if you say the intellect litup with the light of wisdom is superior to the path of selfless-action, then why do you lead me, O Keshava, to the performance of terrible Karmas?

(Holy Gita 3:1)

And a little later, he says this:

Arjuna said: O Krishna, you teach renunciation of action, and at the same time, the Yoga of action. Please tell me decisively, which is better of the two?

(Holy Gita 5:1)

You see! It is no wonder that *Arjuna* says these words, since the disciplines like the *Yoga* of Wisdom (*Buddhi*), which dictates the equanimity of mind, or the *Yoga* of Knowledge (*Samkhya*), which prescribes the understanding of the Intuitive-Self, or other such *Yogic*-disciplines that demand much higher subtlety in seeking the Truth, do seem easy, since there is not much grossness in their adaptation and application, and they seem quite direct in their approach because by nature they seem to be an effective remover of ignorance and darkness.

And, they do seem quite appealing, and hence, naturally more attractive than *Karma-Yoga*. Therefore, because of these reasons, many seekers choose to take these direct paths to enlightenment by living life in isolation and contemplating upon the Truth, and thus, try to escape the hassle of *Karma-yoga* (Action-in-nonattachment), which demands engagement with the world, and no escape from the duties of daily life.

But somehow, Lord *Krishna*'s view is different on this. It's true that He starts out His exposition of eternal wisdom with *Samkhya* (Knowledge of the Intuitive Self), and explains quite clearly how wrong is the understanding of man and how deluded he is; however, he chooses *Karma* (Action-in-nonattachment) as the first option to reach the enlightenment, **"Therefore, perform your duties in daily life – Holy Gita 3:8,"** and He gives a very good reason for it **(Holy Gita 3:3-3:7)**.

Surely, it seems logical that if we could just read the holy books and gain all sorts of sacred knowledge, we should become enlightened by the light of wisdom, but in reality that does not happen. Sorry! It just does not work that way since sacred knowledge is quite different than the secular knowledge when it comes to leaning.

No matter how much knowledge we earn and accrue by our holy labor, but unless that Knowledge becomes integrated in us, it has no meaning, no significance, except that it enables us to talk about it, and speak of it so that we feel as if we are endowed with it. It creates such a confidence in holy text that we do not even hesitate in preaching others and presenting ourselves to the world as if we are filled with the sacred wisdom; but that is as far as it goes.

Sadly, more often than not, this is exactly what happens to folks who choose to stroll on the avenues of *Samkhya* (Knowledge) and pathway of *Buddhi* (Wisdom) to reach directly the pinnacle of enlightenment, and prefer not to walk the long-path of *Karma* (Selfless-action), which demands a faithful fulfillment of ones natural duty with extreme nonattachment and rendering of their lives to the life they have been given through the ordinance of *Karma*.

No doubt! The mediation upon the Self in isolation and contemplation upon the Truth in seclusion is great; but, the physical separation alone from the objective world by adopting a life of solitude by abandoning the natural life ordained by *Karma* does not easily erase the subtle sensuality that continues to crave through the subjective mind.

Too bad that such behavior is not unusual by any means; in fact it occurs more often than not. Though it is hard to get acknowledgement from folks that are victim of such misguiding, but that does not mean that it is not very common among those that bid to adopt the path of *Samkhya* (Knowledge) or *Buddhi* (Wisdom) or *Sanyasa* (Renunciation) or other spiritual disciplines that discourage external earthly engagement.

In the following verse, Lord God says that it is hypocritical for someone who does not acknowledge his lust for sensual things upon which his mind continually hovers internally, and externally he projects as if he has risen beyond them and gives an impression that he has overcome his passion.

Such condemnation from the Incarnated God comes in the form of a warning so that we really get this truth firmly into ourselves that path of *Samkhya* (Knowledge), or of *Sanyasa* (renunciation), or of any other such *Yogic* avenue that abandons the path of *Karma* is not safe at all, as there is a great danger of falling into prey to hypocrisy of sensual detachment from the alluring objective world:

Those who have restrained the organs of actions, but continue to think of the objects of the senses, are foolish and hypocritical.

(Holy Gita 3:6)

The senses in body do not easily forget the taste of pleasure in sensual things. So abandoning the involvement with them alone does not erase the recollection of pleasure that one gets out of them, and it does not eliminate the taste of it from his thoughts as one continues to ponder upon them even after he has separated himself from their environment.

And if such is the case, which is what generally happens, then all holy labor results only in further darkness in the seeker since it gives him a false sense of growth in purity and piousness due to his gain in textual holy knowledge and wisdom, which of course is superficial and shallow and by no means represents the genuinely induced understanding that is deeply integrated in his inner self and has become a part of his authentic being.

So this is where lies the biggest challenge for a seeker who avoids the difficult path of *Karma-Yoga* and adopts a direct path to enlightenment by engaging with the subtle disciplines like *Yoga* of Knowledge (*Samkhya*), *Yoga* of Wisdom (*Buddhi*), *Yoga* of Renunciation (*Sanyasa*), and others like them.

Look at the verse below **(Holy Gita 5:6)**, where Lord *Krishna* gives response to questions posed by *Arjuna* in verses quoted above **(Holy Gita 3:1, 5:1)**, and discloses the fact that **"path of Samkhya (Knowledge) is beset with troubles,"** and is filled with obstacles for the very obvious reason that even though the spirit desires to contemplate upon the higher truth, the body and mind do not cooperate and continue to mediate upon alluring things of appealing earthly enjoyments.

Oh! Hear these words of wisdom by Lord Jesus Christ as documented in gospel of Mark that warns the believer to not become the victim of temptations:

Watch ye and pray, lest ye enter into temptation. The spirit truly is ready, but the flesh is weak.

(Holy Bible, Mark 14:38)

The humanity of the incarnated God can be easily witnessed through these words of Jesus as He speaks of fleshly temptations.

So as we can see, Lord *Krishna* prefers *Karma-Yoga* over other *Yogic*-approaches even though it may be considered a bit inferior by some, but still He finds it most fit due to the fact that it is most feasible, practical, easy to adopt, and extremely essential to reach the enlightenment since it purifies and establishes the soul in her natural perfection.

But, O Mighty-armed Arjuna, without Karma Yoga the path of Samkhya is beset with troubles. The Sage who pursues Yoga (having attained renunciation) hastens to the attainment of Brahman.

(Holy Gita 5:6)

Therefore, just because the spiritual discipline of *Samkhya* (Knowledge) seems to be a direct ladder for ascension of soul to enlightenment and to the state of pure consciousness – the Self-realization, it does not mean that it is the best way for a seeker to adopt, since the path of Knowledge is not as easy as one generally may think of it as it surely is filled with troubles.

Also, besides the problem of lingering desires in the craving heart, there lies another danger for the seeker of *Samkhya*, which is of ego that may grow in him as a result of his growth in holy knowledge. Though not many become aware of it; however, there is a good possibility of its happening especially when the sacred learning is done without any true humility and meekness and without true integration of that knowledge into daily life. Please know that this happens more often than not, as the holy knowledge often makes one quite arrogant of his spiritual richness.

Oh! The sense of being wise and holy that rises in one after gaining the higher Knowledge makes him very proud and egoistic just the way the possession of any worldly richness does.

As a result, the knowledge received without humility becomes infected with the disease of ego and pride, which not only stops all spiritual growth, but brings the spiritual downfall for the seeker. And since this happens in extreme subtleness, so it often goes unnoticed; and thus, one begins to conduct openly in arrogance and pride that rises out of ego due to false sense of holiness.

Since gaining the scriptural knowledge in *Hindu* philosophy is not all that easy as it is in other religions due to the fact that in place of just one main holy book like Christianity has Holy Bible, Judaism has Torah, Islam has Holy Quran, *Hinduism* has numerous of such sacred manuscripts, which were revealed to prophets **(Veda-Vyasa)** of ancient times and still do not have the translation in common languages.

No wonder, Holy *Ramayana* is the most read holy book among *Hindus*, since it is written in Hindi and has translation available in other languages as well, and also because, it does not present just the pure knowledge as Holy Gita does or the Upanishads do, but much story telling about the life of incarnated God, Lord Rama.

This is why having a spiritual-teacher (Guru) is regarded a must for a *Hindu* seeker so that one could be given a good foundation in knowledge of the truth of God. In fact there is a wide belief among *Hindus* that without a Guru one cannot attain *Moksha* (*Liberation*), since without guidance from a spiritual-teacher how could one find salvation for his soul?

Well, whether one agrees with such thought or not, one has to agree that in *Hinduism*, it is not easy to grow in scriptural knowledge. So when one accomplishes such a feat, he is regarded a bit highly in spiritual realm. This is one of the reasons why *Hindu* sages and saints, the *Sadhus* and *Swamis*, are regarded quite highly, since the common belief is that they have acquired Knowledge, and have come to know the Truth.

So when one acquires godly wisdom and becomes versed in holy text of *Hindu* tradition, it is very natural for him to feel quite special in community of Hindu believers, particularly when looked upon through the spiritual considerations; but that has a danger because it often multiplies person's ego and grows him in holy-arrogance.

Therefore, the genuine humility is essential for all holy learning since in it lies the attitude that is suitable and worthy to receive the higher Knowledge, properly and effectively. Otherwise, as often is the case, the ego and pride destroy the spiritual growth of the seeker and makes him blind to his own truth.

The thought that one has to have much textual holy knowledge to grow in God, though is quite popular, yet is highly inaccurate. The growth in textual knowledge does not grow one closer to God; the obedience and abidance to what one knows of Him does. It is not the learning of more words of wisdom what makes one know God, but the abidance in His goodness and grace does. It is not being the expert in holy knowledge but the taking of refuge in His sanctuary and being surrendered and submitted to His will and being faithfully reliant upon His provisions what brings one closer to God and establishes his intimate communion with Him.

Still, it is not that we should not try to learn the scriptural knowledge, because we should; in fact, we ought to read and learn from holy books daily; but, our main focus must be upon living by what we already have learned and what God has taught us thus far rather than vigorously engaging in multiplying our expertise in holy know-how.

Surely, it is good to know the scriptures as best as we can because that is the direct source of Knowledge; but knowing scriptures only teaches what the truth is, and does not automatically convert it into our belief. The truth becomes our belief only when we live it and wear it upon our soul, because only then it gets incorporated in us in a way that it becomes an integral part of our inner being.

No doubt! We need the understanding of the truth as it has been unfolded in our Holy books, but not just by reading it, but by learning and living and experiencing it in our daily lives and infusing it into us by walking the holy path that has been laid down by the scriptures.

True! That we can gain the knowledge of God from holy books, but infusion of Truth does not occur by reading and learning alone. The truth grows in us only when we learn of Him through that knowledge and grow in our relationship with Him by abiding in His refuge and living by His advocated commandments and walking the daily walk that He has ordained for us in holy text.

Oh! God speaks the Truth directly to our hearts when we seek His fellowship through our intimate communions.

Surely, the holy texts help us understand the Truth about God and Creation, and enable us to grasp many mysteries about Existence, but by no means, their expertise is a pre-qualification for comprehension of His truth and Reality.

Please know that knowing the Truth is good but only a little; only a little is far superior to knowing a whole lot of it and not practicing enough.

For example, we all can agree intellectually, that God is everything and that He is all in all; and I am sure, quite unhesitatingly, we all can declare that God alone is as He is the only reality there is and nothing else, but how many among us really believe in such claim when it comes to behaving in its accordance? I am sure we all know what our honest answer is going to be!

Surely, only a few among thousands!

Let us look at the following verse and try to realize how hard it is to find such a blessed person who has arrived this understanding that God is all in all; that *"Vasudevah* **(God) alone is all this."**

I am sure, we all can claim to know God but how many among us are such chosen souls who really can stand by this truth. The words of Holy Gita declare how difficult it is to find such a blessed soul, because such Truth-realized men are in scarcity and are very rare to be found:

After many lives (of progressive spiritual evolution) one acquires wisdom and worships Me with the vision that *"Vasudevah* alone is all this." It is extremely difficult to find such a great soul.

(Holy Gita 7:19)

Yes! It is true that most of us has comprehended mentally this truth that *"Vasudevah* **(God) alone is all this,";** that God is all in all; that God alone is; but, it surely has not become our conviction; and that is why, though we say we do, yet we do not truly believe in its reality.

No wonder why Holy Gita says that **"It is extremely difficult to find such a great soul,"** because there are only a few blessed ones who have arrived to such high state of consciousness where they believe that God is all in all and they live by this conviction; their daily life is a witness to this truth.

Oh! The union with God comes in truly knowing the truth that He alone is. In such understanding alone, when the recognition of individual existence begins to cease, the soul begins to merge with the oneness of God. And thus, even while living in the human body, spiritually her separation from the Creator comes to an end as she merges with Him and becomes His oneness.

And once we have comprehended the reality that God is all in all, that He alone is, that He is what exists and also what exists not, there is nothing more left to be known, **"Having known which nothing more shall remain here to be known – Holy Gita 7:2;"** there in nothing more to be understood and comprehended; there is no more knowledge remained to be gained.

The true knowledge is none else but knowing that God is all in all, and that He is in everything and everything is in Him. The understanding and realization of His omnipresence in all creation, **"The entire world is pervaded by Me – Holy Gita 9:4,"** is the highest wisdom there is, **"This knowledge is the King of all knowledge the King of all secrets – Holy Gita 9:2."**

Do we ever hear that *Sant Kabir*, saint *Soor-Daas* or Sage *Raheem* were great holy scholars? That they were expertise in sacred text? That they were the *Pandits* of holy scriptures? No, very certainly not! But can anyone doubt that they were not Self-realized souls?

Therefore, the quantitative knowledge is no measure of wisdom, but understanding and realization of the reality of God's omnipresence and His omniscience is. Whoever understands this and lives life in conviction of Oneness with God, he gets released from all bondage, and becomes eternally free from all manacles of mortality. Never again he is born, nor dies; and never again he visits any *Karmic* world even in times of Creation and Dissolution:

> **Having taken refuge in this knowledge and having attained oneness with Me these Sages are neither born at the time of creation nor are they affected at the time of the universal dissolution.**

> **(Holy Gita 14:2)**

Fourth: The true renunciation (Sanyasa) brings liberation even in this world, not to mention hereafter.

By nature, the renunciation (*Sanyasa*) implies freedom from bondage since a renounced life is a life of non-attachment; it is a life that is free from dominance of desire. Once a person has successfully relinquished his passion, he is free from all bindings. No more he is held captive of temptations; and thus, no more he remains a prisoner of *Karma*.

However, the successful adoption of *Sanyasa* (*Yoga* of renunciation) is not all that simple since there is no easy way to be free from desire. Surely, through renunciation, which is often adopted externally and not internally, one can minimize the interaction with the objective world to avoid its temptation, but the inner craving still lives on **(Holy Gita 3:6)**.

The infection of infatuation does not cure as easily. The attachment and desire continue to hover over mind and thoughts for a long time until one has arrived the state of Self-contentment **(Holy Gita 4:20).**

The external renunciation of the physical world mostly results in suppression of lustful feelings and emotions. The intentional denial of desires and their outright non-recognition does not abolish them for good but only suppresses them. On the surface they seem to have died but underneath they continue to live even often without much conscious acknowledgement.

Thus, the renunciation, if not practiced properly, meaning if it is not adopted internally, it would not produce the right result that it is supposed to, which of course is the deliverance of man from desire and freedom from bondage to all cravings.

Since passion is deeply embedded in man, the external abandonment would only mask its face but would never extinguish it with its entirety, or even weaken it sufficiently so that it does not effectively hinder the spiritual progress.

Oh! The desire is such a flame that burns deep inside man's heart and does not get extinguished by relinquishment of the outer world.

To attain the goal of human liberation from passion, the *Yogic*-practice of renunciation has to be applied internally, wherein the liberation of soul from attachment comes not by the denial of the world but by the denial of the 'self' brought through the higher understanding and wisdom.

It is the self-denial which is what is required if one longs to be free from attachment and wishes his deliverance from bondage. Look at these words of Lord Jesus, which unfold the mystery of how one can become His true disciple and how he can successfully walk closely with Him by saying that one has to embrace death to his lower 'self' even while living in this world and constantly deny his inner man because he is often severely marred by passion and infatuation:

Then said Jesus unto his disciples, If any man will come after me, let him deny himself, and take up his cross, and follow me.

(Holy Bible, Matthew 16:24)

If one desires to be the disciple of Jesus, then he has no other way but to take up his cross and accept death of his very own 'self'. Only through complete denial of the 'self' can he become able to follow Him. Surely, the death of the 'self' is the way of soul's resurrection to everlasting life in God.

In following words Lord *Krishna* unveils the secret of true renunciation, and says that for it to be meaningful, it must be rooted in *Karma-Yoga* – the Selfless-action; because, life of selflessness purifies the soul and reinstates her in divine wisdom. When one is endowed with wisdom, through the light of the Spirit, one becomes well-established in his 'Self'; and thus, he becomes forever liberated from passion and infatuation, and therefore, does not remain a captive of *Karma*:

O Conqueror of Wealth (*Arjuna*) if one attains renunciation by the practice of *Yoga* (*Karma Yoga*) dispels all doubts by wisdom and becomes established in the Self he is never bound by *Karmas* (actions)

(Holy Gita 4:41)

The beautiful thing about it is that even though the eternal liberation from bondage comes after the soul has ceased the body and become free from the good and evil *Karma*, her freedom begins as soon as she becomes established in her true Self through the light of wisdom attained by practicing the inner-renunciation (*Sanyasa*).

Thus you will become free from the bondage of good and evil *Karmas* and being united with the *Yoga* of renunciation liberated even in life you will attain Me.

(Holy Gita 9:28)

Surely, the complete deliverance of the soul from hold of *Karma* comes only after the physical death of her embodiment, but her spiritual freedom from bondage begins to reign from the very day she arrives the home of true renunciation. Thus, for man who has attained true *Sanyasa*, he already has attained the life of true liberty; his days are already filled with everlasting peace and contentment.

As we can see that the word of God, **Holy Gita 9:28**, promises that such a sage, who has become a true *Sanyasi* (one who is well established in the *Yoga* of renunciation), attains Him while he is still living, because in abandonment of his desires through self-renunciation, lies such a freedom, which has tracks leading to eternity.

Fifth: The Bhakti Yoga (the Yoga of love and devotion) is a direct connection between man and God, which paves his way to permanent union with Him.

There is one secret, which is beautifully exposed in the following verse which we must know, if we ever desire to know God; because, this is one of those truths that must be deeply infused in our heart and soul if we ever wish to have union with Him.

Listen to these words of Lord God that clearly tell of what place the love and devotion has in His heart?

By Supreme Devotion he knows Me what and who I am in reality and having thus known Me fully he enters into Me.

(Holy Gita 18:55)

Isn't there a depiction of the fact of how so dearly He adores the one who loves Him; and how out of love He reveals Himself to the man of devotion by blessing him with the vision of Truth that enables him to know and become united with Him.

These words of Lord God give glimpses of *Bhakti Yoga* – the spiritual discipline of love and devotion – and expose the way of communion with Him through deep affection and adoration. The striking fact about this verse is that one comes to know God only **"by Supreme Devotion."**

And once one knows God, his 'knowing' becomes his entrance into God, **"He enters into Me;"** meaning he exists in God with his entirety and God becomes his abode. So the 'knowing' becomes the submerging of one's individuality into the oneness of God.

You see! Knowing is not just learning of Him but integrating of His knowing into inner Self and ultimately becoming Him; that is what the true knowing of God is all about.

The following words of the *Upanishad* speak of this truth in such a way that they unveil the ultimate reality of what becomes of the one who comes to know God:

In truth who knows God becomes God.

(Mundaka Upanishad, Part 3, Chapter 2)

Oh! The ultimate reality of 'Knowing of God' is the 'Becoming of God'; meaning, after knowing God, the singularity of individual existence merges with its entirety into the unity of Oneness of the universality of God.

So from verse above, **Holy Gita 18:55**, it is clear that love and devotion are such a medium that enjoin the heart of man with the heart of God. It is such a thread that connects the 'created' with the Creator. Undoubtedly, *Bhakti* is such a power that enables man to enter into the live presence of his Maker and to commune with Him in a very intimate way. Wow!

Hear these words of Holy Gita where she joyfully unveils the secret of how can one approach God and reach His closeness? She boldly declares that through love alone is God attainable. According to her, the unwavering devotion is the only way through which man can reach the reality and truth of God and understand who He truly is:

Within whom abide all these beings, by whom all this pervaded, that Supreme Being is attainable <u>by unswerving devotion to Him alone</u>, O *Partha*!

(Holy Gita 18:55)

What better confirmation do we need than these words of Lord God Himself that applaud love and devotion as the only avenue that leads to Him!

The scriptures in all holy books repeatedly exalt this truth, that through love and devotion alone God can be reached; that *Bhakti* is the only way of attaining God.

So this spiritual discipline (so called *Bhakti-Yoga*), which is based on love and devotion, is nothing but truly falling in love with God; it is being absolutely crazy about Him, and being utterly forgetful of oneself in His thoughts and living life as if he has no life outside of God.

If we look at the philosophy of this *Yogic*-approach, it all makes sense, since not only God is a God of love, **"I am the God of Love – Holy Gita 10:28,"** but **"God (He) is love."** Therefore, what else could connect with Him better than the love and affection, devotion and dedication?

The holy word says that if one loves not God, he knows not God, since God Himself is the Love. So how can one know God and not know love, because without love, knowing of God is just not possible:

He that *loveth* not *knoweth* not God; for <u>God is love</u>.

(Holy Bible, John 4:8)

Beloved! God keenly desires to be loved. This is why, the love and devotion, the worship and *Bhakti*, is the easiest way to have communion with Him; it is such a medium that enables man to communicate his raw emotions and feelings to God without any fabrication.

Why God longs for our love? Because His true essence is of love! And since our genesis is in Him **(Holy Gita 9:17)**, our true essence is also of love. So if the true essence of both, the Maker and the 'made' is of love, then any relationship between the two has to be of love. After all, if God is love and He is our creator, then we are created by Love, sustained by Love, and eventually salvaged by Love to be united with Love.

Seek to know him from whom all beings have come, by whom they all live, and unto whom they all return. He is Brahman.

(Taittiriya Upanishad, 3. 1-6)

The good thing about 'love' is that we all know it; we all have experienced it; and we all have been naturally taught and trained in it. Love is such an inheritance from God that not only humans, even the birds and animals are blessed with it; even they recognize love and know how to operate in it.

Oh! Love is intrinsically known to all living beings.

However, the problem is that unlike all other creatures, human love is often tainted with selfishness and self-centricity. More often than not it is contaminated with vices like lust and lasciviousness, and gluttony and greed.

So even though the quintessence of love is of light since it emanates from God and carries the radiance of His spirit, it still is often dark due to defilement caused by the perverted human-heart, which destroys its purity, and debases its piousness.

Now the question is why love, which is of God, gets so tarnished, and becomes so ungodly? After all, God is not only **'the God of love'** but also **"God (He) is love;"** so it has to be like Him. If God is Holy and hallowed, immutable and unchangeable, then so should be love; meaning, the essence of love should be the same as of God. And in truth, so it is!

But if we take it to be true, then the question is: How come love, which has the soul of purity and piousness, and is of unchangeable essence, is so often tarnished and tainted, and seems to be changing?

The answer lies in the fact that even though the desire of expression of love is inherent in all creatures (not just human), the way of expression is not, which of course, depends upon the nature of the one who is expressing it and also to whom it is being expressed. And thus, the way of expression of love changes the form of love.

Surely, the essence of love is always the same but when we express it towards our parents, siblings, wife, husband, children, friends, relatives, and all others who are dear to us, its form changes from person to person, relation to relation; so it is not the same for all as it differs depending upon to whom we are offering.

We communicate love variably because the expression of love depends deeply upon our relationship with the person to whom we communicate it, and also upon our emotions and feelings and intent with which we express it. No wonder, love has so many looks and so many varying faces, because every expression of it has so many variables associated with it.

This is why, though the soul of love is always the same since she is of God who is love, her spirit is different every time she communicates it since communication of love is dependent upon to whom it is being expressed and with what heart it is being communicated!

It means God's love is the same as ours but only in its essence and not in its expression, because God expresses love in perfect purity and piousness, but we do it in selfishness and self-centricity and defile it with lust and greed, and contaminate it with all kinds of impurities that hover in human heart.

Coming back to the point that we all know what love is since we all have experienced it in one form or the other, the only thing we need to work on is how to express it and express it properly so that it could be acceptable to God.

Hear the words of the Psalmist, whose love longs to be acceptable in the sight of God:

Let the words of my mouth, and the meditation of my heart, be acceptable in thy sight, O LORD, my strength, and my redeemer.

(Holy Bible, Psalms 19:14)

So the key in expression of love and devotion to God is that it should be as such that it is acceptable to God, and that it finds favor in His sight; and that it is after His heart so that He receives it with much fondness. If God does not enjoy the offered love, then of what good it is? So the offered love and devotion has to be of God's liking, otherwise, it is of no good!

Now the question for each one of us is: Does our love and devotion meet the expectations of God? Does it merit high against His measures, and does it find favor in His sight? Meaning, is our *Bhakti* that we exercise in our daily life, acceptable to God? Well, let's look into it.

Since in *Hindu* tradition, the religion is so deeply integrated with its culture, there is hardly a day goes by when one does not perform some kind of religious rituals and rites. The daily *Pooja* and *Aarti*, prayer and worship, are quite popular practices among *Hindus*. It is a daily thing for many to read holy books like Holy *Ramayana* or Holy Gita, and sing hymns and praises to exalt God, and convey ones love and devotion to Him.

But does all this is sufficient to say that we love God? Is standing in front of a holy picture or statue and singing hymns and pronouncing prayers and engaging in all kind of worship and doing all kinds of *Pooja* enough for our claim? Do all the rituals and rites, which we perform almost on a daily basis, fulfill the entirety of our love for Him? Do our holy thoughts and mental adorations meet the demands imposed by our claimed love, and do they satisfy the expectations rising out of that claim? Is all that spirituality, which is a part of our common daily life, enough to justify our proclamation of love for God?

Surely, such holy practices are quite common, not only among *Hindus* but among folks of all religions, as most believers across all societies offer their love and devotion to God in one form of worship or the other and convey their prayers and praises to Him.

So, it can be said without any exaggeration that a man of religion is often involved in offering his love and devotion to God in ways professed and practiced by his belief system; but the question is: how much of his holy labor is adequate and acceptable to God?

Of course, it is easy for us to hold opinions about the others, but we surely have the responsibility to judge our own love and devotion to God and see if it meets His standards and is in conformance to His expectations. Such examination is a must for each one of us because how else we would know if we are spiritually on the right track or not!

I highly recommend this exercise to all, but especially to those that are genuinely involved in seeking higher grounds of spirituality, because most of us would discover one of the most disheartening facts, that all what we do in our religious realm, is nothing but only a small token of recognition of our love for God.

To love God, we need to submit and surrender ourselves to Him, and completely let go of ourselves for His sake. We need to resign our entirety to Him and accept His refuge willingly and joyfully. We need to move into in His sanctuary and continually stay in His presence and be available to His services and remain ready to respond to His instructions at all hours of the day. We need to make God our only business as nothing else should ever be of any interest to us.

Thus, we need to make Him the center of our existence – the main focus of our life – the very soul of our being, of course, by loving Him with our body, mind, soul, and everything else **(Holy Gita 18:65)**.

Throughout all scriptures, God has spoken quite clearly how does He desire to be loved? We can take any holy book and find out what God has to say about how does He wish to be loved and worshipped?

In Holy Gita alone, there are so many such texts that speak of how God desires to be approached and adored, exalted and glorified. Please hear the cravings of His heart that are so audible to an ear that earnestly desires to listen to what God has to say about loving Him:

> **<u>Fix your mind in Me</u>, <u>be devoted to Me</u>, <u>worship Me</u>, and <u>bow down to Me</u>. Having thus surrendered yourself to Me with your spirit united with Me, you will surely attain Me.**
>
> **(Holy Gita 9:34)**

From these words where Lord *Krishna* summarizes it all in just few words and tells us how to love and adore Him, it is quite evident that not only God expresses the desire for our love and devotion, but He also opens up His heart to show His expectations about it.

He says, **"Fix your mind in Me," "be devoted to Me," "worship Me,"** and **"bow down to Me;"** which certainly makes us feel like He is almost repeating Himself. Well, why does God use such expressions that are so close to each other in their meaning? We can be very sure that these expressions are not redundant; but then, what is He saying?

Surely, if we read these words with a little diligence we can easily figure out that through these expressions, Lord God wants to make sure that we get the point. And of course the point is, that we ought to love and adore Him in every which way we can; we ought to exalt and glorify Him whichever way possible.

Beloved! This is how God desires to be loved and be adored!

According to Holy Bible, in the book of Deuteronomy (Old Testament), when God speaks to Moses and gives him the Commandments for His people Israel to abide by, the most important holy directive among them, which of course is the greatest of all, is the 'Commandment of Love for God' **(Holy Bible, Deuteronomy 6:5).**

Is it is coincidence? Very definitely, not!

It is the same commandment that was recalled back and repeated fifteen hundred years later by Lord Jesus Himself, as quoted in all four gospels of Holy Bible (New Testament). Here are the words from the book of Mark:

And thou *shalt* love the Lord thy God with all thy heart, and with all thy soul, and with all thy mind, and with all thy strength: this is the first commandment.

(Holy Bible, Mark 12:30)

And what do they have to say? Simply that, just be of God in each and every way possible. God wants us to love Him with our mind, heart, soul, spirit and everything else; meaning, our whole essence has to be devoted and dedicated to His exaltation and glory. That's it! That's the bottom line.

Loving God does not mean just loving Him as a concept and adoring Him as a notion; not so! In all truth, loving God means living and abiding in Him, and experiencing and expressing life through Him. That is what loving God means.

Now, can we see how do these words of Holy Bible are so much similar to those quoted from Holy Gita only few paragraphs back, **"*Manmana Bhav, Madbhakta Bhav, Madyaji, Maam Namaskarah* – Fix your mind in Me, be devoted to Me, worship Me, and bow down to Me – Holy Gita 9:34?"** Of course, the words are different, but meaning is the same. Both instruct man that his highest priority in life is to love God with all his being. Isn't it!

To understand how important it is for Lord God that we remember His instruction about loving Him during all our days, please make a note of the fact that right before He ends the discourse in Holy Gita, He repeats almost the same words **(Holy Gita 9:34),** again in the following verse:

Fix your mind on Me be devoted to me sacrifice to me offer adoration to Me; you will indeed attain Me - this I truly promise to you because you are my dearly beloved.

(Holy Gita 18:65)

Both verses virtually have the same meaning. Their top part is exactly the same; however, the lower part differs where Lord God not only gives the assurance of our union with Him but also makes a personal promise that we would surely attain Him just because He has most profound love for us.

These words come right before He speaks His final words in Holy Gita, where once more Lord God reminds us that we must love Him, always. He also tells how and why should we love Him, and what would happen if we faithfully render ourselves to Him in love and devotion?

Now, through these words, is it not true that Lord God wishes to remind us what is most important to Him? Is it not that He wants to make sure that we remember His most important instruction and not forget that loving God the way He desires to be loved is the only way to make it acceptable to Him? Is it not that He wills us to know that attaining Him is the highest goal of life, which of course, according to His promise is very achievable through His love and devotion; but of course, the love and devotion has to be rendered to Him through absolute surrender and submission?

Beloved! The whole message, which God is conveying through these words, is filled with meaning. A meaning, that is so enormous that it cannot be easily extracted and be comprehended in its entirety.

It unveils the truth that man needs deliverance from *Karma*; that he needs the grace of God so that his soul could be redeemed. It tells that the grace of God is found only when one takes asylum in His sanctuary with absolute surrender and submission.

But of course, this is not possible until first man learns how to truly love God.

By asking man to love Him in every which way he can, God wants to teach him how to be humble and how to be free of ego, because only then he would be able to receive His light and wisdom, and thus, be enlightened with His radiance, which would enable him to know Him and see Him with His true reality and truth.

So after knowing that God desires love from us more than anything else because He is the God of Love **(Holy Gita 10:28)**, and to love Him is our desire, then we ought to do exactly what He has told us to do; that we ought to **"fix your mind in Him,"** **"be devoted to Him,"** **"worship Him,"** and **"bow down to Him;"** meaning, we ought to be so devoted and dedicated to Him that we see our total life through Him.

To make our love and devotion acceptable to God, if this is what He wishes, and this is what He wants us to do, that we love Him unconditionally, and adore Him with all our being and devote ourselves to Him in everyway possible, then that is what we must do.

But how can it be accomplished? How can we love God the way He desires to be loved? Since God is not a person, so how are we to know if whatever way we love Him is good enough? And whatever way we express our adoration and affection to Him, who in truth is un-manifest and is of no from and shape, is acceptable to Him? How do we know this for sure?

Well, if we think that the acts of worship and devotion, the deeds of charity and works of goodwill, the giving away of alms and donations, the engagement in spiritual endeavors and enterprises, the exercises of sacrifices and austerity, the rendering of rituals and rites, the performance of sacraments and sacred services, and all these righteous acts of religiosity are good enough to please God, then we still need to make sure that we are truly right on this? Because, without finding out the correct answer to this question is too big of a gamble, don't you think!

Surely, if we are failing to meet His expectations in our offer of love and devotion, then without any doubt we are in trouble, because we are investing all our holy labor into something that is of not much value in the sight of God.

Beloved! Here is a surprising revelation with which many may not agree that our spiritual walk is very narrow; it does not cover all grounds of love, which we must have for God. Our holiness falls way short of becoming a true homage to Him; our holy efforts do not even come close to achieve any acceptable merit in His sight.

Oh! Whatever we do in love for God is very little in comparison to what we do for love of ourselves; whatever we do to please Him is nothing in comparison to what we do to please ourselves. And that is a fact, which we cannot deny!

We all can examine our hearts and find out this quite saddening truth.

Now, if this is what we call loving God then obviously it is very easy to love Him, because then, all we need is to offer Him love and devotion through our prescribed holy ritual and rites, and worship Him with through payers and praises, and by bringing flowers and sweets to His altar. And that's it!

But is it enough? Sadly, the truthful answer arrived through higher understanding is 'No'. Because to love God means to love His creation, to love His created beings. So, there lies our challenge. Can we really love all of God's creation? Can we really love all beings He has formed and shaped? There we face the greatest challenge in loving God.

No wonder, the greatest commandment of love that God has given to man in Old Testament of Holy Bible is complemented with its true meaning by Lord Jesus Christ in New Testament when He spoke these words:

> **And Jesus answered him, The first of all the commandments is, Hear, O Israel; The Lord our God is one Lord:**
>
> **And thou *shalt* love the Lord thy God with all thy heart, and with all thy soul, and with all thy mind, and with all thy strength: this is the first commandment.**
>
> **And the second is like, namely this, Thou *shalt* love thy _neighbour_ as thyself. There is none other commandment greater than these.**
>
> **(Holy Bible, Mark 12:29-31)**

He makes it very clear that equally important to the commandment of 'To love God' is the commandment of **'to love thy neighbor as thyself'**. In a way the first one is truly not complete unless it is complemented by the second one. So unless one learns how to love his neighbor, he would not be able to learn how to love God. The entirety of 'Loving God' includes the extremities of 'loving the neighbor'. Thus, the claim, that one loves God but without loving his neighbor, bears no meaning.

So by saying, **"Love thy neighbour as thyself,"** the Lord God makes sure that we know how to love Him properly and sufficiently. In fact, to make sure that we understand it fully, He even goes one step further to clarify it, and demands that we love not only the neighbor who is ours friend, but also the one who is our foe:

> **But I say unto you which hear, <u>Love your enemies</u>, <u>do good to them which hate you</u>.**
>
> **(Holy Bible, Luke 6:27)**

Through these explicit words, Lord Jesus not only commands us to Love God and teaches us how, but also issues a challenge to rise in His love so high that we become enabled to love not only our friends but also our enemies.

Having such sense of renewed understanding as dictated by these scriptures that encapsulates the entirety of how to love God so that it is pleasing to His heart, let us question once more how can we learn how to attain it adequately and pleasingly? How can we worship and exalt Him with a dedication and devotion that is according to His word and holy instruction?

My firm belief is that we all are capable of doing it, but only by being fully rendered to Him, and not by our empty ritualistic ways, hollow worship, and void love and devotion!

Please look into your heart and discern diligently and honestly, and see if you can deny the fact that our whole worship and devotion that we render to God is void and vain because we offer it to Him as a ritual. It is just a routine that we perform because it makes us feel good; it makes us feel holy and hallowed; and it gives us a sense that we are righteous and justified.

And even if it is not a routine, it still is pretty much empty since it does not carry such dedication and devotion, the surrender and submission that is required to make it fully acceptable to God. How often or offerings are hollow and empty, void and vain!

So, the bitter truth is, that no matter how we take comfort in our holy ways, most often they are nothing but vanity; no doubt!

Oh! To love God, we need to have a spiritual vision that sees beyond the religious metaphors, beyond our holy rituals and rites, beyond daily worship and prayer. We should not be satisfied by our traditional holy chores like visiting the temples and attending the holy gatherings. Even the scheduled meditation and contemplation should not be the high points of our holy day.

You see! All these holy things that we do in order to remain a faithful follower of our holy religion are not enough to please God. Too bad, that our holy mind believes that such exercises are sufficient and are satisfactory services to God to receive His graces.

Well, one does not have to agree with me as he can judge it for himself. All he has to do is to stand against the word of God in verses, **Holy Gita 9:34, 18:65**, and measure his love and devotion for Him, and see it for himself.

The truth is that no matter how great we believe our holy life is, none of this has much merit in the sight of God, because all this does not consists of the most essential element of *Bhakti* (love and devotion), which manifest its true essence only through absolute submission and surrender to God and loving our neighbor we love ourselves.

Loving God is not limited to just few customary rituals and rites, few sacred activities of sacrifice and austerity, few moments of meditation and contemplation. No, not so!

It is a continual thing like an unbroken deliberation that unceasingly prolongs throughout all hours of the day, never halting even for a minute, never taking any breaks, never ceasing to take a pause, but constantly adoring God through our actions of love and light, day and night, diligently and devoutly, with absolute surrender and submission, in utmost

285

purity and piousness, and with a willful and joyful heart that rejoices the blissful abidance in Him.

Of course, realistically saying, no one can meet such standards of adoring God with perfect love and devotion. We all would fall short in one way or the other. We all would fail in such dedication and devotion; but that is alright.

The inadequacies in our efforts are okay as long as our intentions are pure, and our heart is fully devoted to loving God and as long as we are fully dedicated to Him with our absoluteness. God sees not what and how much we have accomplished in our holy ways, but with what heart and soul we have rendered ourselves to His exaltation and His glorification.

So, the true *Bhakti-Yoga* is not just another spiritual discipline that is practiced only at certain set times of the day, but is a way of life in which each and every moment is lived in love of God; but of course, with the sole purpose to please Him and with no other goal in mind.

Thus, the *Yoga-of-devotion-and-love* is nothing but a life that is totally given to God in love with full faith and trust in Him, and with total reliance upon Him.

In such faithful and focused follow-up of this *Yoga*, God is not only known with utter simplicity but with tremendous vitality; He is revealed not only in understanding but in vivacious living reality. His Truth is not just comprehended as wisdom, but is witnessed as manifestation of His words.

Oh! In the vigor and vitality of this *Yoga* is seen the expressed reality of God in lives of those that love Him with the entirety of their essence and have their mind, heart and soul fully dedicated to Him as His liveliness in their days becomes the witness of His returned love.

Surely, we are the most selfish people if we love Him because we need something in return; if we seek any reciprocation of our devotion. Such love has no value and worth for God, and it holds no merit in His sight.

Therefore, our love has to be of highest degree that never seeks any return or reciprocation from God, not even any recognition and acknowledgement. We must love Him just for the sake of His love and for no other purpose.

In fact our love should be so pure and holy, so unselfish and untainted that we love Him not because we desire salvation for our soul but because we just love Him. That's all!

Oh! His salvation comes to us because He is our Salvation. In Him, we are naturally salvaged, redeemed, and resurrected to true life; in Him we are naturally reinstituted back to our eternal form.

Thus, when we take a look at our love and devotion for God, we see how insufficient and inadequate it is; how faulty and flawed it is; how defiled and besmirched it is!

Beloved! Just loving God through our rituals and rites, and worshipping Him through our traditional ways is not enough. Offering flowers and sweets, chanting His name, singing hymns and prayers are all good, but it is not enough. Our customary holy ways must be complemented with a life that is surrendered and submitted to God. Our thinking and thoughts, ambitions and aspirations, goals and resolutions, plans and preparations, expeditions and explorations, missions and pursuits, all must align with the mind of God; they all must be fully given to Him with our joyful submission.

Our love and devotion has to be pure and pious, otherwise our unholy offerings would never be acceptable to God who is most holy and hollowed. How can He ever be interested in sacrifices that are tainted with selfishness and self-centricity, ego and pride, and are laced with lust and lasciviousness? Why would an utterly sacred God ever accept gifts of love that are glutted with gluttony and greed, and are defiled by all kind of vice?

Beloved! Know that the best way to adore God is by living a life that is holy and hollowed, and is in complete harmony with His will. Surely, such a spiritual path is the best of *Bhakti-Yoga* – the spiritual discipline of love and devotion.

Therefore, with absolute surrender and submission, we must take refuge in God and abide in His sanctuary willfully and joyfully. We must focus upon Him, always; and should never let our sight go off Him no matter what!

And thus, in each and everything, we all must pursue Him first by making Him the center of our universe, and become the disciples of *Bhakti-Yoga* – the spiritual discipline of love and devotion.

Sixth: God is attainable through love alone.

Surely *Bhakti* – the love and devotion to God with a heart of submission and surrender – is an unfailing way of His attainment, **"That Supreme Being is attainable by unswerving devotion to Him alone, O *Partha*! – Holy Gita 8:22,"** because when we love and adore God so unceasingly, it pleases Him the most, and in return, He reveals Himself to us and allows us to come close to Him.

Since God is extremely merciful and kind, so when we offer Him unselfish love and devotion, He receives and reciprocates it by giving His love million times more; He returns it by bestowing multitudes of graces, **"O *Partha*, however the person adores Me, in the same manner I bestow My grace on him – Holy Gita 4:11."**

Of course, through His unending graces, not only we receive the prosperity of this world but also cherish the riches of eternal world, and become enlightened with the radiance of His spirit.

Oh! We become infused with His love and light; we become lighted with His radiance and wisdom; we become filled with His knowledge and understanding; and we become embodied with His Truth and Reality, **"As an act of divine compassion, dwelling within their self, I destroy the darkness born of ignorance with the shining lamp of wisdom – Holy Gita 10:11."**

When such divine and eternal affluence dawns upon our spirit, God dwells in us live and we become the living witness of His goodness and grace; we become breathing projection of His liveliness, **"But those who worship Me with devotion I am in them and they are in Me. – Holy Gita 9:29."** Lord God says that in love and devotion, He lives in us and we become projection of His liveliness; and we live in Him and He becomes the source of our liveliness.

Beloved! In such surrender and submission, where one has taken total refuge in God, lies the life eternal; in it lies the doorway to the abode of everlasting peace and joy:

O *Bharata* take refuge in Him alone with all your being. By the Grace of God you will attain supreme peace and supreme abode.

(Holy Gita 18:62)

Like many other scripture verses, in following verse also, God says that in love <u>alone</u>, man attains His abode; that in devotion alone, he reaches His Reality:

O *Arjuna*, the scorcher of your foes, <u>it is by single-minded devotion alone</u> that I can be known, seen in reality, and also entered into.

(Holy Gita 11:54)

The word '**alone**' here is highly significant because it leaves no room for any other way but 'love and devotion' that brings union of man with His creator. This is the only avenue there is that enables man to know who God truly is. There are all kinds of disagreements in theologies of various religions; however, they all agree that love is the way to God, and it is the way of God.

However, there seems to be a paradox, since in Holy Gita alone there are multitudes of references where Lord God repeatedly says that He is very reachable through so many other spiritual approaches, which He himself speaks of with so much enthusiasm and passion.

This gives rise to a question, why just like the above verse, in so many other scriptural texts, it is written so profoundly that love and devotion alone is the way to God **(Holy Gita 11:54)**? Why does Lord God use the word '**alone**' and singles out the devotion and love from all other *Yogas*, and anoints it with such a high merit and calls it 'the only way' to Him? Why does He seem contradictory to His own words when He says that, "**it is by single-minded devotion <u>alone</u> that I can be known, seen in reality, and also entered into;**" that through unceasing devotion alone He is reachable? Why?

After all, as described in several preceding sections, God is attainable through other *Yogas* (spiritual disciplines) as well, which He Himself speaks of so passionately not only in Holy Gita but in our holy books as well; so what is the justification of Him saying that in love **alone** He is attainable? Why God seemingly has created such a paradox? Why He has stated a truth at one place and then something to contradict it at another place? Why?

Well, the simplest of answers to this question can be found by raising another simple question: Can we ever fully merge into something without becoming it? Can we ever become one with something without liquidating our individuality into its singularity? Of course, never! Hopefully, this fact alone dissolves all the confusion. But let us try to understand it anyway!

Since God is love and He is the God of Love **(Holy Gita 10:28)**, so how can we ever merge with Him without becoming 'love'? How can we become one with His wholeness of love without us first abandoning our individuality into oneness of Love?

But since the 'becoming' has to begin somewhere before we fully 'become', the *Yoga* of *Bhakti* (love and devotion) begins to make sense, since it opens the door of our merger with God, Who is Love, and paves the way for our union with Him by transforming us into love. But please mind that only through His grace alone such 'becoming' of us is possible.

So love is such an essentiality that is a must, before we can ever inch forward towards God.

Of course, God is the home of all virtue, so our merging with Him requires us to become that virtue. But becoming of any virtue takes place in us only when 'love' lays down a path for it, when love first becomes our way; only then all the transformation of our inner person takes place.

Merging with God means becoming one with Him in all and every sense, as no individuality is left thereafter. So if He is Love, we become Love; if He is Light, we become Light; if He is Knowledge, we become Knowledge; if He is Bliss, we become Bliss; and thus, we become everything God is. Our merging becomes complete in us only when we become who He is.

But all the becoming is dependent upon first our becoming of 'Love' as love is that eternal and divine instrument that paves the way for all other 'becoming'; it is that virtue that is a must to flourish and nurture all other virtue in us.

For example through *Jnana* (Wisdom) one becomes light, and through *Samkhya* (Knowledge) one becomes Knowledge, but can he become these virtues without first becoming vessel of love? Surely not!

Similarly, not just the Wisdom and Knowledge, but every virtue of God, we become it only when love first forms the way for it. This is the fundamental understanding, which we all must have in order to begin our walk on spiritual grounds rightly and effectively.

Since God is love, hence all *Yogas*, all spiritual disciplines, all holy trails, which lead to Him, must pass through this destination before we can ever arrive their finality – the eternal destiny – the ultimate reality of the Paradise.

Therefore, it does not matter what *Yoga* we adopt, we must operate in love since it is an unavoidable essentiality. This is exactly what Lord God is trying to make us aware of in verse, **Holy Gita 11:54**, that love is a <u>must</u> in all recipes for arriving to the reality and truth of God.

Seventh: In truth, various Yogas are not as disjoint as they seem to be.

While listening to the greatness and grandeur of various *Yogas*, one gets the feeling that these spiritual disciplines are quite different from each other since they have very different looks due to the fact that they wear different disciplinary masks, but quite surprisingly, underneath their external appearance, which reflects the makeup of their *Yogic*-philosophy, they all have the same spirit – the spirit of love and light.

This secret unfolds only when one rises to such levels of higher understanding where he has the vision of Truth and sees rightly the reality of God.

Then he understands that even through the spiritual disciplines differ in their adaptation and application due to differences in their *Yogic*-philosophies and dispositions in operating principles, but the most potent central law is the same that operates as the very life in them and is the common essence in all; and that universal law, which is the heart and soul of all *Yogic*-restraints, is of course the law of love and light.

The fundamental principle involved in such understanding is that love is the way to light, and light is the way to liberty.

Therefore, no matter what spiritual approach we adopt, we must walk from the darkness to light, which is only possible if we could demolish the walls of ego and pride, and rise above our deeply infused self-centricity through the power of love.

You see! In love are rooted all *Yogic*-approaches since no spiritual discipline is of any good unless it has the power to remove darkness and bring light into the soul; but that happens only when love dawns upon her and begins to cleanse her.

By cleansing the impurities, love reestablishes the soul in purity and piousness where she begins to reflect the radiance of God. Once the glitter of God begins to glow upon her face, and His wisdom endows in her spirit, the soul finds freedom from all fetters of *Karma*, and becomes liberated from all bondage. Well, when that day comes, with new wings of eternal liberty, the soul flies towards the high skies of heavens to be united with God.

Thus, as we can see, no matter what spiritual path we adopt, and no matter what holy trail we follow, the eventual end of all avenues is always the same – which is the love and light of God – the ladder that leads the soul to eternal kingdom, and escorts her to the magnificent abode of *Moksha*.

The most unrevealed secret is that all the spiritual disciplines are intertwined with each other, and the reason for their entanglement is that they all have to operate in love, because without love they will not be effective since love is what leads a seeker to light.

Considering the established truth that the intuitive Self-knowledge and divine wisdom is the ultimate destination of all spiritual journeys, the various *Yogic*-paths, regardless of how diverse they are, must merge into the avenue of love, so that they could be directed towards the single source of light, which is God.

The wisdom says that the spiritual paths are the entry points to the Kingdom of God. But once we have made the entry, the distinction between the door through which one enters and the other doors disappears quickly. In there, we become the citizen of the same country – the country of God – which is the country of love and light.

God has provided various types of *Yoga* so that we could choose and adopt according to our suitability and liking. After all, we all are made differently; we all have our likings and *dis-likings*. Certain things are suitable to us and certain other are not; not everything is made to our suitability. So it makes sense that God has provided all kinds of *Yogic*-paths so that we all could choose a spiritual discipline that is most appropriate and suitable to us.

Otherwise, *Yogas* are like the colors of a rainbow, whose brilliance beautifies the whole sky not because the glow of any single color is splendid, but because the brilliance of the whole band formed by the assimilation of all kinds of colors is so marvelous and magnificent, that rainbow smiles in the sky as a divine glory.

Such is the colorful union of *Yogas*, and such is their rainbow-look, that at one end of which glows the Knowledge (*Samkhya*) while at the other glitters the Selfless-action (*Karma*); these are two ends of spectrum of Yogic-disciplines, **"Since ancient times I have taught two paths: the Yoga of Knowledge – Holy Gita 3:3,"** and in between gleams the beauty of all remaining *Yogas* along with them. While one end, which is of *Samkhya* (the path of Knowledge), is highly subtle, the other end, which is of *Karma* ((the path of Selfless-action), is utterly gross.

Only the ignorant considers the seemingly diverse spiritual disciplines (*Yogas*) as being different approaches, and regards them to be the separate channels to reach enlightenment, but the wise regards them otherwise and thinks of them as varying channels of the same band with only difference that they each provide individual appeal to spiritual seekers in terms of suitability of their nature and ease of adaptability.

What we need to understand is that these *Yogas*, which look so different from outside, are in fact very complementary to each other. Without contributions from others any one of them would not be as effective since they all depend upon each other's feed. Therefore, no matter what *Yoga* a person begins with and with what *Yogic*-practice he initializes his spiritual journey, there comes a point on the way, where he has to integrate all other *Yogas* into his holy endeavors, otherwise not much progress can he make from that point on.

Here is the explanation, why?

It is a proven fact that *Karma-Yoga* is very essential to all seekers, otherwise, why Holy Gita would emphasize it so much? The reason for it is that Selfless-action is a natural first step towards enlightenment since it initiates those spiritual transformations in a seeker, which are essential to a point that they are almost mandatory; meaning, without them he would not be eligible for any meaningful spiritual attainments.

Therefore, *Karma-Yoga* is a must thing if a devotee wishes to climb the ladder of Self-enlightenment, because without the power of action-in-love (action-in-nonattachment), the soul would never be purified and renovated to become fit for the divine revelations.

The *Yoga* of Selfless-action has this unique quality that it prepares one for true enlightenment; it increases purity by dissolving impurities; it enhances holiness by overcoming un-holiness; it drives out the indwelling darkness and makes the soul ready to receive the divine light and wisdom.

In other words, it creates spiritual perfection in man through purification **(Holy Gita 5:11)**; thus, it eliminates the inbreathing ignorance in man and prepares him to receive the knowledge and wisdom, and makes him the qualifying recipient of the truth of God. These words of Lord God Himself provide the witness to this truth: **"Men pursuing their own duties with devotion attain spiritual perfection – Holy Gita 18:46."**

Now if we accept the fact that *Karma-Yoga* is an essential element in seeker's growth, we are compelled to accept the practice of *Buddhi-yoga* as well, since without it *Karma-yoga* remains incomplete, **"Therefore, engage yourself in the practice of *Buddhi Yoga*. The performance of actions with a balanced mind is indeed the skill in *Yoga* – Holy Gita 2:50."** It remains ineffective, since it does not have the integration of equanimity of mind. Therefore, we have to adopt them together if we wish to succeed in any of these two *Yogic*-practices.

Consider now *Samkhya* – the *Yoga* of knowledge – the seekers of which, who are quite sure of their wisdom and understanding, often suggest to renounce all actions and avoid all *Karmic*-involvement by escaping the active life as God has given and retiring into a passive life of Renunciation and Knowledge, which they think would be better merited as per word of God since it should lead them to a *Karmic*-life that is of non-bondage.

However, Lord God very clearly puts down the idea by firmly stating the fact that the *Yoga*-of-action (*Karma*) is better than the renunciation-of-action **(Holy Gita 5:2)** by giving reason that the path of *Samkhya* (characterized by the renunciation of all actions) is very difficult to walk since **"without *Karma-Yoga* the path of *Samkhya* is beset with troubles – Holy Gita 5:6;"** and that the *Yoga*-of-selfless-action is almost an essentiality for *Yoga*-of-Knowledge.

So if we do not adopt the path of Selfless-action (*Karma*) along with path of Knowledge (*Samkhya*), it will be hard to walk on it simply because the inner-purification that we need to have before we are ready to receive the knowledge would not be there; henceforth, it would not work! And that is what Lord God is hinting here by saying that without action-in-nonattachment, the path of Knowledge will be filled with troubles.

Of course, the underneath reason for essentiality of adoption of *Karma-Yoga* while practicing the *yoga* of *Samkhya* (Knowledge) is that unless we arrive spiritual cleanliness in ourselves and attain sufficient purity of mind, how can there be any comprehension of the Truth and Knowledge? How can we fill in something of utmost purity in the vessel that is badly defiled and unclean?

In other words, we can read all kinds of holy text, understand it, talk about it, and even hold intelligent discussions on it; but all that remains void of true understanding of God; it remains annulled of His Reality and Truth, of course, unless first the contamination from our mind has been wiped off and our soul has been sufficiently purified.

Now, let us think the other way around and ask: Can we reach enlightenment through Selfless-action alone and not have Knowledge? Can we reach closeness of God and not know who He is? Is it possible? Of course, not!

Similarly, can we become fully established in Renunciation (*Sanyasa*) and not have selflessness in action (*Karma-Yoga*) or not love God (*Bhakti-Yoga*), or not have Equanimity-of-mind (*Buddhi-Yoga*) or not know the truth of God (*Samkhya-Yoga*)?

Well, the answer clearly tells that the spirituality is a multi-dimensional holy walk. No matter what *Yogic*-dimension we adopt and no matter what spiritual discipline we choose to follow, our real growth in enlightenment comes only when we begin to grow in all dimensions.

In the beginning we are often focused upon one *Yogic*-practice because somehow for whatever reasons that looks attractive to us. However, once we move forward in our spiritual journey, we come to a juncture where the paths of all *Yogas* merge, and from there on we become a traveler of a singular path – the path of love – the path of self-purification.

While traveling on this path, we surely are transformed into someone very new who looks nothing like the old-self, and we begin to shape into what God has wanted us to be when He created us. This Transformation that takes place in us as per His will is multi-directional as we do not just grow in the dimension that we choose as our initial path to enlightenment but in all dimensions of spiritual evolution.

This phase comes in our life only when we have taken total refuge in God, and have fully submitted and surrendered to His will; only then we grow not only in one but in all virtue: in selfless-action (*Karma*), in love and devotion (*Bhakti*), in light and wisdom (*Buddhi*), in relinquishment (*Tyaga*) and renunciation (*Sanayas*), in dispassion (*Vairagya*) and detachment, in knowledge (*Samkhya*) and higher understanding, and in every other way that is helpful in bringing us close to God.

Thus, even though our emphasis may be singular in approaching a *Yogic*-path, but if we have yielded ourselves to our seeking of truth and we are given to our expedition to enlightenment, then our spiritual growth would always be multi-dimensional; there is no doubt about that!

Lord God Himself says that *Yoga*-of-action (*Karma*) and *Yoga*-of-Knowledge (*Samkhya*) are not disjoint paths, **"Children (the ignorant)alone speak of Samkhya (the path of** renunciation) as different from *Yoga* (the path of action) – Holy Gita 5:4)." Only the ignorant thinks of them to be distinct and different.

But the wisdom of a wise man is quite the opposite who regards them as being the two sides of the same coin. He sees them as being one because he knows that one without the other really has no true meaning:

The goal that is acquired by renunciation is the same that is attained by *Karma* Yogis. Whoever sees *Samkhya* and *Yoga* as one indeed sees rightly.

(Holy Gita 5:5)

So if according to God, the most subtle path, the *Samkhya* (Knowledge), and the grossest path, the *Karma* (Selfless-action), are not different from each other, then what should we think of those spiritual disciplines that lie in between these two opposite ends of the spectrum?

Thus in truth, *Yogas* are like various footsteps of the same ladder that leads to the same end-resolve – which is the liberation of soul from bondage.

Since *Yogic*-disciplines are intertwined and in many ways are complementary to each other, they help the seeker in their own ways through their individual virtue, and enable him collectively to reach the full vitality of spiritual perfection.

To expound upon it even further, consider the following verse that depicts a good example where Lord God commands us to engage in the battle of life and render our natural duty with the heart of submission and surrender and keep Him in the forefront of our thoughts at all times:

Therefore remember Me at all times and fight. With your mind and intellect surrendered to Me you will attain Me without doubt.

(Holy Gita 8:7)

According to these holy words, we ought to live like a *Karma* Yogi and fight the battle of daily life just the same as *Arjuna* of *Mahabharata*, and engage in it with full advisement and empowerment of God that we receive from Him through our joyful and willing submission to Him.

297

Now, why does God ask us to do this? How does it benefit us?

Beloved! I am glad that we are asking this question. Know the secret that it benefits us in most divine way because it teaches us how to become surrendered and submitted to God, and be given and yielded to Him, which is impossible to do on our own.

Of course, in such yielding alone comes the life of non-bondage, since all empowerment of life then comes not from the 'self' but from God, and then, there is no 'self' present in action, and neither is the 'doer' in its performance.

The entire day is ordained and put forth by God – discerned and directed by God – formed and shaped by God – authorized and empowered by God – achieved and accomplished by God. The 'self' does <u>nothing</u> since he is entirely surrendered and submitted, given and yielded to God. And thus, only God renders it all.

Oh! The empowerment of God dawns upon our day and the deliverance from bondage bestows upon our soul only when God is the sole business of our day; when all our abilities and capabilities become abandoned in His power and potency; and when all our resources to support and sustain the day are derived from His ever available empowerment and inexhaustible provisions; and surely, when our life becomes such a holy pursuit where God is the foremost thought heading each and every effort and He is involved in all engagements of the day, then there is victory – only victory and no defeat.

Then there is no failure in our lives, because no matter what else happens, and what results in which way, we yet attain Him with absolute certainty, **"Having thus surrendered yourself to Me, with your spirit united with Me, you will surely attain Me – Holy Gita 9:34)."** And that's all what really matters to us anyway because what else could be a better outcome of life?

So as we can see, in these words above, **(Holy Gita 8:7)**, God commands us to adopt the *Yoga* of Selfless-action, but with love and devotion (*Bhakti*). He asks us to remember Him at all times, of course, with an attitude of total submission and surrender, and by rendering our mind and intellect. He instructs us to engage in life with implied sense of duty, which of course according to His words must be rendered selflessly as a *Karma-Yogi*.

This presents a good example where we find that various spiritual paths are not as disjoint as many believe them to be. In verse above, **(Holy Gita 8:7),** the Lord instructs us to engage in life dutifully but with constant and continual adoration of Him (by exercising *Yoga* of *Bhakti*) while rendering all actions in complete surrender and submission (by exercising *Karma-Yoga*).

And, when we render ourselves in such a manner and become worshipper of God through our selfless actions, and begun to live as a dedicated *Karma-Yogi* in our daily life, and adore God in each and every way as a *Bhakti*-Yogi, we attain God with absolute certainty.

The main point to understand is that our good work alone does not make connection with God, no mater how greatly it is done; it is the lighted heart underneath our holy action, which puts us closer to Him; it is the loving spirit that is filled with devotion, which brings us into His presence and makes us acceptable to His sight.

Oh! It is the love and light underneath the action which paves the way of non-bondage for the soul.

Here is another verse, virtually with the same meaning but of course with different words, that provides further witness to this fact that we must render all actions of our common daily life as a *Karma*-Yogi, and while engaged in them we must continuously meditate upon God with the attitude of submission and surrender and be a *Bhakti*-Yogi:

He who remembers Me constantly with his mind unflinchingly devoted to Me for that ever controlled Yogi I am easy of attainment O *Partha*!

(Holy Gita 8:14)

Surely, it is our focus upon God, which is the most important thing in life, as He should be our center in all things. It means it is not what we do, but with what attitude and mindset, and with what heart and spirit we do, counts the most in the sight of God.

Therefore, as we can see, each spiritual discipline serves a particular purpose in our self-transformation; each one helps us in some way in getting ready to receive the wisdom and understanding of God without which we cannot hope to understand His truth.

So, we must not treat various *Yogas* as being different and disjoint, but consider them as being the multiple colors of one rainbow, because in such enlightened vision alone we can understand God's incomprehensible being and be able to see the most colorful flints of His infinite majesty and magnificence.

10

Man's Highest Privilege
~
That He is the Author of His Life

The significance of human embodiment does not sink in us till we understand clearly that it is the only window of opportunity there is for the soul where she could bring any change in her *Karmic*-course; that life as man is the only chance she has if she desires to alter her *Karmic*-fate and ever has any hope to attain the eternal liberation.

However, such understanding does not come easily, especially not till we see a good composite of the total *Karmic*-reality of the soul. Because not until we see the futility of all other lives but human, we realize that all other *Karmic*-suffering besides what the soul endures as human has no real value, as all others are only a payment to due *Karma* with no other rewards whatsoever. It is only the human life where the rewards of her sorrow and suffering could be as high as her salvation – her perpetual freedom from bondage – the *Moksha*.

Once it becomes clear that all other embodiments of the soul but human, do not yield much lasting good for her, the life as human becomes the point of focus, since in it alone she is enabled and empowered to do something about her release from bondage.

Therefore, we must learn the specifics of *Karmic*-realities of the soul during human embodiment, from the moment she wears the most privileged body and takes birth as man, till the time she ceases her fleshly home and parts from this mortal world.

Well, in an effort to create such understanding, let us summarize briefly what facts we have learned so far about the *Karmic*-confinements of the soul:

A – According to the laws of *Karma*, when the soul (*Atman*) ceases a human body, then if not released from bondage, she begins her next *Karmic*-cycle, and is set forth on such a journey of *Karmic*-consequences, which forces her to pass through countless embodiments and compels her to wander in various *Karmic*-worlds.

B – For her good deeds (*Punya*) the soul travels to worlds of pleasure and enjoys the gratification of the high heavens (*Swarga Lokas*), and for her bad deeds (*Papa*) she descends down to the deeps of hell (*Narka Lokas*) and suffers the misery and pain of condemned domains. However, at the end of it all, when her time in those *Lokas* is up, she falls back to earthly provinces and returns to this world of body, blood and bones again.

C – To express and exhaust the due *Karma*, the soul passes through countless embodiments and experiences their pleasure and pain, but not much else meaningful is accomplished by her through it all, since all non-human lives serve one and only purpose, which is to exhaust *Karma* and lighten her *Karmic*-burden; that's all!

D – As the soul passes through the tunnel of Transmigration and goes from one body to another, she carries with her all subtlety that she had at the end of her previous human embodiment, and keeps everything intact till she embodies as human again.

Meaning, at the end of her *Transmigrational* journey (of non-human embodiments), the composite of the subtlety surrounding the soul is the same as she had at the time when she parted away from her previous home of human flesh.

The *Prakriti*, ego, desire and attachment, *Raga* (love, passion, desire) and *Dwesha* (hatred, dislike), and all other elements that composed the inner person in her last human flesh, are still there with her as they were carried with her while she passed through countless births and death and wandered as nomad spirit in various higher and lower worlds.

E – So when the soul is born again as human, she has the same surrounding sensual subtlety, **"He draws the senses and carries them to the body that he obtains - Holy Gita 15:8,"** and the intellectual empowerment, **"He is united with the intellect that he had cultivated in his past lives – Holy Gita 6:43,"** as she did at the time when she parted away from her previous human body with only one exception that now she has a new body and new physical world surrounding her.

From this brief summary of *Karmic*-cycle, it becomes quite clear that if we wish to map out only the meaningful path of the spiritual evolution of the soul, we can do so by connecting the two dots in her *Karmic*-journey – the end of one human life to the beginning of next – and thus, hypothetically eliminating all detours that the soul takes by wandering meaninglessly through of *Karmic*-worlds of varying consciousness and assuming all kinds of countless non-human embodiments.

After all, only human lives are consequential in determining *Karmic*-path of the soul, since all other embodiments serve no other real purpose but to make her suffer the immeasurable consequences of *Karma*, and force her to go through all kinds of experiences of pleasure and pain.

It means at the time of her birth as human, the soul is virtually at the same point in her spiritual evolution where she was at the end of her previous human embodiment. And now she is ready to pickup right where she left off and to begin travel on that journey again.

So if we overlook everything else but human embodiments of the soul, then we can visualize how her spiritual evolution progresses from one human life to the next and be able to see the direction she is heading to.

Since whatever the surrounding sensual subtlety the soul has at the end of one human embodiment, she gets it back at the beginning of next **(Holy Gita 6:43)**. Therefore, any logical mind can see that her journey through human lives is almost seamless except that she gets a new fleshly vessel each time.

With this concise but a clear view of soul's *transmigrational* journey where only her human embodiments matter in terms of what really affects her *Karmic*-course, let us explore some facts that can truly enhance our understanding of what human life is all about:

First: Since Karma is a phenomenon of 'cause' and 'effect', the human life is both; it is born out of 'effect' of life in past, and becomes the 'cause' of life to be born in the future.

Of course, all life, which the soul endures in any form, human and non-human, is an expression of *Karma* that she has created during her past human embodiments **(Holy Gita 8:3)**. It means the human life of present also is an 'effect' of what has taken place during her previous human lives, which surely are its 'cause'.

Thus, looking through the *Karmic*-philosophy, human life is both – the 'cause' as well as the effect – since it is the 'effect' of previous human lives, and is the 'cause' of the human lives that are yet to come in the future.

This fact that human life is not only the 'effect' but also the 'cause' is very important for us to understand, since it unfolds the mystery of what human life is capable of.

Second: Even though we have no control over the 'cause', but we certainly do over the 'effect'.

Surely, the current human life is the 'effect' of previous human lives that caused it, but it also is the contributing 'cause' for future human lives; meaning, it is not only the 'effect' of previous human lives but also is the 'cause' for future human lives that are yet to come through *Karmic*-ordinance. Thus, even though we have no control on the 'effect', we certainly do on the 'cause'.

Of course, we all know that life comes to us exactly as it has been pre-ordained by God according to our due *Karma*; and we have no choice in receiving it, but to accept it whether we like it or not. So the 'effect' of previous *Karma* is there in the form of our current life: the environment, the events and happenings, and the daily unfolding of life moment by moment; and we are to accept it as it comes without any choice, without any reservations. True!

However, how do we respond to life that comes to us as preordained, is still under the power of our 'freewill'. We have total freedom in our response to it, don't we, as there are no restraints imposed upon us of any kind!

So even though we have no control over the 'effect', meaning the life comes to us as it has been preordained according to the previous *Karma*, which is its 'cause', we still are free in how we react to it and what kind of 'cause' we become in creating the future life as its 'effect'.

Beloved! No matter how bad the life is and no matter how distastefully it falls upon us, but how do we receive it is still totally up to us; we can receive and respond to it any way we want to. Yes! It's true that we have no control over how it descends upon us, but through our freewill we still have the power to raise it to any level we want to.

Of course, there is no guarantee for anything, but surely, this is the power, which we human have, that can change our *Karmic*-course since through the ability of our freewill we can choose to react anyway we want to; meaning, either we can choose to act in goodness and grace of God and create good *Karma*, and henceforth, create good 'effect' in the form of good future life; or, we can choose to act in badness and wickedness of our self-centric self and create bad *Karma*, and henceforth, create bad 'effect' in the form of bad future life.

Oh! It all is at our disposal; it all is up to our choosing!

Third: We are the authors of our lives.

Surely it does not seem that way, however, it is true that we are the true authors of our lives!

Although I agree that our common belief is that the life we are living has been preordained; meaning, each moment that we live, befalls upon us as pre-determined as nothing in life happens arbitrarily. How often we hear folks complaining "What is supposed to happen would happen!" It's true, no argument there!

However, what we do not realize that, "What is supposed to happen, has not been decided by something else, but by what we have made to happen." Nothing is going to popup in life by itself as each and every moment of it is an outcome of some action(s) that we have rendered in our past.

You see! By living the present, we are not just expressing our past *Karma* but also are creating the *Karma* for future; meaning, we are not just living the present moment and experiencing life as created by the *Karma* of the past, but through the *Karma* of our current actions, we also are creating the life for our future.

Thus, even though on one side we are totally helpless in choosing life for ourselves, since it is coming to us through the ordinance of Karma and we have no control over it; however, we are fully capable of creating life in any form and fashion we want to due to the fact that we are fully privileged to create whatever *Karma* we like by reacting and responding to *Karmically* ordained life accordingly.

Just the way, the happiness and sorrow of the present moment depends upon how did we live that frame of time in our past which created it, the same way, the happiness or sorrow of that future frame of time, which the present moment would create, would depend upon how do we react and respond to it now.

So through our life of the present, we are not just helplessly expressing the preordained *Karma* but also creating confidently new *Karmic-life* for our future through the tremendous power of 'freewill'; meaning, while living the preordained life, we are continually forming and shaping new life for our future through the privileged power of 'freewill that God has endowed and empowered us with.

Thus, regardless of how we are living life, we are constantly and continually authoring new life for ourselves; of course, the quality of which is solely dependent upon how we render ourselves to the life of present that comes to us as preordained.

Fourth: The harmful Karma is created not only by dreadful actions but also by those simple and insignificant ill actions that are part of our common daily life.

A sin, no matter how little it is, is still a sin; it still has severe consequences; it still creates bad *Karma*; it still has its ill *Karmic*-penalties. No matter how insignificant it is, it still has sorrow and suffering that would be forced upon the soul to bear.

But most of us do not mind much, committing little sins during our day since we do not consider their sinfulness as being serious. The reason being, that when we think of sin, our mind immediately goes to heinous acts like murder or robbery, and never goes to those little sins that have become a natural part of our common daily life.

For example: lying here and there, being dishonest every now and then, acting deceitfully whenever we need to, behaving in animosity and jealousy with those whom we do not like, conducting arrogantly and egoistically at times to show our power and authority, treating others with coldness and cruelly, are just few such sins that we never consider as being sin and operate in them more often than not, in fact, almost on daily basis.

You see! Our mind is so corrupt that these kinds of sins do not even register in its radar. As a result, we do not fear committing them since we do not consider them grave enough; or we can say that we have become so numb to sin that we do no sense any wrong in them.

Hear these words of Lord God and judge it for yourself if this is not a portrait of today's man:

Driven by insatiable desire, filled with pride, hypocrisy and arrogance, holding evil ideas due to delusion, they work with impure resolves.

Given to innumerable worries which last only in death, considering the enjoyments of the sense

pleasures as the highest goal, they feel convinced that this is all.

Bound by the fetters of numerous desires, obsessed by lust and anger, they strive for acquiring wealth by adopting unrighteous means, for the sake of gratifying the senses.

"I have obtained this today, I will fulfill this desire as well. This is already in my possession, that wealth will also come under my possession. ...

I have destroyed this enemy. Others will be also destroyed by me. I am the supreme Lord. I am the enjoyer, the perfect one, I am endowed with power, I am happy...

I am wealthy and born in a noble family, who is equal to me? I will perform *Yajna*, give wealth in charity, will rejoice." Thus deluded by ignorance - ....

Confused because of many evil desires, entangled by the snares of infatuation, intensely attached to the gratification of the senses, they fall into foul hell.

Holding themselves adorable in their own eyes, devoid of humility, intoxicated with wealth and pride, they perform *Yajna* in name only for the sake of ostentation, without observing the scriptural injunctions.

Ever addicted to egoism, force, conceit, lust and anger, they hate Me who abide in their bodies as well as in the bodies of others, and are full of maliciousness.

(Holy Gita 16:10-18)

Clearly, this is a pretty good description of mentality that today's humanity has. Beloved! Can we deny it?

When we read such scriptural words, we think that they apply to others and not to us. In ego and pride, ignorance and darkness, we never entertain even the faintest idea that we also are the criminals in the virtuous sight of God; that we also are the violators of His moral law; that we also are the breakers of His righteous rule; that we also are the transgressors in His consecrated country; that we also are the criminals in His upright kingdom.

Just because our violations are not as grave as of robbers and murderers, does not mean that we are not guilty of crimes against His righteousness.

Each one of us can map his day against the violations as listed in verses above **(Holy Gita 16:10-18)**, and see for himself that even though we are not the vicious violators and cold convicts of laws of secular government, yet how many offences do we still commit each and every day against the spiritual administration and authority of God.

Isn't this our reality, that we are intoxicated by power and prosperity, driven mad by name and fame, consumed by lust and lasciviousness, marred by gluttony and greed, and completely taken over by the pursuit of worldly wealth? Isn't pleasure our greatest passion and infatuation our highest engagement?

Of course, it is!

And now, please pay attention and look at what is the *Karmic*-fate of those whose life fits the mold as described above by the words of Lord Himself:

These cruel haters of Myself, the worst among men, who are involved in sinful deeds, I hurl them into demoniac wombs.

O Son of *Kunti*, having entered into demoniac wombs, deluded from birth after birth, unable to attain Me, they continue to fall into lower births.

(Holy Gita 16:19-20)

Oh! They are hurled into the demonic wombs – so says the incarnated God, Lord *Krishna*.

What a sad end of the one who commits crime against the justice-system of God where the penalty of sin could be as grave as him being thrown into gutters of hell, where his soul continues to fall deeper and deeper into lower births.

Undeniably, today's man has become so immoral that he has become spiritually bankrupt. He is living a life which is burdening his soul with the heavy load of sin, and he is drowning in the filth of *Karma* day by day.

He does not realize, that after death, the sinful trail of his unrighteous life will be retraced by *Karma*, and then, he will be held responsible for each and every evil and immoral action that he has committed to enrich himself materially on this earth. He has forgotten that he would be held accountable for each and every breath taken in sinfulness, and that, each guilty conviction would force him to suffer severe consequences of his bad *Karma*.

Beloved! Whether we accept or not, operating in selfishness and self-indulgence is a normal mode of our behavior. May be not with all, but it is true at least for most of us. So how can we deny that conducting in sin is not in integral part of our daily life, because it very definitely is!

But how many among us really see this truth straight? Not many, quite surely! However, that does not mean that these little acts of sin do not have any *Karmic*-consequence, because they surely do.

If the *Karmic*-Laws are true, which they are as per *Hindu* scriptures, then not only the acts of horrible sins create the horrible *Karma*, but even the simple daily actions like thinking ill or talking bad about someone, to which we hardly ever pay any attention, also yield quite a harmful *Karma*.

The validation of this *Karmic*-rule comes from many holy books that document and dictate quite severe *Karmic*-consequences for those ill actions that we most often do in our common daily life, of course, without much hesitation since we do not realize how serious those offences are.

The problem is that selfishness and self-indulgence have veiled our wisdom to a point that we have lost the sensitivity to sin; we have become extremely ignorant of not only the severity of our actions but also the penalties they incur.

As a result, we have becomes disabled to apprehend the reality, that our little actions of ill resolves, our small vile acts of sin, our tiny deeds of hidden wickedness, all such minor offences against the righteousness of God, which seemingly appear to be so insignificant, are actually quite harmful since they do yield the stern consequences for us and produce awful *Karma*.

I am sure that in our common thinking we never see of ourselves as guilty of such crimes; however, can we deny that often our day is tainted with thoughts and actions of anger, jealousy, deceit, greed, hatred, and revenge? What about them? What about those acts of vice and wickedness? Don't they have any consequences? Don't they have any *Karmic-percussions*? Oh! Surely, they do!

Of course, we all have the right to our own judgment; we all are free to think that, may be whole world is like that, but not me. Well, if it happens to be true for someone, and he is without such sins during his day, then that is just great! I am happy for him, and admire him for living a life of such purity and piousness. I wholeheartedly hold him high for his days are free of such evils and his daily engagements are so holy and hallowed. But we are not going to find one like that so easily.

So, let us look deep in our heart and take an honest peek at how do we pass our day from dawn to dusk, and examine what emotions and feeling, what desires and determinations, what resolution and inclinations drive our day, and then see if we still find ourselves free from such indictments, specially after judging it against the backdrop of the truth that *Karma* is mainly dependent upon the motive and intent and the extent of willingness in engaging in effort behind an action rather than just its gross appearance. And then see if we still feel cozy about ourselves? Or, have we changed our view and find ourselves guilty of ill deeds, not just once a while, but more often than not?

The naked truth is that for most of us, our day goes by in doing whatever it takes to add more abundance to our lives; which means we perform all kinds of actions, which by no means are right and just. Our ever unquenched lust and greed to have more physical prosperity, our hungry ambitions and desires to attain and accumulate more worldly wealth, force us to do all kinds of evil all day long. Since everybody else does it, so it does not register as evil to us.

I know all this sounds harsh but the reality cannot be ignored; the imperfection has become our natural being, which is very opposite to what our true nature is – of purity and perfection.

Now-a-days, committing common ills are very much within the normalcy of our acceptable behavior. It is no surprise that no body raises eyebrows and yells a foul when we commit such sins almost daily and engage in them as if they are part of our regular response.

Oh! We are morally so drained and righteously so declined that such daily corruption has become a part of our justified skills. We exalt ourselves for being successful even if we succeed by illegal means. We measure success in life by how much power and authority, how much wealth and prosperity, how much name and fame we have; and it does not matter how do we do it and how do we reach there. Surely most of us do not care for any of that as long as we acquire success and rise to higher levels of human success.

We are so blinded to our own truth that we fail to see our own reality – the reality of our filth and sludge, our own grunge and grime. We fail to see that we are full of ego and pride, extremely lustful and greedy, and driven by never-ending ambitions and desires.

Therefore, no matter how much we argue against it, the reality still stands, that during our lifetime, due to these unaccounted ill actions that we commit daily without worrying about their *Karmic*-percussions since they hardly ever show up on our moral radar, almost all of us would generate so much bad *Karma* that it would keep us under its cruel captivity for a inestimable time to come.

The consequences of our daily sin would be so long-lasting that they would compel our soul to endure the life of all kinds of dreadful domains and force her to pass through the sufferings of countless lower births before she could ever have any hope to be born again as human.

And beloved! That's our truth, whether we agree and accept it, or disagree and deny it!

Fifth: We are fully enabled to create any kind of life we want to for our future, the good or bad – it is totally up to us.

Of course, we have no say in what kind of life we have at present as it is as per *Karmic*-ordinances, however we have the power to shape life of our future since it would be created by the *Karma* of our present.

So even if the life of present moment is most unpleasant and miserable, we still have the capacity to create a moment of joy in our future that would result from the *Karma* of this moment but only if we choose to live it in goodwill and joy. Now whether we do it or not is up to our choosing. Surely, we are free to opt to live it anyway we like; whether we respond to it with good or bad, is totally up to us; and that would decide whether we have just formed and shaped a good moment for our future or bad.

This is why, when life becomes ugly due to percussions of *Karma* of the past, a fool and ignorant complains and often responds to it with anger and bitterness; however, the wise knows that he can do nothing in what has already happened, and accept even the bitter *Karma* patiently and cheerfully, but knows well that he has the power to change its course now, so he operates with goodness and grace and creates joyful future for himself.

Surely, we all can benefit greatly by such attitude but only if we could rise above our emotions and feelings, and understand that we hold such a great power in our hands that enables us to build our future filled with peace and joy even during the times of turbulence and turmoil. Just by conducting with wisdom, we can form and shape our future to a highest degree of meaningfulness even while passing through all kinds of adversities and hardships, and going through most devastating circumstances.

But alas! We hardly ever realize that we endow the most amazing and awesome ability, whose power and potency so definitively enables us to author our upcoming life any way we want to.

It does not matter what kind of circumstances we are currently facing. We surely have no control over them since they are the result of *Karma* of our past; but we still have the power to create good *Karma*, because the exhaustion of the old has no bearing over the formation of the new, since the experience of old *Karma* has no say in the one that is being created now.

There is no doubt that even during the worst and ugliest moments one has the power and privilege to live with happiness and joy, and with peace and contentment. He has the endowment of such authority in himself that he can prevail over the worst of circumstances and conduct himself with altruism and unselfishness, with virtue and righteousness, with magnanimity and nobility, and with generosity and thoughtfulness, but of course, only if he could rise above his emotions and feelings of that moment affecting his inner tranquility and harmonious equilibrium and realize his endowed empowerment.

Quite undoubtedly, one has the ability and authority over it all; however, whether he chooses to exercise it or not is another matter. Surely making the choice to stay firm in his resolution to endure the adverse moments with decency and dignity, honesty and honor, character and candor, morality and uprightness, is always within the power and potentiality of his freewill.

So quite certainly, we all are empowered to create our future life in any manner we want to. We have been given the privilege to model our coming days and fashion our tomorrows in any way that pleases us. Now what do we do with this power and privilege is up to us. Whether we create nice and bright future for ourselves or we make it dark and ugly is our own choice.

Surely, God has given man the gift to form and shape his future life and has endowed him with the power to author it according to his own will; He has given Him the blank canvas to draw its picture anyway he likes and has given him the brush to paint it in any colors that please him.

However, the truth is that most of us more often than not fail to respond properly to life; and when I say 'properly', I surely mean to refer to respond to it in a way God would like us to respond, which frequently is quite different than what we may regard to be proper.

The reason for such discrepancy is due to the fact that a response that is 'right' in our smartness, in fact, may not be right according to the wisdom of God; and hence, it may not be 'proper' because the proper response always means a response that is righteous and virtuous, moral and upright in the sight of God.

So a right response does not always constitute a proper response because self-rightness is often quite the opposite to righteousness of God. Therefore, a response that is enacted in self-rightness and not in the righteousness of God creates *Karmic*-percussions and brings bondage.

This is why God has instituted the 'natural duty' for man, so that by rendering it, he could exhaust and express his preordained *Karma* 'properly and justly' by rendering his natural obligations without being tainted by any sin, **"because by performing duties born of one's own nature, one does not incur sin – Holy Gita 18:47."** And thus, he could be spiritually purified and be able to attain the vision of light and love, which eventually could lead Him to the sanctuary of God where through His grace he could find the eternal liberation for his soul.

But how often man chooses to render his duty exactly the way God has laid it out for him? Surely not very often!

Even though the word of God commands us to render our duty as if it were our most holy service to Him, **"By adoring Him through the performance of one's own duty, one attains spiritual perfection – Holy Gita 18:46,"** but how many among us really heed His instruction but fail! Even among those that are considered to be great and glorious, virtuous and upright, moral and noble, and benign and benevolent, do not fully meet their natural obligations and falter in fulfilling their inherent duties.

Oh! But only if we could do that! Would we not then be blessed to attain our salvation by finding the way to God's refuge where His grace could redeem our soul from bondage and enable us to unite with Him?

> **Having taken refuge in Me, he who performs all his duties at all times, he attains the Eternal and imperishable Abode by My Grace.**
>
> **(Holy Gita 18:56)**

Surely, we would!

But alas! Most of us respond to life though rightly, but our rightness is not necessarily the rightness of God. As a result, we surely attain high feats in this world but our accomplishments have very little meaning in the Kingdom of God because though our responses to life are 'right' but they are not 'proper' as they are rendered in our own smartness and not in the wisdom of God.

Therefore, to respond to life rightly in true sense would happen only when we would act and behave in a manner that is as per the righteousness of God and not according to our own wisdom, and then, we would head onto the path of non-bondage and non-captivity, which eventually would take us on to the way to everlasting life.

Oh! The power to all good life lies right in our hand; but, whether we exercise that power or not is entirely up to us.

Sixth: In ignorance, we often blame God for ills of life and do not realize that it is our own doing.

How often when we see misery and pain in life, we accuse God for being cruel and cold-hearted.

In anger and frustration, we say wrong things to Him; and we do so without knowing the facts about our own reality and without realizing that whatever we are facing in life is due to our own doing. We fail to understand that whatever misery and pain we have is due to our own ill deeds of the past; and nothing what God did to make it happen, as all has been ordained in our life as per our own *Karma*.

Therefore, before we complain and accuse God to be uncaring and cruel, we must understand that life is regulated by the laws of *Karma*; and that these laws are enforced upon all mortal life without any waivers. So what life we have at present is what we have created ourselves at some point in our past. God has nothing to do with it; by no means He is responsible for it, as all responsibility falls upon us since it were we who created it all through our own actions.

The laws of *Karma* are very clear in this regard. With absolute certainty, we reap what we sow, but with only one unknown, the time. The time is the only variable there is; because it could be in this life or the life next or even beyond. The thing that is very definite is that it would bring fruition of *Karma*, one day in its due time when God finds it proper in His sight.

So whatever we have in life is due to our own *Karma* of the past, which was certain to come as per *Karmic*-ordinances and statues, and now it is here. However, the *Karma*, which we are facing now, necessarily does not have to be from the previous life, because it could be from this life as well; in fact, it could be as recent as from the moment that just passed by.

Thus, the timing of expression of *Karma* is the only variable but not its exhaustion, as that comes as per choice of God. There is no hard and fast rule by which the timing of expression of *Karma* is regulated; at least nothing like that has been dictated in scriptures.

It means our life of present is exactly what we have created it to be in our past. Similarly, please know that every moment of our present life would create some moment of our future. Now, when would that future moment come, is totally up to the determination of God. It really is that simple!

The way it works is that our response to some life of past has formed and shaped this moment of present, and the response to life of the present would form and shape some life of our future.

Meaning, the moment that is currently before us is the result of how we have responded to some moment in our past; and now, how are we going to react to this moment of present is going to shape some moment of our future that would come to us later on.

According to laws of *karma*, this is how all life is formed and shaped. If the present moment is a happy moment, it means our response to some moment in the past that created this moment of our present was very pleasant; and that is why it resulted in a good *Karma*, and henceforth brought such good fruits of happiness during this moment.

But on the other hand if the response to that moment in our past that created this moment was bad and we did not deal with it in love and light, then the present moment would also be bad; meaning it would be unpleasant and ugly.

This is why it is often said that we are the authors of our own life; we are the writers of our own fate; we are the creators of our own future.

No wonder, not only for the for the sake of present but also for our future, we are always encouraged to have positive attitude towards life, so that we could naturally respond to it positively rather than indulging in it negativity, and thus, securing happiness and joy for our present as well as for our future rather than filling it with misery and pain.

Once we understand this truth that it is no one else but we ourselves have formed and shaped the life that we have, since we are its authors, then we begin to realize that whatever misery and pain is in it, is not because God intentionally induced it since He is an unkind and cruel God who cares not for our sufferings, but that such moments of hardship have fallen upon us due to the fact that we have created them ourselves through our bad *Karma* of the past by committing crimes against the righteousness of our Creator.

Of course, as always, God was only a witness in our past when we did the evil and created such *Karma*, and so is He now, when the bad *Karma* of our evil deeds has come to fruition in the form of sorrow and suffering.

So why to blame God, when He only established the laws of *Karma* and gave us the authority to operate them and create whatever life we like. And if we have not created good life for ourselves then it is our fault and certainly not His.

Just by accepting this reality, we can do a great favor to us, because by doing so, we immediately increase our awareness about how we are going to respond to life from this point on; meaning, we would be very watchful of ourselves and would be vigilant in doing our level best in creating good *Karma* so that it creates good life for our future.

But too bad that often we do not understand this reality and even though we accept the coming of *Karma* as the will of God, yet we never realize our responsibility that we have the authority and it is our duty to respond to it rightly and justly.

Following verse of Holy *Ramayana* is very popular because the truth spoken in it is believed quite widely. Just about every one of us believes that whatever God wills, happens; meaning, ordained *Karma* befalls upon us no matter what:

hoihi soi jo rama raci rakha, ko kari tarka baRhavai sakha.

These holy words are translated as follows:

After all, whatever Sri Rama has willed must come to pass; why should one add to the complication by indulging in further speculation.

(Holy Ramayana, Bal-Kanda 51:4)

But the truth spoken in these words often becomes a misguiding force within us since it aids to our attitude to be unreceptive and passive. Due to ignorance and lack of understanding of the truth, we allow it to operate in us negatively, as it encourages acceptance of the reality of the situation but without strengthening our resolve to stand against the unpleasant and difficult circumstances.

Therefore, we often accept defeat by hard times, and do not face them with audacity and courage, because we fail to understand that even though we cannot avoid facing them but we still can respond to them with the highest ability that endows us, since response to life is always a matter of our freewill and is completely under its authority.

Therefore, we should always conduct with courage and strength, joy and peace, regardless of circumstances so that we could always be benefitted by the good *Karma* created by it, and reverse even the *Karmic*-course if the situation was brought upon by the wrath of bad *Karma*.

Seventh: Whether our soul rises or falls in spiritual-progression is completely in our hands.

No doubt, the rise or fall in spiritual-progression of our soul is completely in our hands since what we choose to do in our freewill during this life determines what direction in her spiritual evolution she would head after she parts from this world – the upward or downward.

If her *Karmic*-evolution is upward, she heads towards the high provinces of heavens, and if it is downward, then she

319

rapidly descends down to the deep depths of hell; meaning, the good *Karma* feeds the swing upwards while the bad drives it downwards.

Again, mind you! That as far as the spiritual evolution of the soul is concerned, the wandering in high heavens or drifting in lowly hells has no real significance, and that is not all! There is something else very important, which must be taken into account.

You see! Besides forcing the soul to wander in various *Lokas* (planes of varying consciousness) and compelling her to pass through countless embodiments, the *Karma* also affects soul's surrounding environment. The good portion of *Karma* (*Punya*) increases her wisdom and light, while the bad (*Papa*) multiplies her ignorance and darkness.

Holy Gita says that good portion of *Karma* (*Punya*), which is born out of virtuous actions (*Sattwa*), due to its purity and piousness, gives rise to light and wisdom and multiplies the growth of higher knowledge; however, the bad portion of *Karma* (*Papa*), which is born out of self-centric and egoistic actions that are done out of passion and self-indulgence, due to its impurity and adulteration, gives rise to darkness and delusion, and multiplies the growth of greed and gluttony, and ignorance and heedlessness:

The wise say that the fruits of virtuous actions is Sattwika and pure, the fruit of Rajas is pain, while the fruit of Tamas is ignorance.

From Sattwa proceeds knowledge, from Rajas greed, and from Tamas heedlessness, delusion and ignorance.

Those who are established in Sattwa go upwards, those in Rajas stay in the middle, and the Tamasikas steeped in the worst functions of the Guna, go downwards.

(Holy Gita 14:16-18)

Thus, what happens during human embodiment of the soul, and what kind of *Karma* does she create – the good (*Punya*) or bad (*Papa*) – affects her spiritual evolution; due to good she heads upwards while due to bad she goes downwards.

Now if during each human life, the spiritual evolution of the soul continues to be in the same direction, then of course, depending upon the feed caused by the good *Karma* (*Punya*) or bad (*Papa*), either she would spiritually rise and head towards her perfection **(Holy Gita 6:43)** or she would spiritually fall and head towards the wombs of darkness **(Holy Gita 16:21)**.

So if we look at it wisely, this is the real gain or loss for the soul in terms of her eternity, because going to higher *Lokas* to enjoy heavenly pleasures earned out of her good deeds or be thrown in lower domains to suffer misery of burning hell as a persecution for committed sins, are in fact only the side effects.

Of course, whether the soul rises towards the light and wisdom or she heads towards the darkness and delusion, determines where she would eventually head to?

Oh! Her eternal destiny depends upon whether she finds the light or not, whether she becomes able to see spiritually or not, and whether she is able to understand the Truth or not!

Therefore, what happens in human life for the soul has a very far-reaching effect upon her eternal-destiny. This can set the course of her ascent unto the eternal freedom or throw her on the course of *Karmic*-descent that can lead her to the deeps of bondage to mortality.

Thus, the *Karma* in human life has the potency to 'cause' both kinds of 'effect' for the soul – the good and bad; the good can lead her to higher grounds of enlightenment, while the bad can push her deeper into lower corridors of darkness.

If man's discerning empowerment, the mind, is desire-free, then it is pure; in fact so pure that it could see the path to eternal liberty. But if it is infected by passion and infatuation, it becomes impure; so impure that it could become totally blind, and fall further deep into the wombs of bondage.

It means mind has the power of both: to ascend to skies of eternal freedom and everlasting life if pure; and to descend to endless deeps of bondage and mortality if impure. Meaning, a pure mind can acquire a vision of such a light that it could show man the way to *Moksha* (Liberation), while an impure mind could be so dark that it could drown him in dreadful womb of bondage.

Eighth: Continual upward spiritual evolution of the soul can lead her to the supreme goal – the Moksha.

Surely good *Karma* rewards one with life in heavens, but as we already know, that is not the real gain in terms of eternity of the soul, since sooner or later, once she has enjoyed the heavenly pleasures, she falls back to earthly grounds **(Holy Gita 9:21)**, and in its eventuality wears the human embodiment again.

Thus, not much the soul gains out of heavenly experiences as they are temporary and transient; however, the true gain lies in the fact that when she is eventually reborn as human, she possesses all the spiritual wealth she had earned during her previous human life. With goodness of God, she is given all the treasure of intellect and wisdom, and of knowledge and understanding, which she had accumulated back then **(Holy Gita 6:43)**.

In other words, not the trip to heavens, but getting back in current life her accumulated treasures of higher intellect of the past that she accumulated during her previous human life, is the real reward for her good *Karma*.

Now, if during each upcoming human embodiment, the life is invested in good *Karma* intended to accumulating further intellect and wisdom rather than devoting it to fulfill the desires of heavenly pleasures, then more and more spiritual perfection will dawn upon the soul during each human-life, and more and more she would be able to see the truth and reality of God, which undoubtedly in due course would lead her to His refuge where by surrendering herself to His sanctuary, she would find the salvation for herself through His grace:

Having perfected Yogic-states through many lives, in every birth exercising more self-effort than before, a Yogi brings about the removal of mental impurities, and consequently, attains the supreme goal.

(Holy Gita 6:45)

So if one fails to attain the liberation for his soul in this lifetime because of one reason or the other, but if his spiritual efforts are heading in that direction, then he still is greatly benefited by it, since his holy effort would never go to waste, **"On this path, no effort is ever rendered void, nor is there a risk of a negative result – Holy Gita 2:40."**

Though one should never plan it that way because salvaging the soul in this lifetime is the highest reward of our humanity, but if for some reason we fault and fail, then at least there is some consolation in the fact that all our holy labor would be preserved and protected and be given back to us during our next human birth so that we could begin our spiritual journey again right where we left off during this last attempt.

It means the upwards spiritual evolution always grows the soul in more knowledge and wisdom each time she passes through human embodiment, which only enables her to have a better understanding of the truth and reality of God; thus making her further capable of attaining the ultimate goal of human life – the eternal liberation – of course, which comes only through much graces of God.

11

Grace of God
~
Soul's Only Avenue to Salvation

"I just want to say, that I don't teach anybody to get rid of their ego. No, I teach them to understand it, and see how it came into being and how its functions?" – A wise man once wrote these words to me. What a revelation that was! His words were filled with wisdom, only unveiling the truth, which the saint has comprehended directly through his own enlightening experiences.

The ego is one of the subtlest identities, which is very hard to keep tab on. So if one thinks he has succeeded in getting rid of it by whatever *Yogic*-exercise he practices, let him be exposed unprepared to egotistically assaulted situations and see for himself if his ego flares up or not? Because there is a high probability that his ego will flash like the head of a serpent and would bite like a snake?

You see! Habitually, often we try to fix the things without first understanding them. Well, so is the case with ego too. We try to get rid of it without first comprehending the reality of its workings. Surely we know what ego is, but do we really know how it operates and how it affects? Do we really know the limits of its subtlety and understand the entirety of its influence?

Oh! The honest answer for most of us is 'No'.

Beloved! Just knowing what ego is, is not enough; it needs to be understood; it needs to be watched; it needs to be continually monitored and be under constant surveillance. Ego is so subtle that at times though it is there but we cannot see and recognize it. It is highly dominant and controlling, prevalent and shrewd, and most of all, illusionary and deceptive.

In fact it is so deceptive that it can make a right thing look wrong, and a wrong thing look right, and provide quite a compelling argument for acceptance of its version of presented truth. This is what happens to most of us; our ego and pride deludes and blinds us to our own truth, forget about the truth of others and the truth of God. No wonder even the most wise sometimes gets deceived by its illusions.

One of the most highlighted examples of its deception is the belief it induces in some spiritually self-confident men and make them assured of the idea that liberation of the soul can be attained through man's own *Karma*; meaning, through his own spiritual efforts and endeavors, through his own purity and piousness, through his own sacred learning and knowledge, through his own wisdom and understanding, he can salvage his soul; that through his own holy endeavor he can attain liberation from bondage. This happens to be a thought of extreme deception, which of course is caused by ego born out of false and misleading spiritual confidence.

Thus, not only we see the evil workings of ego in the arrogant and proud, but oftentimes in the one who has amassed tremendous holy wealth through his enormous spiritual toiling. How often we see the harshness in conduct of a man who claims and portrays himself holy and hallowed, sacred and spiritual? How often we hear the words of arrogance from a man who has learned the scriptures and has become master of the holy text?

These are the evils of highly deceptive ego that often surface in men who embody sacred learning and knowledge, and personify purity and piousness, and are supposed to be the knower of wisdom of God. Such learned men become a great example where the sense of the egoistic 'self' blinds a person and misdirects him unto the wrong holy path leading to their spiritual destruction.

Of course, he behaves un-righteously not because he is bad by nature but because this is what ego has done to him and made him so deluded that he has become blind to the truth about himself by his own self-righteousness, and now because of grown darkness he walks the arrogant path of self-glory, and thus gets diverted away from the path of rectitude and righteousness of God.

This is exactly what happens to the one who thinks that he could attain the salvation on his own through his own holy endeavors by purifying himself through prescribed *Yogic*-disciplines and growing into higher enlightenment, thus by cleansing the soul and making her spiritually perfect, and eventually leading her to eternal liberation.

Even though not so often, yet once a while, we come across such men who think that their holy knowledge is enough to pave the way to their 'Self-realization'. They claim that they are so established in Knowledge that they have ceased the sense of self-existence since they believe that they are just the *Atman* and not the body; they declare that they are beyond the reaches of *Karma* since they have transcended it through their accomplished higher understanding of the Truth.

What a grand thought that is, no doubt! And what a marvelous accomplishment it is, I must say!

However, my great fear is that such claims most often are the products of egoistic deception that carry nothing but darkness and delusion. Such philosophical belief is not a path to true knowledge that could lead one to 'Self-realization', but it is a trail of darkness and delusion that is going to make him fall into the gutter of grunge and grime of self-gratification.

Of course, it is not that such a claim is impossible, because the existence of absolute self-denial, after all, is the finality of self-surrender to God; however, the greater possibility exists that such claim has come out of darkness and delusion created by egoistic 'self', which has become irrationally arrogant due to the sense of self-knowledge of scriptures and self-confidence in ones own religious holiness, rather than a true grasp of Self-knowledge and real understanding of the Reality and Truth; because more often than not this is what happens.

Now, let us consider why such a claim, that one can arrive to *Moksha* (Liberation) through his own holy efforts and endeavors, has a great possibility of being wrong. There are at least two solid reasons that can be highlighted:

First: Moksha (Liberation) requires absolute 'self-abandonment', which without the grace of God is impossible to arrive.

Oh! The way of liberation of the soul is the way of self-abandonment, self-dissolution!

And that comes only when the ego is putdown and has been brought under complete control. It is a way of total non-being and non-identification. It requires extinction of all self-assertions, which is only possible through a constant and continual denial of egoistic-existence and a consistent abandonment of the 'self'.

Now, is it possible to arrive to such a state-of-being of perfect 'non-self'? We all should try to find the answer to this question on our own because then we would learn, what a monster we are dealing with. And then, we would also realize how difficult it is to control ego and how hard it is to let go of our 'self' and become a <u>perfect</u> 'non-identity'.

Ask any wise man and he would tell that such perfection of 'non-being', of 'non-identity', and of 'non-self', if not impossible, then to say the least is extremely difficult; and difficult to a point that it may exist only hypothetically. Meaning, one could arrive to such a high state of enlightened existence only in supposition and not in reality.

Simply because, even after much extermination of the egoistic will, the residues of self-centric imperfection always remain even if they are only of a minute degree.

Second: The 'self' cannot extinguish the 'self'.

I cannot eliminate my 'I' by myself – is a simple fact. I do not need to be a genius to understand that. Because once I say, I have overcome my 'I', I am actually telling a lie because the claim I just made came from no other but my own establishment of 'I'.

So the sense of egoistic-self cannot be destroyed by the 'self'; only a power higher than 'self' can accomplish this impossible task. And, that higher power is no other but the higher 'Self' – the Transcendental Supreme Self – the Brahman - the God Himself.

Please hear these words of God that provide witness to this truth:

The Sages say that the senses (Indriyas) are higher than the objects, while higher still than the senses is the mind. The intellect is higher than the mind, and even higher than the intellect is the Supreme Self.

(Holy Gita 3:42)

According to the wisdom depicted in these words, higher than the mind and intellect is the Supreme Self – meaning God.

But what are the mind and intellect? Aren't they the home of ego? Of course, they are! Because even when mind takes on the varied states of existence – Mana (state of Emotion), Chitta (state of Reflection), Buddhi (state of Intellect) – the fourth state, which is of Ego (Ahamkar), always exists. Meaning, ego coexists in mind with all others and remains in it as a cohabitant and as an active partner during all other states. Thus, ego is ever-existent in mind no matter what!

Therefore, one has to rise beyond the periphery of mind if he wishes to find the field that is not under the influence of ego; and that happens to be the domain of Supreme Self – the God Himself.

It means we need God to reach God; we need Him if we wish to attain Him; we need Him if we desire to seek salvation for our soul; we need Him if we want to set our Atman free from the fetters of Karma and secure his eternal liberation from bondage.

So, it is a delusive thought to think that through his own workings one can rise to such high levels of enlightenment where he could reach *Moksha* and salvage his soul from the manacles of mortality.

Oh! Blessed are those who believe that salvation is not earned by works of man but received as a gift through the grace of God!

Here are some thoughts on this subject that are worthy of our serious meditation since they yield sufficient reason in support of the thought that no human is self-sufficient in attaining freedom from *Karmic*-bondage, and they also sufficiently validate the fact that man is never self-empowered in securing the salvation for his soul, no matter how powerful and potent, pure and pious, virtuous and righteous, learned and knowledgeable, wise and prudent he may be.

You see! Man's holy endeavors cannot accomplish this impossible task no matter how great and glorious they are. And if so, then we may wonder for what good they are after all?

Well, following are some explanations and arguments that try to clear the mind about what is the true function of man's holy endeavors? Why on his own he is incapable of attaining liberation for his soul? Why does he need God for it? And how has God paved a way to accomplish this humanly impossible task by laying dawn those tracks on which man could walk and easily arrive to his heavenly home and live his eternity with Him.

First thought: The perfection of soul is impossible without God.

Our common belief is that we have to be perfect to attain *Moksha*, because that is what the state of our being is when we are delivered from bondage and become united with God.

This thinking seems right because how can the human imperfection have union with the perfection of God. Of course, Never! Therefore, it makes sense that we must first become perfect so that we could become eligible to be united and be merged with God; isn't it?

So, as can be expected, all our holy efforts are driven towards the goal to make ourselves spiritually perfect. It is only natural to think like that since the ideal state of existence of the soul is only when she reaches the absoluteness of her spiritual perfection. Well, that is what one tries to attain if he is a seeker of *Moksha* – the spiritual perfection of his soul.

But even though such efforts are essential and useful to our spiritual growth, however, as we would learn below, that such thinking does great harm because spiritual perfection is not a prerequisite for soul's salvation.

However, the idea that to attain *Moksha* one has to be spiritually perfect is so popular that most of us never give ourselves a chance to know the reality that there is no pre-condition to attain the liberation of the soul except that one has to be fully given to God. Thus, ignorance overshadows our spiritual vision and directs our holy walk unto wrong path.

On top of it, we become even more delusional when we misread such scriptural texts that tell that man can reach the spiritual perfection by adopting certain spiritual disciplines and practicing certain prescribed *Yogic*-exercises.

For example, here are the words of Holy Gita that say that if we perform all actions for the sake of God, we would attain perfection, **'Upon doing actions for My sake you will attain perfection – Holy Gita 12:10."** Lord God even gives an example on how a *Karma*-Yogi reaches this spiritual feat, **"*Janaka* and others attained perfection by following the *Yoga* of Action – Holy Gita 3:20."**

Similarly, the scriptures tell that one can achieve perfection through *Sanyasa* (renunciation), **"He attains perfection through renunciation – Holy Gita 18:50."** Yet another holy text dictates that if one has the Knowledge Supreme, then he could be sure to attain perfection, **"Supreme knowledge which is the best of all knowledge knowing which all Sages attained perfection – Holy Gita 14:1."**

These are only some of those examples which describe how to achieve spiritual perfection, which could be considered as the pre-state to our true state-of-being prior to attaining the state of eternal liberation (*Moksha*).

However, if we carefully examine the spiritual approaches, in each one of these *Yogic*-disciplines that have been dictated as means to arrive to such high state of enlightenment, we learn

330

that for most of us to succeed fully on our own in any one of those ways is highly unlikely. They are not as independent and autonomous as we think; they are the works of my 'I' alone.

If we diligently examine these holy texts, we find out that, what is being asked in these examples is impossible to arrive by anyone, no matter how holy he is, unless he first seeks help from God; meaning, no one can meet successfully the condition of dictated spiritual approach perfectly on his own, and henceforth, would always remain short of reaching the high point of total spiritual perfection.

You see! We do not have to accept this conclusion without argument. Therefore, let us realistically consider how much possibility there exists for a human to succeed in any such holy endeavor where he reaches the spiritual perfection hundred percent. Let us investigate the odds a man faces in achieving the absoluteness of any *Yoga*.

And moreover, let us raise those questions that can tear apart the heart of the matter and separate the reality of what is possible by the holy labor of man and what is not?

For example: In today's world, can we ever become hundred percent a *Karma*-Yogi? Meaning, can we ever perform all actions of our day absolutely without any desire for their fruits? Can we ever remove all traces of selfishness in all of our works? And while doing them can we ever become fully established in our mental equanimity?

Or, can we ever arrive to the level of consciousness where our self-being is nothing else but just Knowledge? Can we ever completely renounce the world and become a hundred percent *Sanyasi*? Can we ever attain the total equanimity of mind and be fully established in the highest wisdom? Or, can we ever attain the absolute state of existence as a *Jnana*-Yogi?

To find answers to such questions, we do not have to be an enlightened soul or be a man of high wisdom, because it is not hard at all to realize that the probability of succeeding fully in any one these spiritual approaches is highly remote, even to a point of being very little to none, but only leaving an almost hypothetical possibility aside. Meaning, it is almost imposable for man to attain such enlightened feat of highest consciousness.

No wonder the word of God says that a soul which has realized the truth of God is very rare to be found, **"It is extremely difficult to find such a great soul – Holy Gita 7:19,"** since such wisdom dawns only after many lives of continual spiritual progression, **"After many lives (of progressive spiritual evolution), one acquires wisdom – Holy Gita 7:19."**

Surely, this sounds to be very disheartening, but we must face the reality.

Of course, there are many other spiritual paths beyond what I have given the examples of, that are described in holy books, which seemingly pave the way for man's spiritual perfection and lead him to his salvation, but they all have the same minute statistical certainty of ever arriving to their final destiny of perfection, especially if they try to attain it through their own spiritual potency and not through the power of God.

Because, the possibility of anyone attaining such spiritual perfection that is of the highest degree is almost impossible to none. The simplest argument applied in support of it could be this, that there exists nothing else in God's creation in perfection except God Himself. But it certainly does not forbid the possibility that one can reach a near perfection if not total perfection, even though it is highly remote.

The discussion here is not to prove the point whether I am wrong or right but to get a firm grip that for us to reach the spiritual perfection is highly unlikely, and that means there has to be another way which of course is through God alone where we do not have to be perfect to reach our salvation.

In regard to this, two things need to be understood here. First, arriving to spiritual perfection has a very little possibility; and second, even if one can make it happen, he certainly cannot succeed in it without God. So no matter how we look at it, we need God, regardless.

Of course, without any doubt, there are, and have been in the past, such high souls who have attained the spiritual perfection, and thus found a way to eternal liberation. But they always were in scarcity, and always will be. Such highly enlightened souls will always be rare to be found. And again, they were only spiritually perfect and not perfect in all aspects of their existence.

For example, Lord *Krishna* speaks of king *Janaka* **(Holy Gita 3:20)** and of other holy sages **(Holy Gita 14:1)** who attained such feat, and then through His own words, He repeatedly confirms this fact that man is capable of reaching spiritual perfection.

Regardless, we still cannot deny the reality that reaching to such enlightened state-of-being is highly unlikely, even to a point of being impossible, especially, when we speak of ordinary folks; because, the discussion here is not about those few rare souls who are highly awakened and are capable of such attainment, but about the rest of remaining multitudes of the seekers who are not of such divine capacity.

Thus, knowing the truth about human limitations in regard to his spiritual abilities, we must understand and accept this near-impossibility of reaching spiritual-perfection especially attaining on our own, because if we do that, then our conviction of such reality immediately removes the darkness that lingers in us and makes us believe that we are self-sufficient in our salvation; and we begin to understand how to engage in our spiritual efforts in such a way, that they can pave the way for our eternal liberation through the grace of God by enabling us to seek the total refuge in Him and surrendering ourselves to Him with our entire existence regardless of state of our spiritual perfection.

Beloved! Let us not try to walk this road alone and reach the spiritual perfection by ourselves since on our own the perfection is beyond our efforts anyway, as for that we need God to walk with us; and also, we do not need to be perfect to attain eternal liberation because so says the word of God.

Second thought: The human actions have limitations, and so have their outcome.

We can never deny that human actions have limitations. No works of man are infinite no matter how great and grand they are in their magnitude and magnificence.

There are at least three arguments in its support:

First, all human actions are finite regardless of their enormity; meaning, the infinity of God can never be reached through them since they in themselves are limited and finite. So how can finite reach the infinite; and even when we keep adding finites, the total sum still remains finite.

Second, they are ever tainted with defects regardless of their majesty and magnificence, **"All actions must be renounced since they are associated with defects – Holy Gita 18:3;"** meaning, how can they reach the 'state of perfection' – the state of eternal liberation – when they in themselves are imperfect.

Just these two arguments alone establish the truth that man due to limitation in his actions can never reach the limitlessness of God, henceforth, on his own, can never has union with Him and attain the salvation for his soul.

Now, if we can retain this wisdom in ourselves, we definitely would be much better off, as then we would very easily accept the reality that no matter what we achieve in this world on our own, its merit will always fail to being worthy and deserving the salvation of our soul. Ask any Self-enlightened man who has achieved the state of highest self-awareness and he would tell, that his own effort was never enough to reach such an unreachable state of enlightenment, but he made it there through the grace of God.

Third, since this argument is about the evaluation of what man can accomplish the most through his *Karma*, we are going to consider only his good deeds and not the bad. But even then, regardless of how great and grand are the rewards of his holy works, they are never good enough to lift his soul beyond the heights of *Karmic*-reach.

You see! The *Karma* is like a 'token of a reward' (Remember! we are only talking about good Karma rising out of man's good deeds), which man is forced to cash-in in due time, and whose worth depends upon the evaluated merit of what he has done to earn it. Of course, the reward could be bad or good depending upon the character of his action.

I am calling *Karma* a 'Token of reward' quite intentionally even though I am well aware of the fact that it truly is never a reward because it always is a penalty regardless of how immense and enormous, magnificent and majestic it is. Because anything, which is good and great, is truly good and great only when it yields the ultimate good for us; otherwise, it is not. Thus, in case of *Karma*, even when it is good, it really is not good, since the ultimate fruit of it is only more bondage.

The truth about *Karma* is that, in its eventuality, it is always harmful to the soul because it increases her mortality and forces her to suffer more the misery and pain by furthering her *Karmic*-life **(Holy Gita 14:5),** unless of course, it is without bondage. Then again, the cycle of *Karma* is sustained not only by bad *Karma* but also by good *Karma*. Hence, to call any *Karma* good is a mistake and to call it a reward is absolutely wrong, unless of course, it is bondage-less, which of course, is not the case most often.

However, in our discussion at the moment, I still like to call it a 'Token of reward', because I wish to reflect upon our common and quite popular view of it, which definitely considers the good *Karma* as good and does not perceive it to be bad, even though that is what is its reality.

And this view that *Karma* is a reward tempts not only just a few but most of us who are awakened to the know-how of *Karma* and understand how *Karmic*-cycle operates; and it entices us to work hard so that we could better our *Karma* by doing good deeds, and reap its rewards in 'next-life'.

But as we know by now, that no matter what prosperous lives the soul passes through due to her glorious and gorgeous deeds, which includes trips to higher and heavenly worlds, **"As a result of meritorious deeds they attain the heavens where they enjoy divine pleasures – Gita 9:20,"** and no matter how much enjoyment she experiences through them, she still eventually returns to this world.

After having gone through all those heavenly places and enjoying all those *Karmic*-rewards, she falls back again onto the earthly grounds, **"With the exhaustion of meritorious deeds having enjoyed the expansive pleasures of the heavens they fall into human world – Gita 9:21."**

Karmic-Cycle ~ The Chronic Consequence of Karmic-Bondage

Thus, after experiencing all kinds of heavenly pleasures, which the soul earns through her good *Karma*, at the end of it, she again descends down to the human world; meaning, any ascension into higher *Karmic*-worlds is only temporary and transient; her stay in those highly pleasant provinces does not last forever as in due time it all comes to an end as she eventually falls back to earthly domains.

So, it is more like a detour, which only prolongs soul's misery and furthers her time in bondage to the cycle of birth and death; because, no matter how many pleasures and enjoyments she passes through, in eventuality, she still remains a captive of *Karma* that keeps her enslaved to the repeated cycle of birth and death.

Hence, the ultimate truth about *Karma* is that instead of it being a 'reward', it actually is a debt that demands its payoff, which has to be made by the soul by all means.

And yet another truth is, that no matter how we pay this debt, it is always painful, because even after spending the time in heavenly provinces, the soul again returns to the human world, which is nothing but an ocean of suffering and sorrow, **"This world which is the abode of pain – Gita 8:15."**

But alas! This reality is not reflected in our mentality, which considers good *Karma* to be rewarding since it brings good return in future lives. So we overlook the fact that the eventual end of good *Karma* also is not good because its recompenses do not have any lasting value.

This is why the wise considers all bondage to *Karma* to be evil, and due to this reason he invests his life in getting himself released from its bondage.

No wonder, the human is very special creature of all creatures in the creation of God, as his is the birth, which has the power to take his soul into bondage or out of bondage. Surely, in the hands of man lies the power to sustain the cycle of *Karma* as well as rests the potency to terminate it.

Thus, the truth is that man in his choosing has empowerment of both: to dig deeper into the captivity to *Karma*, or to get out of it and release himself from its grip. It all lies under the power of his freewill.

Nonetheless, choosing to liberate his soul from *Karmic-*bondage does not mean that man's actions, on their own, are capable of doing so, as all of his holy actions, no matter how grand and glorious they are, are still short of such power; his *Karma*, regardless of how majestic and magnificent it is, is still not potent enough to lift his soul to the high grounds of eternal liberty.

Third thought: Man is totally incapable in himself and needs God to succeed in anything of God.

One of the most undermined truths is that man cannot succeed in anything of God unless God helps him attain it. Meaning, on his own man cannot know God. He cannot attain Him through his own efforts and cannot have union with Him through his own holy endeavors.

In other words, man's release from *Karmic-*cycle cannot come through the power of *Karma*. The reason being, the human-action has no such potentiality; it has no such capacity that could do this wonder and pull man out of the *Karmic-*grip.

But often, in his ego and pride, he thinks that his holy ways and spiritual endeavors can take him beyond the *Karmic-*horizons; and thus, he fails to understand the reality that his own goodness cannot take him to the gates of *Moksha* (liberation of the soul).

Too bad! Man's confidence in himself and his sense of self-reliance deludes him with this kind of self-destructive thinking. His trust in his own sanctity and righteousness misguides him to such untruthful beliefs; his assurance in his own smartness and intelligence misleads him to such harmful understanding.

Though it is true that man has the power to affect his *Karmic-*course by actions but only as far as the wandering of his soul in the wilderness of *Karmic-*worlds is concerned, and never beyond it; since from that point on, he is totally helpless and needs help from God.

Oh! This is one of those secrets, which man does not understand until God reveals it to him in His goodness and grace. So not only man needs grace of God to attain salvation but he also needs grace to realize that he needs His grace, because nothing about God can he ever come to know but without Him willing it first. Nothing happens in man about God unless God sanctions it first and induces inclination in him towards it. Surely, it is God who puts the thought in the heart of man, so that he could desire Him in his freewill.

Look to these words of Holy *Ramayana* that verify the truth that God reveals Himself only to those whom He chooses in His will. Only they come to know Him and none else; as only His chosen receives His truth and reality:

> **soi janai jehi dehu janai, janata tumhahi tumhai hoi jai.**

These words are translated as follows:

> **In fact, he alone can know you, to whom You make Yourself known; and the moment he knows You he becomes one with You.**

> **(Holy Ramayana, Ayodhya-Kanda 126-2)**

Therefore, there is no way one can know God unless God wills it first and chooses to reveal Himself to Him. It is always in His choosing only.

Beloved! No matter how learned and knowledgeable, intelligent and smart, we are, this still is a very delusive thought that we can learn of God on our own. Surely, it is a grave mistake to think that through our own understanding and wisdom, and learning and knowledge, we can ever comprehend Him.

Please look at these words the *Upanishad* has to say. Is there any way we could ever prove them wrong? Of course, all knowing of God comes through His graces alone **(Holy Gita 10:11)**:

> **Words and mind go to him, but reach him not and return.**

> **(Taittiriya Upanishad, 2. 9)**

This truth as unveiled by above holy text has been reflected throughout all scriptures, which clearly states that the mental sharpness of man is incapable in penetrating the thick indwelling wall of darkness that hinders the knowledge of God.

Surely, the mind is the media for all understanding but when it comes to knowledge of God, mind has to learn how to be still and cease its reason, and let the reason come to it through the guidance of the spirit. Only then arrives to it the true wisdom and understanding and true knowledge of God.

The *Upanishads* say that our intellectual thoughts seeking true wisdom are returned empty and without any true knowledge of God. The reason for them being void is that they are the instruments of physicality, and hence, they can be applied only to acquire the physical knowledge of this world.

But since God is the Spirit, we can know him only through our spirit and not through anything else. After all, He is formless and without any attributes, without any characteristics and qualities (while speaking about the absoluteness of His existence), and without any *Gunas* (three modes of nature), so how can He ever be known through the instruments of *Gunas*, which is what our mind and intellect are.

To know God, one needs to have the sight that can reach beyond the opaqueness of *Gunas*, **"He is verily called Gunateeta – the one who has gone beyond the Gunas – Holy Gita 14:25."** One has to have the vision that could penetrate their obscurity and reach the light of God. But of course, such vision comes only through His graces.

Look at what *Arjuna* has to say at the end of the discourse parted by Lord *Krishna*, **"My delusion is gone; I have regained my memory by Your Grace – Holy Gita 18:73."** Through these words, he clearly acknowledges that his delusion and ignorance has vanished, because the Lord God has showered His graces upon him **"by Your Grace,"** and not because he has come to understand the Truth and Reality on his own.

Thus, a humble acknowledgement by *Arjuna* provides a strong witness that it is not his wisdom but the grace of God that has destroyed his inner darkness and enabled him to reach the enlightenment:

As an act of divine compassion, dwelling within their self, I destroy the darkness born of ignorance with the shining lamp of wisdom.

(Holy Gita 10:11)

Please know that on our own we can never gain the wisdom of God, as it only comes when He sheds His graces upon us. Though on our own we might become learned in scriptures and train ourselves to be the expertise of the holy text, but we would always remain void and empty of any true knowledge of Him; we would never reach the true knowing of the Reality and Truth; we would never be able to have a good look of the face of God. Surely, any wisdom of God is only through His graces, always, and not through any other goodness that we might have.

Therefore, let us acknowledge it with true understanding that through the mercy and kindness of God alone we can come to know anything about Him. Through His graces alone we can come to realize that the salvation of our soul is the main purpose of life, and that the only way we are going to attain it is also through His graces. There is absolutely no other resource that we have that could help us in this matter.

But alas! Often we travel on the journey of enlightenment in our own power since we are so habitual to do the things on our own. So we treat learning of things of God the same way as learning of any other wisdom of this world, and consider the gaining of His knowledge as the brilliance of our holy endeavors, which it never is.

This is the reason why spiritual life often becomes nothing but a routine of physical but somewhat enlightening exercises. Though, it certainly disciplines our body in some ways and makes us feel as if we have become enlightened, but with all certainty we hardly make any progress towards knowing God and barely grow in His understanding.

Therefore, the realization, that God has to be behind all of our holy endeavors and that only He can make it possible for us to learn anything of Him, is very essential for our spiritual growth; because only with such belief we would be able to grow in His knowledge and wisdom, and only then we would be able to clearly see the view of the Divine, which has been hidden by our egoistic self.

Please hear what God has to say about how overwhelming is the ocean of Maya to all others, but to only those that surrender to Him and believe in His grace. Because only they

340

are able to overcome it; only they are able to cross it; and only they are able to reach to the other side:

This divine Maya of Mine composed of the three Gunas is difficult to cross over but those who surrender to Me they alone are able to cross it.

(Holy Gita 7:14)

God's own words are witness to the reality that only through His grace, can we overcome all obstacles in life, **"You will cross over all obstacles by My Grace – Holy Gita 18:58;"** only through His mercy and kindness can we find our way out of all impediments.

But too bad, that in our ego, we fail to realize this reality and do not learn of our not-so-obvious impotency and helplessness, and do not accept our inability in all matters, especially when it comes to higher understanding.

So even though we are totally disabled and incapacitated without God in comprehending the Reality and Truth, yet in our ignorance we ever remain filled with the confidence of our own capabilities to attain such feats.

No doubt! Such egoistic attitude harms us greatly, since it makes us believe that our righteous deeds are capable to take us the corridors of *Moksha* (Liberation) and bring salvation for our soul; but unfortunately, it is very misleading thought as our upright actions can do nothing more than to clear our spiritual vision so that we could begin to see clearly the truth and reality of God.

Surely, the primary purpose of all righteous works is to remove our darkness and delusion, and raise light in our spiritual sight. All holy sacraments and religious traditions that have been put forth by God are for us to be cleansed off dirt and filth of *Karma* under which our soul (*Atman*) has been buried since her primal conception as *Jiva* (conditioned-soul).

Therefore, what we must know firsthand is that all righteous ways have been instituted by God to waken up our sleeping soul so that she could regain her true awareness and be able to see His light and come to know who in truth He is. And in the wonderment of 'knowing of Him (God)' lies such a heavenly wisdom for the soul, that she ceases her falsely conceived self-individuality and becomes one with Him for all eternity.

Oh, how wonderful are these words of the *Upanishad* that speak of how the tiny soul merges with the infiniteness of God; how she loses her confined self-individuality in the enormity of His being; and how she assumes His greatness by becoming one with Him:

As rivers flowing into the ocean find their final peace and their name and form disappear, even so the wise become free from name and form and enter into the radiance of the Supreme Spirit who is greater than all greatness.

(Mundaka Upanishad, Part 3, Chapter 2)

The holy word tells us that it is the merging of falsely assumed 'self' of the soul into the Oneness of the Transcendental Self, what extinguishes her identity and makes her one with the One Who is all pervading and eternal. Just as a river loses her self-recognition by merging into the ocean, so does the soul also, and becomes one with God by letting go of her false self-identification.

It means it is the total extinction of the assumed 'self' by the soul that brings her amalgamation with God, and of course, such extinction of falsehood comes only when she is fully surrendered to Him, because only through submission and surrender can she attain grace and goodness of God to be free from all egoistic illusions of self-centric assertions.

No wonder, at the end of the discourse, how many times Lord *Krishna* emphasizes surrender to remind us that it is the only way to reach His grace, which is the only avenue for our soul to have union with Him and be eternally liberated from the fetters of *Karma*.

Look at what advice Lord God gives to *Arjuna* while speaking His final words at the end of eighteenth (and last) chapter of Holy Gita:

O *Bharata*, take refuge in Him alone with all your being. By the Grace of God you will attain supreme peace and supreme abode.

(Holy Gita 18:62)

He tells him that in a humble surrender to God is received His unending grace; and in grace alone lies that blissful abode of supreme peace and joy, which is called *Moksha* – the home of eternal liberty.

But too bad! That most of us, due to our egocentric nature, believe that our good deeds and self-righteousness are keys to our liberation, so we exert much emphasis upon doing good deeds and earning good *Karma (Punya)*.

As a result of such thinking, we do all kinds of charities, give donations and perform all sorts of sacrifices; we engage in *Pooja* (worship), *Aarti* (a formal act of adulation), *Yajna* (sacrifices), *Teertha Yatras* (pilgrimages); we do all sorts of holy rituals and rites and sanctify ourselves in so many ways; we worship all kinds of gods and goddesses to attain higher realms of spiritual ground; and we believe that our holy endeavors and sacred sacrifices would make us worthy of receiving the entitlement to the entry into the kingdom of God.

But very disappointingly, none of holy engagements do a whole lot of good for us in terms of attaining salvation, because even though we accumulate tons of good *Karma* but it only increases the *Karmic*-burden for us rather than making it light.

Surely, we rise in *Karmic*-merit by enhancing it's quality through righteous actions, and gain a better berth in higher *Karmic*-worlds but door to salvation still remains shut and we still remain caged in the territory of *Karma*.

However, the true progress towards this goal takes place when we realize our unworthiness, and find our actions incapable of opening the door to the empire of everlasting peace, and accept the truth that only through the grace of God can we ever reach His eternal abode, **"He attains the Eternal and imperishable Abode by My Grace – Holy Gita 18:56."**

Beloved! Our actions are always flawed and imperfect, **"All actions are attended with defects – Holy Gita 18:48,"** so how can they ever yield *Moksha*, which is the abode of perfection?

How can our deeds, which are ever finite regardless of how huge and enormous they are, be enough to bring about something which is infinite? How can the physicality of our body and flesh, which is temporary and transient, produce the permanent blissfulness of the Spirit? How can man, who is so limited by his egoistic ignorance, be able to reach the unreachable limitlessness of God?

Therefore, we must know firmly that we have no capability to reach God on our own, and become fully convinced of the fact that we need Him, as without His grace we would never attain salvation, and without Him holding our hand and walking us through all earthly destinations we would never make it to His heavenly home.

Oh! Of this we must become very convinced, otherwise, the salvation of our soul would never come to pass.

Fourth thought: The only power that can release the soul from the entrapment of Karmic-cycle is the grace of God.

After listening to last few arguments, one may wonder, if all spiritual paths (*Yogas*) are so difficult to succeed as they all point to an almost hypothetical state-of-being, which is almost impossible to arrive, then what are we to do to attain salvation?

This argument leads one to many questions like: How are we to get release from bondage by doing something that possibly can make it happen? If the self-effort is not enough to get *Moksha*, then what is? What else is there that can change this impossibility into a possibility? What other power is there that can join finite to the Infinite? What else is so capable that it can enable the imperfection to become one with Perfection?

By raising such questions and trying to find some answers, we tremendously raise the awareness of God's love in ourselves; because such inquiry, when we make, makes us extremely humble and meek, and leads us to such understanding where we begin to see beyond ourselves, and reach beyond our own potency and power, and begin to look up to those provisions, which God has put in place and provided for our salvation.

Oh! Then we begin to appreciate the greatness of His love. One of our biggest failures in life is that we hardly ever realize

God's loves for us. And even when we do, we still fail to understand the extent of it. We hardly ever get a good grasp of the fact that God loves us infinitely.

Well, just because we fail in understanding of His love, does not mean it is not there.

Of course, due to ignorance about God's love, we miss out on great blessings that He has for us and which he wholeheartedly desires to bless us with; however, we never receive those good fortunes in life just because we never abandon our self-reliance and seek His heavenly endowment with utter humility and meekness.

Beloved! Here is the biggest blessing of all, which God has bestowed upon our grieving soul – the soul that is living in the captivity of *Karma* and suffering the infection of mortality. Here is the decree that God sanctioned and issued for her release from all *Karmic*-imprisonment; here is the His declaration of her independence from all bondage:

Sarva Dharman Parityajaya Mam Ekam Sharam Vrajah, Aham Two Sarva Papebbhyo Mokshyashyami Ma Shuchah

Having renounced all *Dharmas* (involvement in duties and limitations), take refuge in Me alone. I will verily free you of all sins, do not grieve.

(Holy Gita 18:66)

Here is the proclamation of God's protection for those who approach Him in humility, who come to Him in love and seek Him with absolute surrender; here is the statement of promise that proclaims the preservation of those who dedicate themselves to Him in devotion; here is the public-notice of acquittal from all allegations of aggression of those who seek His asylum with a repentant heart; here is the issuance of indiscriminant immunity for all illegal inflictions of those who seek compassionate clemency with contrition and remorsefulness in their soul; here is the declaration of a decree issued by God for those who take His shelter in helplessness and seek His forgiveness for their sins.

Oh! Here is a promise that God has made to overlook all ills of those who abide in His sanctuary and seek His grace with a repentant and reverend heart. Please hear these words and become their witness, where out of love Lord God swears that He would remember their sins no more, no matter how dreadful, grave and unpardonable they are, and promises them the complete clemency from all their crimes against His righteousness.

Beloved! Knowing that man's soul would remain in bondage forever, God has provided him a way to save her from such condemnation just by asking him to seek the total refuge in Him. Just look at the pledge He makes that not even a single blow of fire rising out of the consequences of *Karma* would ever touch his soul again but only if he enters into the His sanctuary by surrendering himself with his entirety and taking a total asylum in Him.

Thus, out of His endless love, God has provided a way to save our soul from further sufferings of separation from Him by allowing us to come to His refuge with our entire existence and be saved through His grace from all censure of sin.

God has granted all of us such a refuge where even the simplest of men, while living a most ordinary life and rendering all his duties through Him, can attain that eternal life with God, where he is fully protected from all prosecution of *Karma*, and is totally preserved from all reproaches of bondage.

Oh! He can attain the impossible, however not on his own, but through his refuge in the sanctuary of God:

Having taken refuge in Me he who performs all his duties at all times he attains the Eternal and imperishable Abode by My Grace.

(Holy Gita 18:56)

Surely, it is the love of God that He gave us such a precious gift of His grace, through which, even without any merit at all, we can receive the salvation for our soul just by entering into His refuge with total humility, and absolute submission and surrender.

But can man be submitted and surrendered to God with His entirety? Can he be yielded to Him with his absoluteness? Can He be given to Him with his wholeness? Can he be rendered to Him with his entire existence?

Oh! Not easy by any means; especially, for man of modern times! His soul is such a slave to his flesh that his self-centricity and selfishness do not allow him to be totally given to God. The evil of ego and pride that is ever-alive in him through his "I', 'Me' and 'Mine' hinders his path to surrender and submission even if he is the most holy and learned. His self-centricity is such a wall that stops him from going to the sanctuary of God.

So looking at this impossibility, no wonder, God gave life of His beloved son Jesus as a ransom to redeem the soul of the most beautifully created creature in His creation – the man – whom He loved so much that He formed and shaped him in His own image and breathed into him His own spirit.

Here are the words of Holy Bible that give testimony of God's love for man and yield an undeniable proof of how he is exceedingly adored in the heart of God; in fact, he is so loved and that God gave His only begotten son to be sacrificed on the cross in exchange for the eternal life for his condemned soul:

For God so loved the world, that he gave his only begotten Son, that whosoever believeth in him should not perish, but have everlasting life.

(Holy Bible, John 3:16)

What more proof, what more witness and what more validation of God's love does man need to believe that he is very loved by Him, and that is why He sacrificed His beloved son, Lord Jesus Christ, to save his soul from the eternal condemnation.

But look at what happened? Even those, for whom He died, do not believe that He came as a Savior; even they do not honor the cause of His death; even they do not exalt Him on the cross; and even they do not credit His sacrifice. What an agony of man's love for God that he believes not His words and seeks not the sanctuary of his Savior who came into this mortal world from heavens to be crucified so that He could save him from the womb of sin and restore him into His own righteousness.

Oh! How many have come to believe Him, and how many have trusted His report? How many have recognized the extent of His love, and how many have appreciated the sacrifice He made? How many have rested their soul into His hands, and how many have received His gift of salvation?

Of course some; but many still deny Him!

So it's no surprise that in his self-righteousness, man denies even God. Sadly nothing is new in it as it has been this way from the very beginning.

Though it does not happen often, yet once a while we can hear the voice of an ignorant saying that there is no need of God in attaining liberation, since he can attain it on his own just by realizing his 'reality', which he can do by acquiring the intuitive knowledge about His 'Self' and reaching the higher understanding of the Truth, of which he thinks he is fully capable of. He believes that the Truth will set him free, and the Truth he is well able to acquire.

Surely, I have to agree with him since it is true what he thinks and believes; after all the Truth – the Knowledge – releases the soul from bondage, as so say the scriptures:

> **And ye shall know the truth, and the truth shall make you free.**
>
> **(Holy Bible, John 8:32)**

However, what is the Knowledge and what is the Truth? Is it not God? Surely through Self-realization, one reaches the Self-salvation, but the realization of truth about the Self is nothing but knowing the reality and truth of God.

Just look at the following words of Lord God where He indirectly cautions man to not fall into such ignorance. He tries to awakens him to the truth that only through His grace can he reach His providence – the land of eternity – as there is no other way but just that. The word 'alone' is highly significant; it is telling us that there is no other power, no other way in this world that can enable us to enter into the heavenly Kingdom:

This divine Maya of Mine composed of the three Gunas is difficult to cross over, but those who surrender to Me, they <u>alone</u> are able to cross it.

(Holy Gita 7:14)

The use of word '**alone**' here is not accidental by any means. Lord God intently uses it to make sure we do not misinterpret the meaning and do not take it in any other way but to understand clearly that His grace <u>alone</u> is the way of rescue for man's soul from the fetters of Maya; that it is the <u>only</u> redeemer she has.

Well, in his ignorance and arrogance, man can deny and disregard God's love as much as he wants to, and not acknowledge and accept it; however, the reality remains, that God's grace is the only savior there for his soul, which falls upon her out to love and love alone, and redeems her from the shackles of sin. Oh! The words of verse, **Holy Gita 18:66**, wear a witness of this truth where Lord God declares man's permanent deliverance from bondage through His grace even though he is totally undeserving of it.

His word promises that even without any worthy qualifications, man can receive salvation for his soul, and attain the most extraordinary blessedness just by humbly seeking the safety and security of His ever-loving sanctuary – Oh! The true refuge of the soul – and enter into His kingdom with a great confidence of having been pardoned from all reprisal for his sins.

Therefore, to make any headway towards the liberation from bondage, it is to our great benefit that with extreme humility we realize our inability of achieving freedom from bondage through self-efforts, and accept the truth that only the grace of God has such potency and power that can save our soul from the gallows of death and mortality.

Fifth thought: God wholeheartedly desires our deliverance from bondage.

Many of us do not understand, that God does not want any soul to perish; in fact, He desires all of them to be saved. This is one of those truths that most of us are not aware of, and in fact, may even find it hard to believe.

The following words of Holy Bible bear witness that God wants every soul to be salvaged; He wishes each one of them to realize and repent for her sinfulness; he desires all to seek salvation through the sacrifice made by the Savior at the Cross, and thus, be reconciled with Him for all eternity:

The Lord is not slack concerning His promise, as some count slackness but is longsuffering toward us, not willing that any should perish but that all should come to repentance.

(Holy Bible, 2 Peter 3:9)

Therefore, it is to our benefit if we keep reminding ourselves that God desires our deliverance from bondage; He wants us to be eternally free from all fetters of *Karma*; He wishes our soul to be salvaged from the scaffold of sin; He covets our *Atman* to be liberated from the manacles of mortality and become eternally established in *Moksha* (Liberation).

Surely, God desires all that! He does wish that our soul be set free from all delusion, which has kept her separated from Him due to her misguided belief in her false self-individuality, and be eternally united with Him.

Though it is not necessarily always possible since *Karmically* imposed circumstances may be so unfavorable that odds are too against the possibility of attaining Liberation (*Mukti*); however, when God grants the soul a human embodiment, He surely hopes that it is her last trip to this world; and that she does not need to visit the corporeal domains again.

With such thought in mind, of course, God arranges all things in life in a manner that they facilitate the proper fulfillment of soul's preordained *Karma*:

He placed all things in the path of Eternity.

(Isa Upanishad)

But not only that He also provides her the best possible spiritual environment **(Holy Gita 6:41)**, so that she could evolve in enlightenment and rise in inner perfection, and become able to clearly see her path to paradise.

Beloved! This is one of the ways how God shows His love towards us, even though we often accuse Him of being so cruel and cold-hearted when we see the sorrow and suffering of human life and wonder why the Creator allows such misery and pain in our world, and why does He not do something about it.

However, all such ill thinking about God is very misguided. Surely when we speak ill of Him, we do it because are living in darkness. In our ignorance, we complain about our Creator because neither we understand His truth nor ours.

We do not realize that all life of present is the consequence of our deeds of the past, and that, God has nothing to do with it, except that He formulated the laws of *Karma* to regulate mortality, and put them in action when He commenced the creation.

So whatever happens in life, we cannot blame God for it, as whatever happens is in ideal accordance to the rules and regulations of *Karma*.

Therefore, let us learn how to not complain and blame God and erroneously hold Him responsible for all the ills that fall upon us due to our deeds of the past. Let us become more sensitive to the thought that God only does His best in giving the soul the best environment she could possibly have within the parameters of her preordained *Karma* so that she could further excel in her spiritual pursuit, and thus, grow more in wisdom and knowledge.

Once our thinking becomes oriented in this fashion, and our understanding in this matter gets adjusted to realize the truth of God correctly and adequately, we begin to appreciate all what God has done for us in terms of providing us with provisions for our redemption.

We also then begin to see that God has not abandoned us in incarceration of bondage, which is due to our own folly, but has provided a way and has made adequate arrangements for our deliverance from sin and restoration of our soul into everlasting life.

In fact if we give further latitude to the thought that God is very desirous of our salvation, then we can expect Him to provide us with an unfailing plan for our rescue from such a critical situation of bondage where we are being held captive by *Karma*, life after life, and without any other hope and any leverage over it.

Also, since God has created human life with a very specific purpose, then obviously He must have provided the details on how to fulfill it. Surely, if He has intended us to be reconciled with Him, then He must have provided the provisions for reconciliation, and if He has desired us to be liberated from the fetters of *Karmic*-bondage, then He must have secured ways for our release from it too.

After all, in His sight, the soul's union with Him is the highest goal of human life, **"He considers Me his highest goal – Holy Gita 7:18;"** therefore, with absolute certainty we must know in our heart that God must have revealed all that knowledge in the scriptures, which we must have in order to get out of the darkness of self-individuality and be forever united with Him.

And since God is a perfect God, we can be very sure that He has already put in place the concrete provisions for our salvation (*Moksha*), because if He is so particular about everything else, then how can He ever be careless and not provide for something, which is of the highest significance to us?

And beloved, so it is! As we have already learned. All our hopes and expectations in God as per His virtue and righteousness are fully correct and have been fulfilled hundred percent. We have already validated this truth. The scriptures are witness to this reality, over and over, as they unveil the way of redemption of man through the grace of God, and eagerly reveal the path for his salvation **(Holy Gita 18:66)**.

But quite unfortunately, only the blessed and sanctified, the humble and meek, finds the way of redemption that has been provided to him through the love of God, and only he receives the greatest gift of His grace given to him for his deliverance from bondage.

As most others, due to ignorance, either never try to walk towards Him, or out of lack of humility and meekness become the victim of spiritual arrogance and get lost on the self-designed holy trails of one kind or the other.

Sixth thought: God does not want to delay our eternal liberation from manacles of mortality.

Please! Get this revelation for good that God does not want any delay in our union with Him. In fact, He wants us to be reconciled with Him right now. He desires us to be united with Him today while we are alive and living in this human body, and not wait for another minute. He wholeheartedly wishes for us to begin enjoying the heavenly experiences in life on earth through the most intimate communion with Him.

This is why He commands us to take refuge in Him **(Holy Gita 18:66)**, and constantly meditate upon His word and continually abide in His love, so that our spirit could unite with His spirit and experience her eternal peace and enjoy communion with Her even now while living in the earthly abodes and not wait till hereafter. In the sight of God, our union with Him should be the first item on our priority list; He has set this goal for us even before we were born, which we must meet with utmost urgency.

Human life is God's main investment in Creation; the salvation of a soul from sin is the reward of His grace; the redemption of the *Atman* from all bondage to *Karma* is the harvest of His love. So the union of human spirit with the spirit of God is His will fulfilled which brings Him the sheer ecstasy of joy:

Likewise, I say unto you, there is joy in the presence of the angels of God over one sinner that *repenteth*.

(Holy Bible, Luke 15:10)

You see, God is not incomplete like us. He is absolute and totally whole, and is a perfect God. He needs nothing; He desires nothing. Though He sustains all worlds, but not because He wants to accomplish anything for Himself, **"There is nothing to be attained by Me – Holy Gita 3:22,"** but because it is a pure joy for Him to provide for His creation

So when we say that God desires this, and God desires that, what we mean to say is that this is what His will is; this is what His plan is; this is what His expectation is; this is what His anticipation is. Therefore, God's expectation and anticipation in anything, no matter how it is stated, actually expresses His desire in that matter; it is a reflection of His will.

Just because God does not express a clear and explicit desire about something, does not mean that He does not have it. Well, if His statues and commandments are not the expression of His desire, then what are they? Surely, they are the expressions of His expectations and anticipations from us.

Therefore, we must believe that God is very interested in our deliverance from sin since His each and every commandment, each and every holy instruction, dictates man to walk on the path of love so that he could attain the vision of light and know the truth of God and attain the liberty for His soul; and thus, with the heart of humility take refuge in His sanctuary and attain the Moksha through His grace. God is very eager for our redemption from the shackles of sin; He is very keen about our release from the captivity by *Karma*; and He is very fervent for our freedom from all bondage; and you know why? So that we could be reconciled with Him and be eternally united.

In this regard, if we diligently seek the wisdom hidden in holy scriptures, we find enough evidence that God desires our reconciliation with Him so that our separation from Him could end for good.

We do not have to look very far to prove this point to ourselves but just dig deep in the verses of Holy Gita and try to answer this question: what is the main theme of the discourse given by Lord God?

The diligently sought answer provides a very tangible proof, that revelations unveiled by the Divine are to awaken man from the deep sleep of ignorance and bring him out of darkness so that he could know the truth about himself (Self) and understand the fact that his soul is living under the captivity of *Karma*, and that now is the time to free her from all chains of bondage so that when her visit ends in this world, she could go to her eternal home for good and not be forced to descend down to these earthly domains again.

In His exposition, not only Lord God reveals the truth about conditioned-soul born as *Jiva* (creature) but unveils ways on how she can get out of darkness and delusion by walking the path of love and light, and provides a provision for her redemption through His grace.

Surely, this is the main theme of the gospel of *SriMada Bhagawada* Gita – the holy love song of God. Well, if not this, then what else?

So the reality is that God desires our salvation more than anything else; that He is very interested in our release from the bondage to *Karma*; that with open arms, He is looking forward to receiving us into His heavenly home when we part from earthly provinces. Please know that God awaits our absolute surrender not each year, not each moth or day, but by each movement, and wishes that we come to Him and take refuge in His sanctuary so that we could be redeemed through His grace and be united with Him eternally.

If this is not true, then what else to make out of His words of verse, **Holy Gita 18:66,** where He commands us to seek refuge in Him with our entirety, so that we could be redeemed from the shackles of sin, and be restored into eternal life with Him?

Seventh thought: Just because God talks about spiritual evolution through many human lives, does not mean He prefers it over attaining Moksha in this life.

Even though God has put in place a continual and slow process of spiritual succession for man to attain freedom from bondage as described in following verse, but that does not mean, this is what He wants us to do, and go through several human lives to reach the ultimate goal of salvation.

Having perfected *Yogic*-states through many lives in every birth exercising more self-effort than before, a Yogi brings about the removal of mental impurities and consequently attains the supreme goal.

(Holy Gita 6:45)

Please do not misunderstand God's words regarding this very important matter of our eternal liberation. God never wants us just to better ourselves in each human life, little by little, and go through numerous lives to attain the freedom from the process of birth and death.

Oh! Ask Him and He would tell that He wants our *Moksha* now; I mean right now; today! He does not desire to delay it even by another minute. Please get this firmly: God desires our deliverance now!

And believe, that He wants to make the current journey to this world as our last; He wants us to break this cycle of bandage for good this time; He wants all this coming and going of our soul to this mortal world to stop; right here, right now.

The holy words quoted above state the truth that the soul (*Atman*) can achieve spiritual perfection by ascending the *Yogic*-ladder through little by little effort in each human life; and by doing so, she can become sanitized and be cleansed of impurities, and thus, eventually become the beholder of the truth of God.

Of course, when the impurities that surround the soul are washed off, the intellect rises to such awareness that it begins to receive the light of the Spirit and it acquires the vision of Truth. And through the vision of truth the soul becomes enabled to see her way to the sanctuary of God, where in His refuge she finds her salvation through His graces; and thus, she finds eternal liberation from bondage.

But reaching the state of such awakening does not necessarily have to come over several human lives. There in no such law against reaching the vision of Truth in a single life.

So, why can't we do it now, in this life?

After all, according to God's own words as stated in the following verse, the ultimate wisdom is what? Of course, the knowing of truth that: **"*Vasudevah* (God) alone is all this;"** that He alone is:

After many lives (of progressive spiritual evolution) one acquires wisdom and worships Me with the vision that "*Vasudevah* alone is all this." It is extremely difficult to find such a great soul.

(Holy Gita 7:19)

So why don't we get established in this wisdom now; in this life; and get over with all coming and going to this world by becoming eternally free from all bondage.

Please make a note that these words speak of the truth quite simply and plainly; they speak of the fact that it takes a continual spiritual progression spanning over several human lives for one to attain such an extraordinary understanding where he comes to know the eventual reality of God that **"Vasudevah (God)alone is all this."** Of course, such realization alone is the ultimate wisdom of all wisdom, and the truth of all truth.

Now, it is true that there is no constraints on how many human lives it will take for a soul to be awakened to the highest consciousness, but who is to say that this life cannot be her last where she could become fully enlightened. Why can't she take the final jump and reach her goal and make this life as her final birth and death?

You see! Described in verse, **Holy Gita 6:45,** is a plan of assurance, which God implemented in case we fail in reaching our goal in this life for whatever reasons, so that we stay on track and finish the job in next human life or after that. But that does not mean that we are not capable of rising to such heights of awakening now, in this life.

Of course, by putting this plan in action God made sure that in case we miss the goal and not get liberated in this life then after going through the troubles of another cycle of *Karma* and enduring another round of suffering of countless lower embodiments, when we eventually come back to this world as human again, we would find everything in tact just the way we leave in this life, so that hopefully, we could finish the task the next time around.

This is His way of saying, that no matter what, our holy effort is insured in His hands, and it can never suffer any loss or destruction, **"A Yogi is never destroyed, neither in this world nor in the next – Holy Gita 6:40;"** that no matter what happens, whether we succeed or not in our holy pursuit of attaining *Moksha*, we can be rest assured that our spiritual labor would not go waste **(Holy Gita 6:43)** but only increase in due time; that our investment made in immortal treasury stays secured and that it would never decrease or get reduced but would only multiply.

This is exactly what these words of God really mean, as they do not encourage the idea that it has to be many more lives before our soul could evolve into full enlightenment; slowly; bit by bit; and hope that some day, eventually, she could be salvaged.

The main purpose God had in mind while implementing this slow but successive provision for salvation of our soul is that He just wanted to make sure that in case we fail to attain freedom from bondage in this life, then during our next, we could pick it up right where we leave off now, and constantly keep marching towards the immortal grounds of eternal liberty:

O Delighter of *Kuru's* Race when he is reborn he is united with the intellect that he had cultivated in his past lives. So he endeavors again to attain the higher rungs of *Yoga* leading to Liberation.

(Holy Gita 6:43)

Eighth thought: The heart of God is that we do not suffer but enjoy life and experience His heavenly peace and joy right here on this earth.

The fact is that the eternal life is not of physical prosperity but of internal richness; it is not of temporal worldly wealth but of endless heavenly riches; it is not of transient pleasures but of long lasting peace and happiness; it is not of temporary satisfaction and contentment but of unending joy and bliss.

Of course, such life cannot be earned by any labor of man as it comes to him only through the grace of God.

Surely, God wholeheartedly desires us to have such heavenly life here on earth, and quite definitely, not at some later time, but right now. So He wants us to enter into His kingdom today, even when we are wearing our fleshly suit and are in our physical form, and begin experiencing the heavenly richness, so that when we die, we only cease our physical existence and leave behind our corporeal experiences but continue to live the indwelling eternal enrichment – the everlasting peace and unending bliss.

Of course, God wants us to have the most blissful life – the life immortal – after our mortal death; but what could be a better way than to somehow enter into it now and begin experiencing it today; and even if it is not exactly hundred percent like it would be after we leave this world and arrive to our eternal destination – the *Moksha* – the salvation, but it surely would be the most exquisite and excellent extension of what we have here on this earth before we move on to heavenly abodes.

12

Freedom from Bondage
~
Man's Ultimate Spiritual Quest

Looking at people and finding them so consumed by their daily quest to build more provisions of life, it seems as if they are planning to live here on this earth forever. There is no talk, no discussion, and no apparent preparation for departure from these mortal grounds; there is no evident sign giving any clue that they are even thinking of this journey of life to end. The finality of life seems no where on their minds – at least so it seems from their preoccupation by the engagements and endeavors of their day.

In general, people are busy, very busy, and hardly have any time to think about what is going to happen after they die. Everyone is tirelessly laboring to gather and collect whatever he can get his hands on; there seems to be a rush to gain as much wealth and prosperity as possible.

It is like a marathon where everyone seems to be so busy in trying to win the race that he has forgotten the truth that one day this life would end, but the race to attain abundance of this world would not end; that the time would come when this body would cease, but the marathon to satisfy the hunger and thirst of its flesh would not cease.

Oh! We are ever busy with building more and more provisions for our lives and are ever consumed by those enterprises that we think would bring fulfillment to our fleshly dehydration, and satisfy our ambitions and desires. Unfortunately, that never happens. After all, we have been trying to satisfy our inner dehydration all our lives, and yet have not succeeded in quenching it. Our flesh still is as thirsty as ever before.

Our whole life has gone by in trying to extinguish our bodily hunger and thirst; but too bad, their flame still goes on like ever before. No doubt, we have completely failed in putting out this embedded blaze that keeps burning in our body day and night.

Well, this is how we are living our days on this earth, which surely gives the impression as if we would occupy this land forever.

Just about each day, we hear that someone among our loved ones has passed away, that someone very dear to us has vanished from our world, that someone has been swallowed by death and we would never see him again, but hearing such things do not deter us in anyway from our preparation seemingly to live here forever.

What we have forgotten that death will not always tip-toe in the neighborhood but will show up at the door one day and will coldly call upon us by our name and forcefully will remove us from our self-built fortified castle which we have built so laboriously. It does not set in our mind that one day soon our soul has to leave the earthly domains and begin an unknown journey into the unfamiliar worlds.

Of course, that day would come, and would come sooner than we can think, when death would make us quit in the middle of our engagements and force us to leave all worldly trades behind, to carry us to attend the judiciary of *Karmic*-constitution. It is just a matter of little wait, as that day is not very far when we would have no power over anything, since along with our body would perish our potency and power over things, and we would helplessly be resting in the mighty hands of *Karma* to face trial for our good and bad deeds.

Surely that day is coming; and the most surprising thing is that we are not ready to receive it; we have not made any preparation for it since it is not a burning issue on our passionately consumed mind.

In life, we plan and prepare for everything, as best as we can, so that we do not fail and falter in any way but succeed in whatever we are engaged in; and we apply all kinds of worldly wisdom and exercise caution at each step of the way in an effort to do things just right to minimize the chances of failures in our endeavors; and thus, approach life with as much readiness as possible.

In fact we are so careful that for any major event in life, we consult our family's spiritual-guide (*Pandit*) so that he cloud tell us the date, day and time when all the stars would align in favor for all things to go right.

How sad though! We organize so vigorously for everything else but remain so unprepared and not care much at all for something that is the most significant event of life after birth – the death.

For most of us, each day goes by without giving much thought to what would happen when the day of departure from this world would come, and we would have no choice but to leave. And we continue to live this way as if life would prolong forever, and the day of death would never come.

But the truth of existence is that it is not a continual journey that lasts forever. As we all know, one day it comes to a halt when all stops moving, and there comes the end. This day comes for each and every life; for some it may come sooner, and for some others it may be later, but it definitely would come. The death is that certainty that never fails, because for each life all else is a variable, except the event that marks its end.

Oh! The death swallows all beings in due time, **"Death is certain for what is born – Holy Gita 2:27;"** therefore, it is certain that we all would ultimately die, sooner or later; whether we plan and prepare for it or not!

One day, all of a sudden, the breathing would fail and the heartbeats would halt; and there would be a dead-silence in all corridors of our inner chamber; not even a ghost of life will be anywhere around our soul when the death would hold her in its palm and ready to take her into another world. Surely, this time would come; for me, for you, and for everyone else!

Of course, we all think about it; surely not daily but time to time. The fear of death is ever haunting and ever recurring; but only so far it goes. After that, we almost become mute in ourselves and not dare to continue this dialogue in ourselves any further for whatever reasons, but we surely do quit on it.

As for reason, a little investigation into the issue reveals that we quit mainly because of our ignorance, misguided understanding, and lack of knowledge of what lies ahead for us after we depart from this world. The sad thing about it is that we allow our inequities in spiritual understanding to rule our *Karmic-destiny*.

Since in life, the pressing issues take precedence, the subject of what lies beyond death gets buried under the multitudes of other priorities. Everything else seems so important that we hardly have any time to spend on a subject that occupies the last place in our minds. We are so dazzled by the glitter and glow of the present that we cannot see the dreadful darkness of our future.

How of little importance is the subject of life-after-death can be seen by the fact that when there is a death in a family and everyone is mourning, in the midst of all this the question that often rises is not what would happen next to the departed soul but what would happen to them that are left behind?

We worry about those that are left rather than the one who is gone? It does not bother us even a bit that we do not know what happened to the beloved soul that just left us, and where has she gone? We do not seem to care anymore about her whereabouts and express no curiosity to know what happened to her after she left the body. Who was so dear to us before death, now we do not seem to care any more?

Can we disagree with any of this? I hope we do not!

This proves my point that life on this earth has so much importance that the life after this life hardly ever takes the forefront in our thinking. Once someone dies, we simply move on to the next phase of life, which is the phase that is without that person. We just rearrange everything to make it work again and we go on.

I agree; what else one can do? So it is quite alright. I am sure we all would agree. Life is like a river; it always flows forward and never stops. So there is nothing wrong the way it flows, because it is supposed to be like this.

But the thing I am trying to bring to our attention is that when the person is alive we do everything we can for his wellbeing, and try whatever it takes to protect and save his life. However, once the person is dead, all our concerns cease. Isn't it!

Because there is not much we can do for him anymore since now he is dead. However, the question is: How many of us really worry about what happens to his soul after she leaves this world?

The honest answer is: Not many! Why? Because, what happens after death is not a burning issue in our mind; it is that simple!

After all, how many among us really care if they attain eternal liberation in this life or not. How many really understand that if they fail to do so and do not get freed from the shackles of bondage, then after death they have to go through another cycle of *Karma* and pass through the immeasurable sorrow and suffering of countless embodiments again? How many are aware of the truth that the salvation of soul is a must during this human life; otherwise, the consequences of failing in this goal are very severe?

Definitely not many! Even though not everyone is blind to this truth, but certainly the majority of folks don't care about this issue. It is such a neglected topic that it has almost no priority in human psyche. And the main reason for such poor attention to this subject is that in common thinking it is quite acceptable; meaning, most of us have no problem in accepting the fact that there will be another birth and then another birth and then another birth and so on. So quite naturally, no body seems to care about it.

Surely, there are some who do think about it and give it a serious thought at one time or the other; but they often wander inside of themselves with lot of questions; unfortunately, often with no clear answers. And that leaves only a few who know the truth; and they are the only ones that are laboring spiritually and striving to attain *Moksha* and trying hard to find eternal liberation for their soul.

There is yet another problem among such believers who do concern themselves with the issue of what would happen to the soul after death, as most of them worry about the 'next-life' rather than worrying about the life-eternal, since many of them believe that deliverance of the soul from bondage is extremely difficult even to a point of being impossible.

With such defeated mindset often the spiritual effort is invested in improvement of *Karma* for 'next-life' rather than being applied towards getting the release from bondage. Of course, not everyone is like that, but this happens to be quite a widely accepted and adopted thought.

However, there are still some, who are blessed to have clear comprehension of truth and reality of God, and they understand the problem of bondage of *Atman*. And it is they who take up on the quest to find freedom for their soul from the captivity of *Karma*. But such chosen souls are only a few and are hard to find, **"It is extremely difficult to find such a great soul – Holy Gita 7:19."**

You see! Even though we are reasonably knowledgeable about basic laws of *Karma* and its bondage, we are yet quite ignorant about it and often have misunderstanding about so many things related to it. For example: one thing we definitely fail to understand is, how deep are the consequences of *Karma*? And how long they keep affecting our future-life?

Surely, there is much ignorance in us about all this and that is why often our spiritual effort goes to waste. Quite sadly, many of us end up harming ourselves instead of doing some good. Our beliefs are so distorted that often we engage in wrong things yielding only wrong results.

No doubt! The lack of understanding on this subject is one of the main causes that we are so lost in our spiritual ways. What we lack the most is awareness of the purpose why we have been made man by the Creator? Surely, there is very little awareness in today's man about why is he born as human? Why God made him a man? And what is the purpose of his life?

These kinds of questions hardly penetrate the typical human-psyche – at least not from the spiritual point of view. Of course, the secular mind always regards the attainment of great and glorious things of this world as the main purpose of man's birth, even though as per word of God, man's magnificent works and glorious deeds are nothing but filthy rags:

But we are all as an unclean thing, and all our *righteousnesses* are as filthy rags; and we all do fade as a leaf; and our iniquities, like the wind, have taken us away.

(Holy Bible, Isaiah 64:6)

Oh! God's wisdom is not the wisdom of this world; that is why the things that hold true value in His sight are not earthly but heavenly; they are not temporary and transient but permanent and perpetual. The true fortunes that man accumulates are not on this earth but are the ones that he secures in the treasury of heaven.

However, man thinks otherwise. Even though in God's sight man's great deeds have no real value except that he becomes recipient of good *Karmic*-rewards, but man still considers earthly attainments as most redeeming and rewarding. What he does not understands that no matter how great are his earthly gains, they yet are not of much value in terms of his salvation since through them he does not make much progress towards his pursuit for eternal life, as that happens only when one resigns himself from the world and turns towards God and surrenders his entirely to His refuge.

So as we can see, this kind of thinking, which is based on worldly wisdom, only underscores our ignorance even more and highlights the lack of understanding even further. Besides, we are the victims of so many misguided beliefs that most of our holy labor goes in vain, and the worst thing about it is that we do not even know it.

No wonder all this has made us so numb to this issue that we do not seem to care about what happens to us after death, and this is why we hardly ever reflect upon this matter as seriously as we ought to and worry about the salvation of our soul (*Moksha*).

Therefore, unless we correct our comprehension about life after death and understand the true purpose of why we are given the human embodiment, not much spiritual progress can we make regardless of how intense are our holy endeavors.

There is one more thing to think about. Since life after death is not an exact science, no one really knows for sure what happens to the soul after she departs from the body. We only know what scriptures tell us.

Of course, various philosophies have their own views based on their religious doctrines. So there are no absolutes, if we make it a subject of human intellect. However, in faith we find some definite answers to such questions, and they come to us without any doubts!

Among *Hindus*, the popular belief is that when one dies, he is born again **(Holy Gita 2:27)**; that after departing from one body, the soul (*Atman*) enters another and embodies as a new creature. This process of birth and death repeats itself until the soul (*Atman*) is freed from bondage of *Karma* and liberated to eternal life (*Moksha*).

It is further believed that *Karma* earned in human life is responsible for determining the future lives of the soul; that after death, she goes to heaven or hell depending upon her *Karma*; that her *Punya* (good deeds) and *Papa* (bad deeds) determine what kinds of future embodiments she is going to have; that good *Karma* takes her to heaven (*Swarga*) and bad takes her to hell (*Narka*); that salvation (*Moksha*) is the eventual end of this repetitive cycle of birth and death.

Though the concept of heaven and hell is quite popular, but since the scriptures are not very precise about them, no one knows exactly what and where they are? Everyone seems to have his own ideas about them. Nonetheless, ignoring who knows how much about it, for just about everyone the rules and regulations of *Karma* boil down to one single principle, that if one does good he gets good.

This thought is heavily applied, not only by those that are spiritually inclined but almost by all, since we all desire good return on our spiritual investments which we make in the form of good deeds. This is why, more often than not, our good works are often driven by the thought of receiving the rewards of good *Karma* not only for this life but also for life after this – so called the *Agala-Janma* (Next-life).

Briefly, this is what our common understanding is about what happens to our soul after we die; and it certainly seems pretty good as far its correctness is concerned. However, surrounding this knowledge, there are so many erroneous believes that have misguided our holy walk and misplaced our spiritual priorities. Undeniably, we are quite misdirected in our holy walk due to all kinds of ignorance and lack of understanding about this issue.

Look at these profound realities of which almost all of us are victims of:

Reality one: 'What would happen after death?' is the last issue on human mind; surely, not many seriously think about it, as this concern is hardly ever on the forefront of man's thought. So, most of us ignore it.

Reality two: Among those few, who do think about what would happen after death, often get hung on the concept of 'Next-life' rather than trying to attain Salvation for their soul now in this lifetime .

Reality three: There is a common belief among *Hindus* that *Moksha* (Liberation) is extremely difficult thing to achieve even to a point that it is almost impossible. Often such misguided belief misleads the spiritual seekers into thinking that attaining *Moksha* is so hard that it is almost beyond them, so they never even try for it. Sadly, the truth is quite the opposite.

Reality four: The spiritual mind that overcomes all such dark beliefs often get victimized by his own holy confidence, which convinces him to believe that man can attain *Moksha* through his own holy labor; and in such egoistic ignorance, he does not realize that the salvation of the soul is attainable only through the grace of God and not through anything else.

Well, here are some more thoughts that are worthy of our reflection:

First thought: *We hardly have any realization that we are the prisoners of bondage to Karma.*

Even though most of us are already quite aware of this truth, but our awareness is dead because if it were alive then we would have been working day and night towards our freedom from bondage and not be lost in enjoying the pleasures and prosperity of this world.

How ridiculous it is that, though we know, yet we behave as if we do not know, and that is why there is no live realization of our dark reality that we are living a life of incarceration; that we are captives of *Karma*; that we are prisoners of mortality; and that we are inmates of the cycle of birth and death.

Oh! How ignorant we are that none of this bothers us? Rather than resisting our custody and confinement by *Karma* and doing something to liberate ourselves from its grip, we happily accept its captivity and celebrate its imprisonment by decorating and beautifying it as much as we can.

Therefore, it is important that we tell ourselves repeatedly that we are in bondage. A reminder of this reality is always good because in all honesty a sincere acknowledgement of this truth is missing in us. In most cases, either it is not there at all, or if it is, then it is very feeble.

Only a blessed soul realizes that life is no more than a fleeting event during the ever-continuing *Karmic*-journey of the soul while traveling towards the eternity. However, she also knows that the momentary life as human that has been granted to her through much graces of God, has the dual power: to put an end to her drifting for good by enabling her to reach the eternal home, or to multiply her nomad wandering even further into wilderness of all kinds of *Karmic*-worlds by alluring her into extremely irresistible earthly engagements.

Due to such awareness a wise-man remains awake and does not get lost in the sensuality of this world. He constantly reminds himself that the consequences of missing this opportunity to release his soul from the fetters of bondage are severe. Just hear these beautiful words of the Upanishad where the heart of one who has realized the Truth of existence is crying to his soul and says:

369

O my soul, remember past strivings, remember ! O my soul, remember that strivings, remember!

(Isa Upanishad)

The awakened heart unlike most others who are ever busy in gathering the abundance of this world, avails the given opportunity, and through the guiding-light of the Spirit, he plans and prepares for his journey into the eternal kingdom that lies beyond all *Karmic*-worlds.

Therefore, it is very important that we remind ourselves of this fact as often as we can and keep it refreshed in our minds since it is the most important issue of our life. The scriptures reveal that our *Karma* is responsible for our mortality; that our *Karmic*-burden is the cause for our embodiments **(Holy Gita 8:3)**. It is that evil, which binds us to the cycle of birth and death and forces our soul to pass through countless embodiments.

As the word 'bondage' suggests, we are in a state-of-being to which we have been bound by compulsion; it is our tenure of service as a slave, servitude or subjugation to the controlling authority of *Karma*.

Therefore, we must remain vigilant of this truth that we are bound to mortality by the compulsion of *Karma*; that we are in its service as a slave to allow its full expression; that we are in the mode of servitude and subjugation to its controlling authority that has the potency even to overwrite the endowed power of our freewill; that our soul is tied to corporeal worlds due to her captivity by *Karma* which forces her to endure inestimable sorrow and suffering of all kinds of births and deaths; and that she would continue to do so until she is relieved of all her *Karmic*-obligations.

Oh! Such consciousness is a must in our lives if we have any hope for making our human embodiment meaningful in any real sense.

Second thought: For soul, there is only one gateway to eternal liberation – the human embodiment.

The truth is that the soul cannot escape the captivity of bondage from any other plane of consciousness (*Loka*), but the plane of human consciousness. Only through this doorway can she ever find her way to eternity; only through human embodiment can she ever attain *Moksha* and reach her salvation.

Drifting in all other *Lokas*, no matter how high they are, does not do any real good to her, since all other *Lokas* (lower or higher) are made only to express *Karma*, where the soul (*Atman*) experiences pleasure and pain depending upon the *Karma* she has to earned. All other planes of consciousness except the one we live in, are the conduits of *Karmic*-exhaustion, and hence, are of no real good.

Therefore, no virtues on those planes, regardless of how great and glorious they are, can enable the soul to rise above the level of *Karmic*-provinces and reach the heights of eternal abode of *Brahman* (God). This earthly plane (*Loka*) is the only providence for the soul from where she can launch her eternal journey to heavenly providence leaving behind all mortal worlds.

Thus, going through any other plane of consciousness is nothing but a detour for the soul as far as her quest for redemption from bondage is concerned, since by passing through them she gains nothing meaningful towards her release from the fetters of *Karma*.

The word of God states quite clearly that after wandering through all other planes of consciousness (*Lokas*), the soul (*Atman*) eventually falls back to this world just because this is her only gateway to glorious grounds of immortality – the Brahma-*Loka* – reaching which she never returns, since there she attains the union with *Brahman* – the Godhead:

All the worlds up to the highest Brahma-*Loka* are characterized by the return of the soul. But he who attains Me for him there is no more of rebirth, O Son of Kunti!

(Holy Gita 8:16)

Once the soul becomes one with God, her assumed individuality ceases to exist and there remains no more birth and death for her. But if somehow that does not happen and the soul is not rescued from bondage, she continues her nomad seemingly inestimable wandering life after life.

Thus, human life is the pinnacle of all embodiments, sitting atop the soul can view the way to eternal providence of God, and through His grace fly her way to His eternal abode. This is why its glory is so exceedingly exalted in all scriptures.

Hear these words of Holy *Ramayana* that sing glory of human form in so many ways, and echo the utter truth about it in such a beautiful manner:

There is no other form as good as human body: every living creature - whether animate or inanimate - craves for it. It is the ladder that takes the soul either to hell or to heaven or again to final beatitude, and is the *bestower* of blessings in the form of wisdom, dispassion and devotion.

Men who fail to adore Sri *Hari* even after obtaining this body, and wallow in the basest pleasures of sense, throw away the philosopher's stone from the palm of their hand and take bits of glass in exchange for the same.

(Holy Ramayana, Uttar-Kanda 121(A).5-6)

The holy book says that when one does not yoke with God and wastes his life in sensual pleasures, he is one of the biggest fools who gives away the most precious gift of God – the human life – in exchange for something that has no real value.

Oh! The human life, which is considered most high because it is the only gateway to eternal kingdom, and which can serve as a raft with which one can cross the ocean of transmigration and reach that providence from where the soul never returns, does not come by as easy since God grants this privilege only through much blessedness:

kabahuka kari karuna nara dehi, deta isa binu hetu sanehi. nara tanu bhava baridhi kahu bero, sanmukha maruta anugraha mero. karanadhara sadagura drRha nava, durlabha saja sulabha kari pava.

These verses are translated as:

Rarely does God, who loves the *Jiva* without any self-interest, graciously bestows on it a human form, which is a veritable raft whereby it can cross the ocean of mundane existence, with My grace for a favorable wind and a worthy preceptor for a helmsman to steer this strong bark - a combination which, though difficult to secure, has been made easily available to it.

(Holy Ramayana, Uttar-Kanda 44:4)

This is why, we cannot afford our life to go waste, and let it pass by without attaining salvation. It is the most precious gift from God that He has given to us in much loving-kindness so that we could end our separation and be united with Him forever.

Therefore, beloved! It is important that we come to our senses and realize that we are in bondage and urgently need deliverance. Because the time is now! And if we do not avail this opportunity, then who knows for how long, may be indefinitely, we would remain in scaffold of bondage, because who knows when we would get another chance to wear human embodiment again.

This human life that God has given to us through much graces, is a rare opportunity to salvage our soul. Of course, for this purpose alone, He has granted this gift and has made us human. So, let us not waste it!

Please know that according to the laws of *Karma*, it is certain, that for most of us, the next human embodiment would not come by as easily; meaning, another chance to liberate our soul from bondage is no where in sight. Surely not many understand this truth, as our common belief is that we would return to this world as human not too long after we die. But quite unfortunately, that is never the case – look at the scriptures, they are very clear about it!

It is really sad that the true value of human life is mostly not understood because we are so consumed in following the tracks that have been already laid for us by the world's value-system, which we embrace without any questioning. We never examine its validity and enquire if it is right for us? We never raise our eyebrows and say that there is something wrong with it.

We just follow what we are taught right from our childhood. We become creatures of a value-system which teaches us that the main goal of life is to make it most fruitful by earning the power and authority, and by accumulating the pleasures and prosperity of this world as much as possible. And that is what we do; we exhaust our life in attaining the glory of name and fame, and collecting the treasures of this world.

In craziness of this rat-race where we measure the futility of life by gauzing who accumulated how much, we waste our life in collecting nothing but worthlessness and vanity, and leave this world empty handed without getting the hold of what we were sent for. Instead of getting freedom from bondage, we part from here with our hands tied with shackles of *Karmic* bondage, in fact, often with stronger grip than what we had when we came into it.

What we do not understand that if we do not make good use of this human life, the next may not come again as easily as we think. We almost never think that we may not get a chance to become human again for a long time, since we all have to take a long journey of other *Lokas* (planes of consciousness), and cross a long stretch of lower births, before we can even hope to embody as human again.

So this is our chance to accomplish for which this life as man has been granted to us by God – which is to attain *Moksha* and reach the eternal liberation.

Third thought: Freedom from bondage is the ultimate goal of human life.

Surely, not many have the consciousness that attaining salvation (*Moksha*) is the ultimate goal of human life. Most of us do not even have the faintest thought of it. The truth is that eternal liberation of the soul is millions miles away in our daily deliberations; her redemption from bondage is no where even close in the meditations of our mind.

Obviously, when there is no awareness of what is the primary purpose of human embodiment, there is no acknowledgment of its immediate need either, and hence, there is no sense of urgency in our thinking and thoughts.

This of course explains our uncaring behavior towards the subject of what happens to us after we die, and it yields a sufficient reason why salvation is often not on *Hindu* mind? This highlights the cause, why often *Moksha* is not a subject of our holy sermon? Why the eternal liberation of the soul is so rarely talked about by our holy teachers?

Please know, that not understanding the true meaning of human life and not realizing why are we born as man, puts us at a great loss, which definitely is not recoverable by any means if not prevented in due time.

And beloved! That time is now, since death could come at any time, and we would have to leave whether we are ready or not. Therefore, we must treat this matter with urgency and have our deliverance before that, so that we are ready to properly leave this world and go to our eternal home and not to wasteful worlds of *Karma*.

The laws of *Karma* present a very dreadful reality that if we miss this opportunity then it is quite possible that we may not get another chance to redeem our soul from the fetters of *Karma* for who knows how long? Because the odds are heavily in favor that it may take countless lives before we are blessed with another such opportunity; and even that would come only if Lord God in His much kindness grants it; otherwise, human life is very rare to come by.

Since human life is the only gateway to reach the eternal grounds, drifting in other higher or lower *Lokas* (planes of consciousness), which the soul has to do due to her *Karmic-*obligations, is just like wandering in the wilderness without accomplishing anything meaningful at all.

Therefore, with absolute confidence we must know that the purpose of our life is to unite with God; He is the final goal of our earthly journey, **"I am the Final Goal – Holy Gita 9:18."**

Through these words, **"One should seek that Abode having attained which one does not return (to the world-process – Holy Gita 15:4,"** how clearly Lord God states that the purpose of human life is to seek that eternal abode, after reaching which, one does not return to this world, since he becomes free from the bondage to all mortality

But sadly, our ignorance has been a problem all along and still is. Ignorance is so deep that many of us do not know the true reason of why are we born? And that is our real problem – the spiritual ignorance – the lack of true Knowledge. Surely, we are here for a purpose. But alas! We do not even know what that purpose is? We are supposed to follow a plan and get something accomplished; but unfortunately, we do not even know what that plan is? Forget about how to execute it?

Oh! Human life is a heavenly gift, which the soul receives only once a while. It is a terrible mistake not realizing what we are doing with that gift given to us by God, and how we are disgracing and dishonoring it by not living it the way it is supposed to be lived.

Rather than living life the way it was intended to be lived by God, we have been living it the way it pleases us. We did not like His preservations, so we created our own protections; we did not like His fortifications, so we constructed our own fortitudes. And this became our passion and love, our affection and adoration.

But why is it like that? Why are we so ignorant about the whole thing? Why do we take this matter so lightly, which is of such a great importance? Why do we not pay attention to the purpose of why we have been born as human and given a highly privileged embodiment?

Oh! It is all because our thoughts are tainted, because our mind is darkened, and because our hearts are perverted. Due to passion and infatuation our intellect is so badly infected that all our discernments are defiled and our resolutions are corrupted.

This is why we do not realize that the main purpose of our life is to attain deliverance from the bondage and liberate our soul from the manacles of mortality so that she could be eternally united with the Creator.

Fourth thought: Through grace of God alone one comes to know that human life is to attain Moksha.

The ignorance is our biggest problem. We live our whole life without realizing its true purpose. We work hard each day but not knowing that all toiling ultimately would end in vanity. Thus, in our ignorance, we badly fail to realize the reality of why are we given the human life by God?

Oh! If one ever grows to such awareness and understands that *Moksha* is the prime goal of human life, he must consider himself a blessed man since only due to much graces of God one reaches such realization. It surely is something to rejoice since in it lies the direct involvement by God; because otherwise, without His participation one never arrives to such a blessed understanding.

Please look around and see how many are there who are spiritually inclined, and are eager and enthusiastic to talk about God? How many are there that are interested in discussing the matters of life after death? How many are there that are concerned whether they are going to heaven or hell; or, they would attain eternal liberation (*Moksha*) or fall down further deep in the ocean of bondage?

Surely not many, as we all know!

This fact alone should comfort those who have become aware of God and know that life has been given to attain salvation, because without His grace such consciousness does not enter human mind.

Oh! Not until God makes man aware of, why is he born, and what is the true purpose of life, he continues to be in deep sleep of ignorance and remains unaware of such reality. Surely, it is He who wakes him up and brings him from darkness to light to show that he is tied to bondage, and that he urgently needs deliverance, which is attainable not by his own goodness but only through the grace of God.

Therefore, let us thank God for His mercy and kindness, that out of love for those who humbly and diligently seek Him, He reveals to them such secrets of life.

So if one has come to know that *Moksha* is the goal of life, then He must also know that God's grace is with him; that God is heavily engaged in His life; that He is very close to him. Just by mere realization of the fact that the sole purpose of life is to live life in love of God and to attain *Moksha*, one can be sure of one thing of utter blessedness that he has already taken the first step on the most delightful journey towards the eternal providence of God. He can be very assured that any effort towards this endeavor can only happen when it has been first sanctioned by God; otherwise, none of this can ever come about.

Isn't it true, when we visit someone, don't we communicate with him and let him know our plans and coordinate with him our visit. Then how can it ever be possible, that we are planning to go and live with our father God, and He is not aware of our plans? Surely, He knows all this, and is fully involved. In fact it is He who is making all the arrangements and provisions for our trip to eternity.

Therefore, we must firmly know in our hearts that not only God is aware of our desire for union with Him but is very willing to do everything He can to make it happen so that we do not fail in our spiritual expedition.

You see! Once we become aware of true purpose of life and realize that we need reconciliation with God, our whole focus begins to shift from this mortal world to the world immortal, though often slowly but quite surely; and we begin to lose the interest in earthly possessions and get attracted to heavenly chattels – the peace and joy. What happens in due time, that we become dull to sensuality of the flesh, and become sharp to peace of our soul, and begin to look forward to remain in the everlasting blissful state of Self-being.

Beloved! The realization of the fact that one needs *Moksha* is not only the starting point but also a significant milestone of that heavenly journey of the soul, which only ends in the eternal empire of God.

Fifth thought: One of the most ill-conceived notions about human life is that in our 'next-life', we are going to be born as human again.

Even though such belief is quite common, it happens to be extremely misguiding, since it reflects a probability that is highly rare. So we set ourselves up for deception by relying upon a notion that is mostly false, and thus, get misguided by our own thinking and belief.

On the basis of what scriptures tell us, it is highly unlikely that for a common man the next *Karmic*-embodiment is going to be of human as there are countless nonhuman embodiments that lie before that. Only after passing through the pleasure and pain of all other creaturely bodies, which are ordained as per *Karma* of this life, the soul is given another chance to embody as human again.

But too bad! This reality goes unnoticed by most of us. We treat it as if it is not there at all. This is why when we speak of 'next-life' in our causal conversations, we usually mean it to be the next human embodiment and not any of the upcoming nonhuman creaturely embodiments that would be ordained by God as per our *karma*.

In other words, there is a built-in mechanism in our belief system that allows us in our thought process to escape the insurmountable misery and pain that are going to incur during all other creaturely embodiments of next *Karmic*-cycle, which our soul would suffer to render her *Karmic*-obligations before she would wear human body again; and thus, it enables us to refer directly the 'next human embodiment' when we speak of 'next-life'.

So as we can see, such a deceptive built-in belief causes us much harm since we become so used to looking at the next human life, and thus, the thought of all other creaturely embodiments disappears from our minds. The intractable experience of sorrow and suffering of all those nonhuman embodiments goes so unacknowledged that it vanishes away from our spiritual deliberations.

The result is that we become blind to our dreadful reality by becoming used to the thought that after death we are coming right back to this world as human again, and never pay any attention to the fact that there is a great probability that we would go through countless other lower lives before we would ever get the chance to be human again.

I know it is not easy to accept this reality but the truth cannot be manipulated into something that we like to hear. Surely, the reality according to scriptures is quite discouraging; because, if we correctly apply the dictated laws of *Karma*, for most of us, the next human life may be as far as eternity.

By now we know it well that the *Karmic*-consequences compel the soul to go through various planes of consciousness – higher and lower – depending upon her good (*Punya*) and bad (*Papa*) *Karma*. It forces her to go through countless lower lives before she embodies as human again. But what does that mean in terms of time-span, we do not fully understand.

Well, following description of consequences of minor bad deeds given by *Narada Purana* is quite discouraging. Here is what it has to say about the penalties for even a common sin like giving a biased judgment or distorting sacred word, and engaging in untruthful holy teaching:

> **nyaye cha dharma shikshayama pakshapatam karoti yah, na tasya niskratir-bhuyah prayaschitah-yutairapih.**

These holy words are translated as:

> **The one who is biased in delivering judgment and is prejudiced and partial in religious teachings, even though he may repent ten thousand times, remains yet unreleased from its sin.**

> **(Narada Purana, Purva Bhaga – Pratham Paad 15:119)**

According to these words, when we calculate the rebirth as human for a common person of today's society, who commits such acts of defilement and engages in vice not once or twice but all day long, the odds compute to be very high; surely, the exercise reveals a dreadful reality for all of us.

It shows that attaining human embodiment is a rare event in the total schema of conditioned-life of the soul (*Atman*), since each *Karmic*-cycle forces her to wear countless nonhuman embodiments that are nothing but vessels of exhaustion of *Karma* made to facilitate the payment of her *Karmic*-dues.

Even for a person, who lives a virtuous life, to be born again as human would not be as easy as commonly believed. The reason being, that *Karma* accumulated during this life would demand exhaustion, and that would force his soul to wear all kinds of embodiments before becoming human again.

Now if this is true for one who lives a virtuous life, then what can we say about other souls in today's time, which, without any doubt, are far more burdened by *Karma* and buried deep under bondage?

To believe that one has not committed much sin in life is a mistake since life in itself is filled with imperfection, as countless daily actions that we perform are laced with defects, **"because all actions are attended with defects – Holy Gita 18:48."** Clearly, no matter how perfectly we render them, we still perform them with much iniquity and imperfection. It means at the end of life there is always a huge burden of *Karma* that has been earned through defective actions, regardless.

Now if the actions are defective, obviously the resulting *Karma* will also be defective? Isn't it? And if the *Karma* is defective, then how can we be without bondage?

This leads us to one simple conclusion that there is no human life that can be lived in total perfection from beginning to the end, regardless of how good it merits in our sight. Thus, at the end of it, it surely would have some *Karma* that has been created with bondage, and hence, would demand exhaustion.

It means the belief that after death we are coming right back to this world as human does not hold much validity if we examine it through the light of scriptural truth. Mind it, please! It is not that it is not possible, but that it is highly improbable for a common man.

Let's look at an example where a man who despite his faith somehow fails to attain *Yogic*-perfection because he yet is not fully established in his Self and his mind still wanders in things of this world. So what happens to him? It is a question that *Arjuna* raises to Lord *Krishna*:

> **O *Krishna*, he who is unable to control himself despite his faith whose mind wanders away from the state of *Yoga* thus failing to attain *Yogic*-perfection what end does he meet.**
>
> **(Holy Gita 6:37)**

As we can see, *Arjuna* wonders about the consequences brought by such a sudden fall of this righteous man, and fears that he may wither away like a cloud, **"Does he not perish like**

a cloud that has been rent asunder by the wind, without finding any support – Holy Gita 6:38."

But contrary to what he thinks, Lord God assures him that this righteous man, even though he may spiritually fall, yet is always in His protection, not only in this life but all life after this:

Lord Krishna answered: O *Arjuna*, a Yogi is never destroyed, neither in this world nor in the next. O Friend, whoever does good does not tread the path of grief.

(Holy Gita 6:40)

From these words of the Lord, it is clear that this man who has almost reached the high levels of *Yogic*-ladder and yet for some reason has faulted in his spiritual pursuit, attains much favor in the sight of God and abides in His graces.

However, look at what happens to this man after he dies? The following verse unveils just that, and reveals a great truth that even such a piously and religiously evolved man wastes countless years in detouring exceedingly pleasurable heavens to express his good *Karma* before returning back to earthly world as man to continue his *Karmic*-progression:

Having fallen from Yoga (after death), a Yogi enjoys heavenly worlds for <u>everlasting</u> years, and then, he is born in the house of those who are pure and prosperous.

(Holy Gita 6:40-41)

According to these holy words, this fallen Yogi, even though has received God's protection in all worlds **(Holy Gita 6:40)**, yet he spends immeasurable time (denoted by the use of words **'everlasting years'**) in heavenly *Lokas* (planes of higher consciousness), and only then he returns to this world as human again. Certainly, depending upon what *Karma* he earns in his life, he is compelled to express it before his soul is given another chance to wear next human embodiment.

So, as we can see, the human life is not attained so easily even by such a highly enlightened soul. Because, due to accumulated *Karma*, not only he has to possibly wear all kinds of creaturely forms but also endure life in other worlds of varying consciousness for immeasurable time before being born as human again.

Of course, God is a sovereign God, so He can grant anything to anyone according to His will. Who is there to say, He can't! Who can challenge Him about His decisions? So if in His delight, He grants someone a human life after he dies and brings him back to this world as human again, who is there to object? Of course, God can do whatever pleases Him, as there are no laws to regulate His will.

However, the implied truth being stated in above verse is that human life does not come as easily as we think; and also, it does not come through our earned wages of *Karma*, but is given to us in much graces of God, but for one purpose alone, which is to attain salvation. Of course, the expression of preordained *Karma* is always there under the conception of each life, lower or higher. Therefore, putting the matter of *Moksha* off till 'next-life' is a grave mistake, because the belief, that we would be back to this world again as human in our next *Karmic*-life, is a very deceptive idea.

The scriptural mathematics proves that such a possibility is highly improbable since there lies so much else in between two human embodiments. There lies an ocean of sorrow and suffering of countless lower lives to cross before one could reach to the other side and embody as human again.

So it is to our benefit if we accept the reality that there is no easy return to earthly environment as human, because we have so much overburdening of *Karma* that would continue to prolong our *Karmic*-suffering for a long time to come.

Therefore, let us not forget that 'next-life' may not be as close as we think. In fact, there are pretty good chances that it could be countless lives away.

Sixth thought: It is a big mistake to put off salvation due to thinking that through likely spiritual evolution it would eventually happen anyway.

To think that if not this life, then there is another one coming right after this is quite a harmful thinking as it only creates illusions. By believing into something that has only a remote possibility to occur, one only deludes himself even further. This has two very obvious problems:

First: The human embodiments do not come as easy and not as frequent as we think since they could be countless lower lives apart.

Second: There is no guarantee that things would progress for better and the soul would evolve towards more enlightenment each time she is given the opportunity to be human and granted the privilege to change her *Karmic*-course.

Of course, based upon the scriptures, the argument certainly holds true that good *Karma*, life after life, would lead one to higher level of intellect and consciousness that would eventually pave his way to freedom from bondage, **"So he endeavors again to attain the higher rungs of *Yoga* leading to Liberation – Holy Gita 6:43,"** but how much certainty does one have that he would remain constant in this spiritual effort throughout all those human births, which he would require to reach such a higher level of enlightenment?

Of course, each human life is controlled and guided by God given human freewill. It means, regardless of how higher grounds of spiritual evolution a man may stands, through his freewill, he yet due to fleshly temptations may choose wrong path and fall onto lower grounds of *Karma*.

Therefore, to think that we would improve our spiritual level little by little in successive human lives as we pass through them, **"Having perfected *Yogic*-states through many lives, in every birth exercising more self-effort than before – Holy Gita 6:45,"** and would attain a gradual increase in our enlightenment, is a huge gamble, because we are looking into an immeasurable time-span to complete this task, and hence, facing limitless risk of falling into unrighteousness since our nature by birth is of sin.

With this argument in mind, who can guarantee that we would continually walk in uprightness and would march straightforward towards the higher levels of enlightenments? Of course, in such thinking, we always face these kinds of risks. We have no assurance in ourselves that it would not happen and we would not fail and fall; and that we would remain firm in our walk on the righteous track in upcoming human embodiments.

Beloved! Counting on future human-lives to attain *Moksha* is not a thought of wisdom at all, since considering its practicality and looking into its reality, we find that it has a very little merit for success. And even though, theoretically, based on the truth as stated by the scriptures, we may be able to justify our rationale, but the odds against it would be at least as high as they are today.

So if this rationale is true, then why not try now and find way to salvage our soul in this lifetime rather than leaving it for future human embodiments. After all, if one is already seeking wisdom in this regard and intellectually inquiring about the salvation of his soul, then in all truth, he is already on his way to redemption.

Of course then, all he has to do is to become firmly committed to this resolution and enter into the sanctuary of God with his entirety where with full confidence he can expect that God would take care of everything else.

Seventh thought: Moksha is not as difficult as it is often believed to be.

This is what plagues the mind of not only those who are ignorant and deluded but even those who are learned and knowledgeable; misguided become not only the unaware and deceived, but even those who understand the problem of bondage and concern themselves with the salvation of their soul; they too often become the victims of such a ill-conceived belief.

Why it is so? Because, so are we taught to think by our holy teachers, and so are we made to believe by our misguided religious beliefs. Over and over, we are told that we should ear better Karma for 'next-life' with the underlying assumption that the next life is going to be of human.

Moksha is just a thought; when it would happen, no one knows; and no one cares to know. Hopefully, it would come during some life by itself. Hopefully, our soul would keep evolving and someday she would find eternal liberation. There are just some faded thought in Hindu mind; no concrete deliberation and discernment.

The eternal liberation of the soul as a far-distant thing, which possibly cannot be reached in this lifetime; and so we do not touch this subject at all and put it off as if it is not our concern.

These kinds of thoughts have made the concept of 'next-life' so prevalent in our holy teachings that *Moksha* is almost a foreign idea, which is hardly ever discussed with any sense of urgency. So we never take a good look at how we can attain it in this lifetime.

Oh! We always hear people talk about *Punya* (good *Karma*) and *Papa* (bad *Karma*); we always hear about going to *Swarga* (heaven) and *Narka* (hell); we always hear about being born in *Agala-Janma* (next-life); we always hear all kind of things like that during our daily casual conversations, and yet there is hardly ever any serious exchange of thoughts about the eternal liberation from bondage and attaining salvation for our soul (*Moksha*).

You see! All kinds of religious subjects get attention in our daily exchanges, but not this, not the salvation of the soul. Hear any holy sermon, and all we get from it, is an encouragement to do better in this life spiritually so that our next-life (*Agala-Janma*) could be better. The focus, more often than not, is upon *Agala Janma* (next-life) and not upon *Moksha* (Liberation).

How often do we hear our holy teachers say that let us try our very best in achieving *Moksha* now, since this human life is our only chance to get out of bondage? How often? How often do they tell us that if we miss this boat, then who knows when we would get another chance again? And who knows after how many lower lives (probably countless), we would be blessed with a human body and be able to avail such opportunity again? How sad!

Something else! The main reason why the idea of 'next-life' is so popular because even the most knowledgeable and learned believes that eternal Liberation is very hard to attain and considers it to be almost impossible. The common belief is that salvation of the soul (Moksha) is not something that comes so easily. Therefore, all we can do is to do better in our holy life and hope that in some future human life, somehow the soul would be redeemed from sin and be released from bondage.

And with this kind of thinking we do not even touch this subject any more and totally avoid the whole matter as if it is of no further concern to us.

Of course, this kind of thinking is so deeply engraved on our mind that we hardly ever take up on this issue and discuss its various specifics, and ignorantly believe such kind of lies about it and accept things that are never true.

Let us ask ourselves: How often do we think of attaining 'Moksha' and how often we talk about the 'next-life'? The answer would provide a strong proof of reality that eternal liberation is no where to be found on our mind; the most we care, if ever do, is about our 'next-life'.

The truth is that we have accepted the captivity by bondage without any resistance, and we are so surrendered to this ill-conceived notion that freedom from bondage is not only difficult but almost impossible. And that is why, not much thought of attaining salvation (Moksha) is ever entertained by us.

In our common psyche, attaining Moksha is considered so beyond reach that common man cannot even dare to think of it. It is regarded so holy of merit that it can only be attained by those that have completely renounced worldly affluence and have chosen to live the most sacred and sanctified life as Sadhu or Swami, sage or saint, and have become Self-realized. They are the only ones that are regarded to be eligible to reach the land of eternal liberation.

Surprisingly, this is where we go very wrong. Because such is never the case as even the most ordinary person has the capacity to reach this highest holy feat and attain salvation for his soul, but of course, through the grace of God and not through his own holy labor.

Oh! In love for man whom he created with so much affection, God has already paved the way for his salvation through His grace; and that is the most joyful news for all mankind.

Eighth thought: The belief that we have to be perfect to attain salvation is totally wrong.

This conviction, that *Moksha* (salvation) is almost impossible, exists in our mind because we believe that we have to be spiritually perfect to have union with God. And since, reaching such perfection is almost impossible, or to say the least is very hard to arrive, attaining *Moksha* is also out of our reach.

True! That this argument seems to hold validity quite well, but let us take it a bit further and find out if the union with God is conditional upon one's being spiritually perfect before hand?

By the law of Creation, no object and no living being that exists and has physical attributes, can ever reach perfection. God is the only one who is perfect as all other – everything and everyone – is made imperfect.

So the idea that the soul has to be perfect to attain salvation does not hold logic since the material world can never be of perfection in its manifestation, but it surely has perfection in its source – God – from whom all has proceeded, **"I am the origin of all beings; all this has proceeded from Me – Holy Gita 10:8."**

It means the perfection of soul comes only after she merges with God and not beforehand. Only after she unites with the Whole, whose part she is, and loses her self-identification in Him, that she herself becomes whole and perfect. Oh! The perfection is not of her but of the One in Whom she merges.

Only when she finds the union with her Source – from whom she has emerged and became an individualized identity – her perfection arrives; because after amalgamation with the Source, the perfection of the Origin becomes her perfection.

Till then, she continues to exist in an imperfect state, no matter what spiritual effort one employs. Though, there exists a possibility for one attaining near perfection but never a complete one since perfection has no existence in material world; it has no corporeal materialization.

An easy support for such argument comes from the fact that existence of life is based upon *Karma* **(Holy Gita 8:3)**; meaning, all conditioned-life of the soul is always due to her bondage – which is nothing but a *Karmic*-imperfection. Thus, no embodiment of the soul can ever exist if she is not grasped by some kind of imperfection since the imperfection is the basis of our physical being. If our soul were perfect, we would not be here. It is that simple!

We exist because we have the imperfection of *Karma* imposed upon our soul. This is why there is a burden of bondage upon her head. Surely, we are in this body because our *Atman* is chained by the shackles of *Karma*; we are a manifested being because our soul is in bondage to mortality.

Thus, the physicality of the soul is the very proof of her imperfect existence. As long as her embodiment continues, her enclosing imperfection also remains. Therefore, we can inarguably say that no matter what we do, we can never reach perfection in our existence as long as we are alive and living in this body.

Now consider these words of fourth *Mahavakya* (the words of supreme utterance), **"Aham Brahmah Asmi – I am Brahman (God),"** which are nothing but the proclamation of a Self-realized soul (*Atman*), who breaks into joy when she realizes that she herself is no other but *Brahman*.

This scriptural truth leads to a question: How can one claim to be *Brahman* and still remain embodied in the human shell? How can he claim to be God and still remain a human? How can he proclaim to be an existence of perfection while still enduring an imperfect existence? How can this be?

The answer is clear, that it is not the perfection of imperfect existence in which the conditioned-soul lives, but the recognition of her intrinsic state of perfection, and (then) her separation from the encapsulating imperfect existence, what brings her union with God and enables her to merge with the only Perfection there is.

The most significant fact to understand is that the proclamation is not made by the embodied *Jiva* (the egoistic conditioned lower-self) but by the soul that has realized her true Self and now knows that she is of perfect nature and regards herself as not being a part of imperfect earthly existence.

It is not the physical self but the true 'Inner-being' who has risen out of the shell of individuality and finally sees his true 'Self' and recognizes that it is the same as the infinite transcendental Self.

So he screams with joy and proclaims to be who he truly is – the *Brahman*, the sole embodiment of Perfection – even though his encapsulating physical-self still remains laced with imperfection – a state that always remains so since nothing can ever reach the existence of absolute non-attribution.

The proclamation that **"Aham Brahmo Asmi – I am Brahman (God),"** made by a Self-realized soul is not done because the body in which the soul dwells has arrived the perfection, but because she has separated herself from the imperfection of her dwelling, and now, she has acquired the knowledge about her Self-being, and has come to know it well that she is not a part of any imperfection but is the part of that Wholeness which is wholly perfect and is the only perfection there is.

Beloved! We must understand this truth if we have any hope to find our way to *Moksha* and know it quite well that the soul does not need to reach perfection before she could be rescued from the fetters of Karma and be salvaged by God; because it simply is not true scripturally. Any such belief is a major hindrance to our holy path, as then, we are only wasting our holy labor in things that would not give us the right and beneficial yields and would not produce right results that could help us move closer to our eternal union with God.

Therefore, to believe that we have to reach the state of perfection to attain *Moksha* is not true; even though it is absolutely true that *Moksha* is the state of supreme perfection of the soul; however, the perfection in soul never comes through her own holy strivings and never arrives before she merges with God, but only after; it is the union with Perfection restores her into perfection.

You see! The 'Self-realization' is not the perfection of the embodiment of the soul (the lower-self) but the recognition of perfection of her true being-*ness* (the higher-Self) who is living in imperfection. As a result, after the realization that her true reality is not the reality of the body but is the reality of the transcendental Self, there is a creation of dissociation between the soul and the imperfect fleshly home that she dwells in.

The sense of her true Self that comes in the soul through Self-realization, which reminds her of intrinsically being of absolute purity and piety, piousness and perfection, creates a distinct disjoint between her and the body by dismantling all egoistic affiliations with it and by dissolving all self-identifications that she used to assert out of mere ignorance; and thus, though she is nowhere close to being perfect, yet becomes an extension of perfection of God even while indwelling the imperfect earthly enclosure – the body.

So, it is not that one becomes perfect first, and then he attains Moksha through Self-realization, but it is the other way around. Once he realizes the truth that his true Self is of perfection and abandons all associations with his imperfect existence even though he still continues to abide in it, he becomes the extension of Perfection. It means, for a man who has become Self-realized and opened the door to Moksha, the perfection is not in his existence as he still continues living in his imperfect body but he surely becomes established in knowledge of his Self-perfection.

So the notion that we need to be perfect to qualify for Moksha should be replaced by the thought that we need to acquire spiritual awareness of the reality of our perfect nature of which we truly are.

The belief that we have be cleansed completely and be without sin before we could be allowed the entry into the holy abode of God, must be replaced by a firm conviction that by taking total refuge in the sanctuary of Perfection, the soul immediately becomes the extension of perfection. And though she still continues to remain surrounded by all kinds of impurities and imperfection, she begins to live in the establishment of Perfection.

Surely it is always good to get rid of any kind of imperfection. But to think that our soul cannot be salvaged and redeemed unless she has attained the total perfection is very wrong. Because no matter how hard we try we can never get rid off our imperfection completely; our physical deficiencies would always remain since it is the basis of our existence; so to think that Moksha will not come until we have arrived to the absoluteness of perfection is very misguiding, and hence, must be abandoned from our holy deliberations.

Definitely, it is an extremely damaging and detrimental belief since it victimizes the seeker by discouraging him from trying his best to succeed in his eternal expedition and by taking his mind away from focused walk towards the ultimate spiritual providence – the *Moksha*. And it harms him badly by distracting him from his primary goal of trying to reach the home of eternal Liberation, and diverting his holy effort towards all kinds of wasteful *Karmic*-destinations.

Since separation from God causes the imperfection of the soul, the only way she would ever reach her perfection is by her union with Him. Oh! Only in union with Him comes her perfection, when His perfection becomes hers, but only after she abandons all of her affiliations and dismisses all her fleshly identifications and relinquishes all of her worldly belongings and totally becomes one with God.

Therefore, we must completely dismiss the belief that we ought to be perfect to attain *Moksha*, as the perfection comes to us not beforehand, but afterward, when through the grace of God get freed from separation and become one with Him and begin to wear His perfection.

Therefore, the idea, which unfortunately is often projected in our holy teachings, that *Moksha* is very difficult to attain, is simply not true. The belief that eternal liberation is extremely difficult to attain is very wrong. Never, we should consider the eternal liberation to be a distant possibility, because it is very easily reachable by anyone who is faithfully willing to surrender his life to the authority of God and joyfully willing to submit his entire existence to His control.

Oh! Over and over, the word of God provides witness to this truth.

Ninth thought: We have to attain salvation before we die and not after; because once we are dead, we can do nothing.

This happens to be the reality of *Moksha*, and if we have any longing for salvation, then we must be mindful of it.

This should serve as a reminder that we have to reach this destiny before the journey of life ends, because the matter of securing eternal life is in the hands of our free-will that we can exercise only when we are alive and not dead. Because, once we are dead, we would cease all command and control over what we can do, as we would have no say on anything after that. So we must do all what we need to do before we die; otherwise, it would remain undone. Hence, *Moksha* must be accomplished while living and not when dead.

Although, it is true that a salvaged soul cannot attain the true reality of salvation until she has been set free from the body, but while continuing to dwell in the flesh, she must arrive to that providence of eternal peace and joy within herself where she is literally liberated from all bondage during all her residual days on this earth.

Even though it is true that the *Atman* merges with *ParamAtman* (Godhead) only after he has abandoned the physical enclosure, but before dismantling his earthly home, he must have a view of his eternal abode. Doesn't it make sense? Of course, it does!

Therefore, before the *Atman* parts away from the noise of this world, he must arrive to that state-of-being where he begins to live in continual peace and joy of *Brahman* (God) and constantly experiences the absolute liberty of *Moksha*. Thus, we have to arrive to *Moksha* when we are alive, and think not that we would reach there after we are dead; as after death we can do nothing since nothing would be in our hands.

The earthly journey ends onto eternal grounds but only if we could touch its outskirts while we are still in earthly domains. This is not something that we would meet all of a sudden after we die, but is something with which we become very familiar much before we ever end into its arms.

So for the one, who is seeking and is on the journey to *Moksha*, this must serve as a guide for his travel towards the providence of eternal life. Surely, he must relentlessly strive to attain freedom in all matters of the day and constantly labor to acquire long-lasting peace and joy by seeking refuge in God and by abiding in His most blissful sanctuary.

His focus should be on achieving the well-established state-of-being within himself where he could continually try to advance towards the lasting enlightenment. He should do all he must, to make sure that he has arrived the state of *Moksha* inside of himself while still living on this earth and has attained the awareness of eternal abode well before he loses the consciousness of this corporeal country.

Tenth thought: *The path of deliverance from bondage has to be chosen by us and not by God.*

One thing should become very clear by now that Moksha, the liberation of the soul, is not some earning of *Karma*, but is a gift of love from God. But that gift has to be received by man by entering into His sanctuary and taking full refuge in Him **(Holy Gita 18:62, 66)**. So the receiving of the eternal liberation of the soul is an act of choice rather than unfolding of an event under the pre-ordinance of *Karma*.

It means one must make a choice in his freewill to initiate the walk which will take him into the presence of God so that he could humbly and thankfully stand before Him and receive the gift of eternal life. Therefore, as we can see, without making this choice, there can be no redemption of man's soul. He must choose it first and only then hope that it happens through the grace of God.

Of course, God is a sovereign God, and so is His will. But since He has made man with 'freewill', He fully honors the granted privilege and does not interfere with his autonomous authority over this most blessed faculty.

Surely, every moment of life, as it unfolds, is preordained by *Karma*; however, man is free to respond to it any way he likes. He has full freedom in it as God has granted him the total power over his discernments and decisions. It is completely up to him how he acts and behaves as it is totally under his privilege, which has been granted to him through God given faculty of 'freewill'.

Please, know it well, that God never interferes in it; never!

It is always man's own will through which he acts and behaves, and not of God; meaning, man's power to act in his freewill is absolute. However, *Karma* forms and shapes the environment and surroundings, situations and circumstances, by inducing temptations and enticements, discouragements and deterrents and other such factors under which the freewill has to operate. As a result, man is often led to choose and act in a certain way through the induced inclinations of the surroundings causing freewill to act in a quite influenced manner; however, it still has full freedom in its expressions.

God never directly forces anyone to do anything. Man always does what he chooses, and does not do what he does not choose.

True, that man does not have the power to salvage his soul from the shackles of *Karma*, he yet has full authority to choose it when God puts forth before him. In other words, it is up to man and man alone to make the choice to save himself from the fetters of bondage since he is the only one who is authorized to do so; in fact it is his natural duty as being human to save himself from falling into the purgatory of hellish world of *Karma* and spare himself from the dreadful consequences of bondage.

Thus, no one else, not even God, can make this choice for him; because, if He did, where would remain the autonomy in man's discernments and decisions operating under the authority of his freewill, which has been endowed to him by the Creator when He made him a special creature and granted this privilege.

This may not sound right but it happens to be true that it is our choice to make to save our soul from the captivity to sin, and not of anyone else's, especially not of God! It is our choice and ours alone, to halt the cycle of *Karma* and put an end to it so that our soul will never have to be subjected to it again and be forced to bear the sorrow and suffering of another embodiment.

Beloved! The endowment of freewill is given to make choice, which we use at each and every moment of life so that we could act according to our own discernment. Therefore, the choice to stop all agony and anguish of our soul (*Atman*) and put an end to all our torture and torment is also ours to make.

Since the decision and the will to act upon that decision lies under our own authority and no where else, the salvation of soul too cannot become a reality unless first we initiate the inclination for its reality and assert our will to attain it.

Oh! We have to make that choice first before we can have any hope for it.

Making choice for *Moksha* is a must because if we do not make this choice, it won't happen; it is not going to come by itself. The human life is regarded as most high since it enables us to make choices; and what choice could be better than to choose to love God and to take sanctuary in Him and through His grace attain salvation for our soul. No wonder, human embodiment is considered so precious by all scriptures.

Therefore, let us not remain ignorant and continue being engaged in things of this world and lose sight of what our future is going to be after we die. Let us not forget that our passion and infatuation consumes our attention so badly that we become insensitive to our own truth and we totally forget what is lying ahead of us. In self-indulgence and self-centricity, let us not become so busy that we do not even think about what is the prime responsibility of our life.

Look at how Holy Gita cautions us to not drown further into bondage, **"He should not drown himself into a degraded condition – Gita 6:5,"** and warns about the consequences of our choices by saying that those who understand the truth and work for their liberation are their own friends, while those who do not, are their own enemies:

> **For one who has conquered his self (lower self) by his Self (higher self) his very self becomes his friend. But for one who has not conquered his self turns out to be his enemy.**

> **(Holy Gita 6:6)**

Surely, it is true that on our own we can never rescue our soul from the shackles of sin, and on our own we can never bring ourselves out of the captivity by the bondage; still, it would happen only when, in our freewill, we make the choice to seek God's sanctuary, and with our whole heart and soul plead to Him for our salvation; only then, He would take the matter in His hands and would make all necessary provisions for our redemption from bondage, but only if it pleases to His heart.

Even when God desires something for us, first He presents it before us; He tempts us with its goodness; He creates desire for it in our heart; and He inspires us to have it. And though He does all those things, He yet never forces us to have it, and never makes it happen on His own, as He always waits for us to choose it. Once we make a choice in our freewill, then if God chooses its manifestation, He then facilitates its materialization.

Beloved! Don't you see that God has already given the invitation to us if we have come to know how important the Moksha is, since only through His grace do we come to such realization. It is as if we have received an invite for the entry into his kingdom. And now whether we respond to it or not is a matter of our freewill. But one thing is for sure that nothing will happen further unless we respond to His invitation and say 'Yes, Lord! I am ready to come Home,' and go to God and plead for His mercy and grace. Only after that, He will take the initiative and set the wheel of salvation in motion. From there onwards, know that God will take charge of our eternal expedition.

Then He would guide and direct it, plan and provide for it. He would initiate it, and He would finish it. He will do it all, but only if first we choose it and willingly submit ourselves to Him and allow Him to manifest it in our life and make it a reality. But if we never choose it, we can be sure that it would never happen, because our 'not choosing' automatically become a choice of 'No'.

Through freewill, God gave us a privilege to choose, which is solemnly sovereign. And if we do not exercise this privilege, then in this case, it will treated as if we have chosen 'No' to the eternal liberation of our soul. Well, that's how God sees it.

And since God never undermines and overwrites our choice, our 'no choice', which in this case represents the choice of 'No' to salvation of soul, becomes the choice of our freewill in His sight; and hence, He would not do anything but honor what we have chosen; and thus, we would continue to live in the slavery to sin, and our soul would continue to endure the captivity by Karma.

Therefore, we must make this choice – the choice to seek the sanctuary of God, as soon as we can; and let Him know that we desire His love and affection, and desperately need His goodness and grace.

With such repentant heart we must go to the altar of God and open up our heart before Him and meekly beseech Him for His mercy and kindness and submit ourselves to Him fully in the hope that He would hear our pleas and accept us into His asylum and grant the eternal safety and security to our sinful soul.

Beloved! This we must do because as per following holy word, if we do not accomplish this feat in this life and attain liberation for our soul, we will be looked as being very ungrateful in the sight of God, and will be considered as the destroyer of our own soul.

jo na tarai bhava saraga nara samaja asa pai, so krta nimdaka mamdamati Atmanhana gati.

This holy text is translated as:

The man who, though equipped with all these resources, fails to cross the ocean of metempsychosis is ungrateful and dull-witted and meets the fate of a self-murderer.

(Holy Ramayana, Uttar-Kanda 44)

We must not forget that God gave us this life as a gift, the purpose of which is not just to live and exhaust our *Karma*, but to express it in His love, and communicate through it His light, so that through His grace we could be sanctified and become bondage free, and thus, become eligible to enter into His eternal empire where we could abide in His presence forever and ever.

Hari OM!

Glossary

Aagami Karma – One of the three (*Sanchit, Aagami, Prarabdha*) types of *Karma*. It is the raw *Karma* that is created in human life.

Agala-Janma – The next' *Karmic*-Birth' / the next *Karmic*-life (embodiment) of the soul.

Ahamkar – The ego.

Akshara – All that what is indestructible.

Arjuna – The main character in Holy Gita after Lord *Krishna*, who is his friend, mentor, and also his charioteer. In the story of *Mahabharata*, when *Arjuna* stands in the midst of the battlefield and faces his own kinsmen to fight to win the rule over the kingdom, he becomes very confused. The thought of imminent destruction and death fills his heart with depression and dejection. So he asks the incarnated God, Lord *Krishna*, his guide and teacher, what is the best course for him that leads to his ultimate good. It is then, that Lord God gives him the discourse of Holy Gita filled with eternal wisdom.

Atman – The soul – the Transcendental Self. The *Atman*, is a part of *ParamAtman* (The Godhead) and is of the same nature as He is, which is of Existence-Consciousness-Bliss (*Sat-Chit-Ananda*).

Bhakti – The devotion. All the spiritual services rendered to God with love while abiding by faith in Him.

Bhishma – The grandsire of the royal family in the story of *Mahabharata*.

Bodha – Revelation of Knowledge.

Brahma – The deity that creates the Creation.

Brahma-loka – The abode of *Brahman* (The Godhead). This is the highest of *Lokas* (The planes of consciousness) represented by absolute purity and holiness.

Brahman – Also called *ParamAtman* (the Supreme *Atman*) – the Godhead; the imperishable, eternal, transcendental Self.

Buddhi – The Intellect.

Chitta – One of the four modes of operation of mind: *Mana, Chitta, Buddhi, Ahamkar (Ego)*. *Ahamkar* is common and coexists with other three.

Dana – The charity.

Dhyana – The act of meditation and contemplation.

Dwehsa – Hatred or dislike; one of the two opposites – love (*Raga*) and hatred (*Dwesha*), like and dislike – with which every man is born.

Dharmakshetra – In the story of Mahabharata, the battlefield *Kurukshetra* is denoted by this word to mean that it is a field of righteousness.

Dhritirashthra – In the story of Mahabharata, the blind King and the father of *Kauravas* that are the embodiment of evil and represent the forces of darkness in the war.

Dronacharya – In the story of Mahabharata, the wise and noble teacher of weaponry in the royal family.

Duryodhana – In the story of Mahabharata, the blind King's oldest son who is highly self-centered and arrogant, and is very egoistic and haughty.

Guna – A mode of nature. All objects in the material world are made of *Gunas* (Modes of nature) as nothing has been made without them.

Gunas – Three modes of nature – *Sattwa* (light), *Rajas* (passion) and *Tamas* (darkness).

Gunateeta – The one who is beyond three modes of nature: *Sattwa, Rajas* and *Tamas* is called *Gunateeta*; of course, only God is as such.

Hastinapur – In the story of Mahabharata, the kingdom of king *Dhritirashthra* over which the war of *Mahabharata* is fought.

Janaka – A king whom Holy Gita exemplifies as a *Karma Yogi* – the one who exercises the spiritual discipline of Action-in-love (Selfless-action).

Janardana – Another name for Lord *Krishna*.

Jiva – The conditioned existence of embodied soul (*Atman*) – the soul as a living being – the transcendental Self embodied as a living creature – the awareness conditioned by *Gunas*.

Jnani – The man of wisdom; who has the intuitive intellect and has the vision for higher truth.

Kama – The human attachment and desire – passion and fervor.

Kalpa – A day of Brahma; considered to be of thousands of years.

Karma-Loka – The planes of *Karmic* consciousness – the fields of *Karma* for the conditioned soul.

Karmic-Lokas – The *Karmic* planes of varying consciousness. All together there are fourteen *Karmic-Lokas*, some higher and some lower than our Loka, the one where we are living in – the Bhumi-*Loka* (Earth). Higher than these fourteen lokas is *Bhrahma-Loka* – the abode of Brahman (The Godhead).

Karna – One of the great warriors in the story of *Mahabharata*. Though he is the oldest brother of *Arjuna*, but he yet sides with the adversary *Duryodhana* because of his personal obligations to him.

Kauravas – In the story of Mahabharata, the sons of the blind king *Dhritirashthra* who represent the evil side in the battlefield *Kurukshetra*.

Keshava – Another name for Lord Krishna.

Kripa – The high priest and the spiritual teacher of the royal family in the story of *Mahabharata*.

Krishna – The incarnated God in higher view of Holy Gita. Otherwise, he is the charioteer of *Arjuna*, who is His disciple and a beloved friend, and who seeks His guidance when becomes very confused in the midst of the battlefield.

Krodha – *The anger.*

Kshara – All that what is destructible.

Kulguru – The title that the spiritual teacher of the royal family holds.

Kunti – The mother of warrior *Arjuna* and all *Pandavas* in the story of Mahabharata.

Kurukshetra – The name of the battlefield.

Liberation – The eternal liberation of the soul from bondage.

Loka – A plane of consciousness.

Lokas – There are fourteen planes of Karmic-consciousness and beyond them is Brahma-Loka – the plane of highest consciousness – the abode of Brahman Himself.

Mahabharata – *Mahabharata* is one of the largest epics in the history of mankind, written about the dynasty of king *Bharata* of India about some five thousand years back.

Mahawakya – The words of the supreme utterance. There are four *MahaVakyas*; 1: *Prajananam Brahman* – the consciousness is *Brahman*; 2: *Tat Twam Asi* – That Thou Are; 3: *Ayam Atman Brahman* – The Self within is *Brahman*; 4: *Aham Brahman-Asmi* – I am *Brahman*.

Maya – The delusive power under Existence that creates the cosmic illusion.

Moksha – The eternal Liberation of the soul from bondage.

Mukti – The eternal Liberation of the soul from bondage.

Narka – The hell. While *Swarga* (The heaven) is regarded as the highest extremity of *Karma Lokas* (The planes of varying consciousness for *Karmic* expressions), *Narka* (hell) is regarded as the lowest.

OM – The word OM denotes *Brahman* – The transcendental Self – The Godhead.

Papa – The bad deeds – which create only bad Karma.

Pandavas – The sons of king *Pandu*, who represent the side of righteousness in the battlefield.

ParamAtman – The supreme *Atman* – The Spirit supreme – The supreme Soul – The Godhead.

Pooja-Aarti – Typical Hindu way of worshipping God.

Prakriti – The nature.

Prarabdha Karma – One of the three (*Sanchit, Aagami, Prarabdha*) types of *Karma*. It is the *Karma* that has matured and is ready to be expressed as life and be exhausted. No exhaustion of *Karma* can ever take place unless first it matures from *Sanchita Karma* and gets converted into *Prarabdha* Karma.

Punya – The good deeds – which create only good Karma.

Puranas – Like *Vedas* and *Upanishads*, eighteen *Puranas* are also *Hindu* holy scriptural books, which are: *Agni, Bhagawata, Bhavishya, Brahma, Brahmanda, Brahma-vaivarta, Garuda, Kurma, Linga, Markenrdiya, Matsya, Naradiya, Padma, Skanda, Vamana, Varaha, Vayu* and *Vishnu*.

Purusha – The supreme soul – the Godhead.

Purushottama – The Man Supreme - the one who is best among men.

Raga – Love or like; one of the two opposites: love (*Raga*) and hatred (*Dwesha*), like and dislike – with which every man is born.

Ramacharitmanas – Also called as Holy *Ramayana* – the most popular holy epic of India beside *Mahabharata*. Holy *Ramayana* describes the story of king *Rama* who according to *Hindu* philosophy is considered to be one of the incarnations of God.

Ramayana – Another name for Ramacharitmanas.

Sadhana – Spiritual exercise.

Sadhu – A sage, a saint.

Samkhya – The *Yogic* discipline of Knowledge.

Sanchit Karma – One of the three (*Sanchit, Aagami, Prarabdha*) types of *Karma*. It is the *Karma* that has been accumulated over previous human lives. At the end of a human life, the earned *Aagami Karma* gets converted into *Sanchit Karma*, which is like a storehouse for all accumulated *Karma*.

Sanjaya – The advisor and the charioteer of the blind king *Dhritirashthra*, who is a visionary as he has the clairvoyant ability granted to him by sage *Vyasa* to see the events of the battlefield.

Sanyasa – The renunciation.

Sanyasi – The one who has adopted renunciation.

Saraswati – The goddess *Saraswati* is considered to be the supreme deity of the Knowledge – the source of all understanding.

Sat-Chit-Ananda – The true nature of the *Atman* (soul) is of Existence-Consciousness-Bliss, which is the nature of Transcendental Self.

Sattwa – The mode of nature of highest virtue and purity.

Shashwatam – The eternal, the perpetual.

SriMada-Bhagawada-Gita – The original name of Holy Gita, which means 'A Song of God'.

Sruti – The deity of the scriptural truth.

Swarga – The heaven.

Tamas – The mode of nature of lowest virtue.

Tapa – The austerity.

Tyaga – The relinquishment

Teertha Yatra – A pilgrimage

Unmanifest – The formless God.

Upanishads – hundreds of holy *Hindu* scriptural books that actually are part of four Holy *Vedas*.

Vairagya – The dispassion.

Vasudeva – One of the most popular names of Lord *Krishna*.

Vedas – The four pillars of *Hindu* scriptures, where each containes hundreds of books of divine wisdom called *Upanishads*.

Vedantic Philosophy – The *Hindu* philosophy, which is described mainly in four holy books called *Vedas*. Each *Veda* is a collection of hundreds of books. They also contain the *Upanishads* in their end part.

Ved-Vyasa – The sage *Vyasa*, the author of Holy Gita and all other *Hindu* scriptural books.

Yajna – sacrifice.

Yogas – Spiritual disciplines as prescribed by Hindu scriptures.

About the Author

Born and raised in India as *Hindu, Vijai Tiwari*, migrated to United states in early seventies. After receiving master degrees in Mathematics and Computer Science, he spent several years working for large companies until he joined Boeing at the Kennedy Space center in late eighties, which launched his career in space technology. Most of his professional accomplishments are in NASA related projects.

Though he never was a man who followed his religious faith, when life took turn and challenged him with questions which seemed much larger than life, he had to search for answers, which he could find no where else but only in the sanctuary of God.

In his awakening what he saw as truth, has become the theme of his writings. This book is a preview of how he sees the Reality and Truth in his enlightened vision. It provides a glimpse of his spiritual thoughts which are not bound by a theology but adhere to deep convictions that have been imprinted upon his spirit through the Seeking of God.

He believes that religion does very little for man as it often harms him rather than doing good. True that Religiosity comfort him much and his holy ways make him feel good about himself, but seeking of God and the realization of Truth, are ever beyond such holy endeavors.

Though human life has been given by the Creator with freewill to live, but God desires man to render it to Him in his absolute surrender and submission so that he could enjoy it greatly by living it in love and light and still find salvation through His grace.

Other Books by The Author

The Divine View of Holy Gita:

The Holy Vedas and *Upanishads* are highly regarded by theologians all over the world, but Holy Gita holds a very special place in the heart of this community.

Holy Gita may be the smallest in volume among the major holy books; however, it is the most complete in its theological exposition. This cornerstone of *Hindu* philosophy reveals not only the wisdom of Holy Vedas and *Upanishads*, but unfolds the spiritual science underneath them.

But the cosmic view of Holy Gita remains hidden to the ordinary eyes as only an awakened vision is able to see her abundant beauty and bountifulness. When a humble heart, longing to know the Truth, devoutly seeks within her verses, her words become alive; her meaning penetrates all ignorance; her radiance illuminates all indwelling darkness.

Because Holy Gita is a gospel of love and light, it is only by touching her soul with such virtue, that we can receive her concealed heavenly wisdom.

The Divine View of Holy Gita is the first book of the author, *Vijai Tiwari*. It is an introduction to the Sacred Reality and Truth that was revealed to him in the timeless tradition of enlightened vision.

Contained in these chapters are direct spiritual insights that are not bound by mere historically based [mediate] theologies but instead spring from a direct [immediate] experience of one man's passionate and personal search for the Truth.

This devotional book seeks the heart of Holy Gita, not through ordinary consciousness and contemplation, but through total immersion in the majesty and magnificence of this holy text. In this book, the author shares his thoughts on the divinity of Holy Gita, which often goes un-ventured and un-comprehended by casual readers, and yields a fresh meaning of her words that has been revealed to him through much graces of the Creator.

The Divine View of Holy Gita was inspired to be written with a four-fold purpose. First, to provide a concise composite of *Hindu* Philosophy based on the scriptural truth as stated in the *Hindu* holy books; second, to shed light on the divinity of Holy Gita and to depict the cosmic view hidden in her verses; third, to address the issue of human bondage, and soul's captivity by *Karma* through the *Karma*-cycle; and fourth, man's release from bondage to sin through the grace of God alone, which he could receive only by absolute surrender to Him and taking total refuge in His sanctuary.

This book not only examines the purpose of human life as revealed through the word of God but also explores how man can fulfill that divine purpose in common daily life.

The intent of this book is not to promote *Hindu* philosophy but rather create a clearer understanding of its doctrine. Above all, the focus of this book is to bring the reader closer to the reality that God can be reached through the purity of love and light. It is neither religion nor its ritual and rites, nor its creeds and canons, but the understanding of higher reality underneath the scriptural truth professed by the religion that is the main subject of this book.

The book emphasizes the truth that one serves God not simply by performing holy works but by doing so within a context of selflessness and with equanimity of mind, not simply through demonstrating one's knowledge of scriptures but through one's humble acceptance of the truth expressed in them, and not by mere observance of the holy ways but through total surrender and submission to the sacred sanctuary of the Divine.

In Search for the Truth:

Though man is not aware of this reality, right from his birth, his soul is intrinsically thirsty for Truth. He is born with this innate desire, and because of it, he drinks water from every well he thinks can quench it. Unfortunately, he still remains unsatisfied, and departs from this world often thirstier than his entrance.

The question is: can man discover this reality on his own? Can he realize that nothing but the union with God will slake his thirst permanently and bring him abiding peace? Also, can he reach Reality and Truth through his own brilliance? Can he desire to know God without God willing it first? And can he reach Him through his own efforts and endeavors? Or, he needs Him to be united with Him?

In Search for Truth discusses this subject in light of scriptures and exposes many mysteries hidden in scriptures as exposed in sacred texts of Holy Gita, Holy *Ramayana*, Holy Bible, Holy *Upanishads*, and other blessed manuscripts, which surely contain the answers to such questions that are ever beyond the brilliance of human mind.

The contents of this book are the descriptions of author's those spiritual recollections that illustrate the striking scenery and overwhelming pleasantry he saw along the way while traveling towards the paradise, the beauty and splendor of which he found utterly overwhelming.

The truth is, that these words are the composed exposures of those sketches of his spiritual development that depict the details of his personal inner struggle as well as his spiritual growth, that occurred while wandering in the wilderness of world of spirituality. Surely, they tell the bits and pieces of story of such a man whose desperate search for light, after his life was doomed to darkness, became the finding of enlightening vision of the higher Truth.

So these words are the witness of the fact that beyond the mundane life of a secular mind lies the extraordinary life of the sacred soul; that beyond the song of passion of this world,

413

echoes the melody of love of eternal empire; that beyond the elegance of outer persona, shines forth the beauty, grace and the elegance of the inner being; that beyond the journey of the egocentric corporeal self, begins the voyage of the altruistic immortal soul; that beyond the glamour and glory of human spirit lies the beauty and splendor of the Spirit of his Creator.

Thus, this book is a documentation of those delightful destinations that a man passed though while desperately searching for truth and looking for God, and is a sincere account of those revelations that he received from God in His unending grace.

It is a collection of those divine disclosures that he got exposed during the awakening of his inner being, and which now have become the most savored experiences of unfolding of his Self within. Surely, these are an assortment of those heavenly views that he conceived in the light of the Spirit as he traveled through the unknown trails of spirituality and marveled upon most glorified spectacles of utterly blissful wonderment.

Liberation of Soul:

Human birth is given to man for the sole purpose of liberating his soul from bondage. But often man employs his life for everything else but that. Even those who are awakened to the higher reality often devote their lives worrying excessively about the 'next life' and investing their spiritual labor in securing prosperity for future reincarnations.

However, in both cases, he misses the essential truth about the human embodiment, which is, that the true purpose of human life is not to accumulate 'good' *Karma* for future lives, but to achieve eternal liberation from the captivity of *Karma*.

Oh! There are only a few, the most blessed ones, who come to know the truth and realize that the salvation of the soul and her redemption from *Karmic* bondage is the highest goal of life, and have full confidence in knowing the fact that it is obtainable not by just some who are holy and hollowed but by anyone who is willing to surrender himself to God with his absoluteness.

The problem lies in the fact that there is tremendous darkness about attaining the eternal liberation of soul (*Moksha*), as most *Hindu* believers are of the thought that *Moksha* is very difficult to attain, which happens to be a very misleading belief.

Such misguidance often leads many to waste the most precious opportunity – the human embodiment – which God has given to them with much hope expecting that they would salvage their soul from the bondage to *Karma* and save her from the claws of sin.

The truth is that man's spirituality is not so much about the salvation of soul as much as it is about him being righteous. Surely, this fact can very easily be verified in all of his spiritual endeavors.

And that is why there is hardly any sense of urgency in the mind of a *Hindu* believer to attain salvation in the current human life, as whenever he thinks about life beyond this life, he generally finds his focus upon the next '*Karmic*-life' (Agala Janma), and not upon the eternal life.

Surely, this is where lies his religious ignorance; this is where he is living in spiritual darkness; this is where he is very misdirected and ill-advised by his holy beliefs.

This book addresses this most important issue of human life and raises all kinds of questions and in doing so, unveils very overwhelming the facts extracted from our scriptures that are related to the subject of Liberation of the Soul.

It also discusses on how to seek the spiritual insight that could correctly guide the growth in knowledge about how to find the right way to reach a truly fruitful and fulfilled religious life, which is fully capable of accomplishing the ultimate goal of human embodiment – of course, the salvation of the soul.

Find out much more on this great subject in the book called 'The liberation of Soul', by Vijai Tiwari, and learn what kind of plan Gad has provisioned and provided man to reconcile him to Himself.

To contact the author, write to:

VijaiTiwari@MissionaryAshram.com

Or

Visit the website: *MissionaryAshram*.com

Additional copies of The Divine View of Holy Gita may be ordered directly from the publisher. Single copies are US$23.50 plus shipping and handling. Contact the publisher for bulk discount prices.

Send check or money order to:

Trafford Publishing
2333 Government Street, Suite 6E
Victoria, British Columbia, Canada, V8T 4P4